Win32 API Programming
with Visual Basic

Win32 API Programming
with Visual Basic

Win32 API Programming
with Visual Basic

Steven Roman

O'REILLY®

Beijing · Cambridge · Farnham · Köln · Paris · Sebastopol · Taipei · Tokyo

Win32 API Programming with Visual Basic
by Steven Roman

Copyright © 2000 Steven Roman. All rights reserved.
Printed in the United States of America.

Published by O'Reilly & Associates, Inc., 101 Morris Street, Sebastopol, CA 95472.

Editor: Ron Petrusha

Production Editor: Jeffrey Liggett

Printing History:

> January 2000:   First Edition.

This book is printed on acid-free paper with 85% recycled content, 15% post-consumer waste. O'Reilly & Associates is committed to using paper with the highest recycled content available consistent with high quality.

ISBN: 1-56592-631-5

To Donna

Table of Contents

Preface

This book is intended for the intermediate- or higher-level Visual Basic programmer. The book has two goals:

- Describe the Win32 API and how to program it from Visual Basic versions 5.0 and 6.0.

- Describe the basic operation of the Windows NT and Windows 9x operating systems.

As you may know, the *Win32 Application Programming Interface*, or *Win32 API* for short, is the programming interface that is used to programmatically control the Windows operating system. More specifically, the Win32 API consists of a collection of functions and subroutines, supplied in a handful of dynamic link libraries (DLLs), that provide programmatic access to the features of the operating system.

The first goal mentioned earlier is a practical one since, as we will see, the Win32 API can be of immense use in extending the power of Visual Basic. The second goal is less practical, but is equally important, since Microsoft's documentation seldom takes into account what the reader knows or does not know. Hence, a grounding in the basics of the Windows operating systems will help VB programmers understand Microsoft's documentation.

Of course, the two goals are not unrelated. Indeed, the purpose of the Win32 API is to implement the services (or features, if you will) of the Windows operating system. Hence, in order to understand the function of the Win32 API, it is important to have some understanding of how Windows itself works.

I should also point out that this book is not intended to be an encyclopedia for the Win32 API. My goal is to present you with enough information to get an overall feel for the Windows operating system and the Win32 API and to allow you to further your education by using Microsoft's documentation, which is seldom as pedagogical as it should be!

Prerequisites

The prerequisites for this book are simple: an intermediate-level (or higher) knowledge of Visual Basic version 4 or later and a desire to stretch VB into the realm of Windows system programming. You may want to do this for a specific purpose—perhaps you are writing a specific application that requires more than VB can handle—or just to learn more about how Windows works without suffering through the very steep learning curve associated with Visual C++–style Windows programming.

You do not need a background in VC++ (or C++ or C) to read this book, nor do you need to have any previous experience with the Win32 API.

What's on the CD-ROM?

The CD-ROM that accompanies this book contains several applications that we discuss in the book. You may want to use these applications and/or modify them to suit your particular needs. Please note that these applications were written as learning tools, not as commercial-grade applications. For instance, they have very little error-handling code and their interfaces are a bit rough in spots. (For example, I paid little attention to issues related to various screen resolutions.)

Note also that the code is for your use only—it is *not* for redistribution. (Incidentally, the prefix *rpi* found on most of these application names stands for *Roman Press Inc.*, which is the name of my computer consulting/publishing company.) If you find any serious problems with an application, or a particularly interesting use or modification, I would appreciate hearing about it by email or via my web site at *www.romanpress.com.*

rpiAPI.bas and rpiExampleCode.bas

The included standard VB 6 code module *rpiAPI.bas* contains the declarations and most of the important utility code used by examples in the book. The more expendable code is contained in the *rpiExampleCode.bas* module. The point is that you may want to use the code in *rpiAPI.bas* in your own projects, but the code in *rpiExampleCode.bas* has more of a one-time-use nature.

Applications

Here are the examples discussed in the book and included on the CD-ROM:

rpiAllocMemory
> An example that is used to demonstrate the *rpiAccessProcess.dll*, which can access a foreign process for memory allocation, data transfer, and more.

rpiBitBlt
> A demonstration of the *BitBlt* function.

rpiClipViewer
> A Clipboard viewer application.

rpiEnumProcsNT and *rpiEnumProces95*
> Display the current processes on a system.

rpiEnumWins
> Shows information about all windows currently in a system.

rpiFileMapping
> Demonstrates memory-mapped files.

rpiGlobalHook
> A global mouse hook example. Uses *rpiGlobalHook.DLL.*

rpiLocalHook
> A local mouse hook example.

rpiPEInfo
> Retrieves information about an executable file.

rpiSpyWin
> Retrieves information about a window.

rpiSubClass
> Demonstrates subclassing.

rpiThreadSync
> Demonstrates thread synchronization (mutexes, events, and semaphores).

rpiDLL
> A DLL with some miscellaneous functions, including *rpiVarPtr*, which does the same thing as VB's undocumented *VarPtr* function on nonstring variables and can be used to simulate *StrPtr*. Also included are the functions *rpiGetTargetByte*, *rpiGetTargetInteger*, *rpiGetTargetLong*, and *rpiGetTarget64*, which perform address indirection in VB.

rpiUsageCount.dll
> A DLL that can be used to tell when a VB application is already running.

The rpiAPIData Application

The CD also contains an application called *rpiAPIData*, which is essentially just a front end for a database that contains tables of the following:

- More than 6,000 Win32 constants and their values

- More than 1,500 VB-style API function declarations

- Approximately 1,000 message identifiers

- About 200 style constants

- More than 400 structure (type) declarations

- More than 600 Win32 data type declarations

Figure P-1 and Figure P-2 show the main windows for this application. The application can be used to extract function, constant, type, and other declarations for use in VB projects. You might even want to turn the application into a VB add-in, something I find extremely useful. (If you need information on creating VB add-ins, let me suggest my book *Developing Visual Basic Add-ins*, also published by O'Reilly.)

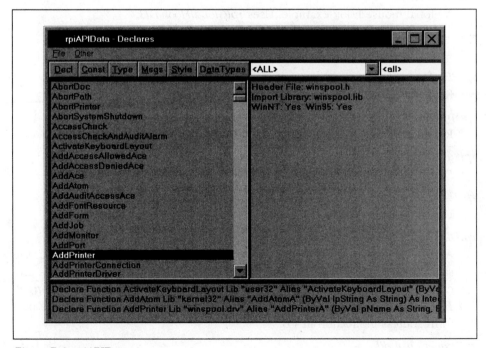

Figure P-1. rpiAPIData

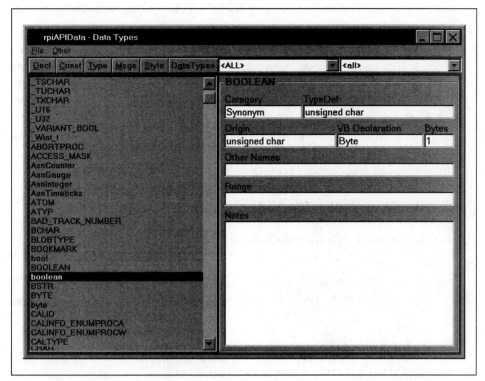

Figure P-2. rpiAPIData: data type view

Resources and References

Win32-related programming, whether in VC++ or VB, is definitely complicated. To do an effective job, you will need good reference material. Aside from this book, I recommend the following:

* As you may know, starting with version 6, Microsoft has moved the entire documentation for Visual Studio (VB6, VC6, VJ6, etc.) to its MSDN Library, a copy of which comes with VB6. Thus, you get documentation not only for VB6, but also for VC6 and the Win32 API. This is without a doubt the most useful documentation for Win32 API programming in VB. In fact, it is about the *only* documentation that I use. (The version of the MSDN Library that is included with Visual Studio is referred to as a *Visual Studio Edition* of MSDN. Frankly, I have not been able to determine how this differs, if at all, from the subscription version of MSDN Library.)

  When I use the unqualified term *documentation* in this book, it refers to the MSDN Library documentation.

  To get quarterly updates, you can subscribe to MSDN for about $100 per year (check it out at *http://msdn.microsoft.com/*). This may be worth doing, since the library also contains some very useful articles, along with the Microsoft Knowledge Base, which is constantly being updated.

• If you want to learn more about the Windows operating system, I can recommend Jeffrey Richter's book *Advanced Windows, Third Edition*, from Microsoft Press. Note, however, that there is no VB code in this book—it is strictly VC++—and it is fairly heavy going. If you want to learn more about the internal workings of Windows NT (which is the Microsoft operating system in *everyone's* future), I recommend *Inside Windows NT* (Second Edition) by David Solomon, also from Microsoft Press. Note, however, that this book is quite technical and contains no code at all.

Conventions in This Book

Throughout this book, I've used the following typographic conventions:

`Constant width`
Used for code blocks and examples, commands, constants, data type names in C, keywords, methods, objects, statements, structures, syntax prototypes, and values.

`Constant width italic`
Used for parameters and variables. Variables are italicized only in body text, not in code blocks.

Italic
Used for filenames, functions, procedures, classes, and URLs. Also used for emphasis and to introduce new terms.

How to Contact Us

We have tested and verified all the information in this book to the best of our ability, but you may find that features have changed (or even that we have made mistakes). Please let us know about any errors you find, as well as your suggestions for future editions, by writing to:

O'Reilly & Associates, Inc.
101 Morris Street
Sebastopol, CA 95472
1-800-998-9938 (in the U.S. or Canada)
1-707-829-0515 (international/local)
1-707-829-0104 (FAX)

You can also send messages electronically. To be put on our mailing list or to request a catalog, send email to:

nuts@oreilly.com

To ask technical questions or comment on the book, send email to:

bookquestions@oreilly.com

For technical information on Visual Basic programming, to participate in VB discussion forums, or to acquaint yourself with O'Reilly's line of Visual Basic books, you can access the O'Reilly Visual Basic web site at:

http://vb.oreilly.com

Acknowledgments

I would like to thank Ron Petrusha, my editor at O'Reilly, and Tara McGoldrick, from the editorial staff, for their help with this challenging book. My special thanks to Matt Childs for doing a careful technical review of this book—not a simple task, to be sure.

Also thanks to the production staff at O'Reilly & Associates, including Jeffrey Liggett, the production editor; Edie Freedman for designing another memorable cover; Mike Sierra for tools support; Rhon Porter for illustrations; David Futato, Jeff Holcomb, and Claire Cloutier LeBlanc for quality control; and Ellen Troutman Zaig for the index.

I

Declaring API Functions in Visual Basic

1

Introduction

As we mentioned in the Preface, this book is intended for the intermediate or higher Visual Basic programmer and has two goals:

- Describe the Win32 API and how to program it from Visual Basic versions 5.0 and 6.0.

- Describe the basic operation of the Windows NT and Windows 9x operating systems.

It is natural to wonder why a Visual Basic programmer would be interested in using the Win32 API. The simple answer is that the Win32 API functions allow the VB programmer to access the raw power of the Windows operating system.

For better or worse, the Visual Basic programming environment per se attempts to shield the programmer from the full power of the Windows operating system. This is partly because of the added complexity that surrounds operating system programming and partly because of the apparent sense on Microsoft's part that VB programmers need to be protected from these complexities (and thus from making more "serious" programming errors than are possible in VB).

To get a better feel for the additional power provided by the Win32 API, let's look at some of the simpler things you will learn to do under Visual Basic using the Win32 API:

- Add tab stops to a VB list box

- Add a horizontal scroll bar to a VB list box

- Add a bitmap to a VB menu

- Determine whether a VB application is already running and prevent multiple instances of the application

- Gather system information, such as which version of Windows is running on a system (Windows 95, 98 or NT), the full pathname of the Windows directory, the screen resolution, or the number of buttons on the user's mouse

- Add an icon to the Windows System Tray

In addition, you will learn several advanced programming techniques that can be used in your VB applications, such as how to:

- Get a list of all running applications

- Synchronize two VB applications so that they can work in cooperation with each other (one application pauses while the other completes a task)

- Extract data from controls that belong to another application

- *Subclass* windows (and controls) to change their behavior

- Install local or global *hooks* to monitor or alter the behavior of the mouse or keyboard

- Inject a DLL into another process space and execute the code in the DLL

- Draw using the Windows GDI drawing functions

- Install a clipboard viewer to save the results of more than one copy operation for later pasting

Finally, you will learn some of the secrets of how Windows operates, so that you can:

- Learn how to map the memory space for a process

- Understand the format of executable files, as well as such things as which functions a DLL exports and which DLLs an executable file uses

What Is the Win32 API?

At the present time, Microsoft offers two 32-bit operating systems—Windows 98 and Windows NT. The Win32 Application Programming Interface, or Win32 API for short, is the programming interface that is used to programmatically control these operating systems. More specifically, the Win32 API consists of a collection of functions and subroutines that provide programmatic access to the features of the operating system.

Generally speaking, application programming interfaces take the form of a collection of functions (we include subroutines in this generic term) that provide the application's services. The Win32 API is no exception. The Win32 API consists of well over 2,000 functions for performing all sorts of operating system services. Table 1-1 shows some categories of Win32 API functions. This table will give you a good idea of the type of services rendered by the Win32 API.

Table 1-1. Some API Function Categories

Bitmap Functions	Message and Message Queue Functions
Brush Functions	Metafile Functions
Clipboard Functions	Mouse Input Functions
Color Functions	Multimedia Functions
Common Dialog Functions	Multiple Display Monitors Functions
Communication Functions	Multiple Document Interface Functions
Coordinate Space and Transformation Functions	Painting and Drawing Functions
Cursor Functions	Path Functions
Data Decompression Library Functions	Power Management Functions
Debugging Functions	Printing and Print Spooler Functions
Device Context Functions	Process and Thread Functions
Dialog Functions	Rectangle Functions
Dynamic Data Exchange Functions	Registry Functions
Dynamic-Link Library Functions	Resource Functions
Error Functions	Scroll Bar Functions
Event Logging Functions	String Manipulation Functions
File Functions	System Information Functions
File System Functions	System Shutdown Functions
Font and Text Functions	Tape Backup Functions
Icon Functions	Time Functions
Keyboard Accelerator Functions	Timer Functions
Keyboard Input Functions	Unicode and Character Set Functions
Large Integer Operations Functions	Window Functions
Line and Curve Functions	Window Station and Desktop Functions
Memory Management Functions	Windows Networking Functions
Menu Functions	

API Icon Functions

To get an idea of what some of these API functions can do, let's take a quick look at the icon-related functions.

CopyIcon
    Makes a copy of an icon

CreateIcon and *CreateIconIndirect*
    Create an icon

CreateIconFromResource
    Creates an icon from raw data in a resource file

DestroyIcon
> Destroys an icon

DrawIcon and *DrawIconEx*
> Draw an icon in a specified location

ExtractIcon, ExtractIconEx, and *ExtractAssociatedIcon*
> Extract icons from an executable file (EXE or DLL)

GetIconInfo
> Retrieves information about an icon

LoadIcon
> Loads an icon from a specified module or application instance

LookupIconIdFromDirectory and *LookupIconIdFromDirectoryEx*
> Search for an icon that matches certain criteria

Other APIs

Microsoft Windows is not the only application that has an API. For instance, it would be reasonable to say the Microsoft Excel object model is the application programming interface for Excel, and similarly, the Word object model is the API for Microsoft Word, and the Data Access Objects (DAO) object model is the API for the Jet database engine.

Even the PC BIOS and the DOS operating system have APIs. These APIs are used by assembly language programmers to gain programmatic access to the BIOS and DOS services. As you might imagine, the BIOS services are very primitive. For instance, the BIOS has disk services to read a disk sector, write a disk sector and format a disk track. The DOS API services are at a somewhat higher level than the BIOS services and so are generally easier to use. This applies especially to the area of disk access (hence the name *D*isk *O*perating *S*ystem). For instance, the DOS API has functions to open and close a file, read from and write to a file, find a file, delete a file, rename a file, and so on. In short, while the BIOS API understands only disk sectors and tracks, the DOS API understands files.

Windows 9x and Windows NT—Two Different Win32 APIs

Anyone who has worked with both Windows 9x and Windows NT knows full well that these are quite different operating systems. They do have very similar user interfaces, but they are quite different underneath the surface.

Aside from the fact that Windows 9x does not support such things as security services and symmetric multiprocessing (using more than one CPU at a time), perhaps the two most significant differences from the API programmer's perspective is that Windows 9x does not support the Unicode character set (except in very limited situations), and it does not protect its own memory from errant applications. As a result, Windows 9x is far less stable than Windows NT.

Curiously, Windows 9x does protect each *application's* memory from access by *other applications*, but it does not protect its *own* memory from access by an application. Therefore, while an errant program cannot corrupt another program, it can corrupt the operating system itself, causing a system-wide crash. On the other hand, Windows NT does protect its own memory from running applications and is thus far less likely to crash as a result of accidental attempts to write to protected memory.

To a casual computer user who does some word processing, keeps checkbook balances on the PC, accesses the Internet, and plays some games, this may not be a major issue. On the other hand, to a serious computer user and especially to a programmer, the more stable the operating system, the less time will be spent waiting for the system to reboot.

For these reasons, I strongly prefer Windows NT. The downside is that Windows NT is less friendly when it comes to some user-interface amenities, and more seriously, it does not have the same breadth of support for hardware devices. Unfortunately, this may be a reason for some to stay away from Windows NT.

In any case, I don't mean to leave the impression that you cannot program successfully in the Windows 9x environment. I did it for many years before switching to Windows NT. It just means that you should expect to get interrupted fairly regularly by system crashes.

Since the two Windows operating systems are so different, it should come as no surprise that each implements the Win32 API differently. Some Win32 API functions are implemented under Windows 9x but not under Windows NT and vice versa. This can make for very awkward coding. For instance, we will need to write two entirely different sets of code to list all of the current processes (running applications)—one that works under Windows 9x and one that works under Windows NT.

Fortunately, the documentation usually makes it clear under which operating systems a given API function is supported.

The Obstacles to Win32 API Programming Under Visual Basic

There are two aspects to learning how to use the Win32 API under Visual Basic:

- Translating Win32 API functions into the language of Visual Basic so that it can be incorporated into a VB application
- Getting an overall sense of the breadth and depth of the Windows API

We will try to accomplish both goals. However, this is not a reference book on the Win32 API, so as far as the latter goal is concerned, the emphasis is on the words *overall sense*. In many respects, the most difficult part of using the Windows API in *any* language is figuring out whether there is a function that will accomplish a desired goal and just *exactly* what that function does! This can be a very difficult (and frustrating) challenge since the Win32 documentation is, shall we say, not always written with absolute clarity in mind.

The documentation for the Win32 API, which is now part of the MSDN Library documentation, is written in the language of Visual C++ (although the API documentation per se does not use object-oriented techniques, unlike Microsoft Foundation Classes, or MFC). Accordingly, we will spend considerable time learning to translate Visual C++ function declarations and data type declarations into the language of Visual Basic. When you are done with this book, you should be just about as comfortable reading a VC++ declaration as a VB declaration.

Lest you think that translating the VC++ declarations of Win32 functions into Visual Basic should be a trivial task, note that Win32 uses literally *thousands* of different "data types" in its function declarations. In order to translate an API function declaration into VB, we must be prepared to replace any of these data types with the dozen or so that VB understands. More seriously, VB treats strings and structures (user-defined types) quite differently than does Win32. Nevertheless, the secret to successful translation is practice, and you will get plenty of that in this book.

Proceed with Circumspection

Of course, the Win32 API is not the only solution to all programming issues. Many tasks can be handled in more than one way. For instance, suppose we (as VB programmers) want to create a text file on the hard disk. We have several choices:

- Use the familiar VB **Open** statement whose complete syntax is:

    ```
    Open pathname For mode [Access access] [lock] _
    As [#] filenumber [Len=reclength]
    ```

- Take advantage of the new FileSystemObject object model found in the Windows Scripting Runtime Library:

    ```
    Dim fso As New FileSystemObject
    Dim ts As TextStream
    Set ts = fso.CreateTextFile("d:\temp\doc.txt", True)
    ```

- Use the Win32 API *CreateFile* function, whose rather formidable syntax is:

    ```
    Private Declare Function CreateFile Lib "kernel32" _
        Alias "CreateFileA" ( _
        ByVal lpFileName As String, _
        ByVal dwDesiredAccess As Long, _
    ```

```
   ByVal dwShareMode As Long, _
   ByVal lpSecurityAttributes As Long, _
   ByVal dwCreationDisposition As Long, _
   ByVal dwFlagsAndAttributes As Long, _
   ByVal hTemplateFile As Long _
) As Long
```

The *CreateFile* function returns a low-level handle to the file. Of course, using *CreateFile* only makes sense when it offers some advantages over the other higher-level and much simpler choices. We will see an example of this in Chapter 10, *Objects and Their Handles*, where we will use the file handle to map a portion of the file directly into memory.

To create a simple text file, it makes more sense to use one of the simpler, higher-level methods. In fact, the FileSystemObject object uses the *CreateFile* API function to accomplish its goal, so why not take advantage of that? Indeed, Figure 1-1 shows the API functions that are imported (that is, used by) the file *SCRRUN.DLL*, which houses the FileSystemObject object. Note that the list includes *CreateFileA* and *CreateFileW*, which are the ANSI and Unicode versions of *CreateFile*. (Incidentally, the program *rpiPEInfo* shown in Figure 1-1 is one of the applications we will create in this book.)

To be sure, the Win32 API is the lowest level accessible to the programmer (VB or VC++). It allows the VC++–programmer to access the full power of the Windows operating system, and it allows the VB programmer to get much closer to this goal than by using VB alone.

When faced with a programming issue, however, it is generally wise to find the highest-level solution, except perhaps in cases where performance is a serious issue. As you will see as you read this book, there are a great many situations in which the Win32 API is that highest level!

Cautions

Working with the Win32 API is not like working with Visual Basic. With the Win32 API, we are much "closer" to the operating system, and there are far fewer protections than under Visual Basic. Indeed, VB is a *very* protected environment, for which we pay a penalty in terms of limited access to the operating system itself and very limited *direct* access to memory.

In particular, when we read or write to memory, we take certain risks (but nothing that a reboot won't fix). If we attempt (either deliberately or inadvertently) to write to or read from protected memory, the operating system will hopefully raise a *General Protection Fault*, or GPF. Figure 1-2 shows an example of a GPF dialog (under Windows NT 4.0).

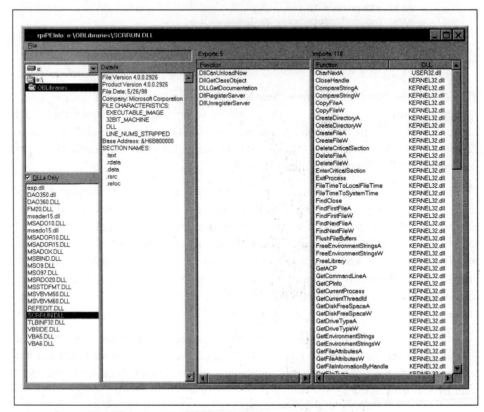

Figure 1-1. Imports of the scripting runtime library

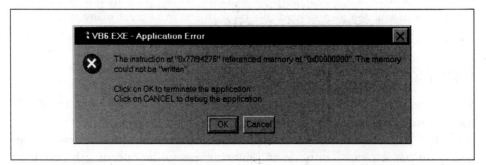

Figure 1-2. A General Protection Fault

Generally speaking, one of two things will happen when we hit the OK button:

- The operating system will abruptly terminate the VB session, but Windows and all other applications will continue to work normally.

- The entire system will become unstable, exhibiting some form of idiosyncratic behavior. *In this case, we may lose all unsaved data and must reboot the system.*

I have been programming using Windows API for some time now, under both Windows 95 and Windows NT 4 (but not under Windows 98), and I can tell you from experience that the latter scenario tends to happen much more often under Windows 95 than under Windows NT, which makes perfect sense in view of our earlier discussion about memory protection. In fact, I have very rarely crashed Windows NT (although it has happened a few times).

In any case, this leads me to the single most important maxim for Win32 API programming (or any programming, for that matter):

> Save all work in all applications, including the VB project, before running any code, especially if it contains API function calls.

2

Preliminaries

In this chapter, we cover some preliminary topics that are required for the remainder of the book.

Character Codes

A *character code* is just a mapping from a set of consecutive integers (starting with 0) to a set of characters. The Windows API uses several different character codes.

ASCII

The original ASCII (American Standard Code for Information Interchange) character code contains 128 characters, including the familiar Roman letters, Arabic digits, and various punctuation marks, mapped to the first 128 nonnegative integers, represented as 8-bit binary numbers. When IBM introduced the PC in 1981, it extended the ASCII character code by adding an additional 128 characters, including some foreign language characters, a very few mathematical symbols, and several graphics symbols for making boxes and the like on a character mode display. This 256-character code is known as the *extended ASCII code*.

ANSI

Microsoft adopted the American National Standard Institute or ANSI character code for use with Windows 1.0 (released in 1985). The first 128 characters and their codes are the same as in ASCII, but the upper 128 characters are different. For some reason, not all of the upper 128 code values were mapped to characters. I have yet to hear a reasonable explanation for this seemingly unnecessary waste of precious resources.

In 1987, Microsoft introduced the idea of a *code page*, which is just a mapping from characters to numbers. IBM's original extended ASCII character code became code page 437 or *MS-DOS Latin US*. All code pages have the same lower 128 characters (in the same places) but the upper 128 characters vary from page to page.

Although code pages proliferated, they did not solve the real problem, which is that 256 characters are simply not enough to satisfy the needs of the entire world! For instance, the Chinese and Japanese languages each have more than 20,000 characters, and there are many hundreds of mathematical and scientific symbols.

DBCS

To accommodate large character sets, the awkward *double-byte character set* (or DBCS) was devised. To say that DBCS is awkward is to be overly kind. We could say a lot more about a character map in which some characters have 8-bit codes whereas others have 16-bit codes! It is not hard to imagine the problems that such a character code creates. For instance, there is no way to determine the number of characters in a binary string from its length!

Fortunately, DBCS is supported only in versions of Windows designed specifically for countries that require this code. We will ignore it completely, but you will see it mentioned in the Win32 documentation.

Unicode

The Unicode project began in 1988. Unicode is a 2-byte character code, allowing for 65,536 distinct characters, which is enough for the foreseeable future. Version 2.0 of the standard includes 38,885 characters. Microsoft uses the term *wide character* as a synonym for Unicode character, although others use the term to represent any 2-byte character code.

The first 256 Unicode characters are the same as in the extended ASCII character code, with the high-order byte of each codeword set to 0. Beyond this, several blocks of contiguous code values are mapped to blocks of related symbols, with lots of room in between blocks for future expansion. For instance, the Greek alphabet lies within the range &H370–&H3FF, along with some other characters (the lowercase alpha has code number &H3B1).

The *Unicode Consortium* is responsible for overseeing the development of the Unicode character set and providing technical information about the code. The Consortium cooperates with the ISO in refining the Unicode specification and expanding the character set. The Consortium consists of major computer corporations (such as IBM, Apple, Hewlett-Packard, and Xerox), software companies (such as Microsoft, Abode, Lotus, and Netscape), international agencies, universities and even some individuals. You can find more information about Unicode and the Unicode Consortium at *http://www.unicode.org/unicode/contents.html.*

It is important to note that when a 2-byte integer (such as a Unicode codeword) is stored in memory, the low-order byte is stored first. For instance, the Unicode codeword &H0041 will appear in memory as 41 00.

Unicode Support Under Windows

Windows NT uses Unicode as its native character code. In other words, Windows NT was designed specifically to use Unicode. It also supports ANSI for compatibility purposes. However, Windows 9x does not support Unicode, except in some special cases. In particular, Unicode is used for all OLE-related API functions and for a handful of other API functions. As I mentioned earlier, this is one of Windows 9x's major shortcomings.

On the other hand, Visual Basic uses Unicode internally to represent strings (whether running on Windows NT or Windows 9x). The lack of full support for Unicode under Windows 9x has significant consequences, as we shall see in Chapter 6, *Strings*.

Parameters and Arguments

Throughout the book, I will try to make the proper distinction between a parameter and an argument—a *parameter* is a placekeeper that is used in the declaration of a function; an *argument* is the actual object being passed to the function. Thus, the parameter appears in the declaration of the function, whereas the argument appears in the call to the function.

IN and OUT Parameters

Generally speaking, a parameter to a function can be used for one of two non-mutually exclusive purposes:

- To send a value to the function
- To return a value from the function

A parameter that is used to send a value to a function is called an *IN* parameter, and one that is used to return a value is called an *OUT* parameter. If a parameter functions in both capacities, it is referred to as an *IN/OUT* parameter. The words IN and OUT are occasionally used in the documentation, but this is rare.

ByVal and ByRef

As you no doubt know, the difference between parameter passing by value and by reference can be summarized as follows:

> Using ByVal asks VB to pass the value of the argument, whereas using ByRef asks VB to pass the address of (that is, a pointer to) the argument.

It is particularly important to have a clear understanding of the differences between passing by value and passing by reference, because when dealing with API function calls, a slip here will generally mean a GPF.

Dynamic Link Libraries

The Windows API functions are implemented in dynamic link libraries (DLLs), so it might be a good idea to briefly discuss DLLs and how they work. We will have much more to say about DLLs later in the book.

A *dynamic link library*, or DLL for short, is an executable file that contains one or more *exportable* functions, that is, functions that can be called from another executable (*EXE* or *DLL*). In many ways, DLLs are much simpler than EXE files, since they do not contain code to manage a graphical interface or to process Windows messages, for instance.

To clarify the terminology, an *executable file*, also called an *image file*, is a file that adheres to the *Portable Executable* (PE) file format specification. These files have the extension *EXE* or *DLL*. To confuse matters, the term executable file is often used to refer to EXE files only. (We will devote an entire chapter to the PE file format.)

Unfortunately, Visual Basic cannot create traditional DLLs. It is capable of creating a very useful form of DLL called an *ActiveX server*. However, these DLLs do not export functions in the traditional manner. Rather, they export *Automation objects*, along with their properties and methods. For this reason, they are also called *Automation servers*. We will speak no more about these special types of DLLs.

To say that DLLs are ubiquitous under the Windows operating system seems like an incredible understatement. For instance, the Windows NT system that I am using to write this book currently has no fewer than 1,029 *distinct* DLLs on the hard disk, taking about 93 megabytes of disk space!

Windows uses several DLLs to house the Win32 API functions. In fact, most of the more than 2,000 functions in the Win32 API are contained in three DLLs:

KERNEL32.DLL
 Exports about 700 functions that manage memory, processes, and threads

USER32.DLL
 Exports about 600 functions that control the user interface, such as creating windows and sending messages

GDI32.DLL
 Exports about 400 functions for drawing graphical images, displaying text, and manipulating fonts

In addition to these DLLs, Windows also includes several other DLLs for more specialized tasks. Following are some examples.

COMDLG32.DLL

   Exports about 20 functions for controlling the Windows common dialogs

LZ32.DLL

   Exports a dozen functions for file compression and expansion

ADVAPI32.DLL

   Exports about 400 functions for object security and registry manipulation

WINMM.DLL

   Exports about 200 multimedia-related functions

Export Tables

Needless to say, a DLL is useless if we cannot determine what functions it exports. (It also helps to have some good documentation!) Each DLL contains a table of names of the functions that the DLL exports. This is called the *export table* of the DLL. (Some functions are exported from a DLL by position only, but we won't worry about that.)

Also, each DLL has an import table that lists the external functions that are called by the DLL. This is called the *import table* of the DLL.

It may surprise you to learn that it is not easy to view the export or import tables of a DLL. It is almost as though there were a conspiracy to hide this information. In particular, Visual Basic has no tools to view these tables. Visual C++ comes with a program called *DUMPBIN.EXE* that can be used for this purpose, and sometimes the Window QuickView utility will show these tables for a DLL.

You might argue that there is no point in knowing just the names of a DLL's exportable functions, because without information about the functions' parameters and return values (that is, how to use the functions), the functions are not very useful. Nevertheless, there are times when the "documentation" forgets to report which of several DLLs exports a given function! In these cases, we can benefit by searching export tables. Also, sometimes the import table of a DLL will give us an idea as to how a certain feature of the DLL is implemented.

In any case, one of the main applications that we will discuss in this book is a PE file information utility, whose main window is shown in Figure 2-1. (The application is included on the CD that accompanies this book.) Writing this application will give us some valuable experience dealing with the Win32 API, and the application may come in handy from time to time as well.

The Role of DLLs—Dynamic Linking

Windows applications, whether written in Visual Basic or Visual C++, are extremely complex—far too complex to be completely self-contained. Indeed, a Windows application requires a great many external functions, including Win32

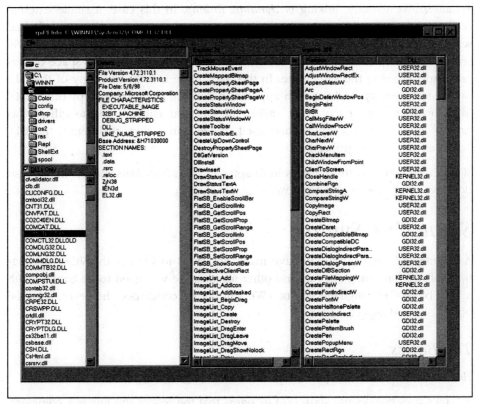

Figure 2-1. PE file information utility

API functions and various VB or C runtime functions that are generally contained in precompiled code modules or *code libraries* of some form.

Generally speaking, there are two ways to incorporate external code into an application. The simplest method is to incorporate the external code *directly* into the application's executable at creation time (that is, at *link* time). This is referred to as *static linking*.

Static linking has both advantages and disadvantages. Among its advantages is simplicity, for it does produce self-contained applications. The problem with this is that a Windows application that contained all code necessary to be entirely self-contained would be prohibitively large.

Static linking also resolves versioning problems, since the executable carries with it its own version of all necessary code. But that also has a downside. If an error is found in an external code module, the executable will need to be relinked with the corrected library. The main problem, however, is that static linking promotes duplication of code. The same code library may end up in several dozen different applications on the same machine.

An alternative to static linking is *dynamic linking*. In this case, a single external code module can service multiple applications. Simply put, an application is linked with *references* to external functions in external *dynamic link libraries*. As we will see, a single physical copy of a DLL can be mapped into the address space of several applications at the same time. In this way, there is only one copy of the DLL in physical memory, and yet each application thinks it has its own copy of the DLL in its own memory space. Thus, calling the DLL's functions is just as efficient as calling code within the application itself. Indeed, in a very real sense, the DLL becomes part of the application.

We will elaborate on these issues in Chapter 13, *Windows Memory Architecture*, so don't worry too much about it now.

Some C++ Syntax

As mentioned earlier, we will have many occasions to look at the VC++ declarations of API functions. For this and other reasons, we will need to be familiar with a little bit of C++ language syntax. (We will not be concerned, however, with the object-oriented aspects of C++.)

The Basics

Here are two basic assumptions about the C++ language syntax:

- C++ uses the double slash (//) to signal that the rest of the line is a comment. This is the analog of Visual Basic's apostrophe.

- Extra whitespace (spaces and carriage returns) is ignored in C++. In particular, no line continuation character is required. For example, the function declaration:

  ```
  VOID CopyMemory(PVOID Destination, CONST VOID *Source, DWORD Length);
  ```

  is equivalent to the more readable:

  ```
  VOID CopyMemory(
    PVOID Destination,   // pointer to address of copy destination
    CONST VOID *Source,  // pointer to address of block to copy
    DWORD Length         // size, in bytes, of block to copy
  );
  ```

  This formatting also allows us to add comments to each parameter declaration, a feature that would be very useful in documenting VB declarations.

- Almost all lines of C++ code end with a semicolon. Curly braces ({}) are used to enclose multiline blocks of code.

- C++ is a case-sensitive language. *This also applies to all of the Win32 API function names!*

Declaring Variables

A variable that is declared in Visual Basic in the form:

```
Dim VarName as VarType
```

is declared in C++ using the more concise syntax:

```
VarType VarName;
```

For instance:

```
Dim x as Long        ' declare a long
```

becomes:

```
int x;          // declare an integer
```

(In C++, an integer is 4 bytes in size.)

Declaring Arrays

To declare an array, such as an integer array with 100 elements, we write:

```
int iArr[100];
```

Note, however, that the index for this array ranges from 0 to 99, so that (unlike in VB), the value `iArr(100)` is invalid. Note also that VC++ uses square brackets rather than parentheses for array indices.

Declaring Functions

A function that is declared in Visual Basic in the form:

```
Function FName(Para1 as Type1, Para2 as Type2,...) as ReturnType
```

is declared in C++ using the more concise syntax:

```
ReturnType FName(Type1 Para1, Type2 Para2,...)
```

For example:

```
Function Sum(x as Long, y as Long) As Long
```

becomes:

```
int Sum(int x, int y);
```

Pointers

Simply put, a *pointer* is a memory address. Under Win32, all memory addresses are 32 bits long. A *pointer variable* (often just called a *pointer*) is a variable of type pointer, that is, a variable that the compiler (VB or VC++) interprets as holding an address. Figure 2-2 shows a pointer variable.

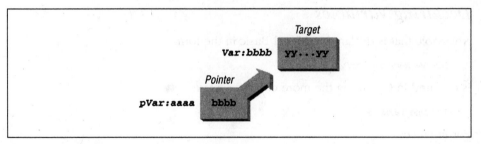

Figure 2-2. A pointer

In this figure, *Var* is a variable of some type or other (integer, long, character, whatever). Its contents are yy...yy and its address is bbbb. The variable *pVar* is a pointer variable. It contains the address of *Var* and so, like all pointer variables, has length 32 bits. We say that *pVar* points to *Var* and that *Var* is the *target* of the pointer. If *Var* has type Integer, for example, we would say that *pVar* is an *integer pointer.*

Pointers and pointer variables are extremely powerful objects, and Win32 makes *extensive* use of them. Accordingly, VC++ fully supports pointers and pointer operations. An example of the influence of pointers on the VC++ language can be seen in *pointer arithmetic,* which can seem quite strange to the uninitiated.

The following code (whose syntax we will discuss in more detail later), declares an integer pointer *pi* and then prints the value of both *pi* and *pi*+1:

```
int i = 1;      // declare integer and initialize
int *pi;        // declare pointer to integer
pi = &i;        // set pointer to point to integer (& is VC++ AddressOf operator)
cout << pi << " / " << pi+1;     // print value of pi and pi+1
```

Surprisingly, the output is:

```
0x0012FF78 / 0x0012FF7C
```

(0x is the prefix that VC++ uses to indicate hex). Note that *pi* + 1 is actually 4 larger than *pi*!

The reason for this is that the VC++ compiler understands both that *pi* points to (holds the address of) a 4-byte integer and that the *only* reason to add 1 to a pointer is to point to the next item (in this case, 4-byte integer) in memory, whose address is 4 greater than the address of the current integer. Hence, it adds 4 (not 1) to the value of the pointer! You can probably see that, while this may seem strange at first, it can be very useful, because it allows us to simply add 1 to any pointer to point to the next item of whatever the target type is: integer, long, character, etc.

Unlike VC++, Visual Basic makes every effort to hide pointers from the programmer. The reason is that programming with pointers can be dangerous in the sense that the accidental (or deliberate) misuse of a pointer can easily result in an attempt to access protected memory. In fact, as we will see in Chapter 13, the Windows operating system deliberately "wastes" some memory address space in order to safely detect the accidental use of the *null pointer*, that is, a pointer to the 0 address. For instance, it is a relatively common mistake to forget to initialize a pointer variable, since this requires defining a target variable, as we did in the previous code. If we forget to initialize a pointer, the result is a null pointer.

In any case, since Win32 uses pointers constantly, we will need to deal with pointers in VB. As it happens, there are some tricks that make this possible. We will be able to do just about anything necessary except call a function using a pointer to that function (which is very easy to do in VC++).

Declaring a pointer in VC++ is easy. It is done using the syntax:

```
targetdatatype *pointervariable;
```

(A space before or after the * is optional, but at least one of them should be included for clarity.) For instance, to declare a pointer to an integer, we write:

```
int *pi;
```

It is possible to declare a pointer variable without knowing the target data type. This is done by writing:

```
void *pWhatever;
```

Incidentally, as we will see, VC++ is replete with synonyms for data types. Thus, you may also see this declaration in the equivalent form:

```
LPVOID pWhatever;
```

where LPVOID stands for *long pointer to a void.*

By Indirections, Find Directions Out

The asterisk (*) is known as the *indirection operator.* It is used both to define a pointer variable (as above) and to get at the value pointed to by a pointer variable, that is, the value of the target variable. For instance, the following code:

```
int i;        // declare integer
int *pi;      // declare pointer
pi = &i;      // set pointer to address of integer
i = 5;        // place value in integer variable

// output to console
cout << "Pointer: " << pi << "  Target: " << *pi;
```

produces the following output to a DOS window:

```
Pointer: 0x0012FF78  Target: 5
```

Note that in the last line, the expression `*pi` means "that which is pointed to by the pointer `pi`" or more succinctly, "the target of `pi`."

Note also that the & operator, called the *address-of* operator, returns the address of its operand. Thus:

```
&var
```

is the address of the variable *var*. This operator is very useful for filling in pointer variables.

Pointers in Visual Basic

The indirection and address-of operators are the key to using pointers in VC++. As it happens, the address-of operator has an undocumented counterpart in Visual Basic and the indirection operator can be faked without too much trouble through the use of the API function *CopyMemory*.

Visual Basic has an undocumented function called *VarPtr*, left over from the days of QuickBasic. The QuickBasic documentation says that *VarPtr* returns the offset of a variable and *VarSeg* returns the segment. The days of segmented addressing are mercifully gone, but *VarPtr* seems to have survived. It now simply returns the address of a variable, that is:

```
. VarPtr(var)
```

is the address of the variable *var*. If you are not comfortable using an undocumented VB function, you can also use the function *rpiVarPtr* from the *rpiAPI.dll* library on the CD that accompanies this book. The expression:

```
rpiVarPtr(var)
```

is equivalent to `VarPtr(var)`. However, for reasons we will discuss in Chapter 6, *rpiVarPtr* does not work on string variables. (This has to do with the translation from Unicode to ANSI that is performed automatically by VB when it calls an external function with a string parameter.)

Incidentally, you might be interested in the C code for this function:

```
int WINAPI rpiVarPtr(int pVar)
{
   return pVar;
}
```

This function just returns its argument. By declaring this function in VB as:

```
Public Declare Function rpiVarPtr Lib "rpiAPI.dll" ( _
   ByRef pVar As Any _
) As Long
```

the argument is passed to the function by reference. That is, VB passes the *address of* the argument to this function, which is unceremoniously returned as a VB `long`.

Note that using `As Any` in the declaration of *rpiVarPtr* prevents VB from checking the data type of the parameter, so we can pass it a variable of any type. This means we don't need to have *rpiVarPtrByte*, *rpiVarPtrInteger*, and *rpiVarPtrLong* functions, for instance. (Again, *rpiVarPtr* does not work on strings.)

To do indirection, we need some way to retrieve the target of a pointer. The simplest way to do this is to use the *CopyMemory* API function, which copies bytes of memory from one address to another address. We will discuss the details of how to use *CopyMemory* in general and how to do indirection in particular in the next chapter. There are also some functions to do indirection in the *rpiAPI.dll* library that accompanies this book.

3

API Declarations

As we mentioned earlier, the Windows API contains well over 2,000 functions. Of course, since the API is intended to be used in the VC++ environment, all of the declarations are in the Visual C++ language (that is, the C++ language with Microsoft's VC++ extensions). Here is an example of an API declaration taken from the Win32 documentation on the MSDN Library CD:

```
LRESULT SendMessage(
   HWND hWnd,          // handle of destination window
   UINT Msg,           // message to send
   WPARAM wParam,      // first message parameter
   LPARAM lParam       // second message parameter
);
```

One possible translation into VB (and there are others, as we will see) is:

```
Declare Function SendMessage Lib "user32" Alias "SendMessageA" ( _
    ByVal hwnd As Long, _
    ByVal lMsg As Long, _
    ByVal wParam As Long, _
    ByRef lParam As Any) _
As Long
```

In this chapter, we want to lay down a few basic principles for making such translations. We will assume that you are familiar with the concepts of passing parameters by value and by reference.

For convenience, we will refer to any procedure (function or subroutine) that resides in a DLL and is intended for export as an *external function*. (The procedure is *external* to the VB application that calls this function.)

The VB Declare Statement

The Visual Basic `Declare` statement is used to call external functions that reside in DLLs. The statement must be used at the module level, rather than the procedure level. There are two syntaxes—one for functions and one for subroutines:

```
[Public | Private] Declare Sub name Lib "libname" _
    [Alias "aliasname"] [([arglist])]
```

and:

```
[Public | Private] Declare Function name Lib "libname" _
    [Alias "aliasname"] [([arglist])] [As type]
```

where the items in square brackets are optional and the bar indicates alternative choices. You can get the complete details on this syntax in the VB help system. Let us discuss some of the highlights.

Public or Private?

When using the `Declare` statement in a standard code module, we can use the `Public` keyword to make the function accessible to the entire VB project. Within a form or class module, however, we must use **Private** or VB will complain.

The Calling Name

The *name* keyword should be replaced by the name of the function, *as we intend to call it from our VB code*. As we will see, at times there are good reasons for this name to differ from the actual function name as defined in the DLL. To use a different name, we must employ the **Alias** syntax, discussed below. It is important to note that, unlike names in VB, *DLL function names are case-sensitive* (as is everything in the VC++ language)!

The Export Library

The phrase:

```
Lib "libname"
```

is used to indicate the source DLL that exports the function. For Win32 API calls, this is usually (but not always) one of the "big three":

KERNEL32.DLL
USER32.DLL
GDI32.DLL

For these three DLLs, you can omit the extension *.DLL* in *libname*, as we did in the example at the beginning of this chapter.

Aliases

As mentioned, there are several reasons for calling a DLL function using a name that is different from its true name, as defined in the DLL. This is done using the `Alias` keyword. Here are three compelling reasons to use aliases.

Avoiding VB keywords and illegal characters

Some API functions have the same names as VB functions. *SetFocus* is a case in point:

```
HWND SetFocus(HWND hWnd);
```

We cannot declare this in VB as:

```
Declare Function SetFocus Lib "user32" (ByVal hwnd As Long) As Long
```

because *SetFocus* is a VB keyword. But we can declare it as:

```
Declare Function SetFocusAPI Lib "user32" Alias "SetFocus" ( _
    ByVal hwnd As Long) As Long
```

In addition, some API functions use characters that are illegal in VB, as with the file functions *_hread*, *_hwrite*, *_lclose*, and so on, which begin with an underscore. We can alias these names to names that omit the leading underscore.

Fortunately, not many API functions either are VB keywords or contain illegal characters, but when it does happen, we would not be able to use them in VB were it not for aliases.

ANSI versus Unicode

The Win32 API functions that use string parameters generally come in two versions—one for ANSI and one for Unicode. The *SendMessage* function defined at the beginning of this chapter is a case in point.

There are actually two different *SendMessage* functions defined in the *USER32.DLL* library. The ANSI version is called *SendMessageA* and the Unicode version is called *SendMessageW* (the W is for wide). In the jargon, we would say that there are two *entry points* for the *SendMessage* function. Rather than sprinkling our code with As or Ws, it makes more sense to make the choice once in the declaration and then use the unadorned word *SendMessage* throughout the code. For one thing, this would make any future changes simpler.

As we have said, Windows NT supports Unicode. It therefore implements the Unicode entry points for API functions that have string parameters. For compatibility, Windows NT also implements the ANSI entry points, but these implementations generally just make the necessary conversions, call the corresponding Unicode version of the function, and convert back to ANSI!

On the other hand, Windows 9x generally does not support Unicode, except for some limited situations. According to Microsoft:

> Windows 95 does not implement the Unicode (or wide character) version of most Win32 functions that take string parameters. With some exceptions, these functions are implemented as stubs that simply return success without modifying any arguments.

This seems rather ill advised. Would it not be better to return a value that does not indicate success when the function has done nothing?

In any case, there are some exceptions to this rule. In particular, Windows 9x does support Unicode entry points in the OLE-related API functions, as well as a handful of other API functions, as shown in Table 3-1.

Table 3-1. The Unicode API Functions Implemented in Windows 9x

EnumResourceLanguages	*FindResourceEx*	*GetTextExtentPoint*
EnumResourceNames	*GetCharWidth*	*lstrlen*
EnumResourceTypes	*GetCommandLine*	*MessageBoxEx*
ExtTextOut	*GetTextExtentExPoint*	*MessageBox*
FindResource	*GetTextExtentPoint32*	*TextOut*

In addition, Windows 9x implements two conversion functions: *MultiByteToWideChar* and *WideCharToMultiByte*.

Let us take special note of the fact that Windows 9x does implement the Unicode version of *lstrlen* (which is called *lstrlenW*). This function returns the number of characters in a null-terminated Unicode character array. This will prove to be useful to us later in the book.

As we will see in Chapter 6, *Strings*, the best course of action for a VB programmer is simply to call the ANSI entry points, since they are compatible with both Windows 9x and Windows NT.

Parameter type declarations

The third reason to use aliases has to do with the type declarations of the parameters in a `Declare` statement. We will examine this issue in detail later in this chapter.

Suffice it to say now that we may want to declare several *versions* of a single external function using different data types for some of the parameters. One reason for this is to take advantage of VB's type-checking capabilities to catch type-declaration errors before they reach the DLL, when they will probably cause a General Protection Fault (GPF). To do so, we will need to use aliases.

The Parameter List

The *arglist* is a list of parameters and their data types. Its (simplified) syntax is:

```
[ByVal | ByRef] varname[( )] [As type]
```

where the optional parentheses following **varname** are required for array variables.

The **type** keyword can be any of the following: **Byte**, **Boolean**, **Integer**, **Long**, **Currency**, **Single**, **Double**, **Date**, **String** (variable length only), **Variant**, user-defined, or object. (Actually, fixed-length strings can appear as procedure arguments, but they are converted to variable-length strings before being passed to the function.)

The VC-to-VB Translation Game Plan

Generally speaking, translating a VC++-style API function declaration into VB involves the following steps:

1. Get the library name (DLL name and path) for the **Lib** clause of the VB declaration.

2. Translate the return type of the function from a VC++ data type to a VB data type.

3. Translate each parameter declaration from VC++ to VB. This involves choosing a VB data type and also deciding whether to use **ByVal** or **ByRef**.

4. Decide upon an alias name, if necessary. This can be done for descriptive reasons or for the reasons discussed earlier.

No doubt the most difficult part of this translation process is the parameter data type translation process, so let us elaborate on this.

Passing Parameters to an External Function

The procedure for parameter declarations and parameter passing for external DLL functions is quite similar to that of ordinary VB functions except in three cases: strings, addresses, and structures (user-defined types). However, handling strings and structures just involves handling addresses, so it all boils down to addresses, that is, to *pointers*. So let us discuss pointers now. We will consider strings in Chapter 6 and structures in Chapter 4, *Data Types*.

The most important thing to remember about parameter declaration and parameter passing when it comes to external DLL functions is that we are really contending with *two* declarations—the defining declaration in the DLL as well as the VB declaration in the `Declare` statement. Our job is to match the VB `Declare` statement to the defining DLL declaration.

In particular, it is important to keep in mind that any `ByVal` and `ByRef` keywords that appear in a `Declare` statement are instructions to Visual Basic, not to the DLL.

An Example to Illustrate the Possibilities

We can illustrate these issues using a simple external function:

```
short WINAPI rpiAddOne(short *pVar)
{
    return ++(*pVar);
}
```

Note that this function expects a pointer to a VC++ `short`, which is the same as a VB integer, as an argument. In other words, we need to pass the address of an integer variable. The function then just increments the value of that integer, but this really doesn't matter; we are interested only in how to declare and pass the parameter.

Now, there are three cases to consider. Note that these are not mutually exclusive—we will often have a choice between them.

Case 1

In some cases, we will have the address of the integer variable in another variable, that is, we will have a pointer to the integer variable. This may happen because this address was returned to us by another API function, for instance. Say the address is in the `long` variable *pTargetVar*. In this case, we want to pass the contents of the pointer variable. For this, we should make the VB declaration (note the alias, because there will be other versions):

```
Public Declare Sub rpiAddOneByValAsLong Lib "rpiAPI.dll" Alias "rpiAddOne" ( _
    ByVal pTargetVar As Long)
```

and then make the call:

```
rpiAddOneByValAsLong pTargetVar
```

Case 2

If we are not given the address, we can always generate it using *VarPtr* or *rpiVarPtr*. Suppose that the target variable is *iTargetVar*. Then we can use the same declaration as in the previous case and make the call:

```
rpiAddOneByValAsLong VarPtr(iTargetVar)
```

In either situation, we are passing the actual address of the integer variable, as desired.

Case 3

If we are not given the address explicitly and do not want to use the *VarPtr* or *rpiVarPtr* functions, we can pass the target variable by reference, letting VB generate and pass its address for us. After all, that is precisely what passing by reference means! In this case, we make a different VB declaration:

```
Public Declare Sub rpiAddOneByRefAsInteger Lib "rpiAPI.dll" Alias "rpiAddOne" ( _
    Var As Integer)
```

and then make the call:

```
rpiAddOneByRefAsInteger iTargetVar
```

Note that the **ByRef** declaration is type-specific, in this case to the type **Integer**.

Passing a Parameter as Any

Many API functions expect a pointer as an argument, but don't care about the type of the target variable. In fact, my *rpiVarPtr* is one such function. To emphasize this fact, I could have defined this function in *rpiAPI.dll* as follows:

```
void* WINAPI rpiVarPtr(void *pVar)
{
    return pVar;
}
```

The parameter declaration:

```
void *pVar
```

says that *pVar* is a void pointer, which is VC++'s way of saying that it doesn't care what the pointer is pointing to. We will encounter void pointers often in API functions.

In any case, since I didn't care what type of pointer was coming in to the function, and since all pointers are VC++ integers, it seemed easier to make the declaration:

```
int WINAPI rpiVarPtr(int pVar)
{
    return pVar;
}
```

The point here is that to use a VB declaration of the form of case 3 above, using **ByRef** parameter passing, we would need a separate declaration (alias) for each target data type, as in:

```
Public Declare Function rpiVarPtrByRefAsByte Lib "rpiAPI.dll" _
Alias "rpiVarPtr" ( _
    ByRef pVar As Byte _
) As Long

Public Declare Function rpiVarPtrByRefAsInteger Lib "rpiAPI.dll" _
Alias "rpiVarPtr" ( _
```

```
    ByRef pVar As Integer _
) As Long

Public Declare Function rpiVarPtrByRefAsLong Lib "rpiAPI.dll" _
Alias "rpiVarPtr" ( _
    ByRef pVar As Long _
) As Long
```

To avoid this, VB supports the **As Any** declaration:

```
Public Declare Function rpiVarPtrByRefAsAny Lib "rpiAPI.dll"_
Alias "rpiVarPtr" ( _
    ByRef pVar As Any _
) As Long
```

This type-insensitive declaration is more flexible, but also has the disadvantage that it suppresses VB's data type checking. This can be dangerous, because if a type error gets past VB and reaches the DLL, it is likely to cause a GPF.

In any case, the use of **As Any** can be a time saver. While some authors advise against it, I say it's up to you. Use it with circumspection and you can save some extra coding work. Use it carelessly and the amount of work you save will pale in comparison to the amount of time you will spend chasing down the cause of GPFs!

ByVal Again

We should conclude with a little-known fact about **ByVal**. Namely, we can override the default **ByRef** setting for an external function—and only for an external function—by including the word **ByVal** in the function call. For example, consider the *CopyMemory* function:

```
VOID CopyMemory(
    PVOID Destination,  // pointer to address of copy destination
    CONST VOID *Source, // pointer to address of block to copy
    DWORD Length        // size, in bytes, of block to copy
);
```

The first parameter is the address of the destination variable of the copy operation. (We will discuss this function in detail a bit later, so don't worry about that now.)

One possible VB declaration of *CopyMemory* is:

```
Declare Sub CopyMemory Lib "kernel32" Alias "RtlMoveMemory" ( _
    Dest As Any, _
    Source As Any, _
    ByVal cbCopy As Long)
```

Thus, the following VB code will copy the contents of the integer variable *iSource* to the integer variable *iDest*.

```
Dim iSource As Integer
Dim iDest As Integer
iSource = 5

CopyMemory iDest, iSource, 2
```

After running this code, *iDest* will contain 5.

Alternatively, we could replace the call to *CopyMemory* with:

```
CopyMemory ByVal VarPtr(iDest), iSource, 2
```

Admittedly, while there is no reason to do this here, there will be cases when we want to pass by value instead of by reference but don't want to create a separate VB declaration for this purpose.

CopyMemory—A VB Hacker's Dream

One of the API functions we will use most often is *CopyMemory*. The purpose of *CopyMemory* is simply to copy a block of memory byte-by-byte from one memory address to another. This opens up a whole new set of possibilities, since VB does not have this sort of capability, except in the rather restricted form of **LSet**, and even then, the documentation recommends against using **LSet** for this purpose.

The *CopyMemory* function has an interesting history. Actually, it is an alias for the *RtlMoveMemory* API function. Apparently, the name *CopyMemory* was first coined by Bruce McKinney, the author of *Hardcore Visual Basic*. Nevertheless, *CopyMemory* is now in the official Microsoft documentation as:

```
VOID CopyMemory(
  PVOID Destination,   // pointer to address of copy destination
  CONST VOID *Source,  // pointer to address of block to copy
  DWORD Length         // size, in bytes, of block to copy
);
```

The keyword **CONST** simply means that the function *CopyMemory* guarantees not to make any changes to the argument *Source*. Since PVOID is a synonym for VOID *, the two parameters *Source* and *Destination* have the same data type— a pointer to a target variable of unknown type.

The simplest VB declaration for *CopyMemory* is:

```
Declare Sub CopyMemory Lib "kernel32" Alias "RtlMoveMemory" ( _
  lpDest As Any, _
  lpSource As Any, _
  ByVal cbCopy As Long)
```

In this case, *lpDest* is the address of the first byte of the destination memory, *lpSource* is the address of the first byte of the source memory and *cbCopy* is the number of bytes to copy (the *cb* in *cbCopy* stands for *count of bytes*).

We will use this form often, but also take advantage of the fact that we can override the `ByRef` setting by including `ByVal` in the call to this function, as described earlier.

A Simple Example

Let us consider an example. The following code:

```
Dim lng As Long
Dim i As Integer
Dim bArray(1 To 4) As Byte

lng = &H4030201

CopyMemory bArray(1), lng, 4
For i = 1 To 4
   Debug.Print Hex(bArray(i));
Next
```

copies the long variable *lng*, byte-by-byte, to the 4-byte array and then prints those bytes. The output is:

```
1 2 3 4
```

This code shows three interesting things. First, the bytes of a long are stored in memory with the lowest order byte stored at the lowest address, as shown in Figure 3-1.

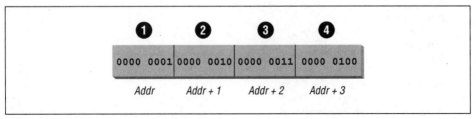

Figure 3-1. The long value &H4030201 stored in memory at address Addr

This method of storing words in memory is referred to as *little endian*. (For more on such things, allow me to refer you to my book *Understanding Personal Computer Hardware*, published by Springer-Verlag, New York.)

Second, the address of a long is the address of the lowest order byte. Third, the code is also one way to extract bytes from an integer or a long.

A More Interesting Example

CopyMemory is very useful for exploring beneath the hood of VB and its interactions with the Win32 API. To illustrate, let's try a little experiment with strings.

Given a VB string, we allocate a byte array, move the bytes from the string to that array, and then examine those bytes.

Here is the code. We will discuss the reason for using `ByVal` with the source string in Chapter 6, so don't worry about that now:

```
Dim sString As String
Dim aBytes(1 To 20) As Byte
Dim i As Integer

sString = "help"

CopyMemory aBytes(1), ByVal sString, LenB(sString)

' Print bytes
For i = 1 To 20
    Debug.Print aBytes(i);
Next
```

The output from this program is:

```
104  101  108  112  0  0  0  0  0  0  0  0  0  0  0  0  0  0  0  0
```

The string officially ends with the first null character (ASCII 0). Note that it appears that the string is in ANSI format—one byte per character. But wait.

Another approach to getting the bytes from the VB string is to declare a long variable and point it to the same character array as the string. We will go into the details of this in Chapter 6, but here is the code:

```
Dim sString As String
Dim aBytes(1 To 20) As Byte
Dim i As Integer
Dim lng As Long

sString = "help"

' Get contents of BSTR variable
lng = StrPtr(sString)

' Now copy as array
CopyMemory aBytes(1), ByVal lng, LenB(sString)

' Print bytes
For i = 1 To 20
    Debug.Print aBytes(i);
Next
```

This time, the output is:

```
104  0  101  0  108  0  112  0  0  0  0  0  0  0  0  0  0  0  0  0
```

which is definitely Unicode (two bytes per character), which seems to contradict the previous output.

As we will see, the fact is that when we pass a string to an external function, such as *CopyMemory*, VB translates the string from Unicode to ANSI. This is why the first output is in ANSI format. However, we were able to bypass VB's translation in the second call to *CopyMemory* by avoiding VB strings altogether. This is why the output is Unicode.

We will explain this in more detail in Chapter 6. For now, we wanted simply to point out how useful *CopyMemory* can be for peering into the inner workings of VB.

Implementing Indirection in Visual Basic

As we mentioned during our discussion of pointers in Chapter 2, *Preliminaries*, *CopyMemory* provides a simple way to implement the C++ indirection operator (*), which retrieves the value of the variable *pointed to* by a pointer variable. In particular, suppose we have a pointer variable *pVar* and we want the contents of the target variable, which in C++ would be easily obtained using the syntax *pVar*.

In VB, we can use the following *CopyMemory* alias:

```
Declare Sub VBGetTarget Lib "kernel32" Alias "RtlMoveMemory" ( _
    Target As Any, _
    ByVal lPointer As Long, _
    ByVal cbCopy As Long)
```

To use this, we need to declare a variable of the same type as the target:

```
Dim Target As TargetType
```

and make the call:

```
VBGetTarget Target, lPointer, BytesToCopy
```

Since *Target* is passed by reference, the function receives the address of this variable. On the other hand, since *Pointer* is passed by value, the function gets the address of the actual target. Thus, the contents of the target are placed in the *Target* variable. Voilà.

If you want to give this a try, just run the following code:

```
Dim Pointer As Long
Dim Target As Integer
Dim i As Integer
i = 123
' Get a pointer
Pointer = VarPtr(i)
' Get the target
VBGetTarget Target, Pointer, LenB(Target)
Debug.Print Target
```

As an alternative, you can use the following functions in the *rpiAPI* DLL.

```
rpiGetTargetByte
rpiGetTargetInteger
rpiGetTargetLong
rpiGetTarget64
```

These functions are defined in the DLL as follows:

```
unsigned char WINAPI rpiGetTargetByte(unsigned char *pByte)
{
    return *pByte;        // return the byte target value
}

short int WINAPI rpiGetTargetInteger(short int *pShort)
{
    return *pShort;       // return the integer target value
}

int WINAPI rpiGetTargetLong(int *pLong)
{
    return *pLong;        // return the long target value
}

__int64 WINAPI rpiGetTarget64(__int64 *p64)
{
    return *p64;          // return the long target value
}
```

Each function takes a pointer to the target variable passed by value and simply returns the target value. Here are the VB declarations:

```
Public Declare Function rpiGetTargetByte Lib "rpiAPI.dll" ( _
    ByVal pByte As Long) As Byte

Public Declare Function rpiGetTargetInteger Lib "rpiAPI.dll" ( _
    ByVal pInteger As Long) As Integer

Public Declare Function rpiGetTargetLong Lib "rpiAPI.dll" ( _
    ByVal pLong As Long) As Long

Public Declare Function rpiGetTarget64 Lib "rpiAPI.dll" ( _
    ByVal p64 As Long) As Currency
```

Dealing with API Errors

In some sense, two types of errors can occur when calling API functions: errors that crash the application and errors that do not crash the application.

When the Program Crashes

If a call to an API function results in a GPF, such as that shown in Figure 3-2, then we might be able to get some help from the memory address shown in the dialog box, but for the most part, we are on our own.

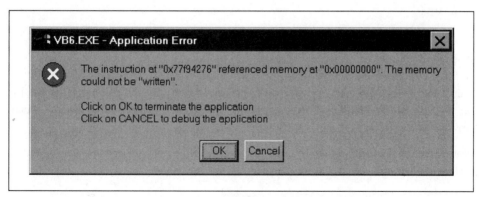

Figure 3-2. A GPF

Here are some things to do, not necessarily in this order:

- Place a breakpoint in your code on the API call that caused the GPF. It may take some experimenting (and several more crashes) to figure out which line actually caused the GPF. Inspect the arguments to the API function very carefully to see if there is an obvious inappropriate value. For instance, often an argument that should be an address or handle is equal to 0. This is definitely going to cause a GPF.

- Check the function declaration for the correct use of **ByVal** and **ByRef**. It is hard to overestimate the number of times that this is the culprit.

- Check the translation from C++ to VB to make sure that the parameters were translated correctly.

When the Program Does Not Crash— Win32 Error Messages

Assuming that a crash does not occur, many API functions will return some useful error information. This can happen in a variety of ways. Some functions return zero on success and a nonzero value on failure. This nonzero value may or may not indicate the source of the problem. You will need to check the documentation to determine the meaning of such returned values. Many API functions return zero on failure and a nonzero value on success. In this case, the return value is no help in tracking down the problem. However, there is still hope.

LastDLLError

Several hundred of the API procedures set an internal error code that is accessible using the *GetLastError* API function, whose syntax is simply:

```
DWORD GetLastError(void);
```

or in VB:

```
Declare Function GetLastError Lib "kernel32" () As Long
```

Apparently, however, Visual Basic may alter the value returned by *GetLastError* before we have a chance to examine that value. Fortunately, VB stores this return value in the LastDLLError property of its **App** object, so we can get at it in this way. The property should be accessed *immediately* after the function call, however.

Note that an API function error does not cause VB to raise an error, so we need to write our own error-trapping code to catch API errors.

FormatMessage

The *FormatMessage* API function can be used to retrieve the text of a Win32 error message, given the error code.

The rather formidable declaration of *FormatMessage* is:

```
DWORD FormatMessage(
    DWORD dwFlags,         // source and processing options
    LPCVOID lpSource,      // pointer to message source
    DWORD dwMessageId,     // requested message identifier
    DWORD dwLanguageId,    // language identifier for requested message
    LPTSTR lpBuffer,       // pointer to message buffer
    DWORD nSize,           // maximum size of message buffer
    va_list *Arguments     // address of array of message inserts
);
```

Here is a VB version:

```
Declare Function FormatMessage Lib "kernel32" Alias "FormatMessageA" ( _
    ByVal dwFlags As Long, _
    lpSource As Any, _
    ByVal dwMessageId As Long, _
    ByVal dwLanguageId As Long, _
    ByVal lpBuffer As String, _
    ByVal nSize As Long, _
    ByVal Arguments As Long _
) As Long
```

We will not go into the details of this complex function. Instead, we will just use it to return a formatted Win32 error message as shown in the *GetErrorText* function below. (Aside from incorporating this code into your VB projects, you could make a small add-in that returns the message from the error code for quick debugging.)

To use the function, you will, of course, need to include the VB declaration of *FormatMessage*, along with the following constant declarations:

```
Public Const FORMAT_MESSAGE_FROM_SYSTEM = &H1000
Public Const FORMAT_MESSAGE_IGNORE_INSERTS = &H200

Public Function GetAPIErrorText(ByVal lError As Long) As String
```

```
Dim sOut As String
Dim sMsg As String
Dim lret As Long

GetErrorText = ""
sMsg = String$(256, 0)

lret = FormatMessage(FORMAT_MESSAGE_FROM_SYSTEM Or _
                FORMAT_MESSAGE_IGNORE_INSERTS, _
                0&, lError, 0&, sMsg, Len(sMsg), 0&)

sOut = "Error: " & lError & "(&H" & Hex(lError) & "): "
If lret <> 0 Then
    ' Check for ending vbcrlf
    sMsg = Trim0(sMsg)
    If Right$(sMsg, 2) = vbCrLf Then sMsg = Left$(sMsg, Len(sMsg) - 2)
    sOut = sOut & Trim0(sMsg)
Else
    sOut = sOut & "<No such error>"
End If

GetErrorText = sOut

End Function
```

Imagine now that we have just called an API function that returns 0 on failure and, according to its documentation, sets *GetLastError*. For example, the following code uses the *GetClassName* function to get the class name of a window from its handle. (We will discuss class names and handles in the chapters on windows.) The function returns 0 if there is an error:

```
Dim s As String
s = String(256, 0)
hnd = Command1.hwnd
lret = GetClassName(hnd, s, 255)

' Check for error
If lret = 0 Then
    MsgBox GetAPIErrorText(Err.LastDllError)
End If
```

If Command1 is a real command button, this should work with no errors. If we replace **Command1.hWnd** with 0, the result will be the dialog box in Figure 3-3.

We will occasionally use the following function, which uses *GetAPIErrorText* to raise an API error. Note that the function adds a sufficiently large number to the original error number so as not to interfere with other error numbers:

```
Public Sub RaiseApiError(ByVal e As Long)
Err.Raise vbObjectError + 29000 + e, App.EXEName & ".Windows", GetAPIErrorText(e)
End Sub
```

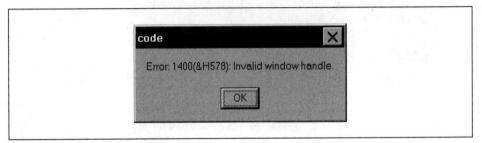

Figure 3-3. An API error message

Now that we have set down some basic principles for dealing with API errors, we may, for the sake of space, ignore these principles for most of the examples in this book.

4

Data Types

In order to understand the Windows API and how to use its functions, it is vital to have a thorough understanding of the concept of a *data type*. Indeed, the Win32 API uses more than a thousand different "data types" (not including structures)!

One of the challenges to successfully using the Windows API from within Visual Basic is to figure out how to translate the required Windows data types into one of only a handful of available Visual Basic data types. This is relatively easy in most cases, but as we will see, there are some tricks when it comes to unsigned data types, strings, and structures.

What Is a Data Type?

It seems like every computer science book that addresses the concept of data type defines the concept somewhat differently. We will adopt a definition that will help us deal effectively with the issue of data type translation between VC++ and VB.

For us, a *data type* (or just *type*) is an object with the following properties:

- A set of values, which we refer to as the *underlying set* for the data type.

- A way to represent the values in computer memory. For those data types for which the representation of every value in the underlying set uses the same number of bits, this number of bits is the *size* of the data type. For instance, under Visual Basic, each member of the Integer data type occupies 16 bits of memory, and so this integer data type has size 16 bits and is thus called a *16-bit data type*. On the other hand, the VC++ integer data type is a 32-bit data type.

- A set of operations that can be performed on the values of this type. It will seldom be necessary for us to enumerate this set of operations explicitly.

- In addition, some data types require an *ancillary data type*. For instance, the ancillary data type for the type *pointer to integer* is the integer data type. More generally, the ancillary data type for a pointer data type is the target data type of the pointer. The ancillary data type for an array data type is the type of the individual array elements. (We won't deal with arrays in which the elements can have different data types.)

Examples of Data Types

To illustrate the definition, let us take a look at a few examples of data types.

The Win32 unsigned integer data type

Under Win32, the *unsigned integer* data type has an underlying set consisting of the mathematical integers from 0 to $2^{32}-1$ inclusive. Each unsigned integer is represented as a 32-bit binary string, so this is a 32-bit data type. The set of operations for this integer data type is the familiar set of binary arithmetic operations, with overflow detection, along with several other types of operations, such as logical operations, which we will not enumerate.

The Win32 integer data type

Under Win32, the *integer* data type (also referred to as the *signed integer* data type) consists of the set of mathematical integers from -2^{31} to $2^{31}-1$ inclusive. Each such value is represented as a 32-bit binary string using *two's complement* representation.

Simply put, two's complement representation uses the leftmost bit, called the *sign bit*, to indicate the sign of the number. Negative numbers have sign bit 1 and positive numbers have sign bit 0. Of course, this has a profound effect on the arithmetic operations that are part of the integer data type, and they are certainly different from the operations of the unsigned integer data type.

We probably should illustrate this quickly. Addition of *unsigned* integers (that is, elements of the unsigned integer data type), works as you might have learned in elementary school:

```
    0100 0000 0000 0000 0000 0000 0000 0000
  +
    0100 0000 0000 0000 0000 0000 0000 0000
    ---------------------------------------
    1000 0000 0000 0000 0000 0000 0000 0000
```

Clearly, this is not correct for the signed integer data type, because the sum of two positive numbers (sign bit = 0) cannot equal a negative number. Thus, addition must be defined differently for these two data types.

We will discuss signed and unsigned data types and the two's complement representation in detail in the next chapter.

The Visual Basic integer data type

Visual Basic's integer data type is not the same as Win32's integer data type (as implemented by VC++, for instance). The VB integer data type is a 16-bit signed data type. In particular, its set of values is the set of integers from -2^{15} to $2^{15}-1$, each of which is represented by a 16-bit two's complement binary string.

The Visual Basic BSTR data type

As we will see in Chapter 6, *Strings*, the data type for a VB string is called the BSTR data type. It is a pointer data type whose ancillary data type is described as a *length-preceded, null-terminated array of Unicode characters*.

Fundamental and Derived Data Types

A *fundamental* data type is one that is not derived from another data type. For instance, the integer and long VB data types are fundamental. A *derived* data type is one that is constructed from fundamental data types. Some examples of derived types are:

- Arrays

- User-defined types (which we will refer to from now on by their C++ name, *structures*)

- Pointers

(Arrays and pointers have ancillary data types whereas structures do not.)

Visual Basic Data Types

The Visual Basic data types are listed in Table 4-1.

Table 4-1. VB Data Types

Type	Size in Bytes	Range of Values
Byte	1	0 to 255
Boolean	2	True and False keywords
Integer	2	–32,768 to 32,767
Long (long integer)	4	–2,147,483,648 to 2,147,483,647
Single (single-precision real)	4	Approximately –3.4E38 to 3.4E38
Double (double-precision real)	8	Approximately –1.8E308 to 4.9E324
Currency (scaled integer)	8	Approximately –922,337,203,685,477.5808 to 922,337,203,685,477.5807

Table 4-1. VB Data Types (continued)

Type	Size in Bytes	Range of Values
Date	8	1/1/100 to 12/31/9999
Object	4	
String (BSTR)	See Chapter 6.	
Fixed-length string	2 bytes for each character	
Variant	16	
Array		
User-defined type (or structure)		

Let us make a few comments about these data types:

- The Boolean data type is a special 16-bit data type with underlying set {True, False}. Nonetheless, True is stored as −1 and False as 0.

- The Byte data type is the only unsigned data type in VB.

- The term *string* is used in an ambiguous way in Visual Basic. We will clarify this in Chapter 6.

- We will often refer to user-defined types as structures (which is the term used in VC++).

- Visual Basic does not have pointer data types, but BSTRs are pointers, as we will see in Chapter 6.

Variants

Variants do not occur very often in Win32 API programming, but they do occur in OLE-related situations, so let us discuss them briefly. A Variant is a special data type that is designed to hold data of different types. It can hold data of any other VB type except fixed-length string. This includes the derived types: array and user-defined type. In addition, a Variant can contain one of four special types of values:

Null
> Indicates that the variable does not contain valid data

Nothing
> A special object type indicating that the Variant has type object (as reported by *VarType*) but does not currently point to a valid Object

Empty
> Indicates that the variable has not yet been assigned a value; that is, the variable is *uninitialized*

An error code
> Indicates that the contents are an error number

To help understand these values and variants in general, we need to take a look at the internal workings of a Variant.

All variants are 16 bytes long. The first two bytes contain a code that indicates the current type of data stored in the Variant. This code is returned by the *VarType* function. Specifically, the return values of *VarType* are shown in Table 4-2.

Table 4-2. The Return Values of VarType

Constant	Value	Description
vbEmpty	0	Empty (uninitialized)
vbNull	1	Null (no valid data)
vbInteger	2	Integer
vbLong	3	Long integer
vbSingle	4	Single-precision floating-point number
vbDouble	5	Double-precision floating-point number
vbCurrency	6	Currency value
vbDate	7	Date value
vbString	8	String
vbObject	9	Object
vbError	10	Error value
vbBoolean	11	Boolean value
vbVariant	12	Variant (used only with *arrays* of variants)
vbDataObject	13	A data access object
vbDecimal	14	Decimal value
vbByte	17	Byte value
vbUserDefinedType	36	Variants that contain user-defined types
vbArray	8192	Array

The *TypeName* function returns a string description of the type stored in a Variant.

The *ShowVariant* procedure in Example 4-1 can be used to peek inside a Variant.

Example 4-1. The ShowVariant Procedure

```
Sub ShowVariant()

Dim i As Integer
Dim aBytes(1 To 50) As Byte
Dim v As Variant

GoSub PrintVariant
Set v = Nothing
GoSub PrintVariant
v = Null
GoSub PrintVariant
```

Example 4-1. The ShowVariant Procedure (continued)

```
v = Empty
GoSub PrintVariant
v = CVErr(123)
GoSub PrintVariant
v = aBytes
GoSub PrintVariant
v = 123
GoSub PrintVariant
v = 100000000
GoSub PrintVariant
v = "ssssssssssssssssssssssssss"
GoSub PrintVariant
v = CSng(1.1)
GoSub PrintVariant
v = 10000000000.9
GoSub PrintVariant
v = CCur(23.34)
GoSub PrintVariant
v = CByte(123)
GoSub PrintVariant
v = True
GoSub PrintVariant
v = #12/12/1998#
GoSub PrintVariant

Exit Sub
PrintVariant:
Dim bVar(1 To 16) As Byte
CopyMemory bVar(1), v, 16
Debug.Print VarType(v) & "/"; TypeName(v) & ":";
For i = 1 To 16
    Debug.Print bVar(i) & "/";
Next
Debug.Print
Return
End Sub
```

The output is:

```
0/Empty:0/0/0/0/0/0/0/0/0/0/0/0/0/0/0/0/
9/Nothing:9/0/0/0/0/0/0/0/0/0/0/0/0/0/0/0/
1/Null:1/0/0/0/0/0/0/0/0/0/0/0/0/0/0/0/
0/Empty:0/0/0/0/0/0/0/0/0/0/0/0/0/0/0/0/
10/Error:10/0/0/0/0/0/0/0/123/0/10/128/0/0/0/0/
8209/Byte():17/32/0/0/0/0/0/0/208/254/31/0/0/0/0/0/
2/Integer:2/0/0/0/0/0/0/0/123/0/18/0/0/0/0/0/
3/Long:3/0/0/0/0/0/0/0/225/245/5/0/0/0/0/
8/String:8/0/0/0/0/0/0/0/116/34/29/0/0/0/0/0/
4/Single:4/0/0/0/0/0/0/0/205/204/140/63/0/0/0/0/
5/Double:5/0/0/0/0/0/0/0/51/51/7/32/95/160/2/66/
6/Currency:6/0/0/0/0/0/0/0/184/143/3/0/0/0/0/0/
17/Byte:17/0/0/0/0/0/0/0/123/0/3/0/0/0/0/0/
11/Boolean:11/0/0/0/0/0/0/0/255/255/3/0/0/0/0/0/
7/Date:7/0/0/0/0/0/0/0/0/0/0/0/160/165/225/64/
```

Note that *TypeName* returns an indication when the data contained in a Variant is an array by appending a pair of parentheses after the type name of the ancillary array type.

Note also that in order to set a Variant to **Nothing**, we must use the **Set** statement, which makes sense because **Nothing** is a special type of object variable.

As you may know, the purpose of the Error data type is to allow a function to return an error code that can be distinguished from an otherwise meaningful numeric return value. For instance, consider the following function:

```
Function vLength(s As String) As Variant
    If s <> "" Then
        vLength = Len(s)
    Else
        ' Convert return value to error code and return
        vLength = CVErr(1)
    End If
End Function
```

This function is meant to return a long value indicating the length of a nonempty string. If the string is empty, the return value is 1. But how do we tell from the return type the difference between an empty string and a string of length 1? The answer is given in the following code:

```
Debug.Print IsError(vLength("help"))
Debug.Print IsError(vLength(""))
```

The first line returns **False** whereas the second line returns **True**. We trust that you can infer from this trivial little example how to use error codes. (If you are interested, there is more on this issue, along with a whole chapter on error handling, in my book *Concepts of Object-Oriented Programming with Visual Basic*, published by Springer-Verlag, New York.)

Basic VC++ Data Types

The world of data types is considerably more complex in VC++ than it is in VB. We want to deal first with the fundamental data types, as seen by the designer of the C++ language (Bjarne Stroustrup) as well as by Microsoft. Before doing so, let us discuss the concept of a **typedef**.

TypeDefs

The purpose of a VC++ **typedef** statement is to allow the programmer to define a new name, or *synonym*, for an existing data type. The syntax is:

```
typedef type-declaration synonym;
```

For instance:

```
typedef long LPARAM;
```

defines `LPARAM` as a synonym for the `long` data type. It is also possible to `typedef` more than one synonym at a time, as in:

```
typedef long LPARAM, WPARAM;
```

Visual Basic has no direct counterpart to the VC++ `typedef` statement.

Now we can proceed to a discussion of VC++ data types.

Char Data Types

The character data types are the most complex of the fundamental types. This is due primarily to the fact that these types are used to represent the characters that are supported by the operating system, and Windows supports both ANSI and Unicode characters (in general).

Designer of C++

The `char` type is designed to hold the characters of the basic character set used by the operating system.

The `char`, `signed char`, and `unsigned char` data types are different, although they may be implemented in the same manner by the compiler. They each must consume the same amount of memory.

Microsoft

To quote the documentation:

> Type `char` is an integral type that usually contains members of the execution character set—in Microsoft C++, this is ASCII. The C++ compiler treats variables of type `char`, `signed char`, and `unsigned char` as having different types. The `char` type is `signed` by default (but this can be changed through a VC++ compiler switch).

Thus, we should treat `char` as a single-byte signed data type, equivalent to `signed char`, with range −128 to 127. On the other hand, `unsigned char` is a single-byte data type with range 0 to 255.

It follows that `unsigned char` is the more natural type for representing ASCII (or ANSI) characters, which may lead you to wonder why Microsoft chose not to treat `char` as `unsigned` by default. In any case, Microsoft does define the `BYTE` data type as a synonym for `unsigned char`.

Unicode character types

What does Microsoft do about Unicode characters?

VC++ has another data type named `wchar_t`, which is a 16-bit unsigned integer data type that holds wide (Unicode) characters. Thus `char` and `wchar_t` handle the two types of characters in Win32.

VC++ also defines some synonyms for these two character data types:

```
typedef char CHAR;
typedef wchar_t WCHAR;
```

Furthermore, in order to allow programmers to write a single program that can be used under either an ANSI or a Unicode setting, VC++ defines the generic TCHAR data type using conditional compilation as follows:

```
#ifdef  UNICODE

typedef WCHAR TCHAR;
typedef WCHAR TBYTE;

#else

typedef char TCHAR;
typedef unsigned char TBYTE;

#endif
```

(Conditional compilation works in VC++ just like it does in VB.) If the conditional compilation constant UNICODE is defined in a program, then the first set of type-defs are valid:

```
typedef WCHAR TCHAR;
typedef WCHAR TBYTE;
```

Thus, TCHAR and TBYTE are synonyms for the Unicode character WCHAR, which, in turn, is a synonym for wchar_t. On the other hand, if UNICODE is not defined, then TCHAR and TBYTE are synonyms for CHAR, which, in turn, is a synonym for char.

In summary, we have the following character data types (along with their unsigned versions):

char and CHAR
> ANSI character

wchar_t and WCHAR
> Unicode character

TCHAR and TBYTE
> Generic character, could be either ANSI or Unicode (but not both at the same time)

Int Data Types

An integer data type is capable of expressing a whole number within a range defined by the number of bytes allocated to it. C++ supports a number of integer data types.

Designer of C++

Three sizes of integer data types are possible: declared as `short int`, `int`, and `long int`. Using the *sizeof* operator to indicate the number of bits that a data type consumes in memory, we must have:

```
sizeof(short int) <= sizeof(int) <= sizeof(long int)
```

Note the equal signs, however, which allow all three integer types to have the same size.

The size of `int` should have the natural size determined by the machine architecture. Otherwise, the issue of size is compiler dependent. It is not uncommon for `int` to have the same size as either `short int` or `long int`. The following terms are equivalent:

```
short int = short = signed short int = signed short
int = signed int
long int = long = long short int = long short
```

For each type—`short int`, `int`, and `long int`—there are corresponding `unsigned` versions, which have the same size as their `signed` counterparts. The terms `unsigned int` and `unsigned` are synonymous.

Microsoft

As with character data types, Microsoft follows the description of the designer of C++, setting the following sizes for Win32:

```
sizeof(short) = 16
sizeof(int) = 32
sizeof(long) = 32
```

All of the `char` and `int` data types and their variations are considered *integral* data types.

Floating Point Data Types

A floating point data type is capable of representing a number within a fractional component defined by its format and the number of bytes allocated to it.

Designer of C++

There are three floating types: `float`, `double`, and `long double`. Each type, in turn, has *at least* as great precision as its predecessor.

Microsoft

Microsoft also defines these three floating point data types, with sizes:

```
sizeof(float) = 4
sizeof(double) = 8
sizeof(long double) = 8
```

and states that "the representation of long double and double is identical. However, long double and double are separate types." We will have very little occasion to use these nonintegral data types.

Other Data Types

Let us take a brief look at some other commonly occurring data types.

Void

The designer of C++ and Microsoft both define the **void** data type as a special data type that can be used as the return type for functions, but no variable can be declared as having type **void**. This type does have one other use, however, and that is to designate a pointer whose target type is unknown, as in the following example:

```
void *pWhatever;
```

FARPROC

The **FARPROC** data type appears quite often in Win32 API function. It is documented as a "pointer to a callback function." We will discuss callback functions in Chapter 15, *Windows: The Basics*, but the point here is that **FARPROC**, being a pointer, is a 32-bit unsigned long.

Handle

Windows is full of different types of objects, such as windows, bitmaps, fonts, cursors, menus, hooks, metafiles, pens, brushes, and so on. When an object of some type is created, Windows generally returns a *handle* to that object. This handle is used to manipulate the object programmatically. That is, most API functions that manipulate an object require a handle to that object.

Handles are not totally unknown to VB programmers, for we can access the handles of many objects through their *hWnd* property.

Although the type **HANDLE** is a synonym for **void***, the data type occurs so often it seems reasonable to consider it a more or less fundamental data type.

Boolean data types

VC++ also defines some boolean data types:

bool

> A 1-byte data type that takes on the values **true** and **false** (both of which are keywords, as in VB)

BOOL *(remember that VC++ is case sensitive)*

A 32-bit data type that is also designed to take on the values true and false (don't ask me!)

boolean and **BOOLEAN**

Also 32-bit data types that can take on the values true and false

Summary

Table 4-3 summarizes the basic (fundamental and almost fundamental) VC++ data types that we will see frequently in dealing with Win32 API function declarations.

Table 4-3. Basic VC++ Data Types

Type	Size in Bytes	Closest VB Counterpart	Range of Values/Notes
char	1	Byte	−128 to 127
signed char	1	Byte	−128 to 127
unsigned char	1	Byte	0 to 255
BYTE	1	Byte	0 to 255
wchar_t	2	Integer	0 to 65,535
TCHAR	1 or 2	Byte/Integer	See "Char Data Types"
(signed) short (int)	2	Integer	−32,768 to 32,767
unsigned short (int)	2	Integer	0 to 65,535
(signed) int	4	Long	−2,147,483,648 to 2,147,483,647
unsigned int	4	Long	0 to 4,294,967,295 ($=2^{32}-1$)
(signed) long (int)	4	Long	−2,147,483,648 to 2,147,483,647
unsigned long	4	Long	0 to 4,294,967,295 ($=2^{32}-1$)
float	4	Long	Approximately −3.4E38 to 3.4E38
double	8	Double	Approximately −1.8E308 to 4.9E324
long double	8	Double	Approximately −1.8E308 to 4.9E324 (Not used often.)
bool	1	Byte	true or false
BOOL	4	Long	true or false
boolean	4	Long	true or false
*	4	Long	Denotes a pointer
void*	4	Long	A pointer to an unknown data type
HANDLE	4	Long	A handle to an object. Officially a void*.
FARPROC	4	Long	Pointer to a callback function

Table 4-3. Basic VC++ Data Types (continued)

Type	Size in Bytes	Closest VB Counterpart	Range of Values/Notes
__int8, __int16, __int32, __int64	1,2,4, 8	Byte/ Integer/ Long/none	Microsoft specific. Not used often.
LONGLONG	8	Double	64-bit signed integer. Not used often.
VARIANT	16	Variant	Same as the VB Variant

As you can see from Table 4-3, we will not have too much trouble converting from a basic VC++ data type to a VB data type. The main complication concerns the fact that VB does not have unsigned versions of its types. We will discuss this issue when we talk in more detail about the nature of signed (two's complement) and unsigned representations in the next chapter.

Translating Derived Data Types

It might seem as though once we understand how to translate fundamental data types from VC++ to Visual Basic, it should be more-or-less routine to translate derived types as well. This is true with one or two exceptions.

After all, since pointers are 32 bits in length, a VC++ pointer should be translated as a VB long. It doesn't matter what the data type of the target is, at least as far as translating the pointer data type itself. Of course, we will probably need to translate this target data type as well.

Also, an array in VC++ is an array in VB—only the ancillary data type needs translating.

There is a wrinkle, however, when it comes to translating VC++ structures into VB structures (user-defined types). We will discuss the matter of structure *member alignment* in detail (with experiments) a little later.

Win32 Typedefs

Although the fundamental VC++ data types number only about a dozen, it sometimes seems a cruel fact that Win32 defines literally *hundreds* of synonyms for these data types through **typedef** statements.

VC++'s various **typedef** statements are contained in a set of more than 300 *include files*. These are text files that usually have extension *.h*.

The rpiAPIData Utility

The CD that accompanies this book contains a database application called *rpiAPI-Data*. This application can display data on Win32 data types, as shown in Figure 4-1.

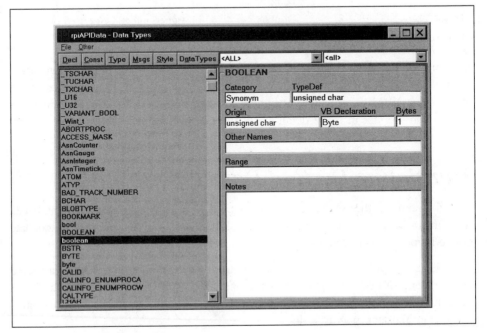

Figure 4-1. rpiAPIData: data type view

rpiAPIData, which is little more than a front end for a database of Win32 type-defs, makes it easier to cut through this typedef alphabet soup and find the basic VC++ data type that most closely corresponds to a given synonym. The database contains more than 650 typedefs.

Before we continue, it is worth reiterating that, unlike VB, VC++ and Win32 are case-sensitive environments. This case-sensitivity is bound to catch all of us sooner or later.

We should point out that the include files contain many hundreds more typedefs than are included in the database. However, there is no need to catalog these individually, because they can often be easily recognized.

First, many typedefs are used to define both ANSI and Unicode versions of the same data type. For instance, the keywords OPENFILENAMEA and OPENFILENAMEW are the ANSI and Unicode versions, respectively, of the same data type (in this case, a structure). Accordingly, there are two typedefs defining OPENFILENAME (as with the TCHAR typedef discussed earlier in "Char Data Types").

Second, Win32 is fond of defining new data type synonyms for pointers by prefixing the target data type name with either a P, NP, or LP. To illustrate, consider the `int` data type. Win32 makes the following typedefs:

```
typedef int* PINT;
typedef int* LPINT;
```

This happens for hundreds of different base data types. In an effort to make the *rpiAPIData* application more usable, it seemed appropriate not to include these variations.

In case you are wondering, the prefixes NP and LP stand for *near pointer* and *far pointer*, respectively. This terminology is a remnant of the days of 16-bit Windows and Intel 80286 processors, when addresses were written in a *segment:offset* format in order to accommodate the fact that CPU registers were 16 bits wide and could therefore address only $2^{16} = 64KB$ of memory. A near pointer was a pointer within the same 64KB memory segment, and thus required only an offset value. A far pointer pointed to another memory segment. If this is not familiar terminology, then you can consider yourself fortunate. (For more on all of this, allow me to suggest my book *Understanding Personal Computer Hardware*, published by Springer-Verlag, New York.)

The designers of VC++ seem very fond of making typedefs using other typedefs. For instance, we find in two different include files:

```
typedef unsigned long DWORD;
```

and:

```
typedef DWORD LPARAM;
```

This is not a problem for VC++ programmers, but it does create a problem for us. After all, a VC++ programmer couldn't care less what size an LPARAM data type is, because he or she just uses the **LPARAM** keyword, as in:

```
LPARAM lparam;
```

However, we need to replace LPARAM with a suitable VB data type, so we need to know its size!

Thus, from our perspective, it would have been nice if all typedefs were given in terms of some small set of basic data types, Instead, we must engage in *typedef chasing*. The origin field in Figure 4-1 is intended to refer (more or less) to the end of this chase, that is, to the *basic* type from Table 4-3, for which the name in question is a synonym.

Please note that this is the first incarnation of *rpiAPIData* and it no doubt has many errors. *Caveat emptor!* Please send me an email when you find errors.

Why All These Typedefs?

There is a reason why Microsoft makes so many typedefs (although one could argue that the situation has gotten a bit out of hand). Simply put, the numerous typedefs are intended to clarify programming code. (You can be the final judge of that.)

For instance, according to the Win32 documentation, an LPARAM is an unsigned long with a particular mission in life—it is a 32-bit message parameter. To be more specific, it appears in the *SendMessage* API function declaration:

```
LRESULT SendMessage(
    HWND hWnd,          // handle of destination window
    UINT Msg,           // message to send
    WPARAM wParam,      // first message parameter
    LPARAM lParam       // second message parameter
);
```

Thus, for instance, the VC++ variable declaration:

```
LPARAM avar;
```

tells us that *avar* is intended to hold a 32-bit message parameter, for use in *SendMessage*. The alternative is:

```
unsigned long avar;
```

which tells us nothing about the intended use of *avar*.

The point is that the **LPARAM** **typedef** imparts a *meaning*, or *interpretation*, to any variable declared using that synonym. Otherwise, there is no difference between the declarations:

```
LPARAM avar1;
unsigned long avar2;
```

If two data types are linked by a **typedef** statement, as in:

```
typedef DWORD LPARAM;
```

we may refer to them as *synonymous* data types.

An Example

We will get plenty of practice doing data type translation throughout the book, but let us pause now to do a short example—translating the *SendMessage* function:

```
LRESULT SendMessage(
    HWND hWnd,          // handle of destination window
    UINT Msg,           // message to send
    WPARAM wParam,      // first message parameter
    LPARAM lParam       // second message parameter
);
```

Since the Win32 documentation says that *SendMessage* is exported by *USER32.DLL*, and since we want the ANSI entry point, we can do a partial translation as follows:

```
Declare Function SendMessage Lib "user32" Alias "SendMessageA" ( _
    HWND hWnd, _
    UINT Msg, _
    WPARAM wParam, _
    LPARAM lParam) _
As LRESULT
```

Next, we need to translate the data types from VC++ to VB and decide on the use of `ByVal` or `ByRef` for each parameter.

Checking the origin and VB Declaration fields for each data type in the *rpiAPI-Data* utility gives the following table:

VC++ Type	Origin	VB Type
LRESULT	long	Long
HWND	void*	Long
UINT	unsigned int	Long
WPARAM	unsigned int	Long
LPARAM	long	Long

Next, we check the meaning of the parameters in the documentation. According to this documentation, the *hWnd* parameter holds a handle to the window that will receive the message. Since VB thoughtfully provides us with this handle as returned by the hWnd property, we should pass the parameter by value, as in:

```
Sendmessage(lstWhatever.hWnd,. . .
```

The *Msg* parameter is a constant that identifies the message (the message ID). Again we pass this by value.

The parameters *WPARAM* and *LPARAM* are "message-specific" values, so we don't get much of a clue from the *SendMessage* documentation as to whether to pass these by value or by reference. Indeed, this may depend upon the message being sent.

Thus, we arrive at the following VB declaration for *SendMessage*:

```
Declare Function SendMessage Lib "user32" Alias "SendMessageA" ( _
    ByVal hwnd As Long, _
    ByVal lMsg As Long, _
    wParam As Any, _
    lParam As Any _
) As Long
```

As it happens, we often can be more specific about the declarations of *wParam* and *lParam* when using this function in a particular situation.

For instance, to search for an item in a list box, we would send the message LB_
FINDSTRING, that is, *wMsg* should be set to the symbolic constant LB_
FINDSTRING. We will discuss how to find the value of symbolic constants in the
Chapter 16, *Windows Messages*.

In this case, *wParam* is the index of the list box entry from which to start the
search, or −1 to start from the beginning. Clearly, we will pass this number by
value. Also, *lParam* is the string to search for. We will discuss strings in the next
chapter, but for now we note that the appropriate choice is:

```
ByVal lParam As String
```

Thus, for sending the LB_FINDSTRING message (and a great many other LB messages), we can use the declaration:

```
Declare Function SendMessageByString Lib "user32" Alias "SendMessageA" ( _
    ByVal hwnd As Long, _
    ByVal lMsg As Long, _
    ByVal wParam As Long, _
    ByVal lParam As String _
) As Long
```

Similarly, when *lParam* is a long, we can use the declaration:

```
Declare Function SendMessageByLong Lib "user32" Alias "SendMessageA" ( _
    ByVal hwnd As Long, _
    ByVal lMsg As Long, _
    ByVal wParam As Long, _
    ByVal lParam As Long _
) As Long
```

Structures and User-Defined Types

We mentioned earlier that there is a potential wrinkle when it comes to translating VC++ structures into VB user-defined types. Although this wrinkle appears
very rarely, it is important to understand it, especially since Win32 uses literally
hundreds of structures in its function declarations.

We might think at first that it is simply a matter of translating each member's data
type from VC++ to VB. For instance, the VC++ structure:

```
struct tagMisaligned {
    char aByte;
    short int anInteger;
}
```

might be translated as:

```
Type utMisaligned
    aByte As Byte
    anInteger As Integer
End Type
```

Unfortunately, there is a problem.

When Visual Basic stores a structure in memory (and only in memory—this does not apply to storage on disk) it *aligns* the members of the structure on what are referred to as their *natural boundaries*. Quite simply, the *natural boundary* of a variable that takes up n bytes of memory is any memory address that is a multiple of n. Thus, we have:

- A byte variable can be located at any memory address.

- An integer variable is located at a memory address that is a multiple of 2.

- A long variable is located at a memory address that is a multiple of 4.

- A double variable is located at a memory address that is a multiple of 8.

- A pointer variable, which includes the VB string type BSTR, is located at a memory address that is a multiple of 4.

- A Unicode character is located at a memory address that is a multiple of 2. In particular, this applies to the characters in a fixed-length string.

In addition, the entire structure is aligned on a memory address that is divisible by 4, but this is not relevant to the issue at hand.

Let's test this with the structure:

```
Public Type utMisaligned
    aByte As Byte
    aLong As Long
    anInteger As Integer
    aString As String
End Type
```

The following code makes a copy of the bytes of the structure as Windows sees that structure:

```
Dim i As Integer
Dim aBytes(1 To 50) As Byte
Dim ma As utMisaligned

ma.aByte = &H11
ma.aLong = &H22334455
ma.anInteger = &H6677
ma.aString = "help"

CopyMemory aBytes(1), ma, LenB(ma)

' Print the length of ma using both Len and LenB
Debug.Print "Len:" & Len(ma), "  LenB:" & LenB(ma)

' Print the byte array
For i = 1 To LenB(ma)
    Debug.Print Hex(aBytes(i)) & "/";
Next
Debug.Print
```

The output is:

```
Len:11          LenB:16
11/0/0/0/55/44/33/22/77/66/0/0/B4/4A/20/0/
```

This shows first that `Len(ma)` and `LenB(ma)` report different values. As the VB documentation states, `Len(ma)` returns the number of bytes used by the structure itself, which is 1 + 4 + 2 + 4 = 11 (a VB string is a 4-byte pointer). On the other hand, `LenB(ma)` returns the number of bytes used to *store* the structure in memory, which, in this case, is 16. Looking at the byte array, we see:

- 1 byte for *ma.aByte*
- 3 bytes of padding so that *ma.aLong* can start on its natural boundary
- 4 bytes for *ma.aLong*
- 2 bytes for *ma.anInteger*, which does not require realignment since it is already on its natural boundary
- 2 bytes of padding so that *ma.aString* can start on its natural 4-byte boundary
- 4 bytes for *ma.aString*, which is an address

Fortunately, the vast majority of API structures have members that are naturally aligned, so the VB user-defined type exactly mirrors the VC++ structure. In the rare cases where the members of a VC++ structure are not naturally aligned, we must resort to some manual realigning. Since this situation is rare, it is simpler to use a third-party program for this purpose. An alternative would be to create a byte array and carefully fill it with data at the appropriate locations.

Flags

A *flag* is a binary word that indicates the state of a certain object. Often, flags are 1 bit long. For instance, to indicate whether or not a window is active requires only a single bit—0 for inactive and 1 for active. On the other hand, some flags require more than one bit. As you no doubt know, an *n*-bit flag can represent any of 2^n states.

In Win32, several flags are often embedded in a single 16-bit or 32-bit word, which would generally be defined as an `unsigned short` or `unsigned int`, respectively. Often the entire word is referred to as a flag.

Thus, it is important to be able to get at the individual bits of a flag. This is easy to do in VC++ and not too much harder in VB.

Let us first discuss a bit of terminology. When a numeric variable is being thought of as a flag, we will refer to it as a *binary word*. The word is also said to be *bit-significant*. The *least significant bit* is the rightmost bit, which is also referred to as bit 0. (The term *least significant* loses its meaning for bit-significant words, but the terminology is still used.)

Setting a bit means setting the bit to 1, and *clearing* a bit means setting the bit to 0.

Masking Bits

Visual Basic's logical **And**, **Or**, and **Not** operators also function as bitwise operators, meaning that when applied to numeric data types, they perform bitwise conjunction and disjunction, respectively. In particular:

```
0 And 0 = 0
0 And 1 = 0
1 And 0 = 0
1 And 1 = 1

0 Or 0 = 0
0 Or 1 = 1
1 Or 0 = 1
1 Or 1 = 1

Not 0 = 1
Not 1 = 0
```

These operators can be used to set or clear any bit position within a binary word. To set a bit position, we **Or** it with a 1. To clear a bit position, we **And** it with a 0.

For instance, if x is an integer, then we can set its sixth bit by writing:

```
x Or 100000 (binary)
```

Of course, VB does not recognize binary words, so we have the choice between:

```
x Or &H20
```

and:

```
x Or 2^5
```

This also makes it easy to extract the bit, as in:

```
FifthBit = IIf((x And &H20) = 0, 0, 1)
```

It can be a bit tedious trying to figure out what number to use as a mask. Here are some guidelines that use Table 4-4.

- Masks are more easily constructed in hexadecimal format.

- To set up a mask for *clearing* bits in a 16-bit word (for instance), begin by writing the all 1s mask:

  ```
  (1111) (1111) (1111) (1111)
  ```

  Next, change the 1 to a 0 in those positions that you wish to clear. For instance, to clear positions 0, 2, 5, and 10, use the mask:

  ```
  (1111) (1011) (1101) (1010)
  ```

Convert this to hexadecimal using Table 4-4. This gives &H0FBDA, so to clear these positions, write:

```
x = x And &H0FBDA
```

- To set up a mask for *setting* bits in a 16-bit word (for instance), begin by writing the all 0s mask:

```
(0000) (0000) (0000) (0000)
```

Next, change the 0 to a 1 in those positions that you wish to set. For instance, to set positions 1, 7, 8, and 15, use the mask:

```
(1000) (0001) (1000) (0010)
```

Convert this to hexadecimal using Table 4-4. This gives &H8182. So, to set these positions, write:

```
x = x Or &H8182
```

- If you want to set some bits and clear others, this should be done in two steps.

Table 4-4. Some Hex/Binary Equivalents

Hex	Binary
0	0000
1	0001
2	0010
3	0011
4	0100
5	0101
6	0110
7	0111
8	1000
9	1001
A	1010
B	1011
C	1100
D	1101
E	1110
F	1111

Symbolic Constants

To put it simply, Win32 is full of symbolic constants—well over 6,000 of them. These constants are defined in include files (files with extension *.h*) along with the typedefs. For instance, the *Winbase.h* file contains the following constant definition:

```
#define MAX_COMPUTERNAME_LENGTH 15
```

In VB this is equivalent to:

```
Public Const MAX_COMPUTERNAME_LENGTH = 15
```

Now, VC++ programmers can include the appropriate include files in their programs with a statement such as:

```
#include <Winbase.h>
```

and then use the constants by name. In VB, we need to add a **Const** statement for each constant that we want to use. However, the problem is that the Win32 documentation does not give the values of these constants because VC++ programmers don't need to know them!

Accordingly, VB programmers need a good text searching utility that can be used to search through include files. For instance, searching for lines that contain both **#define** and **MAX_COMPUTERNAME_LENGTH** turns up the declaration of this constant.

An additional problem arises when searching in this way because a given **#define** statement may be part of a conditional compilation clause and we need to examine the entire clause to be certain that we have the correct value.

5

Signed and Unsigned Data Types

In this chapter, we will take a close look at signed and unsigned data types. The topic is one of special importance in view of the prevalence of unsigned data types in the Win32 API, their complete absence in Visual Basic, and the frequent difficulty of translating an unsigned value into its corresponding signed value.

Signed and Unsigned Representations

We have seen that VC++ and the Win32 API use both signed and unsigned integral data types, whereas VB has only one unsigned type—the Byte data type. This can create a problem when an API function either expects or returns an unsigned data type. To understand just what is involved, we need to take a look at the internal workings of these data types and how they are represented in memory.

The place to start is with some carefully defined terminology. We will couch our examples in terms of 16-bit words, but what we say applies equally to words of any length.

A *16-bit word* is simply a string of 16 binary bits, as in:

```
w = 1111000011110000
```

The key point is that a binary word is *not* a number until and unless it is given an *interpretation* as a number. It is just a string of bits.

There are two common ways in which integers are represented as 16-bit words in most computers, including PCs: the *unsigned representation* is used to represent only nonnegative integers, and the *two's complement signed representation* is used to represent both negative and nonnegative integers. The latter is generally abbreviated in Microsoft's documentation as the *signed representation,* and we may do so as well, although there are other types of signed representations (including the *one's complement signed representation* and the *signed magnitude representation*).

It is important to understand that it is not the number itself that is signed or unsigned, it is the *representation* of the number as a binary word that is signed or unsigned. Numbers are neither signed nor unsigned. (A number can be positive, negative, or zero, but that is not the same thing as signed or unsigned—all numbers have a sign.) Thus, the commonly used term *signed integer* is highly misleading. It should be read as *signed representation of the integer*. Nevertheless, this terminology is so common and so convenient that we will use it as well.

When we declare an integer variable in Visual Basic and give it a value, as in:

```
Dim i As Integer
i = 5
```

VB represents the integer using the two's complement signed representation. In this, we have no choice. Put another way—when VB interprets a binary word as an integer, it does so using the two's complement binary representation of that word. Period. On the other hand, VC++ is more flexible, allowing us to choose the representation, as in:

```
unsigned int ui;
ui = 65000;
int i;        // or signed int i;
i = -30000;
```

Here *ui* is an unsigned integer, that is, *ui* is represented in memory by VC++ as a (32-bit) binary word using the unsigned representation. On the other hand, *i* is a signed integer, that is, *i* is represented in memory using the two's complement signed representation.

Why Two Different Representations?

The reason for using an unsigned representation for integers is simple: by using an unsigned representation, we can represent larger positive integers than when using a signed representation. In exchange, we give up the ability to represent negative numbers.

In particular, a 16-bit word that uses the two's complement signed representation can represent any integer in the range −32768 to 32767, whereas a 16-bit word that uses the unsigned representation can represent integers in the range 0 to 65535.

There are compelling reasons to include both signed and unsigned representations in a programming language. It is probably not necessary to comment on the fact that a language would be hampered significantly if it could not represent negative numbers. On the other hand, an unsigned representation is useful for two reasons.

- When we want to do arithmetic with positive numbers only, we get a larger range of values using an unsigned representation. This happens with addresses, for instance. If the word size of a computer is, say, 32 bits, then the most natural way to access all 2^{32} possible memory addresses is by using an unsigned representation.

- Many numeric data types do not require the use of arithmetic. For instance, window handles are 32-bit numbers, but it makes no sense to add, subtract, or otherwise manipulate these numbers. They are strictly for identification purposes. Thus, the HANDLE data type is an **unsigned long** data type.

It is time that we consider how the two's complement signed and unsigned interpretations actually work.

Unsigned Representation

When a 16-bit word is interpreted as unsigned, we simply count up from 0 in binary, as in the following list (the double arrow ↔ stands for "represents"):

```
0000 0000 0000 0000 ↔ 0
0000 0000 0000 0001 ↔ 1
0000 0000 0000 0010 ↔ 2
     .
     .
     .
0111 1111 1111 1111 ↔ 2^15 - 1 = 32767
1000 0000 0000 0000 ↔ 2^15 = 32768
     .
     .
     .
1111 1111 1111 1111 ↔ 2^16 - 1 = 65535
```

Thus, the unsigned interpretation of 16-bit words allows us to represent all integers in the range 0 to $2^{16}-1=65535$.

As you probably know, each position in a binary number represents a power of 2, just as each position in a decimal number represents a power of 10. Table 5-1 is a template for creating unsigned representations of numbers. Each column is simply a successive power of 2.

Table 5-1. A Template for Unsigned Representations

2^{15}	2^{14}	2^{13}	2^{12}	2^{11}	2^{10}	2^9	2^8	2^7	2^6	2^5	2^4	2^3	2^2	2^1	2^0
32768	16384	8192	4096	2048	1024	512	256	128	64	32	16	8	4	2	1

Table 5-2 shows an example of filling in this template to find the unsigned representation of the integer 50000. By successively subtracting powers of 2, starting with the largest one that fits, we arrive at:

    50000 = 32768 + 16384 + 512 + 256 + 64 + 16

Next, we place these numbers in the third row of Table 5-2 and then put 1s underneath the numbers and 0s everywhere else. This gives a fourth row in Table 5-2, from which we get the unsigned representation:

    1100 0011 0101 0000 ↔ (unsigned) 50000

Table 5-2. An Unsigned Example: Representing 50000

2^{15}	2^{14}	2^{13}	2^{12}	2^{11}	2^{10}	2^9	2^8	2^7	2^6	2^5	2^4	2^3	2^2	2^1	2^0
32768	16384	8192	4096	2048	1024	512	256	128	64	32	16	8	4	2	1
32768	16384					512	256		64		16				
1	1	0	0	0	0	1	1	0	1	0	1	0	0	0	0

Signed Representation

The strategy used in two's complement representation is to use the leftmost bit as an indicator of the sign of the number. The leftmost bit is called the *sign bit*. If the sign bit is a 0, the word is interpreted as a nonnegative integer. If the sign bit is 1, the number is interpreted as a negative integer:

    0xxx xxxx xxxx xxxx ↔ nonnegative integer
    1xxx xxxx xxxx xxxx ↔ negative integer

The Signed-Magnitude Representation

The most obvious way to fill in the other bits is with the *magnitude* (or *absolute value*) of the number. For example, to represent the positive number 5, we would write:

    0000 0000 0000 0101 ↔ 5

since the binary representation of 5 is 101. For the negative number –5, we would simply change the sign bit:

    1000 0000 0000 0101 ↔ –5

This method of representing both positive and negative numbers is called the *signed-magnitude representation.* It is very simple, but not very useful. One problem is that arithmetic with numbers represented in this way requires taking special cases based on the sign of the number. (Just try adding the binary representations for 5 and –5.) Also, there are two representations of the number 0 (+0 and –0):

    0000 0000 0000 0000 ↔ 0
    1000 0000 0000 0000 ↔ 0

The Two's Complement Representation

The *two's complement representation* is a much better approach and is used by most modern computers. It is easy to describe using a table. The analog of Table 5-1 for the two's complement signed interpretation is Table 5-3. The only difference between this table and Table 5-1 is the negative sign in the first column.

Table 5-3. A Template for Two's Complement Signed Representations

-2^{15}	2^{14}	2^{13}	2^{12}	2^{11}	2^{10}	2^9	2^8	2^7	2^6	2^5	2^4	2^3	2^2	2^1	2^0
-32768	16384	8192	4096	2048	1024	512	256	128	64	32	16	8	4	2	1

To illustrate, Table 5-4 computes the signed representation of the integer −15536. Note that it is the same as the *unsigned* representation of 50000:

```
1100 0011 0101 0000 ↔ (signed) -15536
```

Table 5-4. A Signed Example: Representing −15536

-2^{15}	2^{14}	2^{13}	2^{12}	2^{11}	2^{10}	2^9	2^8	2^7	2^6	2^5	2^4	2^3	2^2	2^1	2^0
-32768	16384	8192	4096	2048	1024	512	256	128	64	32	16	8	4	2	1
-32768	16384					512	256		64		16				
1	1	0	0	0	0	1	1	0	1	0	1	0	0	0	0

Since the only difference between Table 5-1 and Table 5-3 is that the numbers in the first column are negative, it is clear that a binary word with a sign bit of 0 represents the same integer using either the signed or the unsigned representation. Put another way, for integers in the range 0 to 32767, the two representations are identical.

Also, since the sum of all of the numbers in the first row of Table 5-3 is −1, it is clear that a number is negative if and only if its sign bit is 1.

Following is a list that shows how signed representation works. The list is ordered by increasing binary word. Note the sudden change from positive to negative integers in the middle of the list.

```
0000 0000 0000 0000 ↔ 0
0000 0000 0000 0001 ↔ 1
0000 0000 0000 0010 ↔ 2
  .
  .
  .
0111 1111 1111 1111 ↔ 2^15 - 1 = 32767    ' positive
1000 0000 0000 0000 ↔ -2^15 = -32768    ' negative
1000 0000 0000 0001 ↔ -2^15 + 1 = -32767
```

.
.
.

```
1111 1111 1111 1101 ↔ −3
1111 1111 1111 1110 ↔ −2
1111 1111 1111 1111 ↔ −1
```

Why Is It Called Two's Complement?

The reason that it is called this has to do with how we take the negative of a number that is represented in this form. Consider any number x written in two's complement form. Let us use the number in Table 5-4 ($x = -15536$):

```
x ↔ 1100 0011 0101 0000
```

Consider now the ordinary complement of this binary word; that is, the word obtained by changing all 0s to 1s and all 1s to 0s:

```
xᶜ ↔ 0011 1100 1010 1111
```

Adding the two binary numbers gives:

```
x + xᶜ ↔ 1111 1111 1111 1111
```

Note that this will be the result no matter what number we start with.

But the binary word consisting of all 1s is the representation of the number −1, so we have:

```
x + xᶜ = −1
```

from which it follows that:

```
x + (xᶜ + 1) = 0
```

or:

```
−x = xᶜ + 1
```

Thus, to get the negative of a number, we take the complement of its signed representation and then add 1. The resulting binary word is called the *two's complement* of the original binary word. Thus, to get the negative of a number that is represented in two's complement form, just take the two's complement of the number's binary representation..

Translating Between Signed and Unsigned Representations

Now we come to the heart of the matter—translation between signed and unsigned representations. There are two issues to consider.

First, we may need to pass to an API function a number that is too large to fit in the corresponding VB signed data type. For instance, we may need to pass a 16-bit representation of a number in the upper "unsigned" range 32768 to 65535, say for example the number 50000. In VC++, we could simply write:

```
unsigned short usVar;
usVar = 50000;
```

but in VB, the code:

```
Dim iVar As Integer
iVar = 50000
```

will produce an Overflow runtime error. Note that we cannot use the code:

```
Dim lVar As Long
lVar = 50000
```

because the function is expecting a 16-bit binary word.

The second problem is the reverse. Suppose, for example, that an API function wants to return a 16-bit value in the range 32768 to 65535, such as 50000. Of course, the return value must be in a VB variable (since we are working in VB). But VB will interpret the variable as having a signed data type. In fact, it will interpret the number as –15536 because, as we have seen, this number has the same *signed* representation as the number 50000 has *unsigned* representation. So, the question is: "How do we recover the intended value?"

These problems are easy to solve if we look at them in the correct light. Referring to Figure 5-1, the point is that VB will give a 16-bit binary word a signed interpretation, whereas Win32 will give it an unsigned interpretation (we are assuming here that Win32 is expecting or returning an *unsigned* short integer).

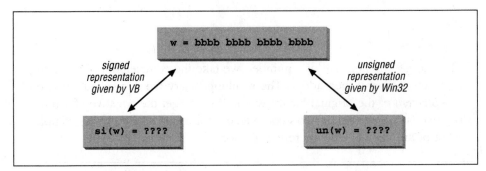

Figure 5-1. Passing numbers between VB and Win32

As in Figure 5-1, if w is a 16-bit binary word, let us write un(w) to denote the number obtained by thinking of w as an unsigned representation and si(w) as the number obtained by thinking of w as a signed representation. Thus, from our previous example in Table 5-2 and Table 5-4, we have:

```
un(1100 0011 0101 0000) = 50000
si(1100 0011 0101 0000) = -15536
```

The point to keep in mind is that we are actually passing or receiving a *binary word*, not a number. VB and Win32 will both interpret this binary word as a number. The difficulty comes when they use different interpretations. VB uses the signed integer interpretation, and Win32 (we are assuming) uses the *unsigned* short integer interpretation.

Thus, referring to Figure 5-1, in passing a number un(w) to an API function, we need to tell VB to pass the number si(w), since Win32 will interpret the binary word w that is actually passed (on the stack) as un(w). Conversely, in receiving a number, VB will see it as si(w), and we need to make the translation to si(w) which, by the way, will require using a larger VB data type to hold the value.

So the whole problem boils down to translating between si(w) and un(w).

We can see how to make these translations by noting that the only difference between Table 5-1 and Table 5-3 is the negative sign in the first column. Accordingly, there are two cases to consider.

The first case is when the number si(w) is nonnegative or, equivalently, the number un(w) is in the lower half of the unsigned range (0 to 32767). (Whether we are passing or receiving, we will know *one* of these numbers!) In this case, the sign bit of w is 0. Hence, as we have seen:

```
un(w) = si(w)
```

Thus, in this case, we can use an ordinary VB integer to pass the number, and, in the other direction, the return value in a VB integer is the actual number (no changes are necessary).

On the other hand, suppose that the number si(w) is negative or, equivalently, un(w) is in the upper range 32768 to 65535. In this case, the sign bit of w is 1. This bit, being in the first column of Table 5-4, contributes a total of 2^{15} to the number un(w). On the other hand, it contributes a total of -2^{15} to the number si(w). Since the contributions from all other columns are the same in both un(w) and si(w), subtracting out the contributions from the first column should produce equal values, that is:

```
un(w) - 2^15 = si(w) - (-2^15)
```

From this, a little algebra gives the two formulas:

```
un(w) = si(w) + 2^16
si(w) = un(w) - 2^16
```

These formulas are the key to all. We can now summarize.

Integers

To pass a number un(w) in the range 0 to 65535 in a VB integer variable, put the number si(w) in the variable. In the other direction, if a VB integer variable receives a number and VB shows this number to be si(w), then the number passed is actually un(w). Here is the relationship between si(w) and un(w).

For si(w) >= 0 or 0 <= un(w) <= 32767(= 2^{15}-1):

```
un(w) = si(w)
```

For si(w) < 0 or 32768 <= un(w) <= 65535(= 2^{16}-1):

```
un(w) = si(w) + 2^16
si(w) = un(w) - 2^16
```

Sometimes a picture is worth a thousand words. Figure 5-2 shows the situation here. When a number lies in the range that is common to the signed and unsigned ranges (0 to 32767), then no changes are required when sending or receiving the number. To send a number in the upper unsigned range, subtract 2^{16} to bring it into the signed range before sending the number. When receiving a number in the lower signed range, add 2^{16} to get the actual number sent (in the unsigned range).

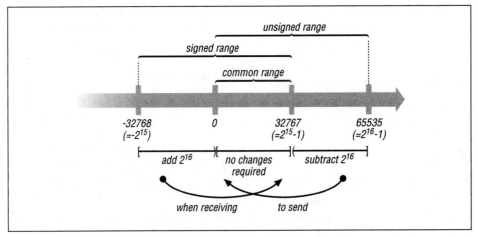

Figure 5-2. Translating between signed and unsigned integers

Longs

Of course, the same principle applies to 32-bit longs.

To pass a number un(w) in the range 0 to 2^{32}–1 in a VB long variable, put the number si(w) in the variable. In the other direction, if a VB long variable receives a number and VB shows this number to be si(w), then the number passed is actually un(w). Here is the relationship between si(w) and un(w):

For `si(w) >= 0` or `0 <= un(w) <= 2`^{31}`-1`:

```
un(w) = si(w)
```

For `si(w) < 0` or `2`^{31}` <= un(w) <= 2`^{32}`-1`:

```
un(w) = si(w) + 2^32
si(w) = un(w) - 2^32
```

Figure 5-3 illustrates the translation process.

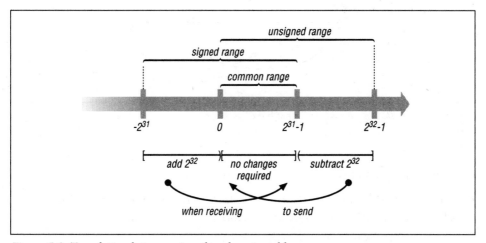

Figure 5-3. Translating between signed and unsigned longs

Bytes

The situation for bytes is actually the reverse of that for integers and longs, since the VB Byte type is *unsigned*. The problem here occurs when the API function expects or returns a *signed* byte. Nevertheless, the principle is exactly the same.

To pass a number `si(w)` in the range –128 to 127 in a VB byte variable, put the number `un(w)` in the variable. In the other direction, if a VB long variable receives a number and VB shows this number to be `un(w)`, then the number passed is actually `si(w)`. Here is the relationship between `si(w)` and `un(w)`:

For `si(w) >= 0` or `0 <= un(w) <= 127 (=2`^{7}`-1)`:

```
un(w) = si(w)
```

For `si(w) < 0` or `128 <= un(w) <= 255 (=2`^{8}`-1)`:

```
un(w) = si(w) + 2^8
si(w) = un(w) - 2^8
```

Figure 5-4 illustrates the translation process.

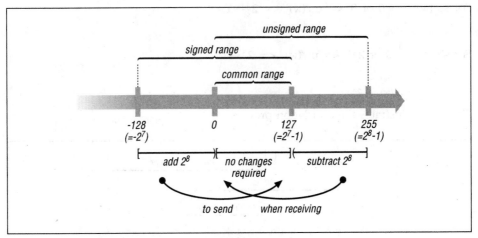

Figure 5-4. Translating signed and unsigned bytes

Examples

Here are some examples:

- Pass a number in the range 0 to 65535 that currently resides in a VB long variable *lng* to an API function with an **unsigned short** parameter:

    ```
    . . . APIFunction(unsigned short param) . . .
    ```

    with VB declaration:

    ```
    Declare . . . APIFunction(param As Integer) . . .
    ```

    Solution:

    ```
    Dim param As Integer   ' same size as the API function's parameter
    If lng >= 0 And lng <= 32767 Then
        param = lng
    ElseIf lng >= 32768 And lng <= 65535 Then
        param = CInt(lng - 2^16)
    Else
        MsgBox "Value out of range for an unsigned short", vbCritical
    End If
    Call APIFunction(param)
    ```

- Pass a number in the range 0 to $2^{32}-1$ that currently resides in a VB **Currency** variable *cVar* to an API function with an **unsigned int** or **unsigned long** parameter:

    ```
    . . . APIFunction(unsigned int param) . . .
    ```

    with VB declaration:

    ```
    Declare . . . APIFunction(param As Long) . . .
    ```

    Solution:

    ```
    Dim param As Long    ' same size as the API function's parameter
    If cVar >= 0 And cVar <= 2^31 - 1 Then
    ```

```
      param = cVar
   ElseIf cVar >= 2^31 And cVar <= 2^32 - 1 Then
      param = CLng(cVar - 2^32)
   Else
      MsgBox "Value out of range for an unsigned int", vbCritical
   End If
   Call APIFunction(param)
```

In the next example, the situation is reversed—the API function expects a signed value but the VB Byte data type is unsigned.

- Pass a number in the range −128 to 127 currently residing in a VB integer variable *iVar* to an API function with a **signed char** parameter (recall that the VB Byte type is unsigned):

  ```
  . . . APIFunction(signed char param) . . .
  ```

  with VB declaration:

  ```
  Declare . . . APIFunction(param As Byte) . . .
  ```

  Solution:

  ```
  Dim param As Byte   ' same size as the API function's parameter
  if iVar >= 0 And iVar <= 127 Then
     param = iVar
  ElseIf iVar >= -127 And iVar <= -1 Then
     param = CByte(iVar + 2^8)
  End If
  Call APIFunction(param)
  ```

- Receive a number in the range 0 to 65535 in a VB integer variable *iVar*, from an API function that has an OUT parameter of type *unsigned short*:

  ```
  . . . APIFunction(unsigned short param) . . .
  ```

  with VB declaration:

  ```
  Declare . . . APIFunction(param As Integer) . . .
  ```

  Solution:

  ```
  Dim lRealValue As Long      ' to hold the real value passed to VB
  If iVar >= -32768 And iVar <= -1 Then
     lRealValue = CLng(iVar) + 2^16
  ElseIf iVar >= 0 And iVar <= 32767 Then
     lRealValue = CLng(iVar)
  End If
  ```

- Receive a number in the range 0 to $2^{32}-1$ in a VB long variable *lVar*, from an API function that has an OUT parameter of type **unsigned int**:

  ```
  . . . APIFunction(unsigned int param) . . .
  ```

  with VB declaration:

  ```
  Declare . . . APIFunction(param As Long) . . .
  ```

  Solution:

  ```
  Dim cRealValue As Currency   ' to hold the real value passed to VB
  If lVar >= -2^31 And lVar <= -1 Then
  ```

```
      cRealValue = CCur(lVar) + 2^32
ElseIf lVar >= 0 And lVar <= 2^31 - 1 Then
      cRealValue = CCur(lVar)
End If
```

- Receive a number in the range 0 to 255 in a VB byte variable *bVar*, from an API function that has an OUT parameter of type unsigned char:

  ```
  . . . APIFunction(unsigned char param) . . .
  ```

  with VB declaration:

  ```
  Declare . . . APIFunction(param As Byte) . . .
  ```

  Solution:

  ```
  Dim iRealValue As Integer   ' to hold the real value passed to VB
  If bVar >= -128 And bar <= -1 Then
      iRealValue = CInt(bVar) + 128
  ElseIf bVar >= 0 And bVar <= 127 Then
      iRealValue = CInt(bVar)
  End If
  ```

Converting Between Word Lengths

Let us conclude our discussion of signed data types with the issue of converting between word lengths. This issue does not arise in API programming, so you may skip it if desired.

To illustrate, suppose we have a number in the signed integer range -32768 to 32767 and we want to place it in a Long variable. What does VB do to the 16-bit signed representation of the number to get a 32-bit signed representation?

If the number is positive, the answer is as expected—VB just puts 16 additional 0s on the left. For instance,

$$0000\ 0000\ 0000\ 1010 \leftrightarrow 5$$
$$0000\ 0000\ 0000\ 0000\ 0000\ 0000\ 0000\ 1010 \leftrightarrow 5$$

On the other hand, what about a negative number?

As an example, consider the negative number -32765, with signed representation:

$$1000\ 0000\ 0000\ 0011 \leftrightarrow -32765$$

Putting 16 0s on the left would produce a *positive* number, so this is not correct. Also, just changing the sign bit does not help—the word:

$$1000\ 0000\ 0000\ 0000\ 1000\ 0000\ 0000\ 0011$$

represents:

$$-2^{31} + 2^{15} + 2 + 1 = -2147450877$$

which is certainly *not* -5.

Suppose instead that we put 16 1s on the left, changing:

    1000 0000 0000 0011 ↔ -32765

to:

    1111 1111 1111 1111 1000 0000 0000 0011 ↔ x

To compute the value of **x**, we look at the contributions of the new bits.

Since the original sign bit contributes -2^{15} to the number -5, but now contributes 2^{15} to the number x, the increase in going from -5 to **x** from this bit alone is:

    2 * (2^15) = 2^16

In addition, the new 1s in positions 16 through 30 contribute an increase of:

    2^16 + 2^17 + . . . + 2^30

to the value of **x**. Finally, the 31st bit, which is the new sign bit, contributes a negative quantity -2^{31}. Adding up all of the changes gives the net change in going from -5 to **x**:

    2*2^15 + 2^16 + 2^17 + . . . + 2^30 - 2^31

Some algebra that I guess you would prefer that I omit shows that this net increase is actually 0:

    2*2^15 + 2^16 + 2^17 + . . . + 2^30 - 2^31 = 0

In other words, there is no change. Hence, **x** = -5!

We have shown that adding 16 1s on the left does not change the number. Put another way, to get the 32-bit signed representation of a negative number from the number's 16-bit signed representation, we just put 16 1s on the left.

We can combine both cases (positive and negative numbers) as follows:

> To get the 32-bit signed representation of a number from the number's 16-bit signed representation, just copy the *sign bit* (whether it be a 0 or a 1) to the left 16 times. This process is called *sign extension*.

6

Strings

The subject of strings can be quite confusing, but this confusion tends to disappear with some careful attention to detail (as is usually the case). The main problem is that the term *string* is used in at least two different ways in Visual Basic!

Just what is a string in Visual Basic? According to the VB documentation, it is:

> A data type consisting of a sequence of contiguous characters that represent the characters themselves rather than their numeric values.

Huh?

It seems to me that Microsoft is trying to say that the underlying set for the `String` data type is the set of finite-length sequences of characters. For Visual Basic, all characters are represented by 2-byte Unicode integers. Put another way, VB uses Unicode to represent the characters in a string. For instance, the ASCII representation for the character h is &H68, so the Unicode representation is &H0068, appearing in memory as 68 00.

Thus, the string "help" is represented as:

```
00 68 00 65 00 6C 00 70
```

Note, however, that because words are written with their bytes reversed in memory, the string "help" appears *in memory* as:

```
68 00 65 00 6C 00 70 00
```

This is fine, but it is definitely *not* how we should think of strings in VB programming. To avoid any possibility of ambiguity, we will refer to this type of object as a *Unicode character array* which is, after all, precisely what it is! This also helps distinguish it from an *ANSI character array*, that is, an array of characters represented using single-byte ANSI character codes.

Here is the key to understanding strings: when we write the code:

```
Dim str As String
str = "help"
```

we are *not* defining a Unicode character array *per se*. We are defining a member of a data type called BSTR, which is short for *Basic String*. A BSTR is, in fact, a *pointer to* a null-terminated Unicode character array that is preceeded by a 4-byte length field. We had better elaborate on this.

The BSTR

Actually, the VB string data type defined by:

```
Dim str As String
```

underwent a radical change between versions 3 and 4 of Visual Basic, due in part to an effort to make the type more compatible with the Win32 operating system.

Just for comparison (and to show that we are more fortunate now), Figure 6-1 shows the format for the VB string data type under Visual Basic 3, called an HLSTR (*High-Level String*).

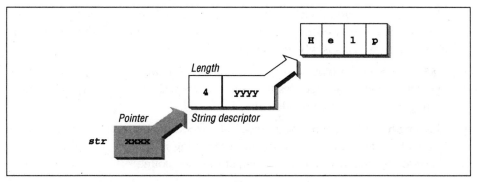

Figure 6-1. The high-level string format (HLSTR) used by VB3

The rather complex HLSTR format starts with a pointer to a *string descriptor*, which contains the 2-byte length of the string along with another pointer to the character array, which is in ANSI format (one byte per character).

With respect to the Win32 API, this string format is a nightmare. Beginning with Visual Basic 4, the VB string data type changed. The new data type, called a BSTR, is shown in Figure 6-2.

This data type is actually defined in the OLE 2.0 specifications; that is, it is part of Microsoft's ActiveX specification.

There are several important things to note about the BSTR data type.

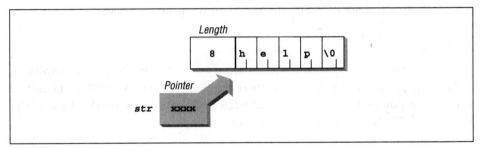

Figure 6-2. A BSTR

- The BSTR is the actual pointer variable. It has size 32 bits, like all pointers, and *points to* a Unicode character array. Thus, a Unicode character array and a BSTR are not the same thing. It is correct to refer to a BSTR as a *string* (or *VB string*) but, unfortunately, the Unicode character array is also often called a string! Hence, we will *not* refer to a BSTR simply as a string—we will refer to it by its unequivocal name—BSTR.

- The Unicode character array that is pointed to by a BSTR *must be* preceded by a 4-byte length field and terminated by a single null 2-byte *character* (ANSI = 0).

- There may be additional null characters anywhere within the Unicode character array, so we cannot rely on a null character to signal the end of the character array. This is why the length field is vital.

- Again, the pointer points to the beginning of the *character array*, not to the 4-byte length field that precedes the array. As we will see, this is critical to interpreting a BSTR as a VC++-style string.

- The length field contains the number of *bytes* (not the number of characters) in the character array, *excluding* the terminating null bytes. Since the array is Unicode, the character count is one-half the byte count.

We should emphasize that an embedded null *Unicode* character is a 16-bit 0, not an 8-bit 0. Watch out for this when testing for null characters in Unicode arrays.

Note that it is common practice to speak of "the BSTR 'help'" or to say that a BSTR may contain embedded null characters when what is really being referred to is the *character array* pointed to by the BSTR.

Because a BSTR may contain embedded null characters, the terminating null is not of much use, at least *as far as VB is concerned*. However, its presence is extremely important for Win32. The reason is that the Unicode version of a Win32 string (denoted by LPWSTR) is defined as a pointer to a *null-terminated* Unicode character array (which, by the way, is *not* allowed to contain embedded null characters).

This makes it clear why BSTR's are null terminated. *A BSTR with no embedded nulls is also an LPWSTR.* We will discuss C++ strings in a moment.

Let us emphasize that code such as:

```
Dim str As String
str = "help"
```

means that *str* is the name of a BSTR, not a Unicode character array. In other words, *str* is the name of the variable that holds the address xxxx, as shown in Figure 6-2.

Here is a brief experiment we can do to test the fact that a VB string is a *pointer to* a character array and not a character array. Consider the following code, which defines a structure whose members are strings:

```
Private Type utTest
    astring As String
    bstring As String
End Type

Dim uTest As utTest
Dim s as String

s = "testing"
uTest.astring = "testing"
uTest.bstring = "testing"

Debug.Print Len(s)
Debug.Print Len(uTest)
```

The output from this code is:

```
7
8
```

In the case of the string variable *s*, the *Len* function reports the length of the character array; in this case there are 7 characters in the character array 'testing'. However, in the case of the structure variable *uTest*, the *Len* function actually reports the length of the structure (in bytes). The return value of 8 clearly indicates that each of the two BSTRs has length 4. This is because a BSTR is a pointer!

C-Style LPSTR and LPWSTR Strings

VC++ and Win32 use the string data types LPSTR and LPWSTR.

An LPSTR string is defined as a pointer to a null-terminated ANSI character array. However, because the only way that we can tell when an LPSTR string ends is by the location of the terminating null, LPSTRs are not allowed to contain embedded null characters. Similarly, an LPWSTR is a pointer to a null-terminated *Unicode* character set with no embedded nulls. (The W in LPWSTR stands for *Wide*, which is Microsoft's way of saying Unicode.) These string data types are pictured in Figure 6-3.

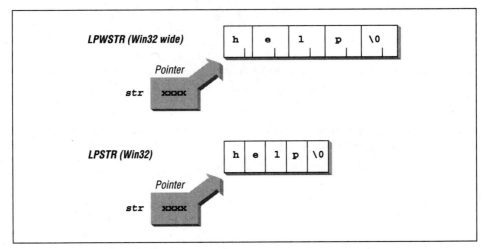

Figure 6-3. LPSTR and LPWSTR data types

We will also encounter the data types LPCSTR and LPCWSTR. The embedded C stands for *constant* and simply means that an instance of this data type cannot (and will not) be changed by any API function that uses this type. Otherwise, an LPCSTR is identical to an LPSTR, and, similarly, an LPCWSTR is identical to an LPWSTR.

Finally, the generic LPTSTR data type is used in conditional compilation, just like the TCHAR data type, to cover both ANSI and Unicode in a single source code. Here are the declarations:

```
#ifdef UNICODE

typedef LPWSTR LPTSTR;      // LPTSTR is synonym for LPWSTR under Unicode
typedef LPCWSTR LPCTSTR;    // LPCTSTR is synonym for LPCWSTR under Unicode

#else

typedef LPSTR LPTSTR;       // LPTSTR is synonym for LPSTR under ANSI
typedef LPCSTR LPCTSTR;     // LPTCSTR is synonym for LPCSTR under ANSI

#endif
```

Figure 6-4 summarizes the possibilities.

Thus, for instance, LPCTSTR is read *long pointer to a constant generic string.*

String Terminology

To avoid any possible confusion, we will use the terms BSTR, Unicode character array, and ANSI character array. When we do use the term *string*, we will modify it by writing VB string (meaning BSTR) or VC++ string (meaning LP??STR). We will avoid using the term string without some modification.

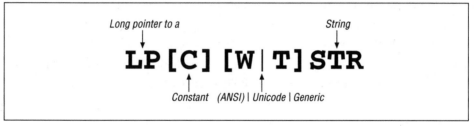

Figure 6-4. The LP...STR mess

However, in translating VB documentation, you will see the unqualified term *string* used quite often. It falls to you to determine whether the reference is to a BSTR or a character array.

Tools for Exploring Strings

If we are going to do some exploring, then we will need some tools. We have already discussed the *CopyMemory* API function. Let us take a look at some additional tools for dealing with strings.

The Visual Basic StrConv Function

The *StrConv* function is used to convert character arrays from one format to another. Its syntax is:

```
StrConv(string, conversion, LCID)
```

where *string* is a BSTR, *conversion* is a constant (described later), and LCID is an optional locale identifier (which we will ignore).

Among the possible constants, and the only ones that interest us, are:

- vbUnicode (which should have been vbToUnicode)
- vbFromUnicode

These constants convert the character array of the BSTR between Unicode and ANSI.

But now we have a problem (which really should have been addressed by the official documentation). There is no such thing as an ANSI BSTR. By definition, the character array pointed to by a BSTR is a *Unicode* array.

However, we can image what an ANSI BSTR would be—just replace the Unicode character array in Figure 6-2 with an ANSI array. We will use the term ABSTR to stand for ANSI BSTR, but you should keep in mind that this term will not be officially recognized outside of this book.

We can now say that there are two legal forms for *StrConv*:

```
StrConv(aBSTR, vbFromUnicode)     ' returns an ABSTR
StrConv(anABSTR, vbUnicode)       ' returns a BSTR
```

The irony is that, in the first case, VB doesn't understand the return value of its own function! To see this, consider the following code:

```
s = "help"
Debug.Print s
Debug.Print StrConv(s, vbFromUnicode)
```

The result is:

```
help
??
```

because VB tries to interpret the ABSTR as a BSTR. Look at the following code:

```
s = "h" & vbNullChar & "e" & vbNullChar & "l" & vbNullChar & "p" & vbNullChar
Debug.Print s
Debug.Print StrConv(s, vbFromUnicode)
```

The output is:

```
h e l p
help
```

Here we have tricked VB by padding the original Unicode character array so that when *StrConv* does its conversion, the result is an ABSTR that happens to have a legitimate interpretation as a BSTR!

This shows that the *StrConv* function doesn't really understand or care about BSTRs and ABSTRs. It assumes that whatever you feed it is a pointer to a character array and it blindly does its conversion on that array. As we will see, many other string functions behave similarly. That is, they can take a BSTR or an ABSTR—to them it is just a pointer to some null-terminated array of bytes.

The Len and LenB Functions

Visual Basic has two string-length functions: *Len* and *LenB*. Each takes a BSTR or ABSTR and returns a long. The following code tells all.

```
s = "help"
Debug.Print Len(s), LenB(s)
Debug.Print Len(StrConv(s, vbFromUnicode)), LenB(StrConv(s, vbFromUnicode))
```

The output is:

```
4        8
2        4
```

showing that *Len* returns the number of characters and *LenB* returns the number of bytes in the BSTR.

The Chr, ChrB, and ChrW Functions

These three functions have different input ranges and produce different outputs. These differences can seem confusing at first—you may have to read the definitions a few times:

- *Chr* takes a long value *x* in the range 0 to 255 and returns a BSTR of length 1. This one character pointed to by the BSTR has Unicode code equal to x. (In this case, the Unicode and ANSI values are actually equal.) Note that, according to the latest documentation, there is no difference between *Chr* and *Chr$*.

- *ChrB* takes a long value *x* in the range 0 to 255 and returns an ABSTR of length 1 (byte). This one byte pointed to by the ABSTR has ANSI code equal to x.

- *ChrW* takes a long value *x* in the range 0 to 65535 and returns a BSTR of length 1. This one character pointed to by the BSTR has Unicode code equal to x.

The Asc, AscB, and AscW Functions

These functions are the inverses of the *Chr* functions. For instance, *AscB* takes a single character (byte) ABSTR and returns a byte equal to the character's ANSI code. To see that the return type is a byte, try running the code:

```
Debug.Print VarType(AscB("h")) = vbByte
```

(The output is **True**.) It may appear that *AscB* will accept a BSTR as input, but in reality, it just takes the first byte in the BSTR.

The *Asc* function takes a BSTR (but not an ABSTR) and returns an integer equal to the character's Unicode code.

Null Strings and Null Characters

To its credit, VB does allow null BSTRs. The code:

```
Dim s As String
s = vbNullString
Debug.Print VarPtr(s)
Debug.Print StrPtr(s)
```

produces the following output (your address may vary, of course):

```
1243948
0
```

This shows that a null BSTR is simply a pointer whose contents are 0. (We will discuss the meaning of *StrPtr* in a moment.) In Win32 and VC++, this is called a *null pointer*. You can probably see the difference between **vbNullString** and

vbNullChar at this point. **vbNullChar** is not a pointer—it is a Unicode character whose value is 0. Thus, at the bit level, the values **vbNullString** and **vbNullChar** are identical. However, they are *interpreted* differently, so they are in fact different.

It is also important not to confuse a null BSTR with an empty BSTR, usually denoted by a pair of adjacent quotation marks:

```
Dim s As String
Dim t As String
s = vbNullString
t = ""
```

Unlike a null string, the empty BSTR *t* is a pointer that points to some *nonzero* memory address. At that address resides the terminating null character for the empty BSTR, and the preceeding length field also contains a 0.

VarPtr and StrPtr

We have discussed the function *VarPtr* already, but not in connection with strings. The functions *VarPtr* and *StrPtr* are not documented by Microsoft, but they can be *very* useful, so we will use them often, particularly the *VarPtr* function.

If *var* is a variable, we have seen that:

```
VarPtr(var)
```

is the *address* of that variable, returned as a long. If *str* is a BSTR variable, then:

```
StrPtr(str)
```

gives the *contents* of the BSTR! These contents are the *address* of the Unicode character array pointed to by the BSTR.

Let us elaborate. Figure 6-5 shows a BSTR.

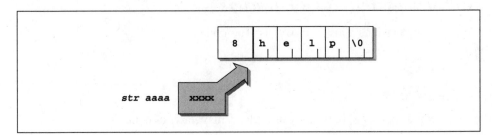

Figure 6-5. A BSTR

The code for this figure is simply:

```
Dim str As String
str = "help"
```

Note that the variable *str* is located at address **aaaa** and the character array begins at address **xxxx**, which is the *contents* of the pointer variable *str*.

To see that:

```
VarPtr = aaaa
StrPtr = xxxx
```

just run the following code:

```
Dim lng As Long
Dim i As Integer
Dim s As String
Dim b(1 To 10) As Byte
Dim sp As Long, vp As Long

s = "help"

sp = StrPtr(s)
Debug.Print "StrPtr:" & sp

vp = VarPtr(s)
Debug.Print "VarPtr:" & vp

' Verify that sp = xxxx and vp = aaaa
' by moving the long pointed to by vp (which is xxxx)
' to the variable lng and then comparing it to sp
CopyMemory lng, ByVal vp, 4
Debug.Print lng = sp

' To see that sp contains address of char array,
' copy from that address to a byte array and print
' the byte array. We should get "help".
CopyMemory b(1), ByVal sp, 10
For i = 1 To 10
   Debug.Print b(i);
Next
```

The output is:

```
StrPtr:1836612
VarPtr:1243988
True
 104  0  101  0  108  0  112  0  0  0
```

This shows again that the character array in a BSTR is indeed in Unicode format. Also, by adding the following lines:

```
Dim ct As Long
CopyMemory ct, ByVal sp - 4, 4
Debug.Print "Length field: " & ct
```

just after the lines:

```
sp = StrPtr(s)
Debug.Print "StrPtr:" & sp
```

we get the output:

```
Length field: 8
```

which shows that the length field does indeed hold the *byte* count and not the character count.

As mentioned earlier, if you do not like to use undocumented functions (and who can blame you for that?), you can use the function *rpiVarPtr* in the *rpiAPI.dll* library on the accompanying CD. You can also simulate *StrPtr* as follows:

```
' Simulate StrPtr
Dim lng As Long
CopyMemory lng, ByVal VarPtr(s), 4
' lng = StrPtr(s)
```

As we have seen, this code copies the *contents* of the BSTR pointer, which is the value of *StrPtr*, to a long variable *lng*.

String Conversion by VB

Now we come to the strange story on how VB handles passing BSTRs to external DLL functions. It doesn't.

As we have seen, VB uses Unicode internally; that is, BSTRs use the Unicode format. Window NT also uses Unicode as its native character code. However, Windows 9x does not support Unicode (with some exceptions). Let's examine the path that is taken by a BSTR argument to an external DLL function (Win32 API or otherwise).

In an effort to be compatible with Windows 95, VB *always* (even when running under Windows NT) creates an ABSTR, converts the BSTR's Unicode character array to ANSI, and places the converted characters in the ABSTR's character array. VB then passes the ABSTR to the external function. As we will see, this is true even when calling the Unicode entry points under Windows NT.

Preparing the BSTR

Before sending a BSTR to an external DLL function, VB creates a new ABSTR string at a location different from the original BSTR. It then passes that ABSTR to the DLL function. This duplication/translation process is pictured in Figure 6-6.

When we first introduced the *CopyMemory* function, we used it to demonstrate this Unicode-to-ANSI translation process. But let's do that again in a different way. The *rpiAPI.dll* library includes a function called *rpiBSTRtoByteArray*, whose purpose is to return the values of *VarPtr* and *StrPtr* on the string that is actually passed to a DLL function. The VB declaration is as follows.

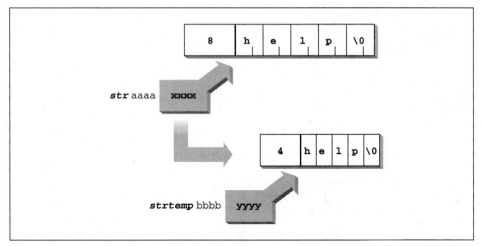

Figure 6-6. Translating a BSTR to an ABSTR

```
Public Declare Function rpiBSTRtoByteArray Lib "???\rpiAPI.dll" ( _
    ByRef pBSTR As String, _
    ByRef bArray As Byte, _
    pVarPtr As Long, _
    pStrPtr As Long
) As Long
```

For its first parameter, this function takes as input a BSTR, which is passed *by reference*. Hence, the address of the BSTR is passed, not the address of the character array. (Thus, we are passing a pointer to a pointer to the character array.)

The second parameter should be set to the first byte of a byte array that the caller must allocate with enough space to accommodate all of the bytes of the BSTR. Failing to do so will definitely crash the application.

The last two parameters are OUT parameters, meaning that the caller just declares a pair of long variables, which the function will fill in. The *pVarPtr* variable will be filled by the address of the BSTR, and the *pStrPtr* will be filled by the contents of the BSTR (which, as we know, is the address of the character array) *as the DLL function sees it*. Thus, we will be able to get a glimpse of what the DLL is actually passed by VB!

The function returns the length (in bytes) of the original string. Finally, in order to convince ourselves that everything is working as it should, the function changes the first character of the original string to an X.

Here is a test run (the function *VBGetTarget* was discussed in Chapter 3, *API Declarations*, under the section "Implementing Indirection in Visual Basic"):

```
Sub BSTRTest()

Dim i As Integer
```

```
Dim sString As String
Dim bBuf(1 To 10) As Byte
Dim pVarPtr As Long
Dim pStrPtr As Long
Dim bTarget As Byte
Dim lTarget As Long

sString = "help"

' Print the BSTR's initial address and contents
Debug.Print "VarPtr:" & VarPtr(sString)
Debug.Print "StrPtr:" & StrPtr(sString)

' Call the external function
Debug.Print "Function called. Return value:" & _
    rpiBSTRToByteArray(sString, bBuf(1), pVarPtr, pStrPtr)

' Print what the DLL sees, which is the temp ABSTR
' Its address and contents are:
Debug.Print "Address of temp ABSTR as DLL sees it: " & pVarPtr
Debug.Print "Contents of temp ABSTR as DLL sees it: " & pStrPtr

' Print the buffer pointed to by temp ABSTR
Debug.Print "Temp character array: ";
For i = 1 To 10
    Debug.Print bBuf(i);
Next
Debug.Print

' Now that we have returned from the DLL function call
' check status of the passed string buffer -- it has been deallocated
VBGetTarget lTarget, pVarPtr, 4
Debug.Print "Contents of temp ABSTR after DLL returns: " & lTarget

' Check the string for altered character
Debug.Print "BSTR is now: " & sString

End Sub
```

Here is the output:

```
VarPtr:1242736
StrPtr:2307556
Function called. Return value:4
Address of temp ABSTR as DLL sees it: 1242688
Contents of temp ABSTR as DLL sees it: 1850860
Temp character array:  104  101  108  112  0  0  0  0  0  0
Contents of temp ABSTR after DLL returns: 0
BSTR is now: Xelp
```

This code first prints the address (*VarPtr*) and the contents (*StrPtr*) of the original BSTR as VB sees it. It then calls the function, which fills in the byte buffer and the OUT parameters. Next, the buffer and OUT parameters are printed. The important point to note is that the address and contents of the "string," as returned by the

DLL function, are different than the original values, which indicates that VB has passed a different object to the DLL. In fact, the buffer is in ANSI format; that is, the object is an ABSTR.

Next, we print the contents of the passed ABSTR, when the DLL has returned. This is 0, indicating that the temporary ABSTR has been deallocated. (It is tempting but not correct to say that the ABSTR is now the null string—in fact the ABSTR no longer exists!)

Finally, note that I am running this code under Windows NT—the translation still takes place even though Windows NT supports Unicode.

The Returned BSTR

It is not uncommon for a BSTR that is passed to a DLL function to be altered and returned to the caller. In fact, this may be the whole purpose of the function.

Figure 6-7 shows the situation. After the ABSTR is altered by the DLL function, the translation process is reversed. Thus, the original BSTR *str* will now point to a Unicode character array with the *output* of the API function. Note, however, that the *character array* may not be returned to its original location. For instance, as we will see, the API function *GetWindowText* seems to move the array. The point is that we cannot rely on the *contents* of the BSTR to remain unchanged, only its address. This will prove to be an important issue in our discussions later in the chapter.

What to Call

Since Windows 9x does not implement Unicode API entry points, for compatibility reasons you will probably want to call only ANSI API entry points in your applications. For instance, you should call *SendMessageA*, not *SendMessageW*. (Nonetheless, we will do a Unicode entry point example a little later.)

The Whole String Trip

Let's take a look at the entire round trip that a BSTR takes when passed to an external DLL.

Assume that we call a DLL function that takes a string parameter and modifies that string for return. The *CharUpper* API function is a good example. This function does an *in-place* conversion of each character in the string to uppercase. The VB declaration for the ANSI version is as follows.

```
Declare Function CharUpperA Lib "user32" ( _
   ByVal lpsz As String _
) As Long
```

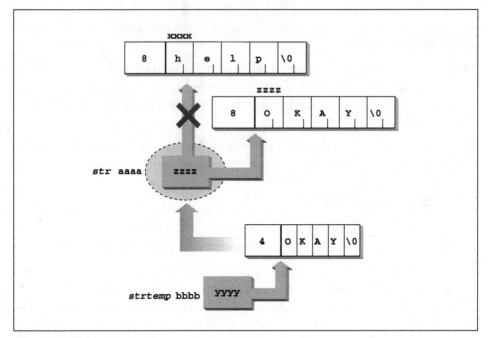

Figure 6-7. The return translation

Under Windows 9x

Under Windows 9x, the following happens to the string argument. Remember that it is the character array *pointers* that are being passed back and forth, not the actual character arrays:

- The BSTR *lpsz* is duplicated as an ABSTR by VB, and the duplicate is passed to the function *CharUpperA*, which treats it as an LPSTR.

- This function processes the LPSTR and passes the result to VB.

- VB translates the LPSTR back to a BSTR.

Note that since most API functions (in this case *CharUpper*) treat BSTRs as LPSTRs, that is, they ignore the length field, we cannot be certain that this field will always be accurate. For *CharUpper*, the length is not changed, so it should remain correct, but other API functions could conceivably change the length of the character array. Unless written specifically for the BSTR format, the function will just null-terminate the new character array, without updating the length field. Thus, we cannot rely on the length field to be valid.

Under Windows NT

Under Windows NT, our string argument will go through the following machinations:

1. The string is translated from a BSTR to an ABSTR by VB and passed to the function *CharUpperA*, which treats it as an LPSTR.

2. This function translates the LPSTR to an LPWSTR and passes the LPWSTR to the Unicode entry point *CharUpperW*.

3. The Unicode function *CharUpperW* processes the LPWSTR and produces an LPWSTR for output, returning it to *CharUpperA*.

4. The function *CharUpperA* translates the LPWSTR back to an LPSTR and passes it to VB, which thinks of it as an ABSTR.

5. VB translates the ABSTR back to a BSTR!

A Unicode Entry Point Example

Under Windows NT, we can call the Unicode entry points and expect to get something meaningful in return. However, VB still makes the BSTR-to-ABSTR translations, and we must counteract this translation. Here is the ANSI version of a call to *CharUpperA*:

```
s = "d:\temp"
Debug.Print s
CharUpperA s
Debug.Print s
```

Under both Windows 9x and Windows NT, the outcome is as expected:

```
d:\temp
D:\TEMP
```

Under Windows NT, we might first attempt the Unicode version thusly:

```
s = "d:\temp"
Debug.Print s
CharUpperW s
Debug.Print s
```

but the result is:

```
d:\temp
d:\temp
```

Clearly, something is wrong. Incidentally, here is what the documentation says about errors in the *CharUpper* function.

> There is no indication of success or failure. Failure is rare. There is no extended error information for this function; do no [sic] call *GetLastError*.

Nonetheless, we know that the problem is that VB is making the BSTR-to-ABSTR translation. So let us try the following code:

```
s = "d:\temp"
Debug.Print s
s = StrConv(s, vbUnicode)
Debug.Print s
```

```
CharUpperW s
Debug.Print s
s = StrConv(s, vbFromUnicode)
Debug.Print s
```

The output is:

```
d:\temp
d : \ t e m p
D : \ T E M P
D:\TEMP
```

What we are doing here is compensating for the shrinking of our BSTR to an ABSTR by expanding it first. Indeed, the first call to the *StrConv* function simply takes each *byte* in its operand and expands it to Unicode format. It doesn't know or care that the string is already in Unicode format.

Consider, for instance, the first Unicode character **d**. Its Unicode code is 0064 (in hex), which appears in memory as **64 00**. Each byte is translated by *StrConv* to Unicode, which results in **0064 0000** (appearing in memory as **64 00 00 00**). The effect is to put a null character between each Unicode character in the original Unicode string.

Now, in preparation for passing the string to *CharUpperW*, VB takes this expanded string and converts it from Unicode to ANSI, thus returning it to its original Unicode state. At this point, *CharUpperW* can make sense of it and do the conversion to uppercase. Once the converting string returns from *CharUpperW*, VB "translates" the result to Unicode, thus expanding it with embedded null characters. We must convert the result to ANSI to remove the supererogatory padding.

Passing Strings to the Win32 API

We can now discuss some of the *practical* aspects of string passing.

ByVal Versus ByRef

Some authors like to say that the **ByVal** keyword is overloaded for strings, meaning that it takes on a different meaning when applied to strings than when applied to other variables. Frankly, I don't see it. Writing:

```
ByVal str As String
```

tells VB to pass the *contents* of the BSTR (actually the ABSTR), which is the pointer to the character array. Thus, **ByVal** is acting normally—it just happens that the content of the BSTR is a *pointer to* another object, so this simulates a pass by reference. Similarly:

```
ByRef str As String
```

passes the *address* of the BSTR, as expected.

IN and OUT String Parameters

There are many API functions that require and/or return strings. Almost all of these functions deal with C-style strings, that is, LPSTRs or LPWSTRs. Some OLE-related functions do require BSTRs. By way of example, the following function is part of the Microsoft Web Publishing API. Note that it uses BSTRs. (Note also that the declaration is kind enough to tell us which parameters are IN parameters and which are OUT parameters. This is all too rare.)

```
HRESULT WpPostFile(
    [in]            LONG        hWnd
    [in]            BSTR        bstrLocalPath
    [in, out]       LONG *      plSiteNameBufLen
    [in, out]       BSTR        bstrSiteName
    [in, out]       LONG *      plDestURLBufLen
    [in, out]       BSTR        bstrDestURL
    [in]            LONG        lFlags
    [out, retval]   LONG *      plRetCode
    );
```

In general, API functions that use strings can do so in three ways:

- They can require a string as input in an IN parameter

- They can return a string as output in an OUT parameter

- They can do both, either in the same parameter or in separate parameters

To illustrate, Example 6-1 shows three API declarations.

Example 6-1. Three Example Declarations

```
// IN parameter example
HWND FindWindow(
  LPCTSTR lpClassName,   // pointer to class name
  LPCTSTR lpWindowName   // pointer to window name
);

// OUT parameter example
int GetWindowText(
    HWND hWnd,           // handle to window or control with text
    LPTSTR lpString,     // address of buffer for text
    int nMaxCount        // maximum number of characters to copy
);

// IN/OUT parameter example
LPTSTR CharUpper(
  LPTSTR lpsz            // single character or pointer to string
);
```

The *FindWindow* function returns a handle to a top-level window whose class name and/or window name matches specified strings. In this case, both parameters are IN parameters.

The *GetWindowText* function returns the text of a window's title bar in an OUT parameter *lpString*. It also returns the number of characters in the title as its return value.

The *CharUpper* function converts either a string or a single character to upper-case. When the argument is a string, the function converts the characters in the character array in place, that is, the parameter is IN/OUT.

How shall we convert these function declarations to VB?

We could simply replace each C-style string with a VB-style:

```
ByVal str As String
```

declaration, which, as we know, is a BSTR data type. However, there are some caveats. First, let us talk about the difference between passing a BSTR by value as opposed to by reference.

Dealing with IN Parameters

The first declaration in Example 6-1:

```
HWND FindWindow(
   LPCTSTR lpClassName,   // pointer to class name
   LPCTSTR lpWindowName   // pointer to window name
);
```

might be translated as follows:

```
Declare Function FindWindow Lib "user32" Alias "FindWindowA" ( _
   ByVal lpClassName As String, _
   ByVal lpWindowName As String _
) As Long
```

This works just fine. Since the *FindWindow* function does not alter the contents of the parameters (note the C in LPCTSTR), the BSTRs will be treated by Win32 as LPSTRs, which they are. In general, when dealing with a *constant* LPSTR, we can use a BSTR.

We should also note that *FindWindow* allows one (but not both) of these string parameters to be set, with the remaining parameter set to a null. In Win32, this parameter that the programmer chooses not to supply is represented by a null pointer—that is, a pointer that contains the value 0. Of course, 0 is not a valid address, so a null pointer is a very special type of pointer and is treated in this way by Win32.

Fortunately, VB has the **vbNullString** keyword, which is a null BSTR (and so also a null LPWSTR). It can be used whenever a null string is desired (or required). Actually, this is not as trivial an issue as it might seem at first. Before the introduction of the `vbNullString` into Visual Basic (I think with VB 4), we would need to do something like:

```
FindWindow(0&,. . .)
```

to simulate a null string for the first parameter. The problem is that VB would issue a type mismatch error, because a long 0 is not a string. The solution was to declare *three* separate aliases just to handle the two extra cases of null parameters. With the introduction of `vbNullString`, this annoyance went away.

To illustrate, in order to get the handle of the window with title "Microsoft Word - API.doc," we can write:

```
Dim sTitle As String
Dim hnd As Long
sTitle = "Microsoft Word - API.doc"
hnd = FindWindow(vbNullString, sTitle)
```

or more simply:

```
Dim hnd As Long
hnd = FindWindow(vbNullString, "Microsoft Word - API.doc")
```

Dealing with OUT Parameters

Now consider the second declaration in Example 6-1:

```
int GetWindowText(
    HWND hWnd,          // handle to window or control with text
    LPTSTR lpString,    // address of buffer for text
    int nMaxCount       // maximum number of characters to copy
);
```

This might be translated to VB as follows:

```
Declare Function GetWindowText Lib "user32" Alias "GetWindowTextA" ( _
    ByVal hwnd As Long, _
    ByVal lpString As String, _
    ByVal cch As Long _
) As Long
```

An HWND is a long value, as is a C-style `int` (integer). In this case, the string parameter is an OUT parameter, meaning that the function is going to fill this string with something useful—in this case, the title of the window whose handle is in the *hwnd* parameter.

Here is an example of a call to this function:

```
Sub GetWindowTitle()

Dim sText As String
Dim hnd As Long
Dim cTitle As Integer
Dim lngS As Long, lngV As Long
```

```
' Allocate string buffer
sText = String$(256, vbNullChar)

' Save the BSTR and Unicode character array locations
lngV = VarPtr(sText)
lngS = StrPtr(sText)

' Search for window with a given class
hnd = FindWindow("ThunderRT5Form", vbNullString)

' If window found, get title
If hnd > 0 Then
    cTitle = GetWindowText(hnd, sText, 255)
    sText = Left$(sText, cTitle)
    Debug.Print sText
        ' Compare the BSTR and character array locations
        ' to look for changes
    Debug.Print VarPtr(sText), lngV
    Debug.Print StrPtr(sText), lngS
Else
    Debug.Print "No window with this class name.", vbInformation
End If

End Sub
```

The output of one run is:

```
RunHelp - Unregistered Copy  -  Monday, December 7, 1998     10:11:53 AM
   1243480        1243480
   2165764        2012076
```

(Don't worry—this unregistered program is mine own.)

We first allocate a string buffer for the window title. We will discuss this important point further in a moment. Then we use *FindWindow* to search for a window with class name *ThunderRT5Form*—a VB5 runtime form. If such a window is found, its handle is returned in the *hnd* parameter. We can then call *GetWindow-Text*, passing it *hnd* as well as our text buffer *sText* and its size. Since the *GetWindowText* function returns the number of characters placed in the buffer, not including the terminating null, that is, the number of characters in the window title, we can use the *Left* function to extract just the title from the string buffer.

Note also that we have saved both the BSTR address (in *lngV*) and the character array address (in *lngS*), so that we can compare these values to the same values after calling *GetWindowText*. Lo and behold, the BSTR has not moved, but its contents have changed, that is, the character array has moved, as we discussed earlier.

Incidentally, since the returned string is null terminated and contains no embedded nulls, the following function also extracts the portion of the buffer that contains the title. This little utility is generic, and I use it often (in this book as well as in my programs).

```
Public Function Trim0(sName As String) As String
   ' Right trim string at first null.
   Dim x As Integer
   x = InStr(sName, vbNullChar)
   If x > 0 Then Trim0 = Left$(sName, x - 1) Else Trim0 = sName
End Function
```

Getting back to the issue at hand, it is important to understand that, when OUT string parameters are involved, it is almost always *our* responsibility to set up a *string buffer*, that is, a BSTR that has enough space allocated to hold the data that will be placed in it by the API function. Most Win32 API functions do not create strings—they merely fill strings created by the caller. It is not enough simply to declare:

```
Dim sText As String
```

We must allocate space, as in:

```
sText = String$(256, vbNullChar)
```

Thus, it is important to remember:

> When dealing with OUT string parameters, be sure to allocate a string buffer of sufficient size.

Note that in some cases, such as *GetWindowText*, the function provides an IN parameter for specifying the size of the buffer. This is actually a courtesy to us, in the sense that the function agrees not to place more characters in the buffer than we specify as the size of the buffer. (I often give the buffer an extra character that the function doesn't know about. Usually, the function includes the terminating null in its reckoning, but why take chances?)

Note that there are other cases in which no such courtesy is extended, so we must be careful.

Consider the case of *SendMessage*, for example. Here is part of what the Win32 documentation says about the **LB_GETTEXT** message, which can be used to retrieve the text of an item in a list box.

> An application sends an LB_GETTEXT message to retrieve a string from a listbox.
>
> ```
> wParam = (WPARAM) index;               // item index [0-based]
> lParam = (LPARAM) (LPCTSTR) lpszBuffer; // address of buffer
> ```
>
> [The parameter *lpszBuffer* is a] pointer to the buffer that will receive the string. The buffer must have sufficient space for the string and a terminating null character. An LB_GETTEXTLEN message can be sent before the LB_GETTEXT message to retrieve the length, in characters, of the string.

Thus, in this case, there is no IN parameter to act as a safety net. If we fail to allocate sufficient space in the buffer, the function will write over the end of our buffer, into unknown memory. If we are lucky, this will crash the program. If we are not lucky, it will overwrite some other data, possibly resulting in logical errors in our program, or crashing a client's program!

However, in this case Windows is not completely devoid of compassion. It does provide the **LB_GETTEXTLEN** message for us to use to first retrieve the length of the item in question. With this value, we can allocate a sufficiently capacious buffer. Example 6-2 shows some sample code. This code extracts the items from a listbox (which might belong to some other application) and places them in our listbox *lstMain*. We will expand this example considerably in Chapter 16, *Windows Messages*. Note the use of two different forms of the *SendMessage* function.

Example 6-2. Using LB_GETTEXT

```
Public Sub ExtractFromListBox(hControl As Long)

Dim cItems As Integer
Dim i As Integer
Dim sBuf As String
Dim cBuf As Long
Dim lResp As Long

' Get item count from control
cItems = SendMessageByLong(hControl, LB_GETCOUNT, 0&, 0&)

If cItems <= 0 Then Exit Sub

' Put items into list box
For i = 0 To cItems - 1

    ' Get length of item
    cBuf = SendMessageByString(hControl, LB_GETTEXTLEN, CLng(i), vbNullString)

    ' Allocate buffer to hold item
    sBuf = String$(cBuf + 1, " ")

    ' Send message to get item
    lResp = SendMessageByString(hControl, LB_GETTEXT, CLng(i), sBuf)

    ' Add item to local list box
    If lResp > 0 Then
        Form1.lstMain.AddItem Left$(sBuf, lResp)
    End If

Next i

Form1.lstMain.Refresh

End Sub
```

An IN/OUT Parameter Example—Watching Out for As Any

Consider now the third and final function in Example 6-1:

```
PTSTR CharUpper(
  LPTSTR lpsz    // single character or pointer to string
);
```

One problem here is that, despite the declaration of *lpsz* as an LPTSTR, the function allows the parameter to be filled with a non-LPTSTR. To wit, the documentation states that the *lpsz* parameter is a:

Pointer to a null-terminated string or specifies a single character. If the high-order word of this parameter is zero, the low-order word must contain a single character to be converted.

For use with string input, we can translate this into VB as:

```
Declare Function CharUpperForString Lib "user32" Alias "CharUpperA" ( _
    ByVal lpsz As String _
) As Long
```

This will generally work, as in:

```
' Convert string
str = "help"
Debug.Print StrPtr(str)
Debug.Print CharUpperForString(str)
Debug.Print str
```

whose output is:

```
1896580
1980916
HELP
```

Let us pause for a moment to inspect this output. The *CharUpper* documentation also states:

If the operand is a character string, the function returns a pointer to the converted string. Since the string is converted in place, the return value is equal to *lpsz*.

On the other hand, the two addresses `StrPtr(s)` (which is the address of the character array) and `CharUpper(s)` seem to be different. But remember the BSTR-to-ABSTR translation issue. Our string *str* undergoes a translation to a temporary ABSTR string at another location. This string is passed to the *CharUpper* function, which then changes the string (uppercases it) and also returns the location of the ABSTR string. Now, VB translates the ABSTR back to our BSTR, but it knows nothing about the fact that the return value represents the location of the temporary ABSTR, so it returns the address of that string!

We can confirm this further by calling the Unicode entry point, just as we did in an earlier example. The following declaration and code:

```
Declare Function CharUpperWide Lib "user32" Alias "CharUpperW" ( _
    ByVal lpsz As Long _
) As Long


' Construct an LPSTR
s = "help"
lng = StrPtr(s)
Debug.Print lng
Debug.Print CharUpperWide(lng)
Debug.Print s
```

returns:

```
1980916
1980916
HELP
```

Now the two addresses are the same, since no translation occurs!

For dealing with characters, we can make the following declaration:

```
Declare Function CharUpperForChar Lib "user32" Alias "CharUpperA" ( _
    ByVal lpsz As Long _
) As Long
```

For instance, calling:

```
Debug.Print Chr(CharUpperForChar(CLng(Asc("a"))))
```

returns an uppercase A.

You might think we could combine the two declarations by using **As Any**.

```
Declare Function CharUpperAsAny Lib "user32" Alias "CharUpperA" ( _
    ByVal lpsz As Any _
) As Long
```

The following code works:

```
s = "help"
Debug.Print StrPtr(s)
Debug.Print CharUpperAsAny(s)
Debug.Print s
```

as does:

```
Debug.Print Chr(CharUpperAsAny(CLng(Asc("a"))))
```

and:

```
Debug.Print Chr(CharUpperAsAny(97&))
```

(which returns the uppercase letter A.) However, the following code crashes my computer:

```
Debug.Print CharUpperAsAny(&H11000)
```

The problem is that the *CharUpper* function sees that the upper word of &H11000 is nonzero, so it assumes that the value is an *address*. But this is fatal. Who knows what is at address &H1100? In my case, it is protected memory.

What Happened to My Pointer?

There is another, much more insidious problem that can arise in connection with passing strings to API functions. As we can see from the *CharUpper* case, the API occasionally uses a single parameter to hold multiple data types (at different times, of course). Imagine the following hypothetical circumstance.

A certain API function has declaration:

```
PTSTR WatchOut(
    int nFlags      // flags
    LPTSTR lpsz     // pointer to string or length as a long
);
```

The documentation says that if *nFlags* has value WO_TEXT (a symbolic constant defined somewhere), then *lpsz* will receive an LPTSTR string (pointer to a character array), but if *nFlags* has value WO_LENGTH, then *lpsz* gets the length of the string, as a long.

Now, if we make the VB declaration:

```
Declare Function WatchOut Lib "whatever" ( _
    ByVal nFlags As Integer
    ByVal lpsz As String _
) As Long
```

we can get into real trouble. In particular, if we set *nFlags* equal to WO_LENGTH, then the following events take place under Windows 9x:

1. We create an initial BSTR string buffer for *lpsz*, say:

```
Dim str As String
str = String$(256, vbNullChar)
```

2. VB creates a temporary ABSTR to pass to *WatchOut*, as shown in Figure 6-8.

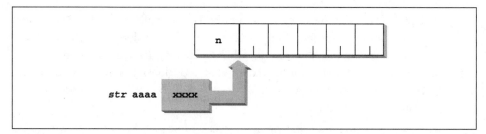

Figure 6-8. Creating a temporary ABSTR

3. As Figure 6-9 shows, because *nFlags* = WO_LENGTH, *WatchOut* changes the pointer, not the character array!

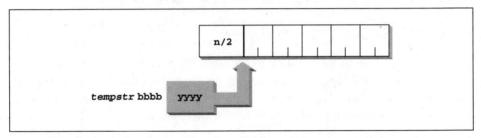

Figure 6-9. Changing the pointer rather than the character array

4. As Figure 6-10 shows, VB tries to translate what it thinks is an ANSI character array at address zzzz of length ????. This is a disaster.

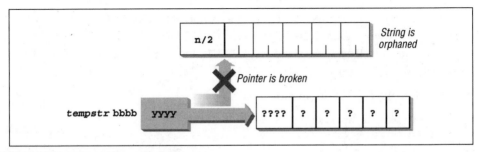

Figure 6-10. The resulting broken pointer

Under Windows NT, the *WatchOut* function changes the original BSTR pointer (instead of an ANSI copy), but this will have the same disastrous effects. Note that even if we somehow are unlucky enough to escape a crash when VB tries to translate the fraudulent ABSTR, the result will be garbage, the program may crash after we send it to our customers, and there is still the matter of the dangling string, whose memory will not be recovered until the program terminates. This is called a *memory leak.*

The problem can be summarized quite simply: occasionally an API function will change a string pointer (not the string itself) to a numeric value. *But VB still thinks it has a pointer.* This spells disaster. In addition, testing to see whether the contents of the BSTR pointer variable have changed doesn't solve the problem, because as we have seen (Figure 6-8), VB sometimes changes the pointer to point to a legitimate character array!

As it happens, the situation described earlier can occur. Here is an important example, which we will play with at the end of the chapter.

The *GetMenuItemInfo* function retrieves information about a Windows menu item. Its declaration is:

```
BOOL GetMenuItemInfo(
  HMENU hMenu,              // handle of menu
  uint uItem,              // indicates which item to look at
  BOOL fByPosition,         // used with uItem
  MENUITEMINFO *lpmii       // pointer to structure (see discussion)
);
```

where, in particular, the parameter *lpmii* is a pointer to a **MENUITEMINFO** structure that will be filled in by *GetMenuItemInfo*. This structure is:

```
typedef struct tagMENUITEMINFO {
    UINT cbSize;
    UINT fMask;
    UINT fType;
    UINT fState;
    UINT wID;
    HMENU hSubMenu;
    HBITMAP hbmpChecked;
    HBITMAP hbmpUnchecked;
    DWORD dwItemData;
    LPTSTR dwTypeData;
    UINT cch;
}
```

Note that the penultimate member is an LPTSTR.

Now, the *rpiAPIData* application on the accompanying CD will automatically translate this to a VB user-defined type, replacing all C data types in this case by VB longs:

```
Public Type MENUITEMINFO
    cbSize  As Long           '//UINT
    fMask  As Long            '//UINT
    fType  As Long            '//UINT
    fState  As Long           '//UINT
    wID  As Long              '//UINT
    hSubMenu  As Long         '//HMENU
    hbmpChecked  As Long      '//HBITMAP
    hbmpUnchecked  As Long    '//HBITMAP
    dwItemData  As Long       '//DWORD
    dwTypeData  As Long       '//LPTSTR
    cch  As Long              '//UINT
End Type
```

Suppose instead that the LPTSTR was translated into a VB string:

```
dwTypeData  As String        '//LPTSTR
```

According to the documentation for **MENUITEMINFO**, if we set the *fMask* parameter to **MIIM_TYPE**, allocate a suitable string buffer in *dwTypeData*, and place its length in *cch*, then the *GetMenuItemInfo* function will retrieve the type of the menu item into *fType* (and adjust the value of *cch*). If this type is **MFT_TEXT**, then the string buffer will be filled with the text of that menu item. However, and this is the problem, if the type is `MFT_BITMAP`, then the low-order word of *dwTypeData* gets the bitmap's handle (and *cch* is ignored).

Thus, *GetMenuItemInfo* may change *dwDataType* from an LPTSTR to a bitmap handle! This is exactly the problem we described earlier. We will consider an actual example of this later in the chapter. Keep in mind also that even if the type is `MFT_TEXT`, the *dwDataType* pointer may be changed to point to a different character buffer.

So if we shouldn't use a string variable for *dwDataType*, what should we do?

The answer is that we should create our own character array by declaring a *byte array* and pass a pointer to that array. In other words, we create our own LPSTR. VB doesn't know anything about LPSTRs, so it will try to interpret it as a VB string.

This even solves the orphaned array problem, for if the API function changes our LPSTR to a numeric value (like a bitmap handle), we still retain a reference to the byte array (we had to create it somehow), so we can deallocate the memory ourselves (or it will be allocated when the byte array variable goes out of scope).

Before getting into a discussion of byte arrays and looking at an example, let us summarize:

> Occasionally an API function will change an LPSTR to a numeric value. *But VB will still think it has a string.* This spells disaster. Moreover, testing to see whether the contents of the BSTR pointer variable have changed doesn't help because VB sometimes changes the original BSTR to point to a legitimate character array. Hence, if there is a chance that this might happen, you should create your own LPSTR using a byte array and use it in place of the BSTR. For safety, you may want to do this routinely when the string is embedded within a structure.

The last point made in the caveat is worth elaborating. Oftentimes an API function parameter refers to a structure, whose members may be other structures, whose members may, in turn, be other structures. This structure nesting can get quite involved. We will see an example when we create our DLL Export Table application. This makes it very difficult to keep track of what the API function might be doing to all of the structure members. The safest thing to do is to *always* use pointers to byte arrays (that is, LPSTRs) and avoid BSTRs completely when dealing with strings embedded in structures.

Strings and Byte Arrays

Of course, a byte array is just an array whose members have type `byte`, for instance:

```
Dim b(1 to 100) As Byte
```

To get a pointer to this byte array, we can use *VarPtr*:

```
Dim lpsz As Long
lpsz = VarPtr(b(1))    ' or rpiVarPtr(b(1))
```

(Even though it doesn't seem so, the letters *lpsz* stand for *long pointer* to *null-terminated* string.) Note that the address of the first member of the array is the address of the array.

Remembering that an LPSTR is a pointer to a *null-terminated* character array, we should initialize the array to nulls:

```
For i = 1 To 100
   b(i) = 0
Next
```

(It is true that VB does its own initialization, but it is not good programming practice to rely on this.)

Translating Between Byte Arrays and BSTRs

To copy a BSTR:

```
Dim s As String
```

to a byte array, we can proceed in a couple of different ways. For a strictly VB solution, we have:

```
s = "help"
Dim b(1 To 8) As Byte
For i = 1 To 8
   b(i) = AscB(MidB(s, i))
Next
```

Another approach is:

```
s = "help"
Dim b(1 To 8) As Byte
CopyMemory b(1), ByVal StrPtr(s), LenB(s)
```

Note that (in both cases) we get:

```
104  0  101  0  108  0  112  0
```

showing that the bytes are reversed in each Unicode integer.

In the other direction, to copy a byte array into a BSTR, VB gives us some help. If *b* is a *Unicode* byte array, we can just write:

```
Dim t As String
t = b
```

For an ANSI byte array *b*, we write:

```
Dim t As String
t = StrConv(b, vbUnicode)
```

Note, however, that the *StrConv* function does not recognize a null terminator in the byte array—it will translate the entire array. Any nulls that are encountered in the array become embedded nulls in the BSTR.

Translating Between BSTRs and LPTSTRs

Let us consider how to translate back and forth between BSTRs and LPTSTRs.

From BSTR to LPWSTR

Getting a BSTR into a Unicode byte array is conceptually easy, because the character array of the BSTR *is* a Unicode byte array, so all we need to do is copy the bytes one by one. Here is a function to translate BSTRs to LPWSTRs:

```
Function BSTRtoLPWSTR(sBSTR As String, b() As Byte, lpwsz As Long) As Long

' Input: a nonempty BSTR string
' Input: **undimensioned** byte array b()
' Output: Fills byte array b() with Unicode char string from sBSTR
' Output: Fills lpwsz with a pointer to b() array
' Returns byte count, not including terminating 2-byte Unicode null character
' Original BSTR is not affected

Dim cBytes As Long

cBytes = LenB(sBSTR)

' ReDim array, with space for terminating null
ReDim b(1 To cBytes + 2) As Byte

' Point to BSTR char array
lpwsz = StrPtr(sBSTR)

' Copy the array
CopyMemory b(1), ByVal lpwsz, cBytes + 2

' Point lpsz to new array
lpwsz = VarPtr(b(1))

' Return byte count
BSTRtoLPWSTR = cBytes

End Function
```

This function takes a BSTR, an *undimensioned* byte array, and a long variable *lng* and converts the long to an LPWSTR. It returns the byte count as the return value of the function. Here is an example:

```
Dim b() As Byte
Dim lpsz As Long, lng As Long
lng = BSTRToLPWSTR("here", b, lpsz)
```

It might have occurred to you to simply copy the contents of the BSTR to the contents of *lpsz*:

```
lpsz = StrPtr(sBSTR)
```

The problem is that now we have two pointers to the same character array—a dangerous situation because VB does not realize this and might deallocate the array.

From BSTR to LPSTR

The function to convert a BSTR to an LPSTR is similar, but requires a translation from Unicode to ANSI first:

```
Function BSTRtoLPSTR(sBSTR As String, b() As Byte, lpsz As Long) As Long

' Input: a nonempty BSTR string
' Input: **undimensioned** byte array b()
' Output: Fills byte array b() with ANSI char string
' Output: Fills lpsz with a pointer to b() array
' Returns byte count, not including terminating null
' Original BSTR is not affected

Dim cBytes As Long
Dim sABSTR As String

cBytes = LenB(sBSTR)

' ReDim array, with space for terminating null
ReDim b(1 To cBytes + 2) As Byte

' Convert to ANSI
sABSTR = StrConv(sBSTR, vbFromUnicode)

' Point to BSTR char array
lpsz = StrPtr(sABSTR)

' Copy the array
CopyMemory b(1), ByVal lpsz, cBytes + 2

' Point lpsz to new array
lpsz = VarPtr(b(1))

' Return byte count
BSTRtoLPSTR = cBytes

End Function
```

From LPWSTR to BSTR

On return from an API call, you may have an LPWSTR, that is, a pointer to a null-terminated Unicode character array. Visual Basic makes it easy to get a BSTR from a byte array—just make an assignment using the equal sign. However, VB doesn't know how to handle a *pointer to* a byte array.

Here is a little utility:

```
Function LPWSTRtoBSTR(ByVal lpwsz As Long) As String

' Input: a valid LPWSTR pointer lpwsz
' Return: a sBSTR with the same character array

Dim cChars As Long

' Get number of characters in lpwsz
cChars = lstrlenW(lpwsz)

' Initialize string
LPWSTRtoBSTR = String$(cChars, 0)

' Copy string
CopyMemory ByVal StrPtr(LPWSTRtoBSTR), ByVal lpwsz, cChars * 2

End Function
```

From LPSTR to BSTR

We can modify the previous utility to return a BSTR from an LPSTR as follows (recall that *Trim0* just truncates a string at the first null character):

```
Function LPSTRtoBSTR(ByVal lpsz As Long) As String

' Input: a valid LPSTR pointer lpsz
' Output: a sBSTR with the same character array

Dim cChars As Long

' Get number of characters in lpsz
cChars = lstrlenA(lpsz)

' Initialize string
LPSTRtoBSTR = String$(cChars, 0)

' Copy string
CopyMemory ByVal StrPtr(LPSTRtoBSTR), ByVal lpsz, cChars

' Convert to Unicode
LPSTRtoBSTR = Trim0(StrConv(LPSTRtoBSTR, vbUnicode))

End Function
```

Example: Using Byte Arrays

Let us demonstrate the use of byte arrays with a simple example using *CharUpper*. We have seen that this function is declared as:

```
LPTSTR CharUpper(
  LPTSTR lpsz          // single character or pointer to string
);
```

This leads to two reasonable translations into VB:

```
Declare Function CharUpperByBSTR Lib "user32" Alias "CharUpperA" ( _
    ByVal s As String _
) As Long
```

or:

```
Declare Function CharUpperByLPSTR Lib "user32" Alias "CharUpperA" ( _
    ByVal lpsz As Long _
) As Long
```

We have seen the first form in action, so let us try the second form.

The following code first converts a BSTR to an LPSTR. Note that we should not convert to LPWSTR, since LPWSTRs are passed to *CharUpperA* without translation by VB; and if we passed an LPWSTR, then as soon as *CharUpperA* encountered the null byte that is part of the first Unicode character in the LPWSTR, it would think the string had ended. Thus, it would capitalize only the first character in the string.

The LPSTR is then passed to *CharUpperA*, which converts it to uppercase. Having saved the LPSTR pointer, we can check to see if it has been changed. If not, we translate the LPSTR back to a BSTR and print it. If the pointer is changed, then we must deallocate the byte array ourselves (or just let the array variable pass out of scope).

Of course, in this simple example, the pointer should not be changed by *CharUpper.* Nevertheless, this same procedure will deal with API functions that may change the pointer:

```
Public Sub CharUpperText

Dim lpsz As Long
Dim lpszOrg As Long
Dim sBSTR As String
Dim b() As Byte

sBSTR = "help"

' Convert BSTR to LPSTR.
BSTRtoLPSTR sBSTR, b, lpsz

' Save LPSTR to check for modification by API function
lpszOrg = lpsz

' Convert to upper case
CharUpperAsLPWSTR lpsz

' If pointer not modified, then convert back to BSTR
' and print
If lpszOrg = lpsz Then
```

```
      Debug.Print LPSTRtoBSTR(lpsz)
   Else
      Erase b
      ' Use new value of lpsz if desired...
   End If

   End Sub
```

Example: Windows Menus

Let us turn to the example involving *GetMenuItemInfo* that we promised earlier. Recall that the *GetMenuItemInfo* function retrieves information about a Windows menu item. Its VB declaration is:

```
Declare Function GetMenuItemInfo Lib "user32" Alias "GetMenuItemInfoA" ( _
   ByVal hMenu As Long, _
   ByVal uItem As Long, _
   ByVal lByPos As Long, _
   ByRef lpMenuItemInfo As MENUITEMINFO _
) As Long
```

where, in particular, the parameter *lpmii* is a pointer to a **MENUITEMINFO** structure that will be filled in by *GetMenuItemInfo*. This structure is:

```
Public Type MENUITEMINFO
   cbSize  As Long
   fMask   As Long
   fType   As Long
   fState  As Long
   wID  As Long
   hSubMenu  As Long
   hbmpChecked  As Long
   hbmpUnchecked  As Long
   dwItemData  As Long
   dwTypeData  As Long
   cch  As Long
End Type
```

According to the documentation, if we set the *fMask* parameter to **MIIM_TYPE**, allocate a suitable string buffer in *dwTypeData*, and place its length in *cch*, then the *GetMenuItemInfo* function will retrieve the type of the menu item into *fType*. If this type is **MFT_TEXT**, then the string buffer will be filled with the text of that menu item. However, and this is the problem, if the type is **MFT_BITMAP**, then the low-order word of *dwTypeData* gets the bitmap's handle. Thus, in this case, *GetMenuItemInfo* will change *dwTypeData* from an LPSTR to a bitmap handle!

Figure 6-11 shows a menu with a bitmap. We will discuss how to create such a menu in VB using the Win32 API in Chapter 21, *Bitmaps*.

Example 6-3 shows the code used to get the text for each of the items in this menu.

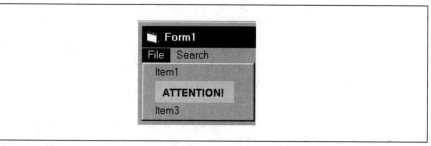

Figure 6-11. A menu with a bitmap

Example 6-3. Getting Menu Text

```
Public Sub GetMenuInfoExample

Const MIIM_TYPE = &H10        ' from WINUSER.H
Dim uMenuItemInfo As MENUITEMINFO
Dim bBuf(1 To 50) As Byte
Dim sText As String

' Initialize structure
uMenuItemInfo.cbSize = LenB(uMenuItemInfo)
uMenuItemInfo.fMask = MIIM_TYPE
uMenuItemInfo.dwTypeData = VarPtr(bBuf(1))
uMenuItemInfo.cch = 49

' Get menu text
For i = 0 To 2
   ' Must reset count each time
   uMenuItemInfo.cch = 49

   ' Get TypeData before
   Debug.Print "Before:" & uMenuItemInfo.dwTypeData

   ' Call API
   lng = GetMenuItemInfo(hSubMenu, CLng(i), -1, uMenuItemInfo)

   ' Get TypeData after
   Debug.Print "After:" & uMenuItemInfo.dwTypeData

   ' Print text -- CAREFUL HERE
'    sText = StrConv(bBuf, vbUnicode)
'    Debug.Print sText

Next

End Sub
```

Here is what happens as this code executes.

The first loop (`i = 0`) presents no problems, and the output is:

```
Before:1479560
After:1479560
```

Observe that the buffer pointer had not changed. Hence, the commented code that prints the menu text would run without error.

The second loop also runs without error (as long as the statements involving *sText* are commented out). The output, however, is:

```
Before:1479560
After:3137668829
```

As the documentation suggests, *GetMenuItemInfo* returns the bitmap's handle in *uMenuItemInfo.dwTypeData*. Thus, we have lost the pointer to the buffer *sBuf*. On the third loop, the program will crash, because the third call to *GetMenuItem-Info* will try to write the menu text for the third item to an imaginary buffer at address 3137668829 = &Hbb0506dd. If this memory is protected (as it probably is), you will get a message similar to the one I got in Figure 6-12.

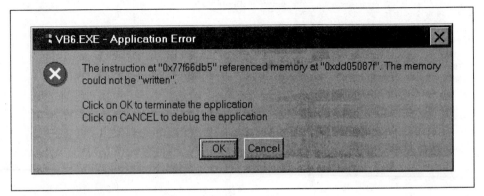

Figure 6-12. Whoops

Note that if we uncomment the lines of code that print the menu text, the code will probably crash when we come to these lines during the second loop.

To fix this code, we need to pay attention to when the pointer changes and correct the problem, as in Example 6-4.

Example 6-4. A Corrected Version of Example 6-3

```
Public Sub GetMenuInfoExample

Dim uMenuItemInfo As utMENUITEMINFO
Dim bBuf(1 To 50) As Byte
Dim sText As String
Dim lPointer As Long

' Initialize structure
uMenuItemInfo.cbSize = LenB(uMenuItemInfo)
uMenuItemInfo.fMask = MIIM_TYPE
uMenuItemInfo.dwTypeData = VarPtr(bBuf(1))
uMenuItemInfo.cch = 49
```

Example 6-4. A Corrected Version of Example 6-3 (continued)

```
' Get menu text
For i = 0 To 2
    ' Must reset count each time
    uMenuItemInfo.cch = 49

    ' Save buffer pointer
    lPointer = uMenuItemInfo.dwTypeData

    Debug.Print "Before:" & uMenuItemInfo.dwTypeData

    ' Call API
    lng = GetMenuItemInfo(hSubMenu, CLng(i), -1, uMenuItemInfo)

    Debug.Print "After:" & uMenuItemInfo.dwTypeData

    ' Check for pointer change
    If lPointer <> uMenuItemInfo.dwTypeData Then
        Debug.Print "Bitmap!"
        ' Restore pointer
        uMenuItemInfo.dwTypeData = lPointer
    Else
        ' Print text
        sText = StrConv(bBuf, vbUnicode)
        Debug.Print sText
    End If

Next

End Sub
```

The output is:

```
Before:1760168
After:1760168
Test1
Before:1760168
After:1443168935
Bitmap!
Before:1760168
After:1760168
Test3
```

Note that if we had declared *uMenuItemInfo.dwTypeData* of type String, then as soon as *GetMenuItemInfo* changed the pointer to the bitmap handle, VB would think it had a character array at that location. We can't even watch out for this and reset the pointer, because the change might have been legitimate.

The previous discussion and the previous example have shown that we need to be *very careful* about BSTRs. In short, there are two issues that must be addressed:

- A BSTR undergoes a BSTR-to-ABSTR translation when passed to an external function.

- A BSTR may have its value changed to a non-BSTR value (such as a handle or length) by an external function.

Note that these issues must be addressed even when a BSTR is embedded in a structure.

In any case, the translation issue is generally not a problem, since VB does the reverse translation on the return value. However, the other issue can be a fatal problem. The only way to avoid it completely is to manually replace any BSTRs by LPSTRs, using a byte array.

Getting the Address of a Variable of User-Defined Type

An API programmer often needs to get the address of a variable of user-defined type. Consider, for example, the structure:

```
Type utExample
    sString As String
    iInteger As Integer
End Type

Dim uEx As utExample
```

Suppose we want to find the address of the variable *uEx*. First, note that the address of a structure variable is the same as the address of its first member.

Now consider the following code:

```
Debug.Print VarPtr(uEx)
Debug.Print VarPtr(uEx.sString)
Debug.Print VarPtr(uEx.iInteger)
Debug.Print
Debug.Print rpiVarPtr(uEx)
Debug.Print rpiVarPtr(uEx.sString)
Debug.Print rpiVarPtr(uEx.iInteger)
```

whose output is as follows.

```
1243836
1243836
1243840

1243824
1243820
1243840
```

As you can see, *VarPtr* reports the address as you would expect: the address of *uEx* is the same as the address of *uEx.aString*, and the address of *uEx.iInteger* is 4 bytes larger, to account for the 4-byte BSTR.

On the other hand, the *rpiVarPtr* is susceptible to BSTR-to-ABSTR translation, which occurs on the member of the structure that is a BSTR.

The relationship between the first and second address in the second group may look strange until we remember that each *call* to *rpiVarPtr* produces a translation, so we cannot compare addresses from two separate calls, both of which involve translations!

On the other hand, the third address is the address of the original integer member. There is no translation in the call:

```
Debug.Print rpiVarPtr(uEx.iInteger)
```

because there are no BSTR parameters. Thus, we can use an external function such as *rpiVarPtr* to compute the address of a structure provided the structure has at least one non-BSTR parameter. In this event, we get the address of one such parameter and count backwards to thebeginning of the structure.

7

System Information Functions

Let us put some of what we have learned to immediate practice. One of the areas of the Win32 API that we can use profitably even without knowing much about how Windows itself works is the area devoted to system information.

There are several API functions that can be used to gather information about the computer upon which the functions are running. The Win32 System Information functions are listed in Table 7-1.

Table 7-1. System Information Functions

GetComputerName	*GetSystemMetrics*	*GetWindowsDirectory*
GetKeyboardType	*GetTempPath*	*SetComputerName*
GetSysColor	*GetUserName*	*SetSysColors*
GetSystemDirectory	*GetVersion*	*SystemParametersInfo*
GetSystemInfo	*GetVersionEx*	

Let us look at a few of these functions.

The Computer's Name

The *GetComputerName* function is used to get the current computer's name. The corresponding *SetComputerName* will set the computer's name. The VC++ declaration is:

```
BOOL GetComputerName(
    LPTSTR lpBuffer,     // address of name buffer
    LPDWORD nSize        // address of size of name buffer
);
```

Here the parameters are an LPSTR and a pointer to a DWORD, and the return type is BOOL. A corresponding VB declaration is:

```
Declare Function GetComputerName Lib "kernel32" Alias "GetComputerNameA" ( _
   ByVal lpBuffer As String, _
   nSize As Long _
) As Long
```

According to the documentation, under Windows 9x the *GetComputerName* function will fail if the input size is less than the constant **MAX_COMPUTERNAME_LENGTH** + 1. This constant is defined in *WINBASE.H* as:

```
#define MAX_COMPUTERNAME_LENGTH 15
```

which in VB becomes:

```
Public Const MAX_COMPUTERNAME_LENGTH = 15
```

We can now write a small function to return the computer's name:

```
Public Function GetTheComputerName As String

Dim s As String
s = String(MAX_COMPUTERNAME_LENGTH + 1, 0)

lng = GetComputerName(s, MAX_COMPUTERNAME_LENGTH)

GetComputerName = Trim0(s)

End Function
```

(Recall that *Trim0* is a simple function to trim a string at the first null.) On my system, the return value is:

```
SRCOMPUTER
```

Special Windows Paths

The *GetWindowsDirectory*, *GetSystemDirectory*, and *GetTempPath* retrieve the path to the Windows, Windows System, and Windows temporary files directories. For instance, the *GetSystemDirectory* function is defined as:

```
UINT GetSystemDirectory(
   LPTSTR lpBuffer,    // address of buffer for system directory
   UINT uSize          // size of directory buffer
);

UINT GetWindowsDirectory( _
   LPTSTR lpBuffer,    // address of buffer for Windows directory
   UINT uSize          // size of directory buffer
);

DWORD GetTempPath(
   DWORD nBufferLength, // size, in characters, of the buffer
```

```
    LPTSTR lpBuffer       // pointer to buffer for temp path
);
```

The VB declarations are:

```
Declare Function GetSystemDirectory Lib "kernel32" Alias "GetSystemDirectoryA" ( _
    ByVal lpBuffer As String, _
    ByVal nSize As Long _
) As Long

Declare Function GetWindowsDirectory Lib "kernel32" _
Alias "GetWindowsDirectoryA" ( _
    ByVal lpBuffer As String, _
    ByVal nSize As Long _
) As Long

Declare Function GetTempPath Lib "kernel32" Alias "GetTempPathA" ( _
    ByVal nBufferLength As Long, _
    ByVal lpBuffer As String _
) As Long
```

Each of these functions returns the number of characters placed in the string buffer. The size of the buffers should be set one larger than the symbolic constant:

```
Public Const MAX_PATH = 260
```

Here is some sample code:

```
Dim s As String, lng As Long

s = String(MAX_PATH + 1, 0)

lng = GetWindowsDirectory(s, MAX_PATH)
Debug.Print Left$(s, lng)

lng = GetSystemDirectory(s, MAX_PATH)
Debug.Print Left$(s, lng)

lng = GetTempPath(MAX_PATH, s)
Debug.Print Left$(s, lng)
```

On my system, the output is:

```
C:\WINNT
C:\WINNT\System32
C:\TEMP\
```

Note that, in each case, the documentation says that the return value is the number of characters copied to the buffer, not including the terminating null. This is why we can use the *Left$* function to extract just the return string. On the other hand, the documentation for *GetComputerName* simply says that the return value is nonzero on success, so we used the *Trim0* function instead.

The Operating System Version

The *GetVersionEx* function returns version information about the Windows operating system and can be used to determine whether the system is running Windows 95, Windows 98, or Windows NT. The declaration is:

```
BOOL GetVersionEx(
    LPOSVERSIONINFO lpVersionInformation    // pointer to version info structure
);
```

where *lpVersionInformation* is a pointer to an **OSVERSIONINFO** structure, which is defined as follows:

```
typedef struct _OSVERSIONINFO{
    DWORD dwOSVersionInfoSize;
    DWORD dwMajorVersion;
    DWORD dwMinorVersion;
    DWORD dwBuildNumber;
    DWORD dwPlatformId;
    TCHAR szCSDVersion[ 128 ];
} OSVERSIONINFO;
```

The documentation for this structure is as follows:

dwOSVersionInfoSize

Specifies the size, in bytes, of the **OSVERSIONINFO** structure. This is a common requirement in structures. Since a DWORD is a 4-byte unsigned long and since VB will translate the 128-character string into a 128-byte ANSI character array, the total size is 4*5+128=148. This is also the value returned by the *Len* function, but not the *LenB* function, which doesn't take into account the Unicode-to-ANSI translation.

dwMajorVersion

Indicates the major version number of the operating system. For example, for Windows NT Version 3.51, the major version number is 3. For Windows NT 4.0 and Windows 9x, the major version number is 4.

dwMinorVersion

Indicates the minor version number of the operating system. For example, for Windows NT Version 3.51, the minor version number is 51. For Windows NT 4.0, the minor version number is 0. For Windows 95, the minor version number is 0. For Windows 98, the minor version number is 10.

dwBuildNumber

Indicates the build number of the operating system under Windows NT. For Windows 9x, the low-order word contains the build number of the operating system, and the high-order word contains the major and minor version numbers.

dwPlatformId

Identifies the operating system platform, and can be one of the following values:

VER_PLATFORM_WIN32s (= 0)

Win32s running on Windows 3.1

VER_PLATFORM_WIN32_WINDOWS (= 1)

Win32 running on Windows 95 or Windows 98

VER_PLATFORM_WIN32_NT (= 2)

Win32 running on Windows NT

szCSDVersion

For Windows NT, contains a null-terminated string, such as "Service Pack 3," that indicates the latest Service Pack installed on the system. If no Service Pack has been installed, the string is empty. For Windows 95, this string contains a null-terminated string that provides arbitrary additional information about the operating system.

Translating the *GetVersionEx* declaration into VB gives:

```
Declare Function GetVersionEx Lib "kernel32" Alias "GetVersionExA" ( _
    lpVersionInformation As OSVERSIONINFO _
) As Long
```

The intention here is to pass the address of an **OSVERSIONINFO** structure by reference.

To translate the structure definition, we replace the DWORDs with Longs, and the TCHAR array, being fixed length, with either a fixed-length string or a byte array. In the former case, VB will do the usual Unicode-to-ANSI translation, but that's fine:

```
Type OSVERSIONINFO
    dwOSVersionInfoSize As Long
    dwMajorVersion As Long
    dwMinorVersion As Long
    dwBuildNumber As Long
    dwPlatformId As Long
    szCSDVersion As String * 128    ' 128 characters
End Type
```

Let's give this a try:

```
Public Sub PrintVersionInfo

Dim lret As Long
Dim osverinfo As OSVERSIONINFO
osverinfo.dwOSVersionInfoSize = Len(osverinfo)
lret = GetVersionEx(osverinfo)
If lret = 0 Then
    RaiseApiError lret
```

```
Else
    Debug.Print "Version: " & osverinfo.dwMajorVersion & "." _
        & osverinfo.dwMinorVersion
    Debug.Print "Build: " & osverinfo.dwBuildNumber
    Debug.Print "Platform ID: " & osverinfo.dwPlatformId
    Debug.Print "String: " & osverinfo.szCSDVersion
End If

End Sub
```

(You will find the *RaiseAPIError* function defined at the end of Chapter 3, *API Declarations.*) The output on my system is:

```
Version: 4.0
Build: 1381
Platform ID: 2
String: Service Pack 3
```

Here is a short function that returns the name of the operating system:

```
Public Function GetOSVersion() As String

' Return name of operating system

Dim lret As Long
Dim osverinfo As OSVERSIONINFO

osverinfo.dwOSVersionInfoSize = Len(osverinfo)

lret = GetVersionEx(osverinfo)

If lret = 0 Then
    GetOSVersion = "unknown"
Else
    Select Case osverinfo.dwPlatformId & "/" & osverinfo.dwMajorVersion & "/" &
osverinfo.dwMinorVersion
        Case "1/4/0"
            GetOSVersion = "Win95"
        Case "1/4/10"
            GetOSVersion = "Win98"
        Case "2/3/51"
            GetOSVersion = "WinNT351"
        Case "2/4/0"
            GetOSVersion = "WinNT4"
    End Select
End If

End Function
```

System Metrics

The *GetSystemMetrics* function retrieves metric (measurement) information about the system. The VC++ declarations is simply as follows.

```
int GetSystemMetrics(
    int nIndex      // system metric or configuration setting to retrieve
);
```

This translates into VB as:

```
Declare Function GetSystemMetrics Lib "user32" ( _
    ByVal nIndex As Long _
) As Long
```

The *nIndex* parameter is set to one of 49 different possible constants. The requested measurement (generally in pixels or nondimensional units) is returned by the function.

To give you an idea of the type of information returned, here is a sampling of the constants for this function. All height and width measurements are in pixels:

```
Const SM_CMOUSEBUTTONS = 43         ' Number of mouse buttons
Const SM_MOUSEWHEELPRESENT = 75     ' True if mouse wheel present
                                    ' (Win NT 4 or Win 98 only)
Const SM_SWAPBUTTON = 23            ' True if mouse buttons swapped

Const SM_CXBORDER = 5               ' Width and height of a window border
Const SM_CYBORDER = 6

Const SM_CXSCREEN = 0               ' Width and height of screen
Const SM_CYSCREEN = 1
Const SM_CXFULLSCREEN = 16          ' Width and height of client area for a
                                    ' full-screen window
Const SM_CYFULLSCREEN = 17

Const SM_CXHTHUMB = 10              ' Width of the thumb box in a horizontal
                                    ' scroll bar.

Const SM_CXICONSPACING = 38         ' Dimensions of a grid cell for items in
                                    ' large icon view.
Const SM_CYICONSPACING = 39

Const SM_CYCAPTION = 4              ' Height of a normal caption area.
```

System Parameters

The *SystemParamtersInfo* function is a powerful function for getting or setting system-wide parameters. The function can also update the user profile while setting a parameter. The declaration is:

```
BOOL SystemParametersInfo(
    UINT uiAction, // system parameter to query or set
    UINT uiParam,  // depends on action to be taken
    PVOID pvParam, // depends on action to be taken
    UINT fWinIni   // user profile update flag
);
```

which can be translated into VB as:

```
Declare Function SystemParametersInfo Lib "user32" _
Alias "SystemParametersInfoA" ( _
   ByVal uiAction As Long, _
   ByVal uiParam As Long, _
   pvParam As Any, _
   ByVal fWinIni As Long _
) As Long
```

Note that, for type safety, we can alter the data type of the *pvParam* depending upon the action to be taken.

This powerful function can take at least 90 different *uiAction* values. We will content ourselves with a single example. Note that the function returns a nonzero value on success and 0 on failure. It will set *GetLastError*, so we can use VB's `Err.LastDLLError` value.

System Icon Metrics

We can get or set the characteristics of system icons (such as those that appear on the desktop) using the constants

```
Public Const SPI_GETICONMETRICS = 45
Public Const SPI_SETICONMETRICS = 46
```

For `SPI_GETICONMETRICS`, the documentation says that the parameter *pvParam* must point to an `ICONMETRICS` structure that receives the information. For `SPI_SETICONMETRICS`, the parameter *pvParam* must point to an `ICONMETRICS` structure that contains the new parameters.

In both cases, we must also set the *cbSize* member of the `ICONMETRICS` structure (see the following) and the *uiParam* parameter of *SystemParametersInfo* to the size, in bytes, of the structure.

The `ICONMETRICS` structure has declaration:

```
typedef struct tagICONMETRICS {
   UINT    cbSize;
   int     iHorzSpacing;
   int     iVertSpacing;
   int     iTitleWrap;
   LOGFONT lfFont;
} ICONMETRICS, FAR *LPICONMETRICS;
```

and the `LOGFONT` structure is:

```
typedef struct tagLOGFONT { // lf
   LONG lfHeight;
   LONG lfWidth;
   LONG lfEscapement;
   LONG lfOrientation;
```

```
      LONG lfWeight;
      BYTE lfItalic;
      BYTE lfUnderline;
      BYTE lfStrikeOut;
      BYTE lfCharSet;
      BYTE lfOutPrecision;
      BYTE lfClipPrecision;
      BYTE lfQuality;
      BYTE lfPitchAndFamily;
      TCHAR lfFaceName[LF_FACESIZE];
   } LOGFONT;
```

where:

```
   Public Const LF_FACESIZE = 32
```

There is an important point to note here. Very often one structure will contain *pointers* to other structures. In this case, however, the *lfFont* variable is not a pointer—it is the actual structure. Thus, we must combine the two structures when creating a VB version:

```
   Public Type ICONMETRICS
       cbSize  As Long
       iHorzSpacing  As Long
       iVertSpacing  As Long
       iTitleWrap  As Long
       lfHeight  As Long
       lfWidth  As Long
       lfEscapement  As Long
       lfOrientation  As Long
       lfWeight  As Long
       lfItalic  As Byte
       lfUnderline  As Byte
       lfStrikeOut  As Byte
       lfCharSet  As Byte
       lfOutPrecision  As Byte
       lfClipPrecision  As Byte
       lfQuality  As Byte
       lfPitchAndFamily  As Byte
       lfFaceName As String * LF_FACESIZE
   End Type
```

Note that this structure behaves well with respect to member alignment. (I'll bet you forgot to check that!) We could have used a byte array for *lfFaceName* as well as a fixed-length string. A fixed-length string is easier to use when outputting the return value, however.

Here is some code that uses this function:

```
   Public Sub PrintIconMetrics

   Dim im As ICONMETRICS
   im.cbSize = Len(im)
   lret = SystemParametersInfo(SPI_GETICONMETRICS, Len(im), im, 0&)
```

```
   If lret = 0 Then
      RaiseApiError Err.LastDllError
   Else
      Debug.Print "Hor Spacing:" & im.iHorzSpacing
      Debug.Print "Vert Spacing:" & im.iVertSpacing
      Debug.Print im.lfFaceName & "/"
   End If

   End Sub
```

The output on my system is:

```
   Hor Spacing:101
   Vert Spacing:109
   MS Sans Serif                    /
```

System Colors

The functions *GetSysColor* and *SetSysColors* are used to get and set colors for various system elements, such as buttons, title bars, and so on. These items can also be set by the user through the Display applet in the Control Panel.

The declaration of *GetSysColor* is simple:

```
DWORD GetSysColor(
    int nIndex    // display element
);
```

where *nIndex* can be set to one of many symbolic constants, for example:

```
#define COLOR_ACTIVECAPTION  2
```

In VB this becomes:

```
Declare Function GetSysColor Lib "user32" (ByVal nIndex As Long) As Long

Public Const COLOR_ACTIVECAPTION = 2
```

The return value is the RGB color. In particular, each color gets a byte in the returned unsigned long: red is the least significant byte, green is next, followed by blue. The high-order byte is 0. (These color bytes appear in reverse order in the long because when it is stored in memory, the bytes are reversed.)

The *SetSysColors* function is:

```
BOOL WINAPI SetSysColors(
    int cElements,                // number of elements to change
    CONST INT *lpaElements,       // address of array of elements
    CONST COLORREF *lpaRgbValues  // address of array of RGB values
);
```

Here, *cElements* specifies the number of system elements whose color we want to change, *lpaElements* is a pointer to a VC++ integer array that contains the indices of elements to change, and *lpaRgbValues* points to a VC++ integer array of new RGB color values.

The VB version is:

```
Declare Function SetSysColors Lib "user32" ( _
    ByVal nChanges As Long, _
    lpSysColor As Long, _
    lpColorValues As Long _
) As Long
```

where we must call the function by specifying the first array element for each array parameter.

Note finally that both functions return 0 on success and set *GetLastError*.

The following example will flash the active title bar between its default color and red every 0.5 seconds, finally leaving the title bar in its original state:

```
Public Function FlashTitleBarColor()

Dim i As Integer
Dim lret As Long
Dim SaveColor As Long
Dim lIndices(0 To 0) As Long
Dim lNewColors(0 To 0) As Long

' Get and save current color
SaveColor = GetSysColor(COLOR_ACTIVECAPTION)
Debug.Print "Current color:" & Hex(SaveColor)

For i = 1 To 5

    ' Change to red
    lIndices(0) = COLOR_ACTIVECAPTION
    lNewColors(0) = &HFF
    lret = SetSysColors(1&, lIndices(0), lNewColors(0))
    If lret = 0 Then
        RaiseApiError Err.LastDllError
    End If

    Delay 0.5

    ' Restore original color
    lIndices(0) = COLOR_ACTIVECAPTION
    lNewColors(0) = SaveColor
    lret = SetSysColors(1&, lIndices(0), lNewColors(0))
    If lret = 0 Then
        RaiseApiError Err.LastDllError
    End If

    Delay 0.5

Next

End Function
```

The *Delay* utility is just:

```
Sub Delay(rTime As Single)

'Delay rTime seconds (min=.01, max=300)

Dim OldTime As Variant

'Safty net
If rTime < 0.01 Or rTime > 300 Then rTime = 1

OldTime = Timer
Do
    DoEvents
Loop Until Timer - OldTime >= rTime

End Sub
```

8

Exception Handling

As you proceed through this book, running the sample code and experimenting on your own, you will probably encounter a great many General Protection Faults (GPFs). That is only natural. You've probably decided that there's not much that you can do about the rather unhelpful error display that accompanies each GPF when your code calls the Win32 API. That, however, is not the case. In this chapter, we'll look at how Windows handles system and application errors that occur in Win32 API calls and how you can override its default error handling (or lack thereof) in your Visual Basic code.

Thwarting the General Protection Fault

Before we discuss how to work around GPFs, first consider the following code:

```
Dim lpDest As Long
Dim lng As Long

lng = 5

CopyMemory ByVal lpDest, ByVal VarPtr(lng), 1
```

This code will produce a GPF because I forgot to set the value of the destination address *lpDest*, so it is simply initialized to 0. But writing to memory location 0 causes a GPF, with the accompanying message shown in Figure 8-1.

Of course, once the OK button is selected, Windows will terminate the application abruptly. There is no opportunity to recover from such an error, as we can when writing pure VB code. Or is there?

Here is what is happening. When an exception (another word for error) occurs in a process, Windows looks for an *exception handler* to handle the exception. When Windows creates a process, it installs a default exception handler for the process,

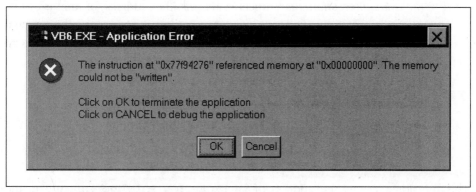

Figure 8-1. Trying to write to memory location 0

called *UnhandledExceptionFilter*. This function is called if the programmer has not installed a replacement exception handler (stay tuned).

UnhandledExceptionFilter first checks to see if the process being debugged is attached to a debugger. If not, as is the case for the VB programmer, the function will display a nasty error message such as the one in Figure 8-1. Subsequently, if the user selects the Cancel button, Windows will start a debugger for the thread. (By default, this is Visual C++ if it is installed on the user's system.) On the other hand, if the user selects the OK button, the *UnhandledExceptionFilter* function simply calls *ExitProcess* to terminate the process in which the thread is running.

Replacing the Default Exception Handler

Now to the point. There is a Win32 API function called *SetUnhandledException-Filter*. To quote the documentation:

> The *SetUnhandledExceptionFilter* function lets an application supersede the top-level exception handler that Win32 places at the top of each thread and process.

The VB syntax for the *SetUnhandledExceptionFilter* function is:

```
Declare Function SetUnhandledExceptionFilter Lib "kernel32" ( _
    ByVal lpTopLevelExceptionFilter As Long _
) As Long
```

where the parameter *lpTopLevelExceptionFilter* is the address of the replacement exception handler.

Thus, we need only to make the call:

```
SetUnhandledExceptionFilter AddressOf NewExceptionHandler
```

where *NewExceptionHandler* is a replacement exception handler in a VB standard code module.

The *SetUnhandledExceptionFilter* function returns the address of the previous exception handler, but we will not need this address. To restore the original default handler, we just call the function with the *lpTopLevelExceptionFilter* parameter set to 0.

The Replacement Exception Handler

The replacement exception handler should have the signature:

```
Function NewExceptionHandler(ByRef lpExceptionPointers As _
                       EXCEPTION_POINTERS) As Long
```

This function receives the address of an **EXCEPTION_POINTERS** structure in the parameter *lpExceptionPointers*. This structure allows the replacement exception handler to get information about the exception. In particular, the structure is defined as follows:

```
Type EXCEPTION_POINTERS
    pExceptionRecord As Long      'pointer to an EXCEPTION_RECORD struct
    pContextRecord As Long        ' pointer to a CONTEXT struct
End Type
```

The second member of this structure is a pointer to a **CONTEXT** structure that contains information about the state of the machine at the time the exception handler is called (that is, at the time of the exception). This structure reports such things as the state of the CPU registers. However, we will not go into this further, since it is not relevant to our discussion.

On the other hand, the first member points to a structure defined as follows:

```
Type EXCEPTION_RECORD
    ExceptionCode As Long
    ExceptionFlags As Long
    pExceptionRecord As Long   ' Pointer to an EXCEPTION_RECORD struct
    ExceptionAddress As Long
    NumberParameters As Long
    ExceptionInformation(EXCEPTION_MAXIMUM_PARAMETERS) As Long
End Type
```

Let us briefly describe the members of this structure.

ExceptionCode

Gives the code number for the exception. The possible values are shown in Table 8-1.

Table 8-1. Exception Codes

Exception Codes	Value
EXCEPTION_ACCESS_VIOLATION	&HC0000005&
EXCEPTION_ARRAY_BOUNDS_EXCEEDED	&HC000008C&
EXCEPTION_BREAKPOINT	&H80000003&

Table 8-1. Exception Codes (continued)

Exception Codes	Value
EXCEPTION_DATATYPE_MISALIGNMENT	&H80000002&
EXCEPTION_FLT_DENORMAL_OPERAND	&HC000008D&
EXCEPTION_FLT_DIVIDE_BY_ZERO	&HC000008E&
EXCEPTION_FLT_INEXACT_RESULT	&HC000008F&
EXCEPTION_FLT_INVALID_OPERATION	&HC0000090&
EXCEPTION_FLT_OVERFLOW	&HC0000091&
EXCEPTION_FLT_STACK_CHECK	&HC0000092&
EXCEPTION_FLT_UNDERFLOW	&HC0000093&
EXCEPTION_GUARD_PAGE	&H80000001&
EXCEPTION_ILLEGAL_INSTRUCTION	&HC000001D&
EXCEPTION_IN_PAGE_ERROR	&HC0000006&
EXCEPTION_INT_DIVIDE_BY_ZERO	&HC0000094&
EXCEPTION_INT_OVERFLOW	&HC0000095&
EXCEPTION_INVALID_DISPOSITION	&HC0000026&
EXCEPTION_INVALID_HANDLE	&HC0000008&
EXCEPTION_NONCONTINUABLE_EXCEPTION	&HC0000025&
EXCEPTION_PRIV_INSTRUCTION	&HC0000096&
EXCEPTION_SINGLE_STEP	&H80000004&
EXCEPTION_STACK_OVERFLOW	&HC00000FD&

ExceptionFlags

A value of 0 indicates a continuable exception. A value of EXCEPTION_ NONCONTINUABLE_EXCEPTION (&HC0000025&) indicates a noncontinuable exception. Any attempt to continue execution after a noncontinuable exception will generate an exception with exception code EXCEPTION_ NONCONTINUABLE_EXCEPTION.

pExceptionRecord

According to the documentation, exceptions may be nested (although the documentation does not say how this can happen). If the *pExceptionRecord* member is nonzero, then it points to an EXCEPTION_RECORD structure that contains information about a nested exception.

ExceptionAddress

This contains the address of the instruction that caused the exception.

NumberParameters

This value is the number of valid entries in the *ExceptionInformation* array (coming next).

ExceptionInformation

> This is used in only one case. When the exception is an access violation (exception code EXCEPTION_ACCESS_VIOLATION), *NumberParameters* is set to 2, and *ExceptionInformation(0)* contains a 0 if there was an illegal read attempt and 1 if there was an illegal write attempt. In either case, *Exception-Information(1)* is the memory address at which the read/write attempt was made.

The documentation states that the replacement exception handler *NewException-Handler* must return one of the following values, which determines the next course of events:

EXCEPTION_EXECUTE_HANDLER

> Causes process termination.

EXCEPTION_CONTINUE_EXECUTION

> Continues execution at the point of the exception. For us, this will simply mean repeating the exception.

EXCEPTION_CONTINUE_SEARCH

> Calls Windows default exception handler.

However, the documentation is addressed to VC++ programmers. We VB programmers have another trick up our sleeves.

To understand this trick, let us recall how VB handles errors within its own code. If an error occurs, VB will check the procedure causing the error for an error handler (On Error …). If none is found, then VB will climb the call stack looking for an active error handler. If none is found, then VB issues its own unpleasant error message and terminates the program.

However, in looking through the call stack, VB will skip over any external procedures—that is, any nonVB code. Figure 8-2 shows the call stack when a breakpoint is reached in a replacement exception handler *NewExceptionHandler*.

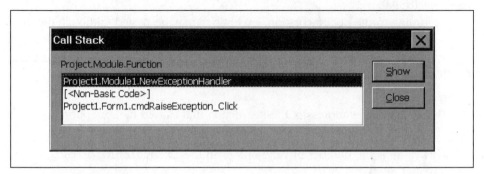

Figure 8-2. The call stack

The first procedure is the Click event shown in Example 8-1, which caused the exception in the *kernel32.dll* library that exports the *CopyMemory* function. Thus, the reference to [<Non-Basic Code>] in Figure 8-2 refers to the external *CopyMemory* function.

Example 8-1. A Click Event That Causes an Exception

```
Private Sub cmdRaiseException_Click()

Dim lpDest As Long
Dim lng As Long

On Error GoTo ERR_RaiseException

lng = 5

CopyMemory ByVal lpDest, ByVal VarPtr(lng), 1

MsgBox "Recovered from GPF"

Exit Sub
ERR_RaiseException:
    MsgBox Err.Description
    Resume Next
End Sub
```

Now, in our replacement exception handler *NewExceptionHandler*, we do three things:

- We collect information about the exception in a string variable, say **sError**.

- We deliberately avoid enabling a VB error handler in *NewExceptionHandler*. In other words, we do *not* use **On Error** in this procedure.

- We deliberately place code in *NewExceptionHandler* to raise a VB error, using the **sError** value as the description of the error, as in:

    ```
    Err.Raise 1000, "NewExceptionHandler", sError
    ```

Now, simply put, if an exception occurs, the call to **Err.Raise** will cause VB to look for a VB error handler. Since none exists in the offending *NewException-Handler* procedure, VB will search the call stack, *skipping over* the external code that caused the exception. Hence, in the case shown in Figure 8-2, the error handler in the cmdRaiseException_Click event will fire, thus displaying the description of the exception in a VB message box, as shown in Figure 8-3.

We now have complete control over what happens next. For instance, in the error-handling code in cmdRaiseException_Click, we call **Resume Next** to continue execution, but of course there are other possibilities. The point is that the VB application will *not* terminate abruptly.

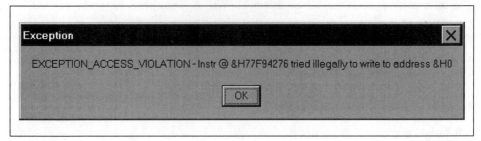

Figure 8-3. A VB message box describing the GPF

Before turning to a complete example, we should mention that this approach to exception handling can be very helpful. However, for the sake of space and clarity of purpose, we will not employ it in the examples in this book.

A Complete Example

Example 8-2 shows the code for the *NewExceptionHandler* replacement exception handler. A complete application is on the accompanying CD.

Example 8-2. The NewExceptionHandler Replacement Exception Handler

```
Function NewExceptionHandler(ByRef lpExceptionPointers As EXCEPTION_POINTERS) As Long

' No need to return a value since Err.Raise will alter execution flow

Dim er As EXCEPTION_RECORD
Dim sError As String

' Make a copy of the exception record portion
' of the passed-in EXCEPTION_POINTERS structure
CopyMemory er, ByVal lpExceptionPointers.pExceptionRecord, Len(er)

' Set up error description string
Do
    sError = GetException(er.ExceptionCode)
    ' Special treatment for access violation -- get addresses
    If sError = "EXCEPTION_ACCESS_VIOLATION" Then
        sError = sError & " - Instr @ &H" & Hex(er.ExceptionAddress) _
            & " tried illegally to " _
            & IIf(er.ExceptionInformation(0) = 0, _
                  "read from address", "write to address") _
            & " &H" & Hex(er.ExceptionInformation(1))
    End If

    ' Check for nested error
    If er.pExceptionRecord = 0 Then Exit Do

    ' Nested error exists
    ' Replace this er by the nested er
```

Example 8-2. The NewExceptionHandler Replacement Exception Handler (continued)

```
    CopyMemory er, ByVal er.pExceptionRecord, Len(er)

    ' New line for next error
    sError = sError & vbCrLf
Loop

' Raise an error to go up the call stack, passing the externally
' generated error!
Err.Raise 1000, "NewExceptionHandler", sError

End Function
```

II

The Windows Operating System

9

Windows Architecture

In this chapter, we give an overview of the architecture of the Windows NT operating system. We have chosen to discuss Windows NT because Microsoft has said that this is the future of Windows. The Windows 9x line will end with Windows 98, so all of us will be running a successor to Windows NT (the first of which is called Windows 2000) sooner or later. At the end of the chapter, we briefly discuss the differences between Windows 9x and Windows NT.

This chapter is meant only to give you a general feeling for the Windows architecture. We will try not to go into more detail than is necessary for this purpose.

Note that we will not discuss the 16-bit Windows operating system. This operating system is by all accounts obsolete, and it no longer seems necessary to compare the two operating systems (except perhaps in passing, in a few rare instances). Thus, the term *Windows* will always refer to one of the 32-bit Windows operating systems.

Processes and Threads

A Windows *application* is a collection of executable programs and support files. For instance, Microsoft Word is a well-known Windows application. A process is a running instance of a Windows application. Note that most applications allow the user to run multiple copies of the application at the same time. Each running instance is a separate process, with its own memory space.

To be more specific, a *process* is a running instance of an application, together with a set of resources that are allocated to the running application.

A *thread* is an object within a process that is allocated processor time by the operating system in order to execute code. In short, threads, not processes, execute program code. Every process must have at least one thread. The purpose of threads, of course, is to allow a process to maintain more than one line of execution, that is, to do more than one thing at a time. In a multiprocessor environment (a computer with more than one CPU), Windows NT (but not Windows 9x) can assign different threads to different processors, providing true multiprocessing. In a single-processor environment, the CPU must provide *time slices* to each thread that is currently running on the system. We will discuss time slices in detail in Chapter 12, *Threads*.

Windows Architecture

Figure 9-1 shows an overview of the Windows NT architecture. Let us review some of the items shown in this figure.

Kernel and User Mode

A Pentium microprocessor has four *privilege levels*, also known as *rings*, that control such things as memory access and access to certain sensitive CPU instructions (such as those related to security). Every thread executes at one of these privilege levels. Ring 0 is the most privileged level, with complete access to all memory and CPU instructions. Ring 3 is the least privileged level.

In order to maintain compatibility with non-Intel systems, the Windows operating systems support only two levels of privilege—Ring 0 and Ring 3. When a thread is running in Ring 0, it is said to be in *kernel mode*. When a thread is running in Ring 3, it is said to be in *user mode*. Low-level operating system code executes in kernel mode, whereas, in general, user application code runs in user mode.

Note that an application thread will switch from user mode to kernel mode when making certain API function calls that require a higher privilege level, such as those that involve accessing files or performing graphics-related functions. In fact, some user threads can spend more time in kernel mode than in user mode!

However, when the kernel mode code is completed, the user thread is automatically switched back to user mode. This prevents the programmer from being able to write instructions that run in kernel mode—the programmer can call only *system functions* that run in kernel mode.

If you are running Windows NT, you can see for yourself when a thread is running in user mode and when it is running in kernel mode. To do this, start the Performance Monitor from the Administrative Tools item on the Start Menu. Select Add To Chart from the Edit menu. Then add % User Time and % Privileged Time from the Counters list. Next, do some graphics-intensive things, such as opening

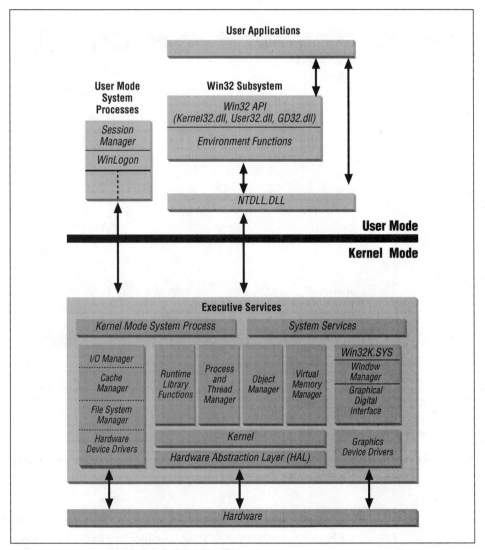

Figure 9-1. Simplified Windows NT architecture

Windows Paint. Figure 9-2 shows the results on my system at a particular moment. The white line is kernel mode percent time.

It is interesting to note that device drivers run in kernel mode. This has two implications. First, an errant device driver, unlike an errant application, can bring down the entire system because it has access to all system code and memory. Second, it is possible for an application programmer to "access" protected resources by writing a fake device driver, although writing device drivers is not an easy task.

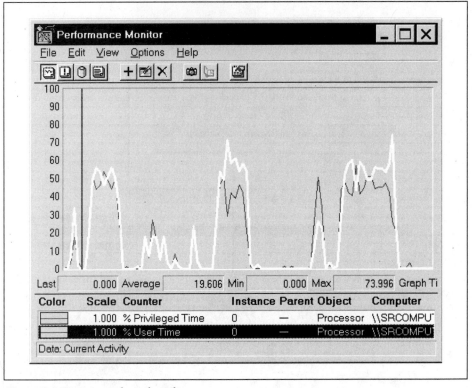

Figure 9-2. User versus kernel mode

Services

Unfortunately, the term *service* is used in a variety of ways in the Windows environment. Here are some of its meanings that are relevant to our discussion.

API service

An API function or subroutine that performs an operating system "service," such as creating a file or drawing some graphics (a line or circle). For example, the *CreateProcess* API function is used to create a new Windows process.

System service

An *undocumented* function that is callable from user mode. These are often called by Win32 API functions to provide low-level services. For instance, the *CreateProcess* API function calls the *NtCreateProcess* system service to actually create the process.

Internal service

A function or subroutine that is callable only from kernel mode. These reside in the lower-level portions of Windows: the Windows NT executive, kernel, or Hardware Abstraction Layer (HAL).

System Processes

System processes are special processes that support the operating system. Every Windows system has the following system processes (and more) running at all times. Note that all of these processes run in user mode except the system process.

- The *idle* process, which contains a single thread that monitors the CPU's idle time.

- The *system* process (unfortunate choice of name), which is a special process that runs only in kernel mode. Its threads are called *system threads*.

- The Session Manager (*SMSS.EXE*).

- The Win32 subsystem (*CSRSS.EXE*).

- The WinLogon process (*WINLOGON.EXE*).

You can verify that these system processes are indeed running by viewing the Processes tab of the Windows NT Task Manager. Also, Figure 9-3 shows the *rpiEnum-ProcsNT* application that we will create in Chapter 11, *Processes*. (We will also create a Windows 9x version.) You can see the idle, system, smss, csrss, and Win-Logon services in the Processes listbox.

Let us look briefly at some of these system processes:

The Session Manager process

The Session Manager (*SMSS.EXE*) is one of the first processes to be created when the operating system boots. It performs important initialization functions, such as creating system environment variables, defining MS-DOS devices names such as LPT1 and COM1, loading the kernel mode portion of the Win32 subsystem (discussed later in this section), and starting the logon process WinLogon.

The WinLogon process

This system service handles user logons and logoffs and processes the special Windows key combination Ctrl-Alt-Delete. WinLogon is responsible for starting the Windows shell (which is usually Windows Explorer).

The system process

This process contains *system threads*, which are kernel mode threads. Windows and various device drivers create system process threads for various reasons. For example, the memory manager creates system threads for performing virtual memory tasks, the cache manager uses system threads for managing cache memory, and the floppy disk driver uses a system thread to monitor the floppy drives.

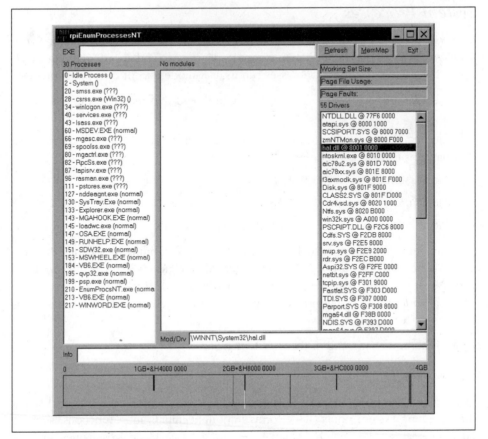

Figure 9-3. rpiEnumProcsNT

The Win32 Subsystem

The Win32 subsystem is the main subject of this book. It is one type of Windows *environment subsystem*. Other Windows environment subsystems (not pictured in Figure 9-1) include POSIX and OS/2. POSIX stands (more or less) for "portable operating system based on UNIX," which provides *limited* support for the UNIX operating system.

The purpose of an environment subsystem is to act as an interface between user applications and relevant portions of the Windows executive. Each subsystem exposes different functionality from the Windows executive. Every executable file is *bound* to one of the subsystems.

In fact, if you look at an executable file (*EXE*) with Windows' built-in QuickView viewer, you will find a line such as:

```
Subsystem:   Image runs in the Windows GUI subsystem.
```

This says that the executable is bound to the Windows GUI subsystem, which is another way of saying that it is bound to Win32. If you use QuickView on a command-based executable (such as *ftp.exe*, found in the Windows system directory), you will see the line:

```
Subsystem:   Image runs in the Windows character subsystem.
```

This is a console-based Win32 application.

As we have seen, the Win32 subsystem houses the Win32 API, in the form of DLLs, such as *KERNEL32.DLL*, *GDI32.DLL*, and *USER32.DLL*.

It is interesting to note that under Windows NT 4.0, Microsoft moved part of the Win32 subsystem from user mode to kernel mode. In particular, the kernel mode device driver *WIN32K.SYS* controls the display of windows (with a lowercase w), screen output, keyboard and mouse input, and message passing. It also contains the Graphical Device Interface library (*GDI.DLL*), used for drawing graphical images and text.

Calling a Win32 API function

When an application calls a Win32 API function in the Win32 subsystem, one of several things may happen:

- If the subsystem DLL (such as *USER32.DLL*) that exports the API function contains all code necessary to execute the function, it will do so and return the results.

- The API function may require that additional code within the Win32 subsystem (but outside of the DLL that exports the function) be called in support of the function.

- The function may need the services of an undocumented system service. For instance, to create a new process, the *CreateProcess* API function calls the undocumented system service *NtCreateProcess* to actually create the process. This is done through the *NTDLL.DLL* function library, which helps make the transition from user to kernel mode.

The Windows Executive

Windows executive services make up the low-level kernel mode portion of Windows NT and are contained in the file *NTOSKRNL.EXE*.

Executive services are sometimes divided into two groups: the *executive* (upper layer) and the *kernel* (lower layer). The kernel is the lowest layer of the operating system, performing the most fundamental services, such as:

- Thread scheduling
- Exception handling

- Interrupt handling
- Synchronization of processors in a multiprocessor system
- Creating kernel objects

Here are some of the major portions of the executive:

Process and Thread Manager
This component creates and terminates both processes and threads, using the services of the low-level kernel.

The Virtual Memory Manager
This component implements virtual memory, which we will discuss in some detail in Chapter 13, *Windows Memory Architecture.*

The Input/Output Manager
This component implements device-independent input/output and communicates with device drivers.

The Cache Manager
This component manages disk caching.

The Object Manager
This component creates and manages Windows executive *objects.* Windows uses objects to represent its various resources, such as processes and threads.

Runtime Libraries
These components contain runtime library functions, such as string manipulation functions and arithmetic functions.

The Hardware Abstraction Layer (HAL)

The hardware abstraction layer (or HAL) is a kernel mode library (*HAL.DLL*) that provides a low-level interface with the hardware. Windows components and third-party device drivers communicate with the hardware through the HAL. Accordingly, there are many versions of HAL to accommodate different hardware platforms. The appropriate HAL is chosen when Windows is installed.

Differences Between Windows 9x and Windows NT

Let us outline briefly some of the major differences between the Windows 9x and Windows NT operating systems.

- Windows NT supports *symmetric multiprocessing* (SMP), that is, Windows NT can use more than one processor at a time. The term *symmetric* refers to the fact that Windows NT treats each processor equally and assigns operating system threads (or user application code) to all processors at different times (as opposed to dedicating one processor for the operating system).

- Windows NT runs on platforms other than Intel-based systems. For instance, Windows NT will run on a PowerPC-based system.

- Windows NT is a true 32-bit operating system, whereas Windows 9x contains a considerable amount of 16-bit code that has been ported from Windows 3.1. As a result, under Windows 9x, portions of operating system memory are accessible from user mode, making Windows 9x far less stable than Windows NT.

- Windows NT implements significant file system security, which is missing from Windows 9x.

- Under both operating systems, applications may share memory. However, under Windows NT, only those applications that specifically request a shared memory resource can see this memory, whereas under Windows 9x, all shared memory is visible by all running programs.

10

Objects and Their Handles

Windows is full of objects. A *kernel object* is a data structure whose members are accessible only by the Windows kernel. Examples of kernel objects are:

Process object
: Represents a process

Thread object
: Represents a thread

File object
: Represents an open file

File-mapping object
: Represents a memory-mapped file, that is, a file whose contents are directly mapped to virtual memory addresses and used like physical memory

Pipe object
: Used to send data between processes

Event object
: A thread synchronization object used to signal when an operation has completed

Mutex object
: A thread synchronization object that can be used across multiple processes

Semaphore object
: Used for resource counting, to signal a thread when a resource is available

In addition to kernel objects, there are also user objects and GDI objects, such as menus, windows, fonts, brushes, and mouse cursors.

Handles

One of the characteristics of an object is that it has a *handle* that is used to identify it.

Although kernel objects are not directly accessible from user mode, the Windows API provides user-mode functions for manipulating these objects. This is a form of *encapsulation* that protects the objects from unwarranted tampering. When a kernel object is created through a call to the appropriate API function (such as *CreateProcess, CreateThread, CreateFile,* and *CreateFileMapping*), the function will return the newly created object's handle, which can then be passed to other API functions in order to manipulate the object.

Generally speaking, an object handle is *process-specific*, which means that it is only valid within a given process. On the other hand, some identifiers, such as process IDs, are *system-wide*, which means they are valid throughout all processes. We will have occasion to use both process handles and process IDs from time to time.

Usage Counts

Kernel objects are *owned* by the Windows kernel, not by the process that created the object (or any other process). As we will see, objects can be shared by multiple processes in a variety of ways. Each process that uses an object has its own process-specific handle to that object.

In view of this, the kernel must maintain a *usage count* for each object. When that count reaches 0, the kernel will destroy the object, but not before. In this way, the process that created an object can *close* its handle (by calling the *CloseHandle* API function), but the object will not be destroyed if some other process currently has a handle to the object.

We note also that kernel objects have security attributes that can be used to restrict access to the object. In fact, this is one of the main features that distinguishes kernel objects from user and GDI objects.

Object Sharing Across Process Boundaries

There are several ways in which an object can be shared among processes:

Inheritance

When a process (that is, a thread within the process) creates a kernel object, it can specify that the object's handle be *inheritable* to child processes that the parent process may subsequently create. In this case, the value of the child's handle is the same as the value of the parent's handle.

Handle duplication

The *DuplicateHandle* function is defined as:

```
BOOL DuplicateHandle(
    HANDLE hSourceProcessHandle,    // handle to the source process
    HANDLE hSourceHandle,           // handle to duplicate
    HANDLE hTargetProcessHandle,    // handle to process to duplicate to
    LPHANDLE lpTargetHandle,        // pointer to duplicate handle
    DWORD dwDesiredAccess,          // access for duplicate handle
    BOOL bInheritHandle,            // handle inheritance flag
    DWORD dwOptions                 // optional actions
);
```

This function allows a handle in one process to be duplicated into another process. The new process-relative handle in the target process may have a different value than the source handle, but this is of no concern since the handles are process-relative.

Named objects

Many kernel objects can be given a *name* when they are created. Names are valid system-wide, which means that any other process can access the object by using its name (assuming that it knows the name, of course). For instance, the last parameter in the *CreateFileMapping* function:

```
HANDLE CreateFileMapping(
    HANDLE hFile,                                   // handle to file to map
    LPSECURITY_ATTRIBUTES lpFileMappingAttributes,  // optional security attributes
    DWORD flProtect,                                // protection for mapping object
    DWORD dwMaximumSizeHigh,                        // high-order 32 bits of object size
    DWORD dwMaximumSizeLow,                         // low-order 32 bits of object size
    LPCTSTR lpName                                  // name of file-mapping object
);
```

can be used to specify a name for the file mapping.

Assume, for instance, that we have created a file-mapping object named MyFMO. Another process can call *OpenFileMapping* with this name as its last argument. The function will return a process-relative handle to this object for use by the second process. Alternatively, the second process can call *CreateFileMapping*, using the object's name as its last argument. The system will see that a file-mapping object by this name already exists and simply return a handle to this object. (This does create a potential problem, because a process may think it is creating a new object when, in fact, it is getting a handle to an existing object. The programmer must check the return value of *CreateFileMapping* immediately to determine which is the case.)

Example: File Mapping

Let us conclude this chapter with an example of creating, sharing, and destroying a kernel object. For this example, we will use the *file-mapping object*.

To put it simply, Windows is capable of treating a disk file as though it were part of memory. To do this, a portion of the file is mapped to a block of virtual memory addresses. Memory-related API functions such as *CopyMemory* can then be used to view and alter the disk file contents. When a file is mapped to memory in this way, the file is called a *memory-mapped file*.

Our application will do the following:

1. Create a *file object*, based on an existing file, using the *CreateFile* API function. This function will return a handle to the file object.

2. Use the file handle and the *CreateFileMapping* API function to create a *file-mapping object*. The function returns a file-mapping object handle.

3. Use the file-mapping object handle and the *MapViewOfFile* API function to map a portion of the file to memory. This function assigns a block of virtual memory addressed to the file. The base address of this block is the handle for the file-mapping view.

4. Use the base address and the *CopyMemory* function to read the file and then write to the file. The program just toggles the case of the text of the sample file *Mapped.txt*.

5. Finally, close all handles.

Since the code from this example will be used in two VB applications (to demonstrate object sharing) and since you might want to use it in your own applications, the best place for it is in a class module. In fact, it is not difficult to create a class named *CFileMapping* with all of the necessary properties and methods for creating file objects, file-mapping objects, and memory-mapped views. Example 10-1 shows the entire code for the *CFileMapping* class.

Example 10-1. The CFileMapping Class

```
Option Explicit

Private mFileMappingName As String
Private mFileViewBase As Long
Private mFileMappingHandle As Long
Private mFileHandle As Long
Private mFileName As String


' ------------
' File mapping
' ------------
' Create a handle to console output
Private Declare Function CreateFile Lib "kernel32" _
```

Example 10-1. The CFileMapping Class (continued)

```
    Alias "CreateFileA" ( _
    ByVal lpFileName As String, _
    ByVal dwDesiredAccess As Long, _
    ByVal dwShareMode As Long, _
    ByVal lpSecurityAttributes As Long, _
    ByVal dwCreationDisposition As Long, _
    ByVal dwFlagsAndAttributes As Long, _
    ByVal hTemplateFile As Long _
) As Long

Const GENERIC_READ = &H80000000
Const GENERIC_WRITE = &H40000000
Const FILE_SHARE_READ = &H1
Const FILE_SHARE_WRITE = &H2
Const OPEN_EXISTING = 3

Private Declare Function CreateFileMapping Lib "kernel32" _
    Alias "CreateFileMappingA" ( _
    ByVal hFile As Long, _
    ByVal lpSecurityAttributes As Long, _
    ByVal flProtect As Long, _
    ByVal dwMaximumSizeHigh As Long, _
    ByVal dwMaximumSizeLow As Long, _
    ByVal lpName As String _
) As Long

Const PAGE_NOACCESS = &H1
Const PAGE_READONLY = &H2
Const PAGE_READWRITE = &H4
Const PAGE_WRITECOPY = &H8
Const PAGE_EXECUTE = &H10
Const PAGE_EXECUTE_READ = &H20
Const PAGE_EXECUTE_READWRITE = &H40
Const PAGE_EXECUTE_WRITECOPY = &H80
Const PAGE_GUARD = &H100
Const PAGE_NOCACHE = &H200

Private Declare Function MapViewOfFile Lib "kernel32" ( _
    ByVal hFileMappingObject As Long, _
    ByVal dwDesiredAccess As Long, _
    ByVal dwFileOffsetHigh As Long, _
    ByVal dwFileOffsetLow As Long, _
    ByVal dwNumberOfBytesToMap As Long _
) As Long

Const SECTION_EXTEND_SIZE = &H10
Const SECTION_MAP_EXECUTE = &H8
Const SECTION_MAP_READ = &H4
Const SECTION_MAP_WRITE = &H2
Const SECTION_QUERY = &H1

Const FILE_MAP_COPY = SECTION_QUERY
Const FILE_MAP_READ = SECTION_MAP_READ
Const FILE_MAP_WRITE = SECTION_MAP_WRITE
```

Example 10-1. The CFileMapping Class (continued)

```
Private Declare Function CloseHandle Lib "kernel32" ( _
    ByVal hObject As Long) As Long
Private Declare Function UnMapViewOfFile Lib "kernel32" _
    Alias "UnmapViewOfFile" (ByVal lpBaseAddress As Long) As Long

Public Property Get FileMappingName() As String
    FileMappingName = mFileMappingName
End Property

Public Property Let FileMappingName(pFileMappingName As String)
    mFileMappingName = pFileMappingName
End Property

Public Property Get FileName() As String
    FileName = mFileName
End Property

Public Property Let FileName(pFileName As String)
    If Dir$(pFileName, vbNormal) <> "" Then
        mFileName = pFileName
    Else
        mFileName = ""
    End If
End Property

Public Property Get FileHandle() As Long
    FileHandle = mFileHandle
End Property

Public Property Let FileHandle(pFileHandle As Long)
    mFileHandle = pFileHandle
End Property

Public Property Get FileMappingHandle() As Long
    FileMappingHandle = mFileMappingHandle
End Property

Public Property Let FileMappingHandle(pFileMappingHandle As Long)
    mFileMappingHandle = pFileMappingHandle
End Property

Public Property Get FileViewBase() As Long
    FileViewBase = mFileViewBase
End Property

Public Property Let FileViewBase(pFileViewBase As Long)
    mFileViewBase = pFileViewBase
End Property

Public Function OpenFile() As Long
' Opens file and gets file handle

mFileHandle = CreateFile(mFileName, _
```

Example 10-1. The CFileMapping Class (continued)

```
    GENERIC_READ Or GENERIC_WRITE, _
    FILE_SHARE_READ Or FILE_SHARE_WRITE, _
    0&, _
    OPEN_EXISTING, 0&, 0&)

OpenFile = mFileHandle

End Function

Public Function OpenFileMapping() As Long

' Create file mapping
mFileMappingHandle = CreateFileMapping( _
    mFileHandle, 0&, PAGE_READWRITE, 0&, _
    FileLen(mFileName), mFileMappingName)
OpenFileMapping = mFileMappingHandle

End Function

Public Function MapFileView() As Long
mFileViewBase = MapViewOfFile( _
    mFileMappingHandle, FILE_MAP_WRITE, 0&, 0&, 0&)
MapFileView = mFileViewBase
End Function

Public Function ReadFromFile(cBytes As Long) As String
' Read from file mapping
ReDim bFile(1 To cBytes) As Byte
CopyMemory ByVal VarPtr(bFile(1)), ByVal mFileViewBase, cBytes
ReadFromFile = StrConv(bFile, vbUnicode)
End Function

Public Function WriteToFile(sWrite As String) As Long
' Return count of bytes written
Dim b() As Byte
Dim lpsz As Long
BSTRtoLPSTR sWrite, b, lpsz
CopyMemory ByVal mFileViewBase, ByVal lpsz, Len(sWrite)
WriteToFile = Len(sWrite)
End Function

Public Function UnMapFileView() As Long
UnMapFileView = UnMapViewOfFile(mFileViewBase)
End Function

Public Function CloseFileMapping() As Long
CloseFileMapping = CloseHandle(mFileMappingHandle)
End Function

Public Function CloseFile() As Long
CloseFile = CloseHandle(mFileHandle)
End Function
```

Note that several of the methods are just wrappers for the API function.

If you open the FileMapping project in the *Code_Mapping* subdirectory of the accompanying CD-ROM and press the command button, the following procedure will be executed. It assumes that the file *Mapped.txt* is in the application directory.

```
Sub DoFileMapping()

Dim sFileName As String
Dim s As String

' Create file
Dim oFile As New CFileMapping

' Set properties
oFile.FileName = App.Path & "\Mapped.txt"

If oFile.FileName = "" Then
    MsgBox App.Path & "\Mapped.txt does not exist", vbExclamation
    Exit Sub
End If

oFile.FileMappingName = "TestFileMapping"

List1.AddItem "Open file: " & oFile.OpenFile
List1.AddItem "Open file mapping: " & oFile.OpenFileMapping
List1.AddItem "Map file: " & oFile.MapFileView

' Read entire file
s = oFile.ReadFromFile(FileLen(oFile.FileName))
List1.AddItem "Read file: " & s

' Reverse case
If s = UCase$(s) Then
    s = LCase$(s)
Else
    s = UCase$(s)
End If

List1.AddItem "Write file: " & oFile.WriteToFile(s) & " bytes"
List1.AddItem "Read file: " & oFile.ReadFromFile(FileLen(oFile.FileName))

List1.AddItem "UnMap file: " & oFile.UnMapFileView
List1.AddItem "Close file mapping: " & oFile.CloseFileMapping
List1.AddItem "Close file: " & oFile.CloseFile
List1.AddItem "*****"
Set oFile = Nothing

End Sub
```

The output is shown in Figure 10-1.

To see how two applications can share the same object—in this case, a file object—just place the *CFileMapping* class into two VB projects. Add the *DoFileMapping* subroutine to the projects and run them both.

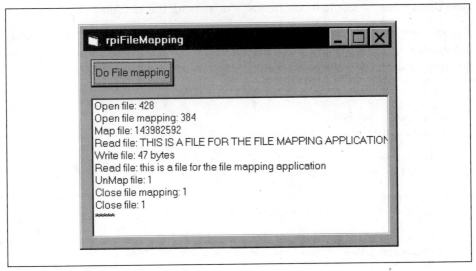

Figure 10-1. The file-mapping application

Coherence

Since we are on the subject of memory-mapped files, we should say a few more words about it. There is nothing to prevent the following from occurring to a single memory-mapped file:

- Have multiple active views based on a single file-mapping object

- Have several file-mapping objects based on the file, perhaps in different processes, each with its own views of the file

- Have one process map a view of the file for writing while another process uses traditional file I/O functions on the file

Needless to say, these possibilities raise questions of what happens when one view changes the data in the file. Here are the facts:

- If only a single file-mapping object is involved, even if that object is shared among different processes, the system will insure that all views based on that file-mapping object are *coherent*, that is, all views see the current state of the data, including any changes made through any of the views. This follows from the fact that all of these views see the same data, since it is stored in a single location in physical memory.

- However, views of the file that are based on *different* file-mapping objects are *not* guaranteed to be coherent.

- There is no guarantee that changes to a file made with traditional file I/O operations (*ReadFile* and *WriteFile*, for instance) will be reflected in file views.

After all, these methods use memory buffers that are different from the buffers used by a file mapping. For this reason, we should *not* mix file-mapping techniques and memory-mapped techniques in the same process.

11

Processes

As we have seen, a *process* is a running instance of an application, together with a set of resources that are allocated to the running application. These resources include:

- A virtual address space.

- System resources, such as bitmaps, files, memory allocations, and so on.

- Process modules, that is, executables that are mapped (loaded) into the process's address space. This includes such things as DLLs, DRVs, and OCXs, as well as the main EXE of the process, which is, unfortunately, sometimes referred to as *the module*. We will elaborate on the issue of modules later in this chapter. However, it is important to understand that the actual module data (and code) either resides on disk or is loaded into physical memory (RAM). However, the term *loaded* has a different meaning with respect to a process's virtual address space. The term *mapped* is more appropriate because this mapping is simply an assignment of virtual addresses to physical addresses. Once a module is loaded into physical memory, those physical addresses can be mapped into multiple virtual address spaces, perhaps using different virtual addresses in each process. The mapping does not necessarily require that any actual data (or code) be physically moved (although it might, as we will see).

- A unique identification number, called a *process ID*.

- One or more threads of execution.

A *thread* is an object within a process that is allocated processor time by the operating system. Every process must have at least one thread. More specifically, a thread includes:

- The current contents of the CPU registers

- Two stacks—one for the thread to use when running in kernel mode and one for the thread to use when running in user mode

- A private storage area for use by subsystems, runtime libraries, and DLLs

- A unique identifier called a *thread ID*

The register contents, stack contents, and storage area contents are referred to as the thread's *context*.

As mentioned, the purpose of threads is to allow a process to maintain more than one line of execution, that is, to do more than one thing at a time. In a multiprocessor environment (a computer with more than one CPU), Windows NT (but not Windows 9x) can assign different threads to different processors at different times, providing true multiprocessing. In a single-processor environment, the CPU must provide *time slices* to each thread that is currently running on the system.

We will devote this chapter to a discussion of processes, leaving threads for the next chapter.

Process Handles and IDs

The distinction between process IDs and handles can be gleaned by looking at the *CreateProcess* API function. One possible VB declaration of this rather complex function is:

```
Declare Function CreateProcess Lib "kernel32" Alias "CreateProcessA" ( _
    ByVal lpApplicationName As String, _
    ByVal lpCommandLine As String, _
    lpProcessAttributes As SECURITY_ATTRIBUTES, _
    lpThreadAttributes As SECURITY_ATTRIBUTES, _
    ByVal bInheritHandles As Long, _
    ByVal dwCreationFlags As Long, _
    lpEnvironment As Any, _
    ByVal lpCurrentDirectory As String, _
    lpStartupInfo As STARTUPINFO, _
    lpProcessInformation As PROCESS_INFORMATION _
) As Long
```

Now, the last parameter is a pointer to a **PROCESS_INFORMATION** structure:

```
typedef struct _PROCESS_INFORMATION {
    HANDLE hProcess;
    HANDLE hThread;
    DWORD dwProcessId;
    DWORD dwThreadId;
} PROCESS_INFORMATION;
```

where, to quote the documentation, the members are as follows.

hProcess

> Returns a handle to the newly created process. The handle is used to specify the process in all functions that perform operations on the process object.

hThread

> Returns a handle to the primary thread of the newly created process. The handle is used to specify the thread in all functions that perform operations on the thread object.

dwProcessId

> Returns a global process identifier that can be used to identify a process. The value is valid from the time the process is created until the time the process is terminated.

dwThreadId

> Returns a global thread identifier that can be used to identify a thread. The value is valid from the time the thread is created until the time the thread is terminated.

Thus, the main differences between a process handle and a process ID (or thread handle and thread ID) are:

- A process handle is *process-specific*, whereas a process ID is valid system-wide. Thus, a process handle, whether it be for the current process or a foreign process, is valid *only* in the process in which it was created.

- Each process has one and only one process ID, but a process may have several process handles, even from within a single process.

- Some API functions require the process ID; others require a process handle.

We should emphasize that although a process handle is process-specific, one process can get a handle to another process. More specifically, if Process A has a handle to Process B, then that handle identifies Process B, but it is valid only in Process A. The handle can be used in Process A to call *some* API functions that relate to Process B. (Don't get too excited about this—Process B's memory is still inaccessible to Process A.)

Module Handles

Every module (DLL, OCX, DRV, etc.) that is loaded into a process space has a *module handle*, also called an *instance handle*. (In 16-bit Windows, these were different objects; in 32-bit Windows, they are the same.)

An executable's module handle is simply the starting or base address of the executable in the process's address space. This makes it rather clear that such a handle has meaning only within the process containing the module.

The default base address of an EXE created using Visual C++ is &H400000. Note, however, that the VC++ programmer can change this default address, and there are important reasons to do so in order to avoid conflict with other modules. (As we will see, relocation of a module due to a base address conflict is costly in terms of both time and *physical* memory.) In addition, modules created by other programming environments may have different default base addresses.

Module handles are often used for calling API functions that allocate resources to the process. For instance, the *LoadBitmap* function loads a bitmap resource from the process's EXE file. Its declaration is:

```
HBITMAP LoadBitmap(
    HINSTANCE hInstance,      // handle to application instance
    LPCTSTR lpBitmapName      // address of bitmap resource name
);
```

The first parameter is the process's instance handle.

Unfortunately, the module handle for a process's EXE is often confusingly referred to as the module handle for the process. Also, the name of the EXE is sometimes referred to as the process's *module name.*

Identifying a Process

The following four items occur frequently in process-related API programming:

- process ID
- process handle
- fully qualified filename of EXE
- module handle of process EXE

The question is: "Given one of these items, can we get the others?" Figure 11-1 illustrates the rather complex answer to this question. The arrows indicate the possibilities.

Getting a Process Handle from the Process ID

It is relatively easy to get a process handle from the process ID, but doing the reverse does not seem possible (at least in any direct way).

We can get a handle to any process from its process ID using the *OpenProcess* function:

```
HANDLE OpenProcess(
    DWORD dwDesiredAccess,    // access flag
    BOOL bInheritHandle,      // handle inheritance flag
    DWORD dwProcessId         // process identifier
);
```

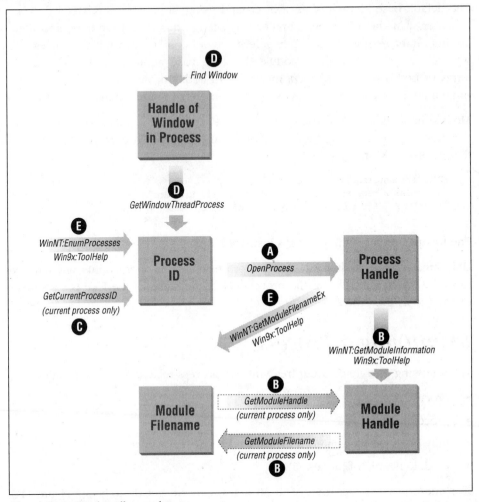

Figure 11-1. IDs, handles, and so on

The *dwDesiredAccess* parameter refers to security rights and can be set to various values, such as:

PROCESS_ALL_ACCESS
Equivalent to specifying all access flags

PROCESS_DUP_HANDLE
Can use the process handle as either the source or target process in the *DuplicateHandle* function (discussed later) to duplicate a handle

PROCESS_QUERY_INFORMATION
Can use the process handle to read information from the process object

PROCESS_VM_OPERATION
Can use the process handle to modify the virtual memory of the process

PROCESS_TERMINATE

Can use the process handle in the *TerminateProcess* function to terminate the process

PROCESS_VM_READ

Can use the process handle in the *ReadProcessMemory* function to read from the virtual memory of the process

PROCESS_VM_WRITE

Can use the process handle in the *WriteProcessMemory* function to write to the virtual memory of the process

SYNCHRONIZE *(Windows NT)*

Can use the process handle in any of the wait functions (such as *WaitForSingleObject*, discussed in Chapter 12, *Threads*) to wait for the process to terminate.

The *bInheritHandle* parameter is set to **True** to allow child processes to inherit the current handle when the current process creates a child process. (The handle value may change, but the point is that the child gets a handle to its parent. We won't be concerned with process inheritance.)

The *dwProcessID* parameter should be set to the process ID of the process whose handle we desire. The *OpenProcess* function returns a handle to the process.

The VB declaration of *OpenProcess* is:

```
Declare Function OpenProcess Lib "kernel32" ( _
    ByVal dwDesiredAccess As Long, _
    ByVal bInheritHandle As Long, _
    ByVal dwProcessId As Long _
) As Long
```

Since getting a process handle from the process ID will come up from time to time, let us create a small function for this purpose. Note that access to the process is for getting information only. The function is:

```
Public Function ProcHndFromProcID(ByVal lProcID As Long) As Long
' DON'T FORGET TO CLOSE HANDLE
ProcHndFromProcID = OpenProcess( _
    PROCESS_QUERY_INFORMATION Or PROCESS_VM_READ, 0&, lProcID)
End Function
```

For Windows NT, we should add an additional flag for use with thread synchronization (discussed in Chapter 12):

```
Public Function ProcHndFromProcIDSync(ByVal lProcID As Long) As Long
' DON'T FORGET TO CLOSE HANDLE
ProcHndFromProcIDSync = OpenProcess( _
    PROCESS_QUERY_INFORMATION Or PROCESS_VM_READ Or SYNCHRONIZE, 0&, lProcID)
End Function
```

It is very important to remember that the returned handle must be closed after it is no longer needed. This is done by calling the *CloseHandle* function:

```
BOOL CloseHandle(
    HANDLE hObject // handle to object to close
);
```

or, in VB:

```
Private Declare Function CloseHandle Lib "kernel32" ( _
    ByVal hObject As Long _
) As Long
```

We will see examples of using *OpenProcess* a bit later in this chapter.

Module Filenames and Module Handles

It is not difficult to go from a module filename to a module handle and vice versa, at least from within the process itself. The *GetModuleFileName* function

```
DWORD GetModuleFileName(
    HMODULE hModule,     // handle to module
    LPTSTR lpFilename,   // pointer to buffer to receive module path
    DWORD nSize          // size of buffer, in characters
);
```

uses the module's handle to retrieve the fully qualified filename (name and path) of the executable file. Note, however, that this function works from within the process in question—we cannot use this function from another process.

Conversely, from within a process, the *GetModuleHandle* function returns the module's handle from its filename (no path here):

```
HMODULE GetModuleHandle(
    LPCTSTR lpModuleName     // module name
);
```

Again, this does not work for retrieving module handles in foreign processes.

These two function declarations can be translated into VB as follows:

```
Declare Function GetModuleFileName Lib "kernel32" _
    Alias "GetModuleFileNameA" ( _
    ByVal hModule As Long, _
    ByVal lpFileName As String, _
    ByVal nSize As Long _
) As Long

Declare Function GetModuleHandle Lib "kernel32" _
    Alias "GetModuleHandleA" ( _
    ByVal lpModuleName As String _
) As Long
```

Given either the module's handle, name, or fully qualified name, the function in Example 11-1 will retrieve the other two items in its OUT parameters.

Example 11-1. Getting a Module's Handle, Name, or Fully Qualified Name

```
Public Function Proc_ModuleInfo(ByRef lHnd As Long, _
    ByRef sName As String, _
    ByRef sFQName As String) As Long

' Algorithm:
' If lHnd = -1 then get EXE handle, name and FQ name
' ElseIf lHnd > 0 then get module name and fully qualified name
' ElseIf sName <> "" then get handle and FQ name
' ElseIf sFQName <> "" then get handle and name

'' Required: Public Const MAX_PATH = 260

Dim lret As Long, x As Integer
Dim hModule As Long, s As String

Proc_ModuleInfo = 0

If lHnd = -1 Or lHnd > 0 Then
    hModule = lHnd            ' Get handle
    If lHnd = -1 Then         ' Get EXE handle
        hModule = GetModuleHandle(vbNullString)
        If hModule = 0 Then
            Proc_ModuleInfo = 1
            Exit Function
        End If
    End If
    ' Get names from handle
    s = String(MAX_PATH + 1, 0)
    lret = GetModuleFileName(hModule, s, MAX_PATH)
    sFQName = Left(s, lret)
    x = InStrRev(sFQName, "\")
    If x > 0 Then sName = Mid$(sFQName, x + 1)

ElseIf sName <> "" Then

    ' Get handle and FQ name from name
    hModule = GetModuleHandle(sName)
    If hModule = 0 Then
        Proc_ModuleInfo = 2
        Exit Function
    Else
        lHnd = hModule
        s = String(MAX_PATH + 1, 0)
        lret = GetModuleFileName(hModule, s, MAX_PATH)
        sFQName = Left(s, lret)
    End If

ElseIf sFQName <> "" Then

    ' Get handle and name from FQ name
    hModule = GetModuleHandle(sFQName)
    If hModule = 0 Then
```

Example 11-1. Getting a Module's Handle, Name, or Fully Qualified Name (continued)

```
        Proc_ModuleInfo = 3
        Exit Function
    Else
        lHnd = hModule
        x = InStrRev(sFQName, "\")
        If x > 0 Then sName = Mid$(sFQName, x + 1)
    End If
End If

End Function
```

Example 11-2 shows some code that exercises this function. The output on my system is shown in Example 11-3.

Example 11-2. Calling the Proc_ModuleInfo Function

```
Public Sub Proc_ModuleInfoExample

Dim sModName As String, sFQModName As String, hMod As Long
Dim lret As Long

hMod = -1: sModName = "": sFQModName = ""
lret = Proc_ModuleInfo(hMod, sModName, sFQModName)

Debug.Print "Handle: &H" & Hex(hMod)
Debug.Print "Name: " & sModName
Debug.Print "FQName: " & sFQModName
Debug.Print

hMod = 0: sModName = "User32.dll": sFQModName = ""
lret = Proc_ModuleInfo(hMod, sModName, sFQModName)

Debug.Print "Handle: &H" & Hex(hMod)
Debug.Print "Name: " & sModName
Debug.Print "FQName: " & sFQModName
Debug.Print

hMod = 0: sModName = "": sFQModName = "C:\WINNT\system32\USER32.dll"
lret = Proc_ModuleInfo(hMod, sModName, sFQModName)

Debug.Print "Handle: &H" & Hex(hMod)
Debug.Print "Name: " & sModName
Debug.Print "FQName: " & sFQModName
Debug.Print

hMod = 2011627520: sModName = "": sFQModName = ""
lret = Proc_ModuleInfo(hMod, sModName, sFQModName)

Debug.Print "Handle: &H" & Hex(hMod)
Debug.Print "Name: " & sModName
Debug.Print "FQName: " & sFQModName
Debug.Print

End Sub
```

Example 11-3. Output from Example 11-2

```
Handle: &HFFFFFFFF
Name: VB6.EXE
FQName: G:\Visual Studio\VB98\VB6.EXE

Handle: &H77E70000
Name: User32.dll
FQName: C:\WINNT\system32\USER32.dll

Handle: &H77E70000
Name: USER32.dll
FQName: C:\WINNT\system32\USER32.dll

Handle: &H77E70000
Name: USER32.dll
FQName: C:\WINNT\system32\USER32.dll
```

Getting the Current Process ID

To get the process ID of the *current* process, we just use *GetCurrentProcessId*, which is declared as:

```
DWORD GetCurrentProcessId(VOID)
```

or, in VB:

```
Declare Function GetCurrentProcessId Lib "kernel32" () As Long
```

This simply returns the process ID. Note that process IDs can be in the upper range of an unsigned long, so a conversion of the return type may be necessary. Note also that this works only for the current process. There is no way (of which I am aware) to get the process ID of a *foreign* process, other than possibly listing all processes and picking the one you want using some other criteria.

Getting the Process ID from a Window

In Chapter 6, *Strings*, we discussed the *FindWindow* function:

```
HWND FindWindow(
  LPCTSTR lpClassName,  // pointer to class name
  LPCTSTR lpWindowName  // pointer to window name
);
```

or, in VB:

```
Declare Function FindWindow Lib "user32" Alias "FindWindowA" ( _
    ByVal lpClassName As String, _
    ByVal lpWindowName As String _
  ) As Long
```

This function uses either the class name or the window's caption to retrieve a handle to the window. From this handle, we can call *GetWindowThreadProcessId*, which retrieves the thread ID of the thread that created the window, as well as the process ID of the process that owns that thread. The syntax is:

```
DWORD GetWindowThreadProcessId(
    HWND hWnd,                 // handle to window
    LPDWORD lpdwProcessId  // address of variable for process identifier
);
```

This function returns the thread ID. Moreover, when the function is passed a pointer to a DWORD in *lpdwProcessId* (as opposed to being passed 0), the function will return the process ID in the target variable.

We can translate this into VB as follows:

```
Declare Function GetWindowThreadProcessId Lib "user32" ( _
    ByVal hwnd As Long, _
    lpdwProcessId As Long _
) As Long
```

Here is a short function that returns the process ID from a window handle:

```
Public Function ProcIDFromhWnd(ByVal hWnd As Long) As Long

Dim lret As Long, hProcessID As Long
lret = GetWindowThreadProcessId(hWnd, hProcessID)
ProcIDFromhWnd = hProcessID

End Function
```

We will discuss window handles in more detail in Chapter 15, *Windows: The Basics*.

Getting Module Names and Handles

A single process generally has many modules loaded in its address space, and this naturally complicates the issue of getting the module handles and names. While it is not difficult to do so, we must unfortunately use entirely different methods in Windows 9x and Windows NT.

Windows NT 4.0 requires the use of a DLL called *PSAPI.DLL* (which stands for Process Status API). This DLL, which is not compatible with Windows 9x, exports functions to enumerate all of the processes in the system, as well as all of the device drivers. It can also get information about all of the modules running in a given process. There will be an example that makes use of this DLL later in this chapter. To enumerate the threads in a Windows NT system, we need to use the Performance Data Helper library (*PDH.DLL*) that comes with the NT Resource Toolkit. However, since we don't have any real need for enumerating threads, we will not do so.

On the other hand, Windows 9x supports the Toolhelp functions in the Windows 9x version of *KERNEL32.DLL*. These functions can be used to take a snapshot of the process space for any process. From this snapshot, we can get all sorts of information, including the current processes as well as the modules and threads for each process. (However, unlike *PSAPI.DLL*, it does not give device driver information.)

This unfortunate situation requires us to write different code for Windows NT and for Windows 9x. Fortunately, Windows 2000 will support Toolhelp. (I only hope it will also continue to support the perfectly good *PSAPI.DLL,* so I don't need to rewrite my code!)

Before looking at an example, however, let us complete the process handle story.

Process Pseudohandles

There is yet another wrinkle in the saga of process handles and process IDs. The function *GetCurrentProcess:*

```
HANDLE GetCurrentProcess(VOID)
```

returns a pseudohandle to the current process. A *pseudohandle* is a kind of lightweight handle. In particular, a pseudohandle is a process-specific number that identifies the process and can be used in calls to API functions that require a process handle.

While pseudohandles sound like ordinary handles, there are some key differences. Pseudohandles cannot be inherited by child processes, as can real handles. Also, a pseudohandle can refer only to the current process, whereas a real handle can refer to a foreign process.

Windows does provide a way to get a real handle from a pseudohandle, by using the *DuplicateHandle* API function, which we discussed in Chapter 10, *Objects and Their Handles.* This function is defined as:

```
BOOL DuplicateHandle(
    HANDLE hSourceProcessHandle,  // handle to the source process
    HANDLE hSourceHandle,         // handle to duplicate
    HANDLE hTargetProcessHandle,  // handle to process to duplicate to
    LPHANDLE lpTargetHandle,      // pointer to duplicate handle
    DWORD dwDesiredAccess,        // access for duplicate handle
    BOOL bInheritHandle,          // handle inheritance flag
    DWORD dwOptions               // optional actions
);
```

Here is some illustrative code, showing how to get process handles and pseudohandles:

```
Public Const PROCESS_VM_READ = &H10
Public Const PROCESS_QUERY_INFORMATION = &H400
Public Const DUPLICATE_SAME_ACCESS = &H2
```

```
Public Sub DuplicateHandleExample()

Dim lret As Long
Dim hPseudoHandle As Long
Dim hProcessID As Long
Dim hProcess As Long
Dim hDupHandle As Long

' Process ID
hProcessID = GetCurrentProcessId
Debug.Print "Current process ID: " & hProcessID

' Pseudohandle
hPseudoHandle = GetCurrentProcess
Debug.Print "Pseudohandle: " & hPseudoHandle

' Duplicate handle
lret = DuplicateHandle(hPseudoHandle, _
   hPseudoHandle, _
   hPseudoHandle, _
   hDupHandle, _
   0&, 0&, DUPLICATE_SAME_ACCESS)

Debug.Print "DuplicateHandle handle: " & hDupHandle

' Handle from OpenProcess
hProcess = OpenProcess( _
   PROCESS_QUERY_INFORMATION Or PROCESS_VM_READ, _
   0&, _
   hProcessID)

Debug.Print "OpenProcess Handle: " & hProcess

' Close real handles
Debug.Print
lret = CloseHandle(hProcess)
Debug.Print "Closing OpenProcess handle: " & hProcess

lret = CloseHandle(hDupHandle)
Debug.Print "Closing DuplicateHandle handle: " & hDupHandle

End Sub
```

This code duplicates the source pseudohandle into the variable *hDupHandle*. It also gets a real (but different) handle using *OpenProcess*. Note that the real handles must be closed. However, pseudohandles do not need to be closed. The output on my system is:

```
Current process ID: 183
Pseudohandle: -1
DuplicateHandle handle: 412
OpenProcess Handle: 392

Closing OpenProcess handle: 392
Closing DuplicateHandle handle: 412
```

Enumerating Processes

Now let us consider the problem of enumerating the processes on a system. As we have said, the technique differs under Windows 9x and Windows NT.

Enumerating Processes Under Windows NT

We will use the following functions from *PSAPI.DLL*:

EnumProcesses
> Enumerates the process IDs for each process in the system.

EnumProcessModules
> Enumerates the handle of each module in a given process.

GetModuleBaseName
> Retrieves the name of a module from its handle.

GetModuleFileNameEx
> Retrieves the fully qualified path of a module from its handle.

GetModuleInformation
> Retrieves information about a module.

GetProcessMemoryInfo
> Retrieves information about the memory usage of a process.

The accompanying CD contains an application called *rpiEnumProcsNT* that displays each process, along with the EXE filename for that process. In addition, the utility displays the modules that are in the selected process's address space and some information related to memory usage by the process. Figure 11-2 shows the utility's main window. The complete source code is on the CD.

Hitting the MemMap button produces a page-by-page memory map (one page is 4 KB) of the selected process's address space, as shown in Figure 11-3. We will discuss this memory map in Chapter 13, *Windows Memory Architecture*.

Clicking the Refresh button starts the process of enumerating the system's processes. The *EnumProcesses* function is:

```
BOOL EnumProcesses(
   DWORD *lpidProcess,    // array to receive the process identifiers
   DWORD cb,              // size of the DWORD array in bytes
   DWORD *cbNeeded        // receives the number of bytes returned
);
```

Since the first parameter is a pointer to the first DWORD in an array of DWORDs, we can pass the first DWORD by reference in VB. Now, a DWORD is actually an unsigned long, so we must use a VB long and do any necessary signed-to-unsigned conversion. However, process IDs are very small numbers (they seem to start at 1 and increase consecutively), and *cbNeeded* is just a count of bytes, so no

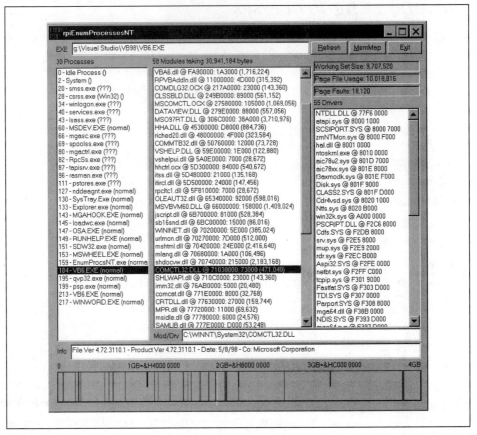

Figure 11-2. Enumerating processes under Windows NT

conversion will be needed for either *DWORD** parameter. Hence, one possible VB
declaration is:

```
Public Declare Function EnumProcesses Lib "PSAPI.DLL" ( _
    idProcess As Long, _
    ByVal cBytes As Long, _
    cbNeeded As Long _
) As Long
```

Note that Win32 supplies no direct way to tell how large to make the *idProcess*
array. The only technique is to guess, try the function, and then compare the
returned value of *cbNeeded,* which contains the number of bytes returned (that is,
four times the number of longs returned), with the size of our array. If the number of longs returned is equal to the size of our array (it is guaranteed never to be
bigger), then we need to increase the size of the array and try again!

The *GetProcesses* procedure shown in Example 11-4 begins with this sort of Terpsi-
chore. Once the processes are enumerated, we sort them and use the *OpenProcess*
function within a For loop to get handles to each process, with which we can call

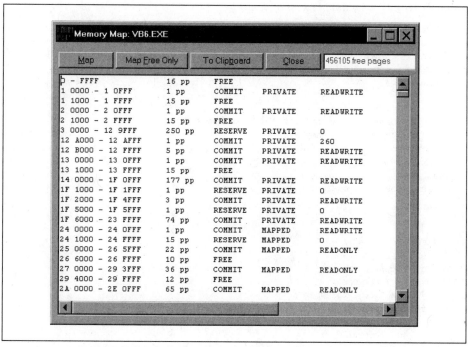

Figure 11-3. A process memory map

such functions as *GetModuleNameEx*. Note that we use the *EnumProcessModules* function to get the first module in each process, since this is always the EXE for the process. (You will find the *RaiseAPIError* function defined at the end of Chapter 3, *API Declarations*.)

Example 11-4. Enumerating Processes

```
Public Const PROCESS_VM_READ = &H10
Public Const PROCESS_QUERY_INFORMATION = &H400

Sub GetProcesses()

' Fills the arrays: lProcessIDs, hProcesses, sEXENames, sFQEXENames
' Sets cProcesses

Dim i As Integer, j As Integer, l As Long
Dim cbNeeded As Long
Dim hEXE As Long
Dim hProcess As Long
Dim lPriority As Long

' Initial guess
cProcesses = 25

Do
    ' Size array
    ReDim lProcessIDs(1 To cProcesses)
```

Example 11-4. Enumerating Processes (continued)

```
    ' Enumerate
    lret = EnumProcesses(lProcessIDs(1), cProcesses * 4, cbNeeded)
    If lret = 0 Then
        RaiseApiError Err.LastDllError
        Exit Sub
    End If

    ' Compare needed bytes with array size in bytes.
    ' If less, then we got them all.
    If cbNeeded < cProcesses * 4 Then
        Exit Do
    Else
        cProcesses = cProcesses * 2
    End If
Loop

cProcesses = cbNeeded / 4

' Sort by processID
For i = 1 To cProcesses
    For j = i + 1 To cProcesses
        If lProcessIDs(i) > lProcessIDs(j) Then
            ' Swap
            l = lProcessIDs(i)
            lProcessIDs(i) = lProcessIDs(j)
            lProcessIDs(j) = l
        End If
    Next
Next

ReDim Preserve lProcessIDs(1 To cProcesses)
ReDim sEXENames(1 To cProcesses)
ReDim sFQEXENames(1 To cProcesses)
ReDim sPriorityClass(1 To cProcesses)

' Now we have the process IDs
' Use OpenProcess to get a handle to each process
For i = 1 To cProcesses

    hProcess = OpenProcess( _
        PROCESS_QUERY_INFORMATION Or PROCESS_VM_READ, _
        0&, _
        lProcessIDs(i))

    ' Watch out for special processes
    Select Case lProcessIDs(i)
        Case 0    ' System Idle Process
            sEXENames(i) = "Idle Process"
            sFQEXENames(i) = "Idle Process"
        Case 2
            sEXENames(i) = "System"
            sFQEXENames(i) = "System"
```

Example 11-4. Enumerating Processes (continued)

```
    Case 28
        sEXENames(i) = "csrss.exe (Win32)"
        sFQEXENames(i) = "csrss.exe (Win32)"
End Select

' If error skip this process
If hProcess <> 0 Then

    ' Now get the handle of the first module
    ' in this process, since first module is EXE
    hEXE = 0
    lret = EnumProcessModules(hProcess, hEXE, 4&, cbNeeded)

    If hEXE <> 0 Then

        ' Get the name of the module
        sEXENames(i) = String$(MAX_PATH, 0)
        lret = GetModuleBaseName(hProcess, hEXE, sEXENames(i), Len(sEXENames(i)))
        sEXENames(i) = Trim0(sEXENames(i))

        ' Get full path name
        sFQEXENames(i) = String$(MAX_PATH, 0)
        lret = GetModuleFileNameEx(hProcess, hEXE, sFQEXENames(i), _
                            Len(sFQEXENames(i)))
        sFQEXENames(i) = Trim0(sFQEXENames(i))

        ' Get priority
        lPriority = GetPriorityClass(hProcess)
        Select Case lPriority
           Case IDLE_PRIORITY_CLASS
               sPriorityClass(i) = "idle"
           Case NORMAL_PRIORITY_CLASS
               sPriorityClass(i) = "normal"
           Case HIGH_PRIORITY_CLASS
               sPriorityClass(i) = "high"
           Case REALTIME_PRIORITY_CLASS
               sPriorityClass(i) = "real"
           Case Else
               sPriorityClass(i) = "???"
        End Select

    End If    ' EXE <> 0

  End If        ' hProcess <> 0

  ' Close handle
  lret = CloseHandle(hProcess)

Next

End Sub
```

When the user selects a process, the utility goes through a very similar procedure to enumerate the modules for the selected process, using *EnumProcessModules*, *GetModuleBaseName*, and *GetModuleFileNameEx*. In addition, it calls *GetModule-Information*, which fills the MODULEINFO structure:

```
Type MODULEINFO
    lpBaseOfDll As Long ' pointer to starting point of module
    SizeOfImage As Long ' size in bytes of module
    EntryPoint As Long  ' pointer to entry point of module
End Type
```

From this structure, we retrieve the size of the module and its base address.

Also, we can get some memory information by calling *GetProcessMemoryInfo*. This fills a structure with all sorts of interesting stuff, but we single out the working set size, the page file usage, and the page fault count. We will discuss memory in more detail in Chapter 13, but, briefly, here is what you need to know:

- The *working set size* is the amount of actual physical RAM that is currently used by the process.

- The *page file usage* is the amount of the Windows page file (swap file) that is being used by the selected process.

- The *page fault count* is the number of times that the process tried to access a memory address that was not currently mapped to actual physical memory. This necessitated a swapping of a memory page out of RAM to make room for the requested page.

Device drivers are also executable files, but they are system-wide, rather than belonging to a specific process. The functions *EnumDeviceDrivers*, *GetDevice-DriverBaseName*, and *GetDeviceDriverFileName* are similar to the corresponding functions for processes and modules.

Once we have module and device driver information, we can create a memory map (at the bottom of the screen). Clicking on a module or driver will change its memory map entry to white for easier identification. Note how the memory map changes as you scroll through the list of processes. We will discuss memory maps in Chapter 13.

Enumerating Processes Under Windows 9x

The Windows 9x version of the previous utility is also on the CD. The main window is shown in Figure 11-4.

The code uses the Toolhelp DLL mentioned in the section "Getting Module Names and Handles" earlier in this chapter. While the Win95 version does not enumerate drivers, it does take advantage of the ability of user mode code to examine the upper region of a process's address space.

Figure 11-4. Enumerating processes under Windows 9x

It is interesting to compare the memory maps in Figure 11-2 and Figure 11-4, both of which are for VB6. In particular, we can see that Windows 9x puts the Win32 (and other) system DLLs in a different location than Windows NT. For example, under Windows NT, *KERNEL32.DLL* is just under the 2GB mark (at address &H77F00000, as shown in Figure 11-2), which is in the area of memory reserved for applications. However, under Windows 9x, this DLL is at the 3GB mark, in the area of memory reserved for the operating system.

In fact, Figure 11-5 shows the upper portion of the memory map of a Win95 process. Note the location of *KERNEL32.DLL* and the other system DLLs. Under Windows NT, this memory area is protected. We will discuss memory maps in more detail in Chapter 13.

Is This Application Already Running?

One of the most often asked questions by programmers is, "What is the best way to tell whether or not a given application is running?"

I can think of several methods for determining whether a particular application is currently running, but I would not be surprised to learn that there are many more. Unfortunately, only one of these methods works for applications that are not created by us in VB.

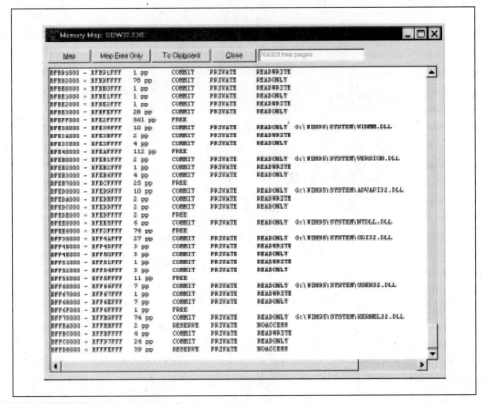

Figure 11-5. The upper portion of a Win95 process space

Using FindWindow

The first method is the simplest, but works only for applications that we create
and only if the application has a uniquely identifiable top level window caption
that does not change. In this case, we can use the *FindWindow* function to see if a
window with that caption exists. There is, however, a subtlety involved here.

To illustrate, here is some code from the Load event of the Clipboard viewer application that we will write later in the book:

```
' Check for running viewer and switch if it exists
hnd = FindWindow("ThunderRT6FormDC", "rpiClipViewer")
If hnd <> 0 And hnd <> Me.hwnd Then
    SetForegroundWindow hnd
    End
End If
```

The problem here is that as soon as this program is run, a form with caption "rpi-
ClipViewer" will be created, so *FindWindow* will *always* report that such a form
(window) exists. However, this is easily overcome with a bit of prestidigitation. In

particular, we change the *design time* caption for the main form to, say, "rpiClip-View." Then, in the Activate event for the main form, we change it to its final value:

```
Private Sub Form_Activate()
Me.Caption = "rpiClipViewer"
End Sub
```

Now, during the Form_Load event, the caption will be "rpiClipView" and thus will not trigger a positive response from *FindWindow*. Indeed, *FindWindow* will only report that such a window exists if there is another running instance of the application, which is precisely what we want.

The SetForegroundWindow problem

Under Windows 95 and Windows NT 4, the *SetForegroundWindow* function:

```
Declare Function SetForegroundWindow Lib "user32" (ByVal hwnd As Long) _
    As Long
```

will bring the application that owns the window with handle *hwnd* to the foreground. However, Microsoft has thrown us a curve in Windows 2000 and Windows 98. Here is what the documentation states:

> Windows NT 5.0 and later: An application cannot force a window to the foreground while the user is working with another window. Instead, *SetForegroundWindow* will activate the window (see *SetActiveWindow*) and call the *FlashWindowEx* function to notify the user.

Unfortunately, Microsoft has decided to take one more measure of control out of our hands by not allowing us to change which application is in the foreground. (To be sure, abuse of this capability leads to obnoxious behavior, but I was not planning on abusing it!)

Fortunately, *SetForegroundWindow* does work if called from within an application—that is, it will force its *own* application to the foreground. This is just enough rope to let us hang ourselves, so to speak.

The *rpiAccessProcess* DLL that we will discuss in Chapter 20, *DLL Injection and Foreign Process Access*, exports a function called *rpiSetForegroundWindow*. The VB declaration of this function is just like that of Win32's *SetForegroundWindow*:

```
Declare Function rpiSetForegroundWindow Lib "rpiAccessProcess.dll" ( _
    ByVal hwnd As Long) As Long
```

The function is designed to work just like *SetForegroundWindow* works under Windows 95 and Windows NT 4, even under Windows 98 and Windows 2000. It does so by injecting the *rpiAccessProcess* DLL into the foreign process space so that the *SetForegroundWindow* function can be run from that process, thus bringing it to the foreground. We will discuss how this is done in Chapter 20. In any case, you should be able to use this function whenever you need *SetForeground-Window* under Windows 98/2000. (By the way, I do believe that this feature should be used only in *very special* situations.)

Using a Usage Count

Conceptually, the simplest approach to this problem is just to have our VB application maintain a small text file that contains a single number serving as a *usage count* for the application and that is located in some fixed directory, such as the Windows system directory. The application can, in its main Load event, check the usage count by simply opening the file in the standard way.

If the count is 1, the application terminates abruptly, without firing its Unload event. This can be done by using the much maligned **End** statement. If the count is 0, the application sets the usage count to 1 and executes normally. Then, in its Unload event, the application sets the usage count to 0. In this way, one and only one instance of the application is allowed to run normally, and it is the only instance that alters the usage count.

Of course, this approach can be made more elegant by using a memory-mapped file, but this brings with it considerable additional baggage in the form of extra code.

Here is some pseudocode for the Load and Unload events of the main form:

```
Private Sub Form_Load()

Dim lUsageCount As Long

' Get the current usage count from the memory-mapped file
lUsageCount = GetUsageCount

If lUsageCount > 0 Then
    MsgBox "Application is already running"
    End
Else
    ' Set the usage count to 1
    SetUsageCount 1
End If

End Sub

Private Sub Form_Unload()

SetUsageCount 0

End Sub
```

We will leave the implementation of this approach to the reader and turn to a somewhat simpler implementation along these same lines.

The rpiUsageCount DLL

As we will see when we discuss the *rpiAccessProcess* DLL for use in allocating foreign memory, an executable file (DLL or EXE) can contain *shared memory*. This memory is shared by every instance of the executable. Thus, if we place a shared variable in a DLL, every process that uses this DLL will have access to this variable.

To be absolutely clear, a shared variable is not the same as a *global* variable. Global variables are accessible to the entire DLL, but each process that loads the DLL gets a *separate* copy of each global variable. Thus, global variables are accessible *within* a single process. Shared variables are accessible throughout the system.

Now, while VB does not allow us to create shared memory in a VB executable, it is very easy to do in a DLL written in VC++.

On the accompanying CD, you will find a DLL called *rpiUsageCount.dll*. The entire VC++ source code is shown in Example 11-5.

Example 11-5. VC++ Source Code for the rpiUsageCount DLL

```
// rpiUsageCount.cpp

#include <windows.h>

// Set up shared data section in DLL
// MUST INITIALIZE ALL SHARED VARIABLES
#pragma data_seg("Shared")
long giUsageCount = 0;
#pragma data_seg()

// Tell linker to make this section shared and read-write
#pragma comment(linker, "/section:Shared,rws")

///////////////////////////////////////////////////////////
// Prototypes of exported functions
///////////////////////////////////////////////////////////
long WINAPI rpiIncrementUsageCount();
long WINAPI rpiDecrementUsageCount();
long WINAPI rpiGetUsageCount();
long WINAPI rpiSetUsageCount(long lNewCount);

///////////////////////////////////////////////////////////
// DllMain
///////////////////////////////////////////////////////////

HANDLE hDLLInst = NULL;

BOOL WINAPI DllMain (HANDLE hInst, ULONG ul_reason_for_call,
                     LPVOID lpReserved)
{
        // Keep the instance handle for later use
        hDLLInst = hInst;
```

Example 11-5. VC++ Source Code for the rpiUsageCount DLL (continued)

```
        switch(ul_reason_for_call)
        {
        case DLL_PROCESS_ATTACH:
                // Initialization here
                break;
        case DLL_PROCESS_DETACH:
                // Clean-up here
            break;
        }
        return TRUE;
}


/////////////////////////////////////////////////////////////
// Functions for export
/////////////////////////////////////////////////////////////
long WINAPI rpiIncrementUsageCount()
{
    return InterlockedIncrement(&giUsageCount);
}
long WINAPI rpiDecrementUsageCount()
{
    return InterlockedDecrement(&giUsageCount);
}
long WINAPI rpiGetUsageCount()
{
    return giUsageCount;
}
long WINAPI rpiSetUsageCount(long lNewCount)
{
    giUsageCount = lNewCount;
    return giUsageCount;
}
```

This DLL has a single, shared long variable, called *lUsageCount*. The DLL exports four functions for use with this variable. (This is more than is needed, but I got carried away.)

```
    rpiIncrementUsageCount
    rpiDecrementUsageCount
    rpiGetUsageCount
    rpiSetUsageCount
```

Here are the VB declarations:

```
    Declare Function rpiIncrementUsageCount Lib "rpiUsageCount.dll" () As Long
    Declare Function rpiDecrementUsageCount Lib "rpiUsageCount.dll" () As Long
    Declare Function rpiGetUsageCount Lib "rpiUsageCount.dll" () As Long
    Declare Function rpiSetUsageCount Lib "rpiUsageCount.dll" () As Long
```

To use this DLL, we just add the code shown in Example 11-6 to the Load and Unload events of the main VB form.

Example 11-6. Calling the rpiGetUsageCount Function

```
Private Sub Form_Load()

Dim lUsageCount As Long

' Get the current usage count
lUsageCount = rpiGetUsageCount

If lUsageCount > 0 Then
    MsgBox "Application is already running"
    End
Else
    rpiSetUsageCount 1
End If

End Sub

Private Sub Form_Unload()

rpiSetUsageCount 0

End Sub
```

The downside of using this DLL is that it uses 49,152 bytes of memory. Also, it does not automatically switch to an already running instance of the application. For this, we still need to use *FindWindow* to get a window handle to use with *SetForegroundWindow* (or *rpiSetForegroundWindow*).

Walking the Process List

Our final approach to checking for a running application is the most obvious one and should always work (although for some reason I get a funny feeling saying "always"). Namely, we walk through the list of all current processes to check every EXE filename (and perhaps even complete path). Unfortunately, as we have seen, this requires different code under Windows NT and Windows 9x. Nevertheless, it is important, so here is a utility that will do the job.

The Windows NT version is *GetWinNTProcessID*. We feed this function either an EXE filename *or* a fully qualified EXE name (path and filename). The function walks the process list and tries to do a case-insensitive match of the name. It returns the process ID of the *last* match and a count of the total number of matches. If the return value is 0, then this application is not running. Examples 11-7 and 11-8 show the code (both versions), including the necessary declarations.

Example 11-7. Walking the Windows NT Process List

```
Option Explicit

' ************************
' NOTE: Windows NT 4.0 only
' ************************
```

Example 11-7. Walking the Windows NT Process List (continued)

```
Public Const MAX_PATH = 260

Public Declare Function EnumProcesses Lib "PSAPI.DLL" ( _
    idProcess As Long, _
    ByVal cBytes As Long, _
    cbNeeded As Long _
) As Long

Public Declare Function EnumProcessModules Lib "PSAPI.DLL" ( _
    ByVal hProcess As Long, _
    hModule As Long, _
    ByVal cb As Long, _
    cbNeeded As Long _
) As Long

Public Declare Function GetModuleBaseName Lib "PSAPI.DLL" _
Alias "GetModuleBaseNameA" ( _
    ByVal hProcess As Long, _
    ByVal hModule As Long, _
    ByVal lpBaseName As String, _
    ByVal nSize As Long _
) As Long

Public Declare Function GetModuleFileNameEx Lib "PSAPI.DLL" _
Alias "GetModuleFileNameExA" ( _
    ByVal hProcess As Long, _
    ByVal hModule As Long, _
    ByVal lpFilename As String, _
    ByVal nSize As Long _
) As Long

Public Const STANDARD_RIGHTS_REQUIRED = &HF0000
Public Const SYNCHRONIZE = &H100000
Public Const PROCESS_VM_READ = &H10
Public Const PROCESS_QUERY_INFORMATION = &H400
Public Const PROCESS_ALL_ACCESS = STANDARD_RIGHTS_REQUIRED Or _
            SYNCHRONIZE Or &HFFF

Declare Function OpenProcess Lib "kernel32" ( _
    ByVal dwDesiredAccess As Long, _
    ByVal bInheritHandle As Long, _
    ByVal dwProcessId As Long _
) As Long
Declare Function CloseHandle Lib "kernel32" (ByVal hObject As Long) _
    As Long

' --------------------

Public Function GetWinNTProcessID(sFQEXEName As String, _
            sEXEName As String, ByRef cMatches As Long) As Long

' Gets the process ID from the EXE name or fully qualified (path/name)
```

Example 11-7. Walking the Windows NT Process List (continued)

```
' EXE name
' If sFQName <> "" then uses this to get matches
' If sName <> "" uses just the name to get matches
' Returns 0 if no such process, else the process ID of the last match
' Returns count of matches in OUT parameter cMatches
' Returns FQName if that is empty
' Returns -1 if both sFQName and sName are empty
' Returns -2 if error getting process list

Dim i As Integer, j As Integer, l As Long
Dim cbNeeded As Long
Dim hEXE As Long
Dim hProcess As Long

Dim lret As Long
Dim cProcesses As Long
Dim lProcessIDs() As Long
Dim sEXENames() As String
Dim sFQEXENames() As String


' ---------------------------------
' First get the array of process IDs
' ---------------------------------
' Initial guess
cProcesses = 25

Do
    ' Size array
    ReDim lProcessIDs(1 To cProcesses)
    ' Enumerate
    lret = EnumProcesses(lProcessIDs(1), cProcesses * 4, cbNeeded)
    If lret = 0 Then
       GetWinNTProcessID = -2
       Exit Function
    End If
    ' Compare needed bytes with array size in bytes.
    ' If less, then we got them all.
    If cbNeeded < cProcesses * 4 Then
       Exit Do
    Else
       cProcesses = cProcesses * 2
    End If
Loop

cProcesses = cbNeeded / 4

ReDim Preserve lProcessIDs(1 To cProcesses)
ReDim sEXENames(1 To cProcesses)
ReDim sFQEXENames(1 To cProcesses)


' -------------
' Get EXE names
' -------------
```

Example 11-7. Walking the Windows NT Process List (continued)

```
For i = 1 To cProcesses

    ' Use OpenProcess to get a handle to each process
    hProcess = OpenProcess(PROCESS_QUERY_INFORMATION Or PROCESS_VM_READ, _
                    0&, lProcessIDs(i))


    ' Watch out for special processes
    Select Case lProcessIDs(i)
        Case 0    ' System Idle Process
            sEXENames(i) = "Idle Process"
            sFQEXENames(i) = "Idle Process"
        Case 2
            sEXENames(i) = "System"
            sFQEXENames(i) = "System"
        Case 28
            sEXENames(i) = "csrss.exe"
            sFQEXENames(i) = "csrss.exe"
    End Select


    ' If error skip this process
    If hProcess = 0 Then
        GoTo hpContinue
    End If


    ' Now get the handle of the first module
    ' in this process, since first module is EXE
    hEXE = 0
    lret = EnumProcessModules(hProcess, hEXE, 4&, cbNeeded)
    If hEXE = 0 Then GoTo hpContinue

    ' Get the name of the module
    sEXENames(i) = String$(MAX_PATH, 0)
    lret = GetModuleBaseName(hProcess, hEXE, sEXENames(i), _
                        Len(sEXENames(i)))
    sEXENames(i) = Trim0(sEXENames(i))

    ' Get full path name
    sFQEXENames(i) = String$(MAX_PATH, 0)
    lret = GetModuleFileNameEx(hProcess, hEXE, sFQEXENames(i), _
                        Len(sFQEXENames(i)))
    sFQEXENames(i) = Trim0(sFQEXENames(i))

hpContinue:

    ' Close handle
    lret = CloseHandle(hProcess)

Next


' ----------------
' Check for match
' ----------------
```

Example 11-7. Walking the Windows NT Process List (continued)

```
cMatches = 0
If sFQEXEName <> "" Then
   For i = 1 To cProcesses
      If LCase$(sFQEXENames(i)) = LCase$(sFQEXEName) Then
         cMatches = cMatches + 1
         GetWinNTProcessID = lProcessIDs(i)
      End If
   Next
ElseIf sEXEName <> "" Then
   For i = 1 To cProcesses
      If LCase$(sEXENames(i)) = LCase$(sEXEName) Then
         cMatches = cMatches + 1
         GetWinNTProcessID = lProcessIDs(i)
         sFQEXEName = sFQEXENames(i)
      End If
   Next
Else
   GetWinNTProcessID = -1
End If

End Function
```

The Windows 9x version uses Toolhelp. The corresponding function (and required
declarations) is shown in Example 11-8.

Example 11-8. Walking the Windows 9x Process List

```
Option Explicit

' ************************
' NOTE: Windows 95/98 only
' ************************

Public Const MAX_MODULE_NAME32 = 255
Public Const MAX_PATH = 260

Public Const TH32CS_SNAPHEAPLIST = &H1
Public Const TH32CS_SNAPPROCESS = &H2
Public Const TH32CS_SNAPTHREAD = &H4
Public Const TH32CS_SNAPMODULE = &H8
Public Const TH32CS_SNAPALL = (TH32CS_SNAPHEAPLIST Or TH32CS_SNAPPROCESS _
                       Or TH32CS_SNAPTHREAD Or TH32CS_SNAPMODULE)
Public Const TH32CS_INHERIT = &H80000000

''HANDLE WINAPI CreateToolhelp32Snapshot(  DWORD dwFlags,
''   DWORD th32ProcessID  );

Public Declare Function CreateToolhelp32Snapshot Lib "kernel32" ( _
   ByVal dwFlags As Long, _
   ByVal th32ProcessID As Long _
) As Long

Public Declare Function Process32First Lib "kernel32" ( _
```

Example 11-8. Walking the Windows 9x Process List (continued)

```
    ByVal hSnapShot As Long, _
    lppe As PROCESSENTRY32 _
) As Long

Public Declare Function Process32Next Lib "kernel32" ( _
    ByVal hSnapShot As Long, _
    lppe As PROCESSENTRY32 _
) As Long

Public Type PROCESSENTRY32
    dwSize As Long
    cntUsage As Long
    th32ProcessID As Long              ' process ID
    th32DefaultHeapID As Long
    th32ModuleID As Long               ' only for Toolhelp functions
    cntThreads As Long                 ' number of threads
    th32ParentProcessID As Long        ' process ID of parent
    pcPriClassBase As Long
    dwFlags As Long
    szExeFile As String * MAX_PATH  ' path/file of EXE file
End Type

Declare Function CloseHandle Lib "kernel32" (ByVal hObject As Long) _
        As Long


' ------------------------


Function GetWin95ProcessID(sFQName As String, sName As String, _
        ByRef cMatches As Long) As Long

' ************************
' NOTE: Windows 95/98 only
' ************************

' Gets the process ID
' If sFQName <> "" then uses this to get matches
' If sName <> "" uses just the name to get matches
' Returns 0 if no such process, else the process ID of the last match
' Returns count of matches in OUT parameter cMatches
' Returns FQName if that is empty
' Returns -1 if could not get snapshot

Dim i As Integer, c As Currency
Dim hSnapShot As Long
Dim lret As Long       ' for generic return values
Dim cProcesses As Long
Dim cProcessIDs() As Currency

Dim sEXENames() As String
Dim sFQEXENames() As String


Dim procEntry As PROCESSENTRY32
procEntry.dwSize = LenB(procEntry)
```

Example 11-8. Walking the Windows 9x Process List (continued)

```
' Scan all the processes.
hSnapShot = CreateToolhelp32Snapshot(TH32CS_SNAPPROCESS, 0&)
If hSnapShot = -1 Then
    GetProcessID = -1
    Exit Function
End If


' Initialize
ReDim sFQEXENames(1 To 25)
ReDim sEXENames(1 To 25)
ReDim cProcessIDs(1 To 25)

cProcesses = 0

' Do first process
lret = Process32First(hSnapShot, procEntry)
If lret > 0 Then
    cProcesses = cProcesses + 1
    sFQEXENames(cProcesses) = Trim0(procEntry.szExeFile)
    sEXENames(cProcesses) = GetFileName(sFQEXENames(cProcesses))
    If procEntry.th32ProcessID < 0 Then
        c = CCur(procEntry.th32ProcessID) + 2 ^ 32
    Else
        c = CCur(procEntry.th32ProcessID)
    End If
    cProcessIDs(cProcesses) = c
End If
' Do rest
Do
    lret = Process32Next(hSnapShot, procEntry)
    If lret = 0 Then Exit Do
    cProcesses = cProcesses + 1
    If UBound(sFQEXENames) < cProcesses Then
        ReDim Preserve sFQEXENames(1 To cProcesses + 10)
        ReDim Preserve sEXENames(1 To cProcesses + 10)
        ReDim Preserve cProcessIDs(1 To cProcesses + 10)
    End If
    sFQEXENames(cProcesses) = Trim0(procEntry.szExeFile)
    sEXENames(cProcesses) = GetFileName(sFQEXENames(cProcesses))
    If procEntry.th32ProcessID < 0 Then
        c = CCur(procEntry.th32ProcessID) + 2 ^ 32
    Else
        c = CCur(procEntry.th32ProcessID)
    End If
    cProcessIDs(cProcesses) = c
Loop

CloseHandle hSnapShot


' ----------
' Find Match
' ----------
```

Example 11-8. Walking the Windows 9x Process List (continued)

```
cMatches = 0
If sFQName <> "" Then
    For i = 1 To cProcesses
        If LCase$(sFQEXENames(i)) = LCase$(sFQName) Then
            cMatches = cMatches + 1
            GetProcessID = lProcessIDs(i)
        End If
    Next
ElseIf sName <> "" Then
    For i = 1 To cProcesses
        If LCase$(sEXENames(i)) = LCase$(sName) Then
            cMatches = cMatches + 1
            GetProcessID = lProcessIDs(i)
            sFQName = sFQEXENames(i)
        End If
    Next
Else
    GetProcessID = -1
End If

End Function
```

12

Threads

Visual Basic itself does not support the creation of threads in a VB application (except in a very limited fashion for ActiveX DLLs and ActiveX controls), although the *CreateThread* API function does work in VB. Moreover, since the proper creation and use of threads requires careful circumspection, I cannot recommend creating threads in VB applications. This does not mean, however, that manipulating existing threads is not useful, as we will see.

Thread Handles and Thread IDs

In general, the story of thread handles, pseudohandles, and IDs parallels that of processes.

We have seen that the *CreateProcess* function returns the thread ID and a thread handle for the first (and only) thread running in the newly created process. Also, the *CreateThread* function returns a system-wide thread ID.

A thread can use the *GetCurrentThreadId* function to get its own thread ID. We have seen that the function *GetWindowThreadProcessId* retrieves the thread ID of the thread that created a particular window (as well as the process ID of the process that owns that thread).

To quote the Win32 documentation:

> The Win32 API does not provide a way to get the thread handle from the thread identifier. If the handles were made available this way, the owning process could fail because another process unexpectedly performed an operation on one of its threads, such as suspending it, resuming it, adjusting its priority, or terminating it. Instead, you must request the handle from the thread creator or the thread itself.

Finally, a thread can call the *GetCurrentThread* function to retrieve a pseudohandle to itself. As with process pseudohandles, a thread pseudohandle is valid only for the calling process and it cannot be inherited. Also as with processes, we can use the *DuplicateHandle* function to get a real handle to a thread from a pseudohandle.

Thread Priority

The term *multitasking*, also called *multiprogramming*, refers to the ability to manage multiple processes (or multiple threads) with a single processor. On the other hand, *multiprocessing* refers to the management of multiple processes or multiple threads with more than one processor.

It is only in a multiprocessor environment that a computer can execute instructions from two different processes at the same time. However, even with a single processor, *task switching* can make it *appear* that more than one process is executing instructions at the same time.

In the older 16-bit Windows operating system, there was only one thread in the entire system. Moreover, 16-bit Windows used a *cooperative* multitasking approach, meaning that each application was responsible for relinquishing the system's thread so that other applications could execute. If a program running under 16-bit Windows was performing a time-intensive task, such as formatting a floppy disk, all other loaded applications had to wait. Worse yet, if an errant program went into an infinite loop, the entire system would become unusable, requiring a cold reboot.

Thread Priority Levels

Win32 is much different. First, it is *multithreaded*, which allows for the possibility of multiprocessing, among other things. Second, it uses a *preemptive* multitasking model, where the operating system controls when and for how long each thread gets CPU time, which is allocated in *time slices*. A time slice is referred to by Windows as a *quantum*.

The length of a quantum is hardware dependent and can actually vary from thread to thread. Just to give a reference point, the base value is 20 milliseconds for Windows 95, 30 milliseconds for Windows NT Workstation (on a Pentium-based system), and 180 milliseconds for Windows NT Server.

Let us explain, in very general terms, how Windows allocates quantums to the threads in a system. The process is quite similar, but not identical, for Windows 9x and Windows NT.

Every thread in the system has a *priority level*, which is a number between 0 and 31. In brief, here are the facts.

- If there are any threads with priority 31 *that require CPU time*, that is, that are *not idle*, the operating system cycles among these threads (without regard to which process they are contained in), giving each of them a time slice in turn. Lower-priority threads do not receive any time slices and thus will not execute. If no priority 31 threads are active, the operating system looks for active threads with priority level 30, and so on. Keep in mind, however, that threads are quite often idle. In fact, just because an application is loaded doesn't mean that *any* of its threads are active. Thus, lower-priority threads do get a chance to execute. Moreover, if the user presses a key that is intended for a process whose threads are idle, the operating system will temporarily assign the CPU to the relevant thread so that it can process the keystroke.

- Priority 0 is reserved *exclusively* for a special system thread, called the *zero page thread*, which clears unused portions of memory. There is also something called the *idle thread*, which runs at priority level 0, polling the system looking for something to do.

- If a thread of a certain priority is running when the operating system determines that a thread of higher priority requires CPU time (for instance, the thread receives a message that a mouse click has taken place), the operating system will preempt the lower-priority thread *immediately*, giving the CPU to the higher-priority thread. Thus, a thread may not be able to complete a given time slice.

- To switch from one thread to another, the system performs a *context switch*. This is the process of saving the state of the CPU (registers and stack) and loading the corresponding values of the target thread.

Assigning Thread Priority

Thread priority is assigned in a two-step process. First, every *process* is assigned a *priority class* when it is created. This class can be read using the *GetPriorityClass* function and changed using the *SetPriorityClass* function. Table 12-1 shows the process priority class names, levels, and the constants used with these aforementioned functions (as well as *CreateProcess*).

Table 12-1. Process Priority Levels

Priority Class Name	Priority Class Level	Symbolic Constant
Idle	4	`IDLE_PRIORITY_CLASS=&H40`
Normal	8	`NORMAL_PRIORITY_CLASS=&H20`
High	13	`HIGH_PRIORITY_CLASS=&H80`
Realtime	24	`REALTIME_PRIORITY_CLASS=&H100`

Most processes should simply be given the normal priority class level. However, for some applications, such as system monitoring applications, it may be more appropriate to assign an idle priority. Realtime priority should generally be avoided because it will initially give the threads in the process higher priority than system threads such as the keyboard, mouse, disk cache-flushing and Ctrl-Alt-Del monitoring threads! It may be appropriate for short-term critical hardware-related processes.

Now, when a thread is first created, its default priority level is set to the priority class level of the process that created the thread. However, the *SetThreadPriority* function:

```
BOOL SetThreadPriority(
    HANDLE hThread, // handle to the thread
    int nPriority   // thread priority level
);
```

can be used to alter a thread's priority. The *nPriority* parameter is used to alter the thread's priority *relative to the priority of the thread's process*. The possible values of *nPriority* and their effects are shown in Table 12-2.

Table 12-2. Thread Priority Level Adjustments

Constant	Thread Priority Level
THREAD_PRIORITY_NORMAL	Priority class level
THREAD_PRIORITY_ABOVE_NORMAL	Priority class level + 1
THREAD_PRIORITY_BELOW_NORMAL	Priority class level – 1
THREAD_PRIORITY_HIGHEST	Priority class level + 2
THREAD_PRIORITY_LOWEST	Priority class level – 2
THREAD_PRIORITY_IDLE	Set thread priority to 1 for all process priority classes except Realtime. In this case, set priority level to 16.
THREAD_PRIORITY_TIME_CRITICAL	Set priority level to 15 for all process priority classes except Realtime. In this case, set priority level to 31.

Thread Priority Boosting and Quantum Stretching

The priority range from 1 to 15 is known as the *dynamic priority range* and the range from 16 to 31 is the *realtime priority range*.

Under Windows NT, a thread whose priority range is in the dynamic range may have its priority temporarily *boosted* by the operating system at various times. Accordingly, a thread's unaltered priority level (set by the programmer through the API functions) is referred to as its *base priority level*. In fact, the Windows NT API function *SetProcessPriorityBoost* can be used to turn *priority boosting* on and off. (This function is not supported under Windows 9x.)

Also, there are occasions when a thread's time slice is temporarily lengthened.

In an effort to smooth operation, Windows will boost a thread's priority or increase its time slice length under the following conditions:

- When a thread is in the *foreground process*, that is, the process whose active window has the input focus
- When a thread first enters its *wait state*
- When a thread leaves its *wait state*
- If a thread is not getting any (CPU time, that is)

Thread States

Threads can exist in one of several *states*:

Ready
> In the pool of threads that are waiting to execute.

Standby
> Selected to run in the next quantum for a processor. Only one thread per processor can be in standby state.

Running
> Executing on a processor.

Waiting (also called idle or suspended)
> In the wait state. When this state ends, the thread either begins executing (running state) or enters the ready state.

Transition
> Ready to run but its stack is paged out to the hard disk page file, rather than being in physical memory. Once the stack contents are returned to memory, the thread enters the ready state.

Terminated
> Completed executing all of its instructions. Subsequently, it may or may not be *deleted*. If not, the system can reinitialize the thread for subsequent use.

Thread Synchronization

When multiple threads are running, it is often important for them to cooperate in some way. For instance, if more than one thread is attempting to access some global data, each thread needs to avoid contaminating the data for the other threads. Also, there are occasions when one thread may need to be informed when another thread has finished a task. This communication may need to take place between threads in a single process or in different processes.

Thread synchronization is a general term that refers to the process of thread coop-eration and communication. Note that thread synchronization needs to involve the system itself, to act as a mediator. (A thread cannot communicate with another thread completely on its own.)

Win32 has several methods for thread synchronization. One method may be more appropriate for a given situation than another method. We will take a brief look at these methods and use some of them in some VB applications.

Critical Sections

One method of thread synchronization involves the use of *critical sections*. This is the only thread synchronization method that does not require the involvement of the Windows kernel. (It is not a kernel object.) However, it can be used to syn-chronize threads only within a single process.

The first step is to declare a global variable of type `CRITICAL_SECTION`, say:

```
CRITICAL_SECTION gCS;
```

We will call this a *critical section object*.

Code that is considered sensitive (or critical) by a given thread is surrounded by a call to the *EnterCriticalSection* and *LeaveCriticalSection* functions, making refer-ence to the critical section object `gCS` (for there may be others):

```
EnterCriticalSection(gCS);
    .
    .
    .
LeaveCriticalSection(gCS);
```

The call `EnterCriticalSection(gCS)` says, in effect: "May I have permission from `gCS` to execute the upcoming critical code?" The call `LeaveCritical-Section(gCS)` says to `gCS`: "I am finished executing critical code. You may now give permission to other threads to execute their critical code."

The *EnterCriticalSection* function checks to see if some other thread has already entered a critical section of code *associated with this critical section object*. If not, then the thread is allowed to execute its critical code—or more properly, not pre-vented from doing so. If so, then the requesting thread is suspended, but a note is made of the request. This is why the critical section object is a data structure—it needs to make notes.

When the *LeaveCriticalSection* function is called by the thread that currently has permission to run its critical code associated with this critical section object, the system can check to see which thread is next in line, waiting for the critical sec-tion object to become free. It can then wake that thread, which will resume execu-tion (during its time slices, of course).

Synchronization Using Kernel Objects

Many kernel objects, including process objects, thread objects, file objects, mutex objects, semaphore objects, file change notification objects, and event objects, can exist in one of two states: *signaled* or *nonsignaled*. It may be helpful to think of these objects as having a lightbulb attached to them, as in Figure 12-1. When the light is on, the object is signaled; when it is off, the object is nonsignaled.

Figure 12-1. A signaled kernel object

To illustrate, when a process is created, its kernel object is nonsignaled. When the process terminates, its kernel object becomes signaled. Similarly, running threads are nonsignaled (that is, their objects are nonsignaled), but become signaled when they terminate. In fact, mutex objects, semaphore objects, event objects, file change objects, and waitable timer objects exist *exclusively* for the purpose of signaling!

The point of all this signaling is that it is possible for a thread to suspend itself until a specified object becomes signaled. For instance, a thread in one process can suspend itself until another process terminates simply by waiting for the other process's kernel object to become signaled.

The functions *WaitForSingleObject* and *WaitForMultipleObjects* allow a thread to suspend itself until the specified object (or objects) is signaled. We will confine our discussion to *WaitForSingleObject*, whose declaration is:

```
DWORD WaitForSingleObject(
    HANDLE hHandle,        // handle to object to wait for
    DWORD dwMilliseconds // time-out interval in milliseconds
);
```

or, in VB:

```
Declare Function WaitForSingleObject Lib "kernel32" _
Alias "WaitForSingleObject" ( _
    ByVal hHandle As Long, _
    ByVal dwMilliseconds As Long _
) As Long
```

The *hHandle* parameter is the handle of the object for which notification of the signaled state is requested, and the *dwMilliseconds* is the time that the calling thread is willing to wait. If *dwMilliseconds* is 0, the function will return immediately with the current signal status of the object. This is how to test the state of an object. The parameter can also be set to the symbolic constant INFINITE (= −1), in which case the calling thread will wait indefinitely.

The *WaitForSingleObject* function puts the calling thread to sleep until the function returns a value. The possible return values are:

WAIT_OBJECT_0
> The object is signaled.

WAIT_TIMEOUT
> The sleep interval specified by *dwMilliseconds* has elapsed and the object is still nonsignaled.

WAIT_ABANDONED
> In the case of a mutex object (only), the mutex was not released by the thread that owned it before that thread terminated.

WAIT_FAILED
> The function has failed.

Example: Waiting for an Application to Terminate

Let us try an example. We want to write a function that will cause a VB application to suspend itself until another application terminates. The other application is identified by its EXE name, which, for this example, is *findtext.exe*. (Of course, you will probably need to change this when you try the example yourself.)

Along with *OpenProcess* and *WaitForSingleObject*, we need the following return values for *WaitForSingleObject*:

```
Public Const WAIT_FAILED = &HFFFFFFFF
Public Const WAIT_OBJECT_0 = 0
Public Const WAIT_TIMEOUT = &H102
```

The *WaitForAppToQuit* function shown in the following code uses some functions that we defined in Chapter 11, *Processes* (and are defined in *rpiAPI.bas* on the CD): *GetWinNTProcessID* and *ProcHndFromProcIDSync*. Note that we need to be a bit careful with error return codes so that we don't use a code returned by *WaitForSingleObject*.

```
Public Function WaitForAppToQuit(sEXEName As String, sFQEXEName As String, _
    lWaitSeconds As Long) As Integer

' Suspend execution until app with specified EXE quits
' or until lWaitSeconds seconds has passed
'
' If sFQEXEName is not empty, use it. Otherwise, use sEXEName.
' Returns 0 on success
' Returns 1 if no process with the specified EXE
' Returns 2 if both sFQName and sName are empty
' Returns 3 if error getting process list
' Returns 4 if cannot get handle to existing process
' Otherwise returns the return value of WaitForSingleObject

Dim lret As Long
Dim hProcessID As Long
Dim hProcess As Long
Dim cMatches As Long
Dim sEXE As String

hProcessID = GetWinNTProcessID(sFQEXEName, sEXEName, cMatches)

If hProcessID <= 0 Then
    ' Error--translate to error code for this function
    If hProcessID = 0 Then
        WaitForAppToQuit = 1     ' no such process
    ElseIf hProcessID = -1 Then
        WaitForAppToQuit = 2     ' no EXE specified
    ElseIf hProcessID = -2 Then
        WaitForAppToQuit = 3     ' error getting process list
    End If
    Exit Function
End If

' Get handle from process ID
hProcess = ProcHndFromProcIDSync(hProcessID)

If hProcess = 0 Then
    WaitForAppToQuit = 4     ' error getting process handle
    Exit Function
End If

' Wait
WaitForAppToQuit = WaitForSingleObject(hProcess, 1000& * lWaitSeconds)

CloseHandle hProcess

End Function
```

Here is some code to try this function out:

```
Public Sub WaitForAppToQuitExample()

Dim t As Long
t = Timer
```

```
lret = WaitForAppToQuit("findtext.exe", "", 10&)
Debug.Print "Return: " & lret

Select Case lret
Case WAIT_TIMEOUT
   Debug.Print "timeout: " & Timer - t
Case WAIT_OBJECT_0
   Debug.Print "resume: " & Timer - t
Case WAIT_FAILED
   Debug.Print "Failed: " & GetAPIErrorText(Err.LastDllError)
End Select

End Sub
```

Before running this code, change the EXE name to one that reflects a running application on your system. If you let the function run to completion, the output will look something like the following:

```
Return: 258
timeout: 10.51171875
```

However, if you start the code and immediately terminate the *Findtext.exe* application, the output will be something like the following:

```
Return: 258
resume: 2.3046875
```

Mutexes

A *mutex* is a kernel object that can be used to synchronize threads running in different processes. A mutex may or may not be owned by some thread. If a mutex is owned by a thread, then the mutex is signaled. If the mutex is not owned by any thread, the mutex is nonsignaled. In other words, for a mutex, *owned* is equivalent to *nonsignaled*.

If a mutex is not owned by any thread, the first thread that calls *WaitForSingleObject* gains ownership of the mutex, in which case the mutex immediately becomes nonsignaled.

In a sense, a mutex is like a *baton* that can be "picked up" by any thread on a first-come-first-served basis.

The point is that when a thread tries to acquire a mutex (pick up the baton) that is already owned (nonsigned) by calling *WaitForSingleObject*, the thread is suspended until the mutex becomes available, which happens when the owner of the mutex releases it (drops the baton).

Mutexes are created by calling the *CreateMutex* function:

```
HANDLE CreateMutex(
   LPSECURITY_ATTRIBUTES lpMutexAttributes, // pointer to security attributes
```

```
        BOOL bInitialOwner, // flag for initial ownership
        LPCTSTR lpName        // pointer to mutex-object name
    );
```

or, in VB:

```
    Declare Function CreateMutex Lib "kernel32" Alias "CreateMutexA" ( _
        lpMutexAttributes As SECURITY_ATTRIBUTES, _
        ByVal bInitialOwner As Long, _
        ByVal lpName As String _
    ) As Long
```

or, to pass **NULL** in the first parameter:

```
    Declare Function CreateMutex Lib "kernel32" Alias "CreateMutexA" ( _
        ByVal lpMutexAttributes As Long, _
        ByVal bInitialOwner As Long, _
        ByVal lpName As String _
    ) As Long
```

The first parameter relates to security and can be set to **NULL** to prevent the handle from being inherited by child processes. The *bInitialOwner* parameter specifies whether the calling thread will initially own the mutex (**TRUE**) and therefore the mutex will be nonsignaled, or whether the mutex will initially be unowned (**FALSE**) and therefore signaled.

The *lpName* parameter is the name of the mutex. This parameter can be set to **NULL** if no name is desired. When a mutex is named, it can be shared among processes. Once a *named* mutex is created by one process, a thread in another process can call *CreateMutex* or *OpenMutex*, using the same name. In either case, the system will simply pass the calling thread a handle to the original mutex. Another way to share a mutex is to call *DuplicateHandle*.

A mutex must be shared in order to work across processes. The reason is simple: to acquire ownership of a mutex (*WaitForSingleObject*) or to release that ownership, a thread must have a handle to the mutex! A thread releases a mutex by calling *ReleaseMutex*:

```
    BOOL ReleaseMutex(
        HANDLE hMutex // handle to mutex object
    );
```

or, in VB:

```
    Declare Function ReleaseMutex Lib "kernel32" Alias "ReleaseMutex" ( _
        ByVal hMutex As Long _
    ) As Long
```

Since mutexes are owned by threads, the problem arises as to what happens if the thread that owns a mutex terminates without first releasing the mutex. The solution is that the system frees the mutex (returning it to signaled state). The thread that called *WaitForSingleObject* using this mutex receives the **WAIT_ABANDONED** return value, which probably indicates that something was wrong with the now-deceased owning thread. It is then up to the waiting thread to decide whether or not to proceed as usual.

Example: Alternating Counters Using Mutexes

To demonstrate the use of mutexes, we will create two small VB applications. Each application counts up to 5 and then pauses while the other application counts to 5. This alternates back and forth. Figure 12-2 shows the main window. (This example will illustrate events as well.)

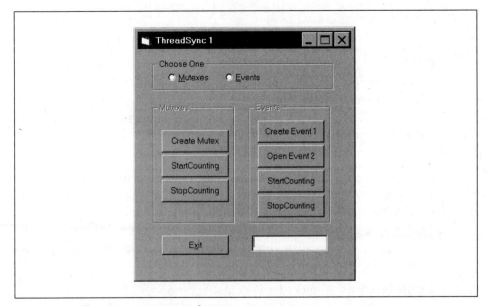

Figure 12-2. Illustrating mutexes and events

To run this example, run both *ThreadSync1.exe* and *ThreadSync2.exe* and place the forms side by side. Then choose the Mutexes option button on each form. Click on each of the Create Mutex command buttons and then on each of the Start Counting buttons. When you get bored, click on both Stop Counting buttons.

The complete code for these almost identical projects is on the CD. The heart of the projects is the following code, which is essentially a loop that counts to 5, releases the mutex, then waits for the mutex to become free again. That's it. Note that each application must release the mutex when done or else the other process will get caught in its wait cycle. The code for this is:

```
Private Sub cmdStartCountingMutex_Click()

Dim c As Long
Dim lret As Long
```

```
    gbStopCounting = False

Do
    c = c + 1
    txtCount.Text = c
    Delay 0.5
    If (c Mod 5) = 0 Then
        ' Release mutex so other process can get it
        lret = ReleaseMutex(hMutex)
        ' Then wait up to 1/2 minute for the mutex to become free again
        lret = WaitForSingleObject(hMutex, 1000 * 30)
    End If
Loop Until gbStopCounting

' To free other process
lret = ReleaseMutex(hMutex)

End Sub
```

Events

Events are used to signal that a certain task has been completed. Unlike mutexes, however, they are not owned by any thread.

For example, Thread A creates an event using *CreateEvent* and sets the event's state to nonsignaled. Thread B gets a handle to the event by calling *OpenEvent* and then calls *WaitForSingleObject* to suspend itself until Thread A completes a certain task and sets the event object to the signaled state. When this happens, the system wakes Thread B, which then knows that the task has been completed by Thread A.

The *CreateEvent* declaration is:

```
HANDLE CreateEvent(
    LPSECURITY_ATTRIBUTES lpEventAttributes,  // pointer to security attributes
    BOOL bManualReset,                        // flag for manual-reset event
    BOOL bInitialState,                       // flag for initial state
    LPCTSTR lpName                            // pointer to event-object name
);
```

This function returns a handle to the event object that it creates. The first parameter determines whether or not the handle is inheritable by child processes. If *lpEventAttributes* is NULL, then the handle cannot be inherited.

If the *bManualReset* parameter is TRUE, when the event is signaled, it remains signaled (unlike a mutex, for example). This implies that *all* threads waiting for the event to become signaled will be waked by the system. Such an event is referred to as a *manual-reset event*, because a waking thread must reset the event to the nonsignaled state if it so desires. On the other hand, if *bManualReset* is FALSE, then the system automatically unsignals the event after waking the *first* thread that is waiting for the event to become signaled. Thus, in this case, only one event is waked, as is the case with mutexes. In this case, the event is called an *auto-reset event*.

The *bInitialState* parameter determines the initial state (TRUE for signaled, FALSE for nonsignaled) of the event. Finally, the *lpName* parameter can be set to the name of the event. This provides a method for event sharing, via the *OpenEvent* function, for instance.

We can translate *CreateEvent* into VB as follows:

```
Declare Function CreateEvent Lib "kernel32" Alias "CreateEventA" ( _
    lpEventAttributes As SECURITY_ATTRIBUTES, _
    ByVal bManualReset As Long, _
    ByVal bInitialState As Long, _
    ByVal lpName As String _
) As Long
```

Alternatively, if we do not want to deal with security issues, we can set *lpEventAttributes* to NULL (0&), in which case we want the following declaration:

```
Declare Function CreateEvent Lib "kernel32" Alias "CreateEventA" ( _
    ByVal lpEventAttributes As Long, _
    ByVal bManualReset As Long, _
    ByVal bInitialState As Long, _
    ByVal lpName As String _
) As Long
```

As with other handles, an event handle should be closed using the *CloseHandle* function.

The *OpenEvent* function is:

```
HANDLE OpenEvent(
    DWORD dwDesiredAccess, // access flag
    BOOL bInheritHandle, // inherit flag
    LPCTSTR lpName // pointer to event-object name
);
```

where the *dwDesiredAccess* parameter can take one of three values:

EVENT_ALL_ACCESS
> Gives full access to the event.

EVENT_MODIFY_STATE
> Enables use of the event handle in the *SetEvent* and *ResetEvent* functions, so that the calling process can change the state of the event (but nothing else). This is important for manual-reset events.

SYNCHRONIZE
> Enables use of the event handle in any of the "Wait" functions (such as *WaitForSingleObject*) to wait for the event's state to be signaled.

The *OpenEvent* function can be declared in VB as:

```
Declare Function OpenEvent Lib "kernel32" Alias "OpenEventA" ( _
    ByVal dwDesiredAccess As Long, _
    ByVal bInheritHandle As Long, _
    ByVal lpName As String _
) As Long
```

The following declarations are also used with events:

```
Declare Function SetEvent Lib "kernel32" (ByVal hEvent As Long) As Long
Declare Function ResetEvent Lib "kernel32" (ByVal hEvent As Long) As Long
Declare Function PulseEvent Lib "kernel32" (ByVal hEvent As Long) As Long
```

Each of these takes an event handle as an argument. *SetEvent* sets the event's state to signaled, and *ResetEvent* unsignals the event. The *PulseEvent* function calls *SetEvent* to release waiting threads, and then calls *ResetEvent* to reset the event to its unsignaled state.

Example: Alternating Counters Using Events

The mutex example in Figure 12-2 also illustrates how the same goal can be achieved using two events. The main code is:

```
Private Sub cmdStartCountingEvent_Click()

Dim c As Long
Dim lret As Long

gbStopCounting = False

Do
    c = c + 1
    txtCount.Text = c
    Delay 0.5
    If (c Mod 5) = 0 Then
        ' Pulse event to signal other process
        lret = PulseEvent(hEvent1)
        ' and wait up to 30 seconds for the foreign event to be signaled
        lret = WaitForSingleObject(hEvent2, 1000 * 30)
    End If
Loop Until gbStopCounting

' To awake other process
lret = SetEvent(hEvent1)

End Sub
```

In this case, each application pulses its own event, signaling to the other application that its counting-to-five task is complete. Then it waits for a corresponding signal from the other application.

Once you have both *ThreadSync.exe* executables running, just click on the Create Event buttons in each project to create their respective events. Then click on each application's Open Event buttons to open the foreign event. Finally, click on the Start Counting buttons to start the counting process. When you get bored, click on the Stop Counting buttons.

Semaphores

Semaphores are used for resource counting. A semaphore is signaled when its *resource count* is positive and nonsignaled when its resource count is 0. In general, a positive resource count indicates that resources are available.

Accordingly, after a thread calls *WaitForSingleObject* and passes the handle of a semaphore, the system checks the resource count for that semaphore. If the count is positive (the semaphore is signaled), the *WaitForSingleObject* function returns, indicating that resources are available to the process (which can proceed to claim those resources). If the resource count is 0 (semaphore is nonsignaled), the system puts the thread to sleep until the resource count becomes positive, which would generally happen when some other process frees this particular resource. For this to work, when a thread frees the resource, it must also release the semaphore, in which case the system increments the resource count.

Thus, semaphores are good for sharing limited resources. For instance, suppose we had three applications that each wanted to print, but the computer has only two parallel ports. By setting up a semaphore with initial resource count equal to 2, we can force the applications to request printing only when there is an available parallel port.

Waiting Can Be Tricky

We should conclude this chapter by mentioning that sometimes waiting can be tricky. The problem stems from the fact that some threads need to be ready at a moment's notice to process messages from other applications. We will discuss messages in Chapter 16, *Windows Messages*, but suffice it to say here that some messages are broadcast to every window in the system. Now, if the thread that manages messages for a particular window is waiting for a signal from some mutex or event, for instance, then it cannot process incoming messages. This will cause a deadlock because the receiving application cannot process the message and the sending application cannot continue until it gets a response to its message!

The solution to this problem is to not send threads that are responsible for message processing into a wait state by calling *WaitForSingleObject*. Fortunately, this is not normally a problem in VB because, as VB programmers, we do not generally write code for threads that process messages.

13

Windows Memory Architecture

In this chapter, we take a look at how Windows NT and Windows 9x use memory. The primary purpose of this chapter is to give you some background on virtual memory and how it is used. As a rule, Visual Basic programmers don't generally need to manipulate memory directly, but we will see one important reason to do so when we discuss accessing foreign processes. In any case, the subject is both interesting and instructive, so I have decided to cover the highlights in this book.

Types of Memory

We should begin by defining our terms. Figure 13-1 shows some of the concepts involved.

Physical Memory

Physical memory is the actual RAM that is installed in a PC. Each byte of physical memory has a *physical address*, which is a number from 0 to one less than the number of bytes of physical memory. For instance, a PC with 64 MB of RAM has physical address &H0000 0000–&H0400 0000 in hex, which is 0–67,108,863 in decimal.

Physical memory (unlike pagefile and virtual memory discussed later) is *executable memory*, that is, memory that can be read or written to by the CPU through its instruction set. Thus, for instance, in the assembly language instruction:

```
mov [si], ax
```

the address in the `si` register must be a physical address in order for this instruction code to actually execute.

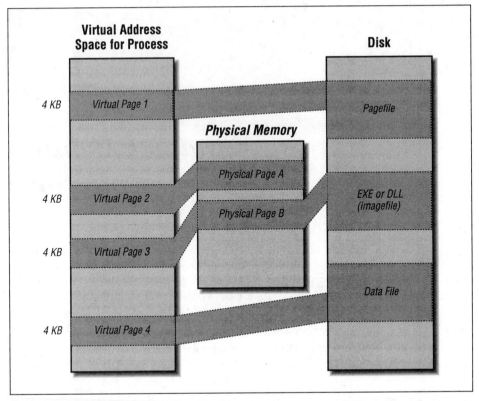

Figure 13-1. Types of memory

Virtual Memory

Virtual memory is simply a range of numbers, referred to as *virtual addresses*. It is nothing more. Thus, while a programmer can refer to a virtual address, Windows cannot access data at that address, since the address does not represent actual physical storage, as do physical and pagefile addresses. In order for code that refers to a virtual address to be executed, the virtual address must be *mapped* to a physical address, where the code or data can actually exist. This is done by the *virtual memory manager* (or VMM). We will discuss the operation of the VMM a bit later. The Windows operating system designates certain areas of virtual memory as *accessible*, that is, accessible to user mode code. All other areas are designated as *reserved*. Which areas are accessible and which are reserved varies with the operating system version (Windows 9x or Windows NT), as we will see in a moment.

Memory Page Frames

As you probably know, the smallest unit of memory that can be addressed is a byte. However, the smallest unit of memory that the Windows VMM deals with is a memory *page*, also called a memory *page frame*. On Intel-style computers, a page frame has size 4KB. We will speak of both *virtual pages* and *physical pages*.

Pagefile Memory

A *pagefile* (also called a *swap file* in Windows 95) is a file that resides on the hard disk. It is used for data and code storage just like physical memory, but is generally larger than physical memory. As we will discuss, Windows uses the pagefile (or pagefiles—there can be more than one) to store information that does not fit in RAM—swapping pages of information between the pagefile and RAM as needed.

Thus, a range of virtual addresses can correspond to addresses in a pagefile, rather than to addresses in physical memory (see Figure 13-1). When this happens, we say that the virtual addresses are *backed* by a pagefile, or *pagefile-backed*.

In general, a set of virtual addresses can be *backed* by physical memory, a pagefile, or indeed *any* file.

Memory-Mapped Files

In Chapter 10, *Objects and Their Handles*, we briefly discussed memory-mapped files and gave an example of file mapping. Simply put, *any file can be used to back virtual memory*, just as a pagefile is used in this way. In fact, a pagefile is a file that exists solely for the purpose of backing virtual memory.

When a file is mapped to memory in this way, the file is called a *memory-mapped file*. Each of the files in Figure 13-1 is memory-mapped. The corresponding virtual pages are *file-backed*.

Recall that the *CreateFileMapping* function is defined as:

```
Private Declare Function CreateFileMapping Lib "kernel32" Alias
"CreateFileMappingA" ( _
    ByVal hFile As Long, _
    ByVal lpSecurityAttributes As Long, _
    ByVal flProtect As Long, _
    ByVal dwMaximumSizeHigh As Long, _
    ByVal dwMaximumSizeLow As Long, _
    ByVal lpName As String _
) As Long
```

This function creates a *file-mapping object*, using the handle of an open file, and returns a handle to the file-mapping object. This handle can be used with the *MapViewOfFile* function:

```
Private Declare Function MapViewOfFile Lib "kernel32" ( _
    ByVal hFileMappingObject As Long, _
    ByVal dwDesiredAccess As Long, _
    ByVal dwFileOffsetHigh As Long, _
```

```
        ByVal dwFileOffsetLow As Long, _
        ByVal dwNumberOfBytesToMap As Long _
    ) As Long
```

to map the file to virtual memory. The starting address of the file mapping in virtual memory is returned by the *MapViewOfFile* function. We can also say that the view is *backed* by the file with handle *hFile*.

Note that if the *hFile* parameter to *CreateFileMapping* is set to –1, then the file-mapping object (and any views created from this object) are backed by the page-file, instead of a specified file.

Shared Physical Memory

Physical memory is said to be *shared* when it is mapped into the virtual address space of more than one process, although the virtual addresses may be different in each process. Figure 13-2 illustrates this concept.

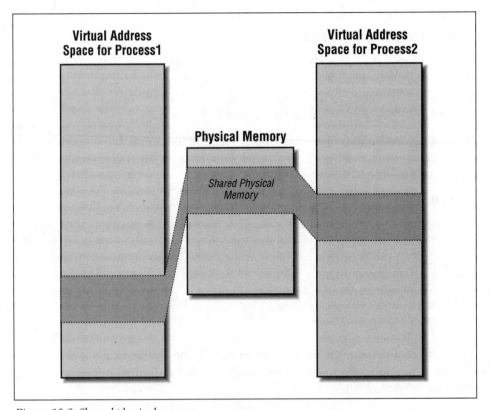

Figure 13-2. Shared physical memory

If a file, such as a DLL, is in shared physical memory, we may refer to the file as being *shared*.

One of the advantages of memory-mapped files is that they are easily shared. As we saw in Chapter 10, naming a file-mapping object makes it easy for more than one process to share the file. In this case, the file's contents are mapped to shared physical memory. Figure 13-3 illustrates this. Note that it is also possible to share pagefile contents through the use of file mappings. In particular, we can create a file-mapping object that is backed by a pagefile simply by setting the *hFile* parameter of the *CreateFileMapping* function to –1.

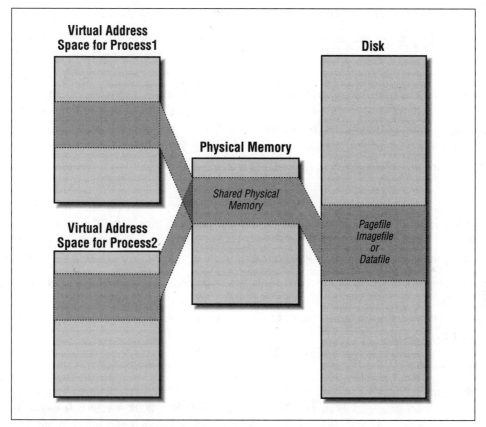

Figure 13-3. A shared file mapping

The Address Space of a Process

Every Win32 process gets a *virtual address space* (also called the *address space* or *process space*) of 4GB. Thus, the code within a process can refer to addresses &H0000 0000 through &HFFFF FFFF (or 0 through $2^{32}-1 = 4,294,967,295$ in decimal). Of course, since a virtual address is just a number, the statement that each process gets its *own* virtual address space is pretty much meaningless. (It is like saying that each person gets his or her own age range, say from 0 to 150.)

However, this statement is intended to mean that Windows does not draw any relationship between Process A's use of the virtual address &H4000 0000, for example, and Process B's use of the same virtual address &H4000 0000. In particular, Windows may (or may not) associate a different physical address to this virtual address for each process.

Windows NT and Windows 9x use virtual memory differently.

Windows NT Address Space Usage

Figure 13-4 shows the general use of a process address space under Windows NT.

Region A

Referring to Figure 13-4, Windows NT reserves the first 64KB of virtual memory for a special purpose and marks it as *inaccessible* to user mode code. When working with pointers, which VC++ programmers must do quite often, it is easy to forget to initialize a pointer. For instance, consider the following code:

```
int *pi;    // declare a  pointer to an integer
*pi = 5;    // point the pointer to an integer value
```

This code will not work. The problem is that a pointer must point to a *variable*, not a value. The first line of code declares a pointer, which initially contains the value 0. That is, it is a *NULL pointer*. The second line of code is thus trying to place the value 5 in memory location 0!

To alert programmers to this commonly made mistake, the lower portion of memory is reserved by Windows (both Windows NT and Windows 9x). As a result, code such as the previous example will cause a GPF, thus alerting the programmer to the error.

Region B

Referring to Figure 13-4, region B starts at the 64KB boundary and reaches up to 64 KB short of the 2GB mark. Thus, region B has size 2GB – 128KB (essentially half the entire address space). Portions of this region are mapped to the main EXE for the application, any application-specific DLLs, and system DLLs, such as *KERNEL32.DLL*, *USER32.DLL*, *GDI32.DLL*, and more.

To illustrate, Figure 13-5 shows the address space of an application called *Designer* (from Micrografx, Inc.). Note the following:

- The main EXE is located at &H40 0000, which is the default base address for a program written in VC++. (I do not know what development environment was used to write *Designer*.)

- An application-specific DLL called *DS70RES.DLL* is located at &H0135 0000, which is somewhat above the EXE.

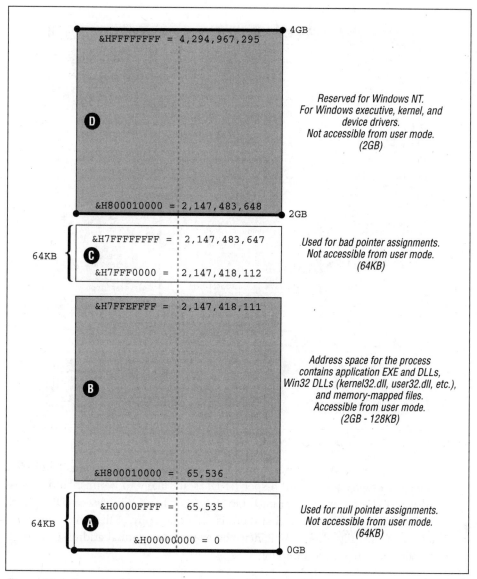

Figure 13-4. Process address space usage under Windows NT

- The next module (*rpcltc.dll*) at &H015B 0000 is a Microsoft DLL.

- There follow several Micrografx and Microsoft DLLs and even a Creative Labs DLL (*sb16snd.dll*)!

- The rest of the DLLs, starting with *COMCTR32.DLL*, are copyrighted by Microsoft. This includes *USER32.DLL* at &H77E7 0000, *GDI32.DLL* at &H77ED 0000, and *KERNEL32.DLL* at &H77F0 0000.

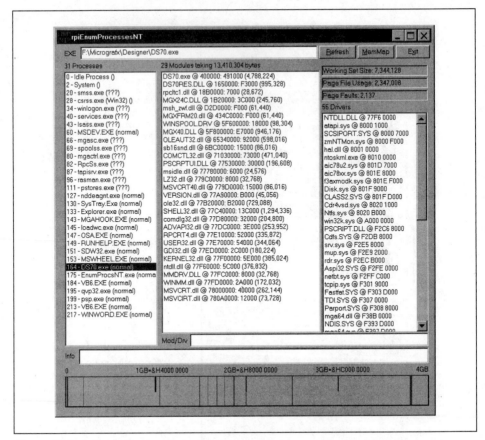

Figure 13-5. An example process space

It is worth remarking that this region may contain both shared and unshared files. For instance, *Designer*'s application-specific DLLs are likely to be unshared (unless other copies of *Designer* are running). On the other hand, the system DLLs, such as *KERNEL32.DLL,* are shared, in that there is only one copy of these DLLs in *physical* memory. Generally, this copy is mapped to the same virtual addresses in each process, but this is not a requirement.

Region C

Referring to Figure 13-4, region C is the 64KB region just below the 2GB mark, where Windows' reserved address space begins. It is used as a kind of barrier that prevents a programmer from using memory addresses that straddle the accessible region B and the inaccessible region D which belongs to Windows.

Region D

This region is reserved for use by Windows NT (the executive, kernel, and device drivers, for example). Applications cannot access memory in this virtual address range. Any attempt to do so will result in an access violation (a GPF).

Windows 9x Address Space Usage

Figure 13-6 shows the general use of a process address space under Windows 9x.

Region A

Referring to Figure 13-6, Windows 9x reserves region A, which is a mere 4 KB in size, for the same purpose as Windows NT reserves the first 64 KB of memory—as an alert for null pointers. This region is protected and will cause an access violation if we attempt to access this memory in user mode code.

Region B

The next region of memory (region B) is used to maintain compatibility with DOS and 16-bit Windows applications. Although it is accessible, a programmer should not use this region.

Region C

Region C is the address space used by application code and its DLLs. Also, Windows modules are placed in this region. For instance, if an application requires a custom control (OCX), the module will be located in this region.

Region D

Windows 9x maps the Win32 system DLLs (*KERNEL32.DLL, USER32.DLL,* and so on) into this address space. These files are shared, meaning that more than one process has access to a single copy of the files in physical memory.

This region of memory is accessible to user mode code (although I certainly would not recommend doing so).

Region E

This region also contains shared Windows files, such as the Windows executive and kernel, virtual device drivers, file system, and memory management code, and so on.

This region of memory is also accessible to user mode code.

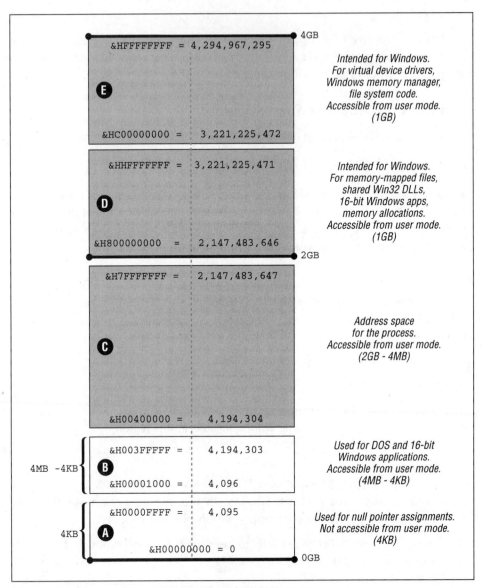

Figure 13-6. Process address space usage under Windows 9x

Example: Using GetSystemInfo

The *GetSystemInfo* API function retrieves some information about address spaces. Its syntax is:

```
VOID GetSystemInfo(
    LPSYSTEM_INFO lpSystemInfo // address of system information structure
);
```

or, in VB:

```
Declare Sub GetSystemInfo Lib "kernel32" Alias "GetSystemInfo" ( _
    lpSystemInfo As SYSTEM_INFO)
```

The system information structure is defined as:

```
struct _SYSTEM_INFO {
    union { DWORD dwOemId;
        struct {
            WORD wProcessorArchitecture;
            WORD wReserved;
        };
    };
    DWORD dwPageSize;
    LPVOID lpMinimumApplicationAddress;
    LPVOID lpMaximumApplicationAddress;
    DWORD dwActiveProcessorMask;
    DWORD dwNumberOfProcessors;
    DWORD dwProcessorType;
    DWORD dwAllocationGranularity;
    WORD wProcessorLevel;
    WORD wProcessorRevision;
}
```

A *union* is a VC++ construct that means that the variable in question can hold more than one data type at different times. For instance, a variable whose type is the following union:

```
union uExample {
    int i;
    char ch;
}
```

can be either an integer or a character. Of course, the system must set aside enough space for the largest possibility, in this case, 4 bytes for a VC++ integer. Naturally, we must do the same.

The SYSTEM_INFO structure contains a union whose members are a DWORD and another structure consisting of two WORDs. Thus, the size of the union is that of a DWORD (or two WORDs), which is 4 bytes.

We can define this structure in VB as:

```
Type SYSTEM_INFO
    wProcessorArchitecture As Long
    dwPageSize as Long
    lpMinimumApplicationAddress As Long
    lpMaximumApplicationAddress As Long
    dwActiveProcessorMask As Long
    dwNumberOfProcessors As Long
    dwProcessorType As Long
    dwAllocationGranularity As Long
    wProcessorLevel As Integer
    wProcessorRevision As Integer
End Type
```

Here is some code that calls *GetSystemInfo*, along with its output on my system:

```
Public Sub GetSystemInfoExample()

Dim si As SYSTEM_INFO
GetSystemInfo si
Debug.Print "Page size: " & si.dwPageSize
Debug.Print "Max app address: " & Hex(si.lpMaximumApplicationAddress)
Debug.Print "Min app address: " & Hex(si.lpMinimumApplicationAddress)
Debug.Print "Application Granularity: " & si.dwAllocationGranularity
Debug.Print "Processor architecture: " & si.wProcessorArchitecture
Debug.Print "Processor count: " & si.dwNumberOfProcessors
Debug.Print "Processor type: " & si.dwProcessorType
Debug.Print "Processor level: " & si.wProcessorLevel
Debug.Print "Processor revision: " & Hex(si.wProcessorRevision)

End Sub


Page size: 4096
Max app address: 7FFEFFFF
Min app address: 10000
Application Granularity: 65536
Processor architecture: 0
Processor count: 1
Processor type: 586
Processor level: 6
Processor revision: 501
```

This reports, as expected, that the page size is 4KB. Also, under Windows NT (which I am running), the minimum address for an application is &H1000 (= 64 KB) as expected from Figure 13-4. Similarly, the maximum application address is &H7FFE FFFF, as expected.

We will explain application granularity later.

According to the documentation, the *wProcessorArchitecture* variable is set to 0 to represent PROCESSOR_ARCHITECTURE_INTEL. (The *dwOemID* parameter is obsolete.) The processor level of 6 indicates a Pentium II processor. The processor revision number 501 is interpreted as Model 5 stepping 1. (For more details, please see the *GetSystemInfo* documentation.)

Allocating Virtual Memory

Each page of virtual address space can be in one of three states:

Reserved
The page has been reserved for use.

Committed
Physical storage is allocated for this virtual page. The storage is either in a pagefile or in a memory-mapped file.

Free

The page is neither reserved nor committed and is therefore currently not accessible to the process.

Virtual memory can be reserved or committed by calling the API function *VirtualAlloc*:

```
LPVOID VirtualAlloc(
    LPVOID lpAddress,        // address of region to reserve or commit
    DWORD dwSize,            // size of region
    DWORD flAllocationType,  // type of allocation
    DWORD flProtect          // type of access protection
);
```

The *flAllocationType* parameter can be set to the following constants (among others):

MEM_RESERVE

This simply reserves a range of the process's virtual address space without allocating any physical storage. (Storage can be allocated with a subsequent call to this function, however.)

MEM_COMMIT

This allocates physical storage in memory or in the paging file on disk for the specified *reserved* region of pages.

The two constants can be combined in order to reserve and commit in one operation.

Separating the process of reserving and committing memory has some advantages. For example, since reserving memory is a very efficient process, if an application should require a large amount of memory, it can reserve the entire amount but commit only the portion that it currently requires, thus spreading out the more time-consuming process of commitment of physical storage.

In fact, Windows itself uses this approach when it allocates a stack for each newly created thread. Windows reserves 1MB of virtual memory for each thread's stack but initially commits only two pages (8KB).

Memory protection

Note that the *flProtect* parameter of *VirtualAlloc* is used to specify the type of access protection to accord the newly *committed* virtual memory (this does not apply to reserved memory). The choices are:

PAGE_READONLY

Gives read-only access to the committed virtual memory.

PAGE_READWRITE

Gives read-write access to the committed virtual memory.

PAGE_WRITECOPY

   Gives copy-on-write access to the committed virtual memory. We will discuss
   this a bit later.

PAGE_EXECUTE

   Enables execute access to the committed virtual memory. Any attempt to read
   or write to the memory, however, will result in an access violation.

PAGE_EXECUTE_READ

   Enables execute and read access.

PAGE_EXECUTE_READWRITE

   Enables execute, read, and write access.

PAGE_EXECUTE_WRITECOPY

   Enables execute, read, and copy-on-write access.

PAGE_NOACCESS

   Disables all access to the committed virtual memory.

In addition, any of these values except PAGE_NOACCESS can be ORed with the following two flags.

PAGE_GUARD

   Designates the pages as *guard pages*. Any attempt to access a guard page
   causes the system to raise a STATUS_GUARD_PAGE exception and turn off the
   guard page status. Thus, guard pages raise a first-access-only alarm.

PAGE_NOCACHE

   Prevents caching of the committed memory.

Let us explain copy-on-write. Suppose that a certain page of physical memory is
being shared by two processes. If the page is marked as read-only, then the two
processes can share the page without problems. However, there may be situations
in which we want to permit each process to write to this memory but not to affect
the other process. By setting the protection to *copy-on-write*, as soon as one process attempts to write to the shared page, the system makes a copy of that page
exclusively for the process that wants to do the writing. Thus, the page is no
longer shared and the other process's view of the data remains unchanged.

We note also that the protection attributes of a page can be changed using the
VirtualProtect API function.

Allocation granularity

Note that if the *lpAddress* parameter is not a multiple of 64KB, then the system
will round down the requested address to the nearest multiple of 64KB. Windows
always reserves virtual memory starting on an *allocation granularity boundary*,
which, in the case of Intel-style processors, is a multiple of 64KB. In other words,
the starting address of any block of reserved memory is a multiple of 64KB.

In addition, the amount of memory that is allocated is always a multiple of the system's page size, that is, of 4KB. Hence, *VirtualAlloc* will round up any memory request to the nearest multiple of the page size.

Incidentally, there are times when Windows allocates virtual memory on behalf of a process, but for Windows' own use. In these cases, Windows does not always follow the rules about allocation granularity boundaries that it follows when allocating memory requested by a programmer (although page size requirements are honored).

The Virtual Address Descriptor

Finally, in case you are wondering, the system keeps track of which virtual pages are reserved in a structure called a *Virtual Address Descriptor* or VAD. This is essential because there is no other way to tell when virtual addresses have been reserved.

Example: Using GlobalMemoryStatus

The API function *GlobalMemoryStatus*:

```
Declare Sub GlobalMemoryStatus Lib "kernel32" Alias "GlobalMemoryStatus" ( _
    lpBuffer As MEMORYSTATUS)
```

reports on a variety of memory-related values by filling in the following structure:

```
struct _MEMORYSTATUS {
    DWORD dwLength;          // sizeof(MEMORYSTATUS)
    DWORD dwMemoryLoad;      // percent of memory in use
    DWORD dwTotalPhys;       // bytes of physical memory
    DWORD dwAvailPhys;       // free physical memory bytes
    DWORD dwTotalPageFile;   // bytes of paging file
    DWORD dwAvailPageFile;   // free bytes of paging file
    DWORD dwTotalVirtual;    // user bytes of address space
    DWORD dwAvailVirtual;    // free user bytes
}
```

In VB, this is:

```
Type MEMORYSTATUS
    dwLength  As Long           'sizeof(MEMORYSTATUS)
    dwMemoryLoad  As Long       'percent of memory in use
    dwTotalPhys  As Long        'bytes of physical memory
    dwAvailPhys  As Long        'free physical memory bytes
    dwTotalPageFile  As Long    'bytes of paging file
    dwAvailPageFile  As Long    'free bytes of paging file
    dwTotalVirtual  As Long     'user bytes of address space
    dwAvailVirtual  As Long     'free user bytes
End Type
```

For example, the code:

```
Dim ms As MEMORYSTATUS
GlobalMemoryStatus ms
Debug.Print "Virtual memory: " & ms.dwTotalVirtual
Debug.Print "Short of 2 GB: " & (2 ^ 31 - ms.dwTotalVirtual) / 1024 & " KB"
Debug.Print "Available Virtual: " & ms.dwAvailVirtual
```

might produce:

```
Virtual memory: 2147352576
Short of 2 GB: 128 KB
Available Virtual: 1965658112
```

Note that the available virtual memory is 128KB less than the 2GBs in the lower half of the total address space of a process, as we would expect from Figure 13-4.

Virtual Memory Management

We want to take a look next at how the Windows virtual memory manager (abbreviated VMM) actually interprets virtual memory addresses as physical addresses.

Translating Virtual Addresses to Physical Addresses: Page Hits

Figure 13-7 shows the translation process when the virtual address is mapped to a physical address. This situation is referred to as a (physical) *page hit*.

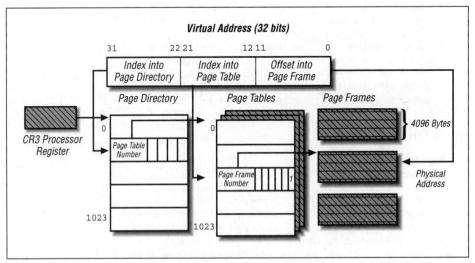

Figure 13-7. Virtual-to-physical address resolution for a page hit

All virtual addresses are divided into three parts. The leftmost part (bits 22–31) contains an index into the process's *page directory*. Windows maintains a separate page directory for each process. The address of this page directory is placed in a CPU register called CR3. (Incidentally, part of the task-switching process is to switch this register so that it points to the incoming process's page directory.) A page directory contains 1024 4-byte entries.

Windows also maintains, for each process, a collection of *page tables*. Each page directory entry contains a page table number, which identifies a particular page table. Thus, Windows supports up to 1024 page tables. (Actually, page tables are created only when needed, that is, when an attempt is made to *access* data or code at a given virtual address, not simply when the virtual memory is allocated.)

The second part of the virtual address (bits 12–21) is used as an index into the page table corresponding to the page directory entry. The page table entry at this index contains, in its leftmost 20 bits, a page frame number that identifies a particular page frame in physical memory.

The third and final part of the virtual address (bits 0–11) is an offset into that page frame. The combination of page frame number and offset into that page frame constitutes a physical address in physical memory.

Since each page table has 1024 entries and there are 1024 page tables, the total number of page frames that can be identified in this manner is $1024 \times 1024 = 2^{10} \times 2^{10} = 2^{20}$. Since each page frame is $4KB = 4 \times 2^{10}$ bytes in size, the theoretical limit of physical addresses is $4 \times 2^{30} = 4GB$.

This rather complex-looking translation scheme has several important advantages. One immediate advantage is that page frames are very small and can easily be kept in memory. It is much easier to find 4KB of consecutive physical memory than, say, 64KB.

However, the main advantage is that a virtual memory address from two processes can be deliberately made to point to different physical addresses or be deliberately made to point to the same physical address!

To illustrate, suppose that Process1 and Process2 both refer in code to the same virtual address. Process1's virtual-to-physical address resolution uses its page directory, and Process2's translation uses its page directory. Thus, while the *indices* into the page directories are the same in both cases, these indices are indices into *different* directories. In this way, the VMM can assure that the virtual addresses in each process resolve to different physical addresses.

On the other hand, the VMM can also ensure that virtual addresses in the two processes, whether they be the same virtual address or not, can resolve to the same physical address. One way to do this would be to have both page directory entries point to the same page table, and thus to the same page frames. In this way, processes can share physical memory.

System page directory and page tables

We should also mention that Windows maintains a *system page directory* to deal with virtual memory reserved for Windows, as well as a corresponding set of *system page tables*.

Format of a valid page table entry

A page table entry is said to be valid when it points to a physical page frame, as in Figure 13-7. Figure 13-8 shows the format of a valid page table entry (some data is omitted).

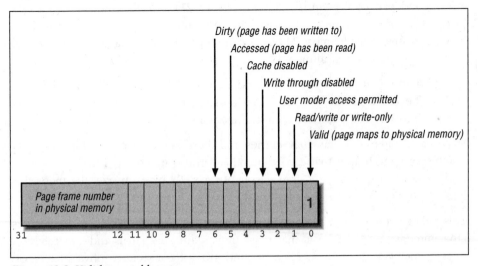

Figure 13-8. Valid page table entry

Note that a page table entry contains flags that describe various properties of the page frame, such as whether or not it has been written to or read from and whether or not access is permitted to this memory from user mode code. The least significant bit is the *valid bit* (also called a *present bit*), signaling that this entry is valid.

Translating Virtual Addresses to Physical Addresses: Page Faults

If a virtual page is not backed by physical memory, but is backed instead by a pagefile, then the translation process will come a cropper, resulting in a *page fault*. The situation is pictured in Figure 13-9.

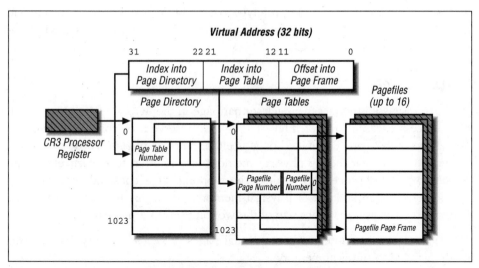

Figure 13-9. Virtual-to-physical address resolution for a page fault

In this case, the system will see that the page table entry is invalid, having its least significant bit set to 0. The format of an invalid page table entry whose page is backed by a pagefile is shown in Figure 13-10.

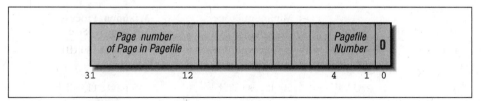

Figure 13-10. A page table entry backed by a pagefile

The fact that the valid bit is 0 tells the system that the page table entry contains a pagefile number between 0 and 15 that identifies the pagefile that backs the virtual address. The page table entry also contains the number of the page within the pagefile that backs the virtual address. The system can then copy that pagefile page into physical memory, change the page table entry from an invalid one to a valid one, and use the 12 bits of the virtual address as an offset into the physical page frame, just as before. This process is referred to as *paging*.

Shared Pages

Our discussion so far concerns unshared physical memory only. The situation for shared physical memory is considerably more complex, and we will not go into the details here, except to say that the VMM uses a concept called *prototype page table entries*. The idea is simply to point the ordinary page table entry in each process with shared memory to a single prototype page table entry, instead of to physical memory. In this way, a single prototype page table entry can point to shared physical memory.

Working Sets

We have discussed the fact that each virtual page in the 4GB virtual address space of a process exists in one of three states—free, reserved, or committed. We can now also say that each committed page is either *valid* or *invalid*. Those pages that are valid, that is, backed by physical memory, are referred to collectively as the *working set* of the process. Of course, the working set is constantly changing, as pages are paged in and out of physical memory. Recall that the *rpiEnumProcsNT* utility also displays the current size of the working set for a process.

The *system working set* describes the virtual pages of *system* memory that are currently mapped to physical memory.

The size of a process's working set is limited by minimum and maximum settings that Windows makes, based on the size of physical memory. The settings are described in Table 13-1.

Table 13-1. Process Working Set Size Limits

Memory Model	Memory Size	Minimum Process Working Set Size	Maximum Process Working Set Size
Small	<=19MB	20 pages (80KB)	45 pages (180KB)
Medium	20–32MB	30 pages (120KB)	145 pages (580KB)
Large	>=32MB	50 pages (200KB)	345 pages (1380KB)

Note that these limits can be changed using the API function *SetProcessWorking-SetSize*:

```
BOOL SetProcessWorkingSetSize(
    HANDLE hProcess,                // open handle to the process of interest
    DWORD dwMinimumWorkingSetSize, // specifies minimum working set size in bytes
    DWORD dwMaximumWorkingSetSize  // specifies maximum working set size in bytes
);
```

Incidentally, setting both of the size parameters to −1 will cause the function to reduce the working set to size 0, thus temporarily removing the process from physical memory.

We also note that the actual size of a process's working set will vary with time, since Windows will increase the working set if it notices that the process is incurring a large number of page faults.

The *system* working set size limits are described in Table 13-2.

Table 13-2. System Working Set Size Limits

Memory Model	Memory Size	Minimum Process Working Set Size	Maximum Process Working Set Size
Small	<=19MB	388 pages (1.5MB)	500 pages (2.0MB)
Medium	20–32MB	688 pages (2.7MB)	1150 pages (4.5MB)
Large	>=32MB	1188 pages (4.6MB)	2050 pages (8MB)

The Page Frame Database

Windows keeps track of the state of each *physical* page of memory in a data structure called the *Page Frame Database*. Each physical page can be in one of eight different states:

Active (or valid)

This page is currently mapped to virtual memory. Thus, it is the target of a working set page.

Transition

On its way to becoming an active page.

Standby

The page was just removed from active status, but it was not modified while active.

Modified

The page has been removed from active status. Its contents were modified while it was active, but have not yet been written to disk.

Modified No Write

Similar to modified but marked so that the contents will not be flushed to disk. Used by the Windows file system drivers.

Free

The page is free but has been written to and is thus not eligible for use by a process.

Zeroed

The page is free and initialized to all 0s by the zero page thread. This page can be allocated to a process.

Bad

The page has incurred parity errors or some other hardware problem and will not be used.

Heaps of Memory

Simply put, a *heap* is a region of virtual memory that has been reserved by Windows. The Win32 API supplies functions for allocating memory from a heap, freeing heap memory, and resizing blocks of allocated memory. In short, these functions provide a more intuitive method for manipulating application memory than *VirtualAlloc* and are especially suited for manipulating a large number of small blocks of memory. Although VB programmers don't have any direct use for heaps, the concept does appear quite often in documentation, so we should discuss it briefly.

Heaps Under 32-Bit Windows

When a process is created, Windows assigns it a *default heap*. That is, Windows initially reserves a 1MB region of virtual memory. However, the system will adjust the size of the default heap as necessary. The default heap is used by Windows itself in a variety of ways. For instance, as discussed in Chapter 6, *Strings*, Visual Basic translates Unicode strings to ANSI for passing to the ANSI entry points of a DLL. Memory for these temporary ANSI strings is obtained from the default heap. The API function *GetProcessHeap* is used to obtain a handle to the default heap. A programmer can also create additional heaps using the *HeapCreate* function, which returns a heap handle.

There are several reasons why a programmer might want to create additional heaps rather than using the default heap. For example, heaps that are dedicated to a particular task are often more efficient. Also, errors made in writing data to heap memory allocated from a dedicated heap will not affect data in other heaps. Finally, allocating memory from a dedicated heap will generally mean that the data is packed more closely together in memory, which may reduce the need for paging data from the pagefile. We should also mention that access to a heap is *serialized*, that is, the system makes each thread attempting access to heap memory wait its turn until other threads are finished. In this way, only one thread at a time can allocate or free heap memory, thus avoiding unpleasant conflicts.

Incidentally, the 16-bit version of Windows supported both a *global heap* and a *local heap*. Accordingly, 16-bit Windows implemented the functions *GlobalAlloc* and *LocalAlloc*. These functions still work, but are not very efficient and should be avoided under Win32. (We will see, however, that they still *must* be used for certain purposes, such as creating a Clipboard viewer.)

Heap Functions

The following functions are used with heaps:

GetProcessHeap
    Returns a handle to the default heap for the process.

GetProcessHeaps
    Returns a list of the handles for all heaps currently used by a process.

HeapAlloc

Allocates a block of memory from the specified heap.

HeapCompact

Defragments a heap by combining free blocks. It can also decommit unused pages of heap memory.

HeapCreate

Creates a new heap in the process's address space.

HeapDestroy

Destroys the specified heap.

HeapFree

Frees a previously allocated heap memory block.

HeapLock

Locks a heap so that only a single thread has access to the heap. Other threads requesting access are suspended until the owning thread unlocks the heap. This provides a form of thread synchronization. This is also how the system enforces thread serialization.

HeapReAlloc

Reallocates a block of memory on the heap. Used to change a block's size.

HeapSize

Returns the size of an allocated heap memory block.

HeapUnlock

Unlocks a heap that was previously locked using the *HeapLock* function.

HeapValidate

Verifies that a heap (or block within a heap) is valid; that is, that it has not been corrupted.

HeapWalk

Allows the programmer to walk the contents of a heap. Used mostly for debugging purposes.

Example: Mapping Virtual Memory

The Win32 API function *VirtualQuery* can be used to get information about the state of virtual memory addresses. The syntax is:

```
DWORD VirtualQuery(
    LPCVOID lpAddress,                       // address of region
    PMEMORY_BASIC_INFORMATION lpBuffer, // address of information buffer
    DWORD dwLength                           // size of buffer
);
```

In VB, this can be declared as:

```
Declare Function VirtualQuery Lib "kernel32" ( _
    ByVal lpAddress As Long, _
```

```
    lpBuffer As MEMORY_BASIC_INFORMATION, _
    ByVal dwLength As Long _
) As Long
```

There is also *VirtualQueryEx*, an extended version of *VirtualQuery* that permits looking at foreign virtual address spaces:

```
DWORD VirtualQueryEx(
    HANDLE hProcess,                     // handle to process
    LPCVOID lpAddress,                   // address of region
    PMEMORY_BASIC_INFORMATION lpBuffer,  // address of information buffer
    DWORD dwLength                       // size of buffer
);
```

or, in VB:

```
Declare Function VirtualQueryEx Lib "kernel32" ( _
    ByVal hProcess As Long, _
    ByVal lpAddress As Long, _
    lpBuffer As MEMORY_BASIC_INFORMATION, _
    ByVal dwLength As Long _
) As Long
```

As expected, the *hProcess* parameter requires a process handle. The *lpAddress* parameter is the starting address on which to report, but it will be rounded down to the closest multiple of the page size (4KB). Both functions return information in the structure:

```
struct _MEMORY_BASIC_INFORMATION {
    PVOID BaseAddress;       // base address of region
    PVOID AllocationBase;    // allocation base address
    DWORD AllocationProtect; // initial access protection
    DWORD RegionSize;        // size, in bytes, of region
    DWORD State;             // committed, reserved, free
    DWORD Protect;           // current access protection
    DWORD Type;              // type of pages
}
```

or, in VB:

```
Type MEMORY_BASIC_INFORMATION
    BaseAddress As Long           'base address of region
    AllocationBase As Long        'allocation base address
    AllocationProtect As Long     'initial access protection
    RegionSize As Long            'size, in bytes, of region
    State As Long                 'committed, reserved, free
    Protect As Long               'current access protection
    Type As Long                  'type of pages
End Type
```

To understand the members of this structure, we need to describe what the function does. Unfortunately, the documentation does a rotten job of explaining this function, but it appears to perform as follows. To aid our discussion, let us refer to the page containing the address *lpAddress* as the *specified page*. Figure 13-11 will help define our terms.

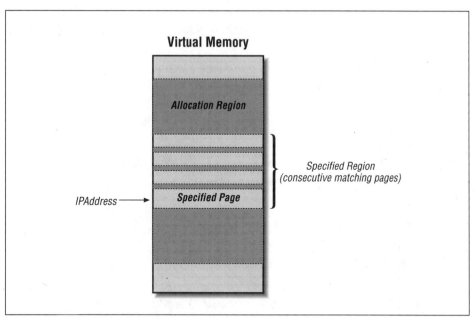

Figure 13-11. The VirtualQuery(Ex) function

The following members of MEMORY_BASIC_INFORMATION are always set by *VirtualQuery(Ex)*:

BaseAddress

    Returns the base address of the specified page.

RegionSize

    The number of bytes from the start of the specified page to the top of the *specified region*. Despite the name, this is *not* generally the size of the *entire* specified region. We will define the term *specified region* later in this chapter.

If the page containing *lpAddress* is free (neither reserved nor committed), the State member contains the symbolic constant MEM_FREE. No other member (except BaseAddress and RegionSize) has meaning.

If the page containing *lpAddress* is not free, the function identifies the *allocation region* containing the specified page, that is, the region of virtual memory that contains the specified page and was originally allocated by a call to *VirtualAlloc*.

Starting at the base address of the specified page, the function examines each successive page in the allocation region, checking to see if it *matches* the specified page in allocation type and protection type. The collection of all consecutive matching pages is the *specified region*. The values in the MEMORY_BASIC_INFORMATION structure refer to this region. Specifically, a page matches the specified page if it satisfies the following two conditions.

- The page has the same *allocation type* as the initial page, as reflected by the flag values: MEM_COMMIT, MEM_RESERVE, MEM_FREE, MEM_PRIVATE, MEM_MAPPED, or MEM_IMAGE.

- The page has the same *protection type* as the initial page as reflected by the flag values: PAGE_READONLY, PAGE_READWRITE, PAGE_NOACCESS, PAGE_WRITECOPY, PAGE_EXECUTE, PAGE_EXECUTE_READ, PAGE_EXECUTE_READWRITE, PAGE_EXECUTE_WRITECOPY, PAGE_GUARD, or PAGE_NOCACHE.

Now we can describe the other members of the MEMORY_BASIC_INFORMATION structure:

AllocationBase

The base address of the allocation region.

AllocationProtect

The *initial* protection type of the allocation region.

State

Either MEM_FREE, MEM_RESERVE, or MEM_COMMIT. Refers to the specified region.

Protect

The current protection type of the specified region.

Type

Either MEM_IMAGE, MEM_MAPPED, or MEM_PRIVATE. Refers to the specified region. The meanings of these constants are as follows: MEM_IMAGE indicates that the region is mapped to an *image* (that is, executable) file; MEM_MAPPED indicates that the region is mapped to a nonexecutable memory-mapped file (such as a data file); MEM_PRIVATE indicates that the region is private, that is, not shared by more than one process.

Finally, we note that these functions return the size of the MEMORY_BASIC_INFORMATION structure.

The following procedure fills a list box with a virtual memory map. You will find this procedure in the *rpiEnumProcsNT* and *rpiEnumProcs95* applications on the CD.

```
Sub MapMemory(lProcessID As Long)

Dim hProcess As Long
Dim lret As Long
Dim meminfo As MEMORY_BASIC_INFORMATION
Dim lCurRegion As Long
Dim sName As String
Dim sItem As String
Dim Tabstops(1 To 5) As Long
Dim bIsFree As Boolean
```

```
lstMain.FontName = "Courier New"
lstMain.FontSize = 9

' Get process handle from process ID
hProcess = ProcHndFromProcID(lProcessID)
If hProcess = 0 Then Stop

lstMain.Clear

' Set tab stops for list box
Tabstops(1) = 4 * 22
Tabstops(2) = Tabstops(1) + 4 * 10
Tabstops(3) = Tabstops(2) + 4 * 10
Tabstops(4) = Tabstops(3) + 4 * 12
SendMessage lstMain.hWnd, LB_SETTABSTOPS, 5, Tabstops(1)

Do
    ' Get info on this region
    lret = VirtualQueryEx(hProcess, lCurRegion, meminfo, LenB(meminfo))

    ' Is it free?
    bIsFree = (meminfo.State = MEM_FREE)

    ' Build item for list box
    sItem = Hex(lCurRegion) & " - " & Hex(lCurRegion + meminfo.RegionSize - 1) _
        & vbTab & meminfo.RegionSize / 4096 & " pp" _
        & vbTab & MemType(meminfo.State)

    If Not bIsFree Then
        sItem = sItem & vbTab & MemType(meminfo.Type) _
          & vbTab & AccessType(meminfo.Protect)
    End If

    ' Get module name. Skip 0, since this gives EXE name.
    If lCurRegion > 0 And Not bIsFree Then
        sName = String$(MAX_PATH + 1, 0)
        lret = GetModuleFileName(lCurRegion, sName, MAX_PATH)
        If lret <> 0 Then sItem = sItem & vbTab & Trim0(sName)
    End If

    ' Display
    lstMain.AddItem sItem

    ' Next start of region
    lCurRegion = lCurRegion + meminfo.RegionSize

    If lCurRegion >= &H7FFEFFFF Then Exit Do
Loop

CloseHandle hProcess

End Sub
```

A portion of the output for one process is shown here:

```
0 - FFFF      16 pp  FREE
10000 - 10FFF   1 pp    COMMIT    PRIVATE   READWRITE
11000 - 1FFFF  15 pp    FREE
20000 - 20FFF   1 pp    COMMIT    PRIVATE   READWRITE
21000 - 2FFFF  15 pp    FREE
30000 - 12CFFF 253 pp   RESERVE   PRIVATE   0
12D000 - 12DFFF 1 pp    COMMIT    PRIVATE   260
12E000 - 12FFFF 2 pp    COMMIT    PRIVATE   READWRITE
130000 - 130FFF 1 pp    COMMIT    PRIVATE   READWRITE
131000 - 13FFFF 15 pp   FREE
140000 - 158FFF 25 pp   COMMIT    PRIVATE   READWRITE
159000 - 23FFFF 231 pp  RESERVE   PRIVATE   0
240000 - 240FFF 1 pp    COMMIT    MAPPED    READWRITE
241000 - 24FFFF 15 pp   RESERVE   MAPPED    0
250000 - 265FFF 22 pp   COMMIT    MAPPED    READONLY
266000 - 26FFFF 10 pp   FREE
270000 - 293FFF 36 pp   COMMIT    MAPPED    READONLY
294000 - 29FFFF 12 pp   FREE
2A0000 - 2E0FFF 65 pp   COMMIT    MAPPED    READONLY
2E1000 - 2EFFFF 15 pp   FREE
2F0000 - 2F2FFF 3 pp    COMMIT    MAPPED    READONLY
2F3000 - 2FFFFF 13 pp   FREE
300000 - 305FFF 6 pp    COMMIT    MAPPED    EXECUTE_READ
306000 - 3BFFFF 186 pp  RESERVE   MAPPED    0
3C0000 - 3C0FFF 1 pp    COMMIT    MAPPED    EXECUTE_READ
3C1000 - 3C7FFF 7 pp    RESERVE   MAPPED    0
3C8000 - 3FFFFF 56 pp   FREE
400000 - 400FFF 1 pp    COMMIT    IMAGE     READONLY G:\Visual Studio\VB98\VB6.
EXE
401000 - 40BFFF 11 pp   COMMIT    IMAGE     EXECUTE_READ
40C000 - 40DFFF 2 pp    COMMIT    IMAGE     READWRITE
```

Two utility functions used in *MapMemory* are:

```
Function MemType(vValue As Variant) As String
' Function returns name of constant for given value.
Dim sName As String
Select Case vValue
    Case &H1000
        sName = "COMMIT"
    Case &H2000
        sName = "RESERVE"
    Case &H4000
        sName = "DECOMMIT"
    Case &H8000
        sName = "RELEASE"
    Case &H10000
        sName = "FREE"
    Case &H20000
        sName = "PRIVATE"
    Case &H40000
        sName = "MAPPED"
    Case &H80000
        sName = "RESET"
```

```
    Case &H100000
        sName = "TOP_DOWN"
    Case &H1000000
        sName = "IMAGE"
    Case Else
        sName = vValue
End Select
MemType = sName
End Function
' ------------------
Function AccessType(vValue As Variant) As String
' Function returns name of constant for given value.
Dim sName As String
Select Case vValue
    Case &H1
        sName = "NOACCESS"
    Case &H2
        sName = "READONLY"
    Case &H4
        sName = "READWRITE"
    Case &H8
        sName = "WRITECOPY"
    Case &H10
        sName = "EXECUTE"
    Case &H20
        sName = "EXECUTE_READ"
    Case &H40
        sName = "EXECUTE_READWRITE"
    Case &H80
        sName = "EXECUTE_WRITECOPY"
    Case &H100
        sName = "GUARD"
    Case &H200
        sName = "NOCACHE"
    Case Else
        sName = vValue
End Select
AccessType = sName
End Function
```

14

Portable Executable Files

In this chapter, we will discuss executable files. Our main goal is to create a VB application that will display various information about a given executable file, including the file's *export table*, which is a list of the functions that the DLL makes available to calling programs. This application is called *rpiPEInfo*.

Executable files are files that have the *Portable Executable File* format, or PE file format. According to the documentation:

> The name "Portable Executable" refers to the fact that the format is not architecture-specific.

However, this seems to be in contradiction to the presence of a *machine flag* in the file (discussed later) about which the documentation states:

> An image file can be run only on the specified machine, or a system emulating it.

In any case, PE files include EXE and DLL files, as well as OCX, DRV, and other files. Unfortunately, however, the term executable file is often applied just to EXE files. (We will *not* do this.) Executable files are also often called *image files*.

By the way, closely related to PE files are the files that are produced by compilers, such as Visual C++. These are called *object files* and have the *Common Object File Format* (or COFF). You will often hear these types of files mentioned in the same sentence with PE files.

The PE file format is extremely complex, and this is no doubt exasperated by the fact that the format is poorly documented in the MSDN library. Our intention is just to give a reasonable amount of detail, but by no means a complete description of the format. You should feel free to skim over some of this material and use it as a reference for future needs.

Module Relocation

As we have mentioned, each module has a *default base address* that is stored in the file itself. The default base address for a DLL compiled under Visual C++ is &10000000 and under Visual Basic it is &H11000000, although these addresses can easily be changed. (In VB, we can change the default base address using the Compile tab of the Project Properties dialog.)

When a module (DLL, OCX, etc.) is loaded into the address space of a process, Windows attempts to place the module at its default base address. However, if there is another module located at that address, a conflict arises and Windows must *relocate* the new module.

There are some interesting and not very well publicized consequences of module relocation that can be important to understand, especially since these consequences can have a negative effect on an application's performance.

The problem with relocation is this. Executable files contain references to memory addresses. For instance, the object code corresponding to the source code:

```
Dim i As Integer
i = 5
```

will contain a reference to a memory location containing data (the number 5). This is a *direct memory reference.*

Also, the function call:

```
Call AFunction(7)
```

is actually a jump to the address of the function *AFunction.* Since this jump is made relative to the address of the **Call** instruction, the object code for this function call will contain the *offset* from the address of the function call to the address of the function itself. This is a *relative memory reference.* Keep in mind that the function *AFunction* may be in the same executable file as the call to that function or it may be in another executable file.

Now, since actual addresses cannot be known at link time (when the executable is constructed), the linker cannot replace the object code for the examples above with the actual addresses. The best it can do is use addresses that are *relative* to some other location in the module.

For a direct reference, the address is relative to the *default* base address of the module. For instance, suppose that the base address of a module is &H10000000. If the memory variable *i* has offset 100 (say) from the start of the module, then the machine language instruction to place the value 5 in that location might look something like the following (in assembly language):

```
mov dword ptr [01000100], 5
```

Note the presence of the base address. In short, *the base address of the executable is hardcoded into the executable.*

A similar problem arises when a call is to a function that is contained in a *different* module (such as another DLL). If the base address of the other DLL is, say, &12000000, the jump instruction would be relative to that base address.

Now, the problem is that there is no guarantee that a module will be loaded at its default base address. In fact, only one module can be loaded at any given address, and, as you can see from our process viewing utility, a process space may have a great many modules. It is not surprising that two modules might have the same default base address.

Fortunately, Microsoft has been careful about assigning default base addresses to its modules in such a way as to minimize conflicts. You can see this by browsing the *rpiEnumProcs* utility. However, all modules that we create in VB (or VC++) will have the same default base address unless we specify otherwise.

In order that a module be relocatable, executable files contain *relocation information* for the *relocatable code* in the file, that is, the code that may need adjustment if the file is not loaded at its default base address. This relocation information is also called *fixup* information or *fixups.*

Now, if a module needs to be relocated for a particular process, its relocatable code needs to be changed for that process, but not for any other process that is using this module. Suppose, for instance, that Process1 has Module1 loaded into its address space at Module1's default address. Process2 wants to load Module1, but it already has a module loaded at Module1's default base address. Thus, Module1 will need to be relocated in Process2's address space, which will necessitate some changes to the relocatable code in Module1. Since Process1 cannot tolerate any changes to the code for Module1, Windows must make a new *physical* copy of Module1 so that it can perform the necessary fixups and map the module into the virtual address space of Process2. This is done using the copy-on-write mechanism that we discussed earlier.

The point, of course, is not only that this copy-on-write process requires additional processor time, but also that the new *physical* copy of the module uses additional precious *physical* memory. Thus, it behooves us to attempt to minimize base address conflicts when creating modules.

The PE File Format

Now we are ready to discuss the format of an executable file. Recall that our main goal is to create the *rpiPEInfo* application that displays various information about a given executable file, including the file's export table.

The overall structure of a PE file is:

- PE file header
    - MS-DOS stub
    - PE signature
    - COFF file header (also sometimes called the PE header!)
    - Optional header
- Section table (table of section headers)
- Sections

Figure 14-1 shows the overall structure in more detail.

The PE File Header

A PE file begins with a *PE file header*, which consists of the following items:

- MS-DOS stub
- PE signature
- COFF file header
- Optional header

MS-DOS stub

The PR file header begins with the *MS-DOS stub*, which is an actual DOS application that by default just prints the message: "This program cannot be run in DOS mode" when the image is run in DOS mode.

The PE signature

Following the DOS stub is the *PE signature*. The PE signature lies at the file offset specified at location &H3C and currently consists of the four bytes:

```
"P"/"E"/NULL/NULL
```

(Of course, there is nothing to prevent a non-PE file from having this signature.)

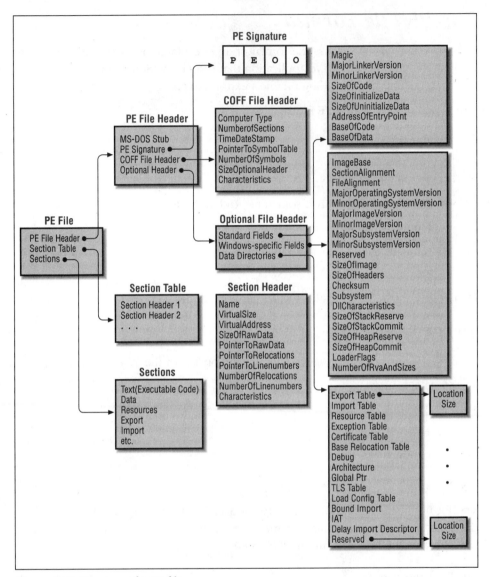

Figure 14-1. Structure of a PE file

COFF file header

The *COFF file header* appears immediately after the PE signature. (The COFF header appears after the signature in a PE file, but at the beginning of a COFF file.) This header contains a variety of information about the file, as shown in Table 14-1.

Table 14-1. The COFF File Header for a PE File

Offset Into Optional Header	Size in Bytes	Field	Description
0	2	Computer type	Required processor type. This value is 0 for unknown and &H14C for Intel and compatible processors.
2	2	NumberOfSections	Number of sections (i.e., number of entries in section table).
4	4	TimeDateStamp	Time and date the file was created.
8	4	PointerToSymbolTable	File offset of the COFF symbol table or 0 if no table is present.
12	4	NumberOfSymbols	Number of entries in the symbol table. This can be used to locate the string table, which immediately follows the symbol table.
16	2	SizeOfOptionalHeader	Size of the PE file optional header.
18	2	Characteristics	Attributes of the file.

The Characteristics flag holds various file information:

IMAGE_FILE_RELOCS_STRIPPED (&H0001)

Indicates that the file does not contain base relocations and *must* therefore be loaded at its preferred (default) base address.

IMAGE_FILE_EXECUTABLE_IMAGE (&H0002)

Indicates that the image file is valid and can be run. If this flag is not set, it generally indicates a linker error.

IMAGE_FILE_AGGRESSIVE_WS_TRIM (&H0010)

Aggressively trim working set. (I do not know how this is done, however.)

IMAGE_FILE_LARGE_ADDRESS_AWARE (&H0020)

The application can handle addresses greater than 2GB.

IMAGE_FILE_BYTES_REVERSED_LO (&H0080)

Indicates that the little-endian memory storage scheme is being used; that is, the least significant byte of a 16-bit word is stored first in memory, followed by the most significant byte. (We have encountered this issue earlier in the book.) All Intel-style PCs use little-endian. (Macintosh computers use big-endian, however.)

IMAGE_FILE_BYTES_REVERSED_HI (&H8000)

Big-endian storage is used.

IMAGE_FILE_32BIT_MACHINE (&H0100)

The PC is based on a 32-bit-word architecture.

IMAGE_FILE_DEBUG_STRIPPED (&H0200)

Debugging information has been removed from the image file.

IMAGE_FILE_REMOVABLE_RUN_FROM_SWAP (&H0400)

If an attempt is made to run the image file from removable media, the file is copied and run from the pagefile (swap file) instead.

IMAGE_FILE_SYSTEM (&H1000)

The image file is a system file, not a user program.

IMAGE_FILE_DLL (&H2000)

The image file is a DLL.

IMAGE_FILE_UP_SYSTEM_ONLY (&H4000)

File should be run only on a UP machine (whatever that means).

IMAGE_FILE_LINE_NUMS_STRIPPED (&H0004)

COFF line numbers have been removed.

IMAGE_FILE_LOCAL_SYMS_STRIPPED (&H0008)

COFF symbol table entries for local symbols have been removed.

IMAGE_FILE_16BIT_MACHINE (&H0040)

Reserved.

The *rpiPEInfo* utility checks for the PE file signature. Finding this signature, the code deciphers the COFF header characteristics flag.

The optional header

The optional header (which is not optional in a PE file, by the way) supplies information to the *loader*, that is, to the Windows system program that is responsible for loading the executable into memory. Unfortunately, this optional header is also referred to as the *PE header* (as opposed to the PE file header)!

The optional header has three parts, which we describe next.

Part 1: standard fields. The standard fields are described in Table 14-2. (Again, don't worry about all of the details of this and other tables. We present them here generally for reference purposes.)

Table 14-2. Standard Fields in an Optional Header

Offset Into Optional Header	Size in Bytes	Field Name	Description
0	2	Magic	An unsigned integer identifying the state of the image file. The most common value is &H10B, indicating a normal executable file.

Table 14-2. Standard Fields in an Optional Header (continued)

Offset Into Optional Header	Size in Bytes	Field Name	Description
2	1	MajorLinkerVersion	Linker major version number.
3	1	MinorLinkerVersion	Linker minor version number.
4	4	SizeOfCode	Size of the code (text) section of the PE file, or the sum of all code sections if there are multiple sections.
8	4	SizeOfInitializedData	Size of the initialized data section of the PE file, or the sum of all such sections if there are multiple data sections.
12	4	SizeOfUninitializedData	Size of the uninitialized data section (BSS) of the PE file, or the sum of all such sections if there are multiple BSS sections.
16	4	AddressOfEntryPoint	Offset of the entry point of the PE file relative to the image's base address when it is loaded into memory. For program images, this is the starting address. Optional for DLLs.
20	4	BaseOfCode	Offset of the beginning of the code section relative to the image's base address when loaded into memory.
24	4	BaseOfData	Offset of the beginning of the data section relative to the image's base address when loaded into memory.

Part 2: Windows-specific fields. The next 21 fields in the optional header contain additional information needed by the Windows linker and loader. Table 14-3 describes these fields.

Table 14-3. Windows-Specific Fields

Offset Into Optional Header	Size in Bytes	Field Name	Description
28	4	ImageBase	The preferred base address of the image when loaded into memory. This must be aligned on an allocation boundary (a multiple of 64KB). The default for DLLs is &H10000000. The default for Windows NT or Windows 9x EXE files is &H00400000.

Table 14-3. Windows-Specific Fields (continued)

Offset Into Optional Header	Size in Bytes	Field Name	Description
32	4	SectionAlignment	Alignment (in bytes) of the PE file's sections when loaded into memory. The default is the page size for the architecture (4KB for Intel).
36	4	FileAlignment	Alignment (in bytes) for the raw data of the sections in the image file.
40	2	MajorOperatingSystemVersion	Major version number of required OS.
42	2	MinorOperatingSystemVersion	Minor version number of required OS.
44	2	MajorImageVersion	Major version number of image.
46	2	MinorImageVersion	Minor version number of image.
48	2	MajorSubsystemVersion	Major version number of subsystem.
50	2	MinorSubsystemVersion	Minor version number of subsystem.
52	4	Reserved	
56	4	SizeOfImage	Size, in bytes, of the image, including all headers.
60	4	SizeOfHeaders	Combined size of MS-DOS stub, PE header, and section headers rounded up to a multiple of FileAlignment.
64	4	CheckSum	An image file checksum, used to catch errors in the file.
68	2	Subsystem	The subsystem required to run this image. See text discussion.
70	2	DllCharacteristics	DLL characteristics.
72	4	SizeOfStackReserve	Size of stack to reserve.
76	4	SizeOfStackCommit	Size of stack to commit.
80	4	SizeOfHeapReserve	Size of local heap space to reserve.
84	4	SizeOfHeapCommit	Size of local heap space to commit.
88	4	LoaderFlags	Obsolete.
92	4	NumberOfRvaAndSizes	Number of data-dictionary entries in the remainder of the Optional Header.

The subsystem field can be one of the following values:

`IMAGE_SUBSYSTEM_UNKNOWN (0)`
Unknown subsystem

`IMAGE_SUBSYSTEM_NATIVE (1)`
Used for device drivers and native Windows NT processes

`IMAGE_SUBSYSTEM_WINDOWS_GUI (2)`
Windows graphical-mode (GUI) image

`IMAGE_SUBSYSTEM_WINDOWS_CUI (3)`
Windows character-mode (CUI) image, that is, runs in a text-based console window

`IMAGE_SUBSYSTEM_POSIX_CUI (7)`
Posix image

`IMAGE_SUBSYSTEM_WINDOWS_CE_GUI (9)`
Runs under Windows CE

Part 3: Data Directory. Each PE file contains several tables and strings that are required by Windows. The *Data Directory* is a table that describes the location and size of these resources. It will prove very important to us in creating the *rpiPEFile* program. The entries in the Data Directory are called *Data Directories*.

Each entry in the Data Directory has the form defined in the following **typedef** and is thus 8 bytes long:

```
typedef struct _IMAGE_DATA_DIRECTORY {
    DWORD   RVA;
    DWORD   Size;   // Size in bytes of item
} IMAGE_DATA_DIRECTORY, *PIMAGE_DATA_DIRECTORY;
```

The RVA field is the *relative virtual address* of the data item (table or string). This confusing field needs some explanation. First, here is what the documentation says:

RVA (Relative Virtual Address)
In an image file, an RVA is always the address of an item once loaded into memory, with the base address of the image file subtracted from it. The RVA of an item will almost always differ from its position within the file on disk (File Pointer).

VA (Virtual Address)
Same as RVA (see above), except that the base address of the image file is not subtracted. The address is called a "Virtual Address" because Windows NT creates a distinct virtual address space for each process, independent of physical memory. For almost all purposes, a virtual address should be considered just an address. A virtual address is not as predictable as an RVA, because the loader might not load the image at its preferred location.

This seems clear enough, and would lead us to think that we could just add the RVA to the base address of the image file when loaded into memory to get the address of the table. However, this does not seem to work. Fortunately, as we will see in the *rpiPEInfo* program, there is an API function called *ImageRvaToVa* that, to quote the documentation:

> . . . locates a relative virtual address (RVA) within the image header of a file that is mapped as a file and returns the virtual address of the corresponding byte in the file.

(I suppose that if all we needed to do was add the RVA to the base address to get the VA, then the *ImageRvaToVa* function, which requires the base address, would not be needed. So something else is probably going on here.)

In any case, Table 14-4 shows the standard Data Directory. Note that this table is not fixed in length and may grow. The NumberOfRvaAndSizes field in the optional header (Table 14-3) gives the number of entries in the Data Directory.

Table 14-4. Data Directory

Offset Into Optional Header	Size in Bytes	Field	Description
96	8	Export Table	Export Table address and size.
104	8	Import Table	Import Table address and size.
112	8	Resource Table	Resource Table address and size.
120	8	Exception Table	Exception Table address and size.
128	8	Certificate Table	Attribute Certificate Table address and size.
136	8	Base Relocation Table	Base Relocation Table address and size.
144	8	Debug	Debug data starting address and size.
152	8	Architecture	Architecture-specific data address, and size.
160	8	Global Ptr	Relative virtual address of the global pointer register. Size member of this structure is set to 0.
168	8	TLS Table	Thread Local Storage (TLS) Table address and size.
176	8	Load Config Table	Load Configuration Table address and size.
184	8	Bound Import	Bound Import Table address and size.
192	8	IAT	Import Address Table address and size.

Table 14-4. Data Directory (continued)

Offset Into Optional Header	Size in Bytes	Field	Description
200	8	Delay Import Descriptor	Address and size of the Delay Import Descriptor.
208	16	Reserved	

The Section Table

After the optional header (and hence the PE file header itself), we find the *section table*, each entry of which is a *section header*. The main bulk of a PE file is contained in sections, of which these entries are the headers. Note that all of the headers come next, followed by all of the sections (rather than a header followed immediately by its section). Each entry of the section table gives, among other things, the offset and size of the corresponding section.

Note that the section table immediately follows the optional header, which is the only way to locate the section table. (The size of the optional header is specified in the COFF file header.) Also, the number of entries in the section table is given by the NumberOfSections field in the COFF file header. (Entries in the section table are numbered starting from 1.)

Each section header (section table entry) has the format shown in Table 14-5 and is 40 bytes in size.

Table 14-5. Format of a Section Table Entry (Section Header)

Offset	Size in Bytes	Field	Description
0	8	Name	An 8-byte, null-padded ASCII string.
8	4	VirtualSize	Total size of the section when loaded into memory. If this value is greater than Sizeof-RawData, the section is zero-padded.
12	4	VirtualAddress	The address of the first byte of the section, when loaded into memory, relative to the image base.
16	4	SizeOfRawData	Size of the initialized data on disk.
20	4	PointerToRawData	File pointer to section's first page within the file. This must be a multiple of the FileAlignment value from the optional header.
24	4	PointerToRelocations	0 for PE files.
28	4	PointerToLinenumbers	File pointer to beginning of line-number entries for the section. Set to 0 if there are no COFF line numbers.
32	2	NumberOfRelocations	0 for PE files.

Table 14-5. Format of a Section Table Entry (Section Header) (continued)

Offset	Size in Bytes	Field	Description
34	2	NumberOfLinenumbers	Number of line-number entries for the section.
36	4	Characteristics	Flags describing the section's characteristics.

Sections

An image file typically has some or all of the following sections:

Text section (executable code)

The text section is named .text and contains the executable code for the file.

Data sections (.bss, .rdata, and .data)

The data sections are named .bss, .rdata, and .data. The .bss section contains uninitialized data, including static variables. The .rdata section contains read-only data, such as literal strings and constants. All other variables are stored in the .data section.

Resource section

This section, named .rsrc, contains information about the resources used by the file.

Relocation section

This section, named .reloc, contains the Fix-Up Table. This table contains entries for all *fixups* for the file. We discussed fixups when we discussed module relocation earlier in this chapter. Basically, fixups are required to make address adjustments in an image file based on its actual load (base) address, which may differ from its default load address.

Export section

The export data section, named .edata, contains information about exported functions and global variables. In particular, the export section begins with a table called the *Export Directory Table*, shown in Table 14-6.

Table 14-6. The Export Directory Table

Offset	Size in Bytes	Field	Description
0	4	Export flags	Reserved.
4	4	Time/date stamp	Time and date the export data was created.

Table 14-6. The Export Directory Table (continued)

Offset	Size in Bytes	Field	Description
8	2	Major version	Major version number.
10	2	Minor version	Minor version number.
12	4	Name RVA	RVA of the ASCII string containing the name of the DLL.
16	4	Ordinal base	Starting ordinal number for exports as listed in the Export Address Table.
20	4	Address table entries	Number of entries in the Export Address Table.
24	4	Number of name pointers	Number of entries in the Name Pointer Table (and Ordinal Table).
28	4	Export address table RVA	RVA of the Export Address Table.
32	4	Name pointer RVA	RVA of the Export Name Pointer Table.
36	4	Ordinal table RVA	RVA of the Ordinal Table.

Incidentally, the Export Address Table contains the *address* of the exported functions in the PE file, but we are only interested in the names of these functions. In fact, our interest centers on the tables shown in Figure 14-2.

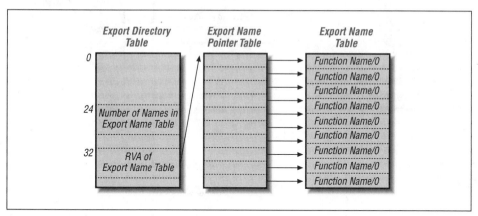

Figure 14-2. The Export Name tables

Note that at offset 32 of the Export Directory Table is the address of the *Export Name Pointer Table* (relative to the image base). This table is an array of pointers into the *Export Name Table*, which, at last, contains the (null-terminated) names of the exported functions. (Since these names may vary in length, we need a pointer to each name.)

As it happens, not all DLLs that export functions appear to have an export section (at least not one named .edata). This means that we cannot simply search for an export section in order to find the Export Directory Table. We must take a different approach in the *rpiPEFile* application. Fortunately, the export table data directory entry (see Table 14-4) seems always to be valid, so we can use this entry to get the RVA of the Export Directory Table.

Import section

This section, called .idata, contains information about functions that are imported by the file. Let us take a closer look at this section. Figure 14-3 shows the details. (Incidentally, in the Hint/Name Table, the documentation says that the name begins at offset 4 in each entry, but experimentation seems to indicate that the correct offset is 2.)

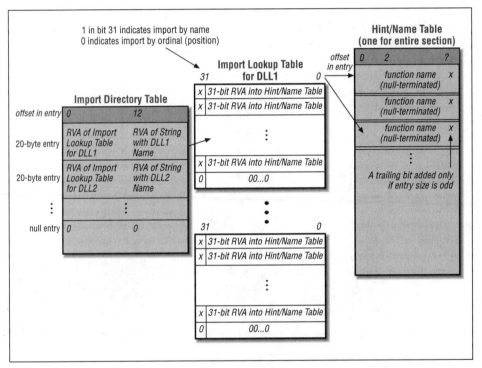

Figure 14-3. Import table section details

The section begins with an *Import Directory Table*. There is one 20-byte entry in this table for each DLL that imports functions to the image file. Let us refer to these DLLs as *import DLLs*. Each entry in this table has two important items for our purposes: the RVA (relative virtual address) of the *Import Lookup Table* for the corresponding import DLL and the RVA of a string that gives the name of this import DLL.

Each entry in the Import Lookup Table for an import DLL is a 32-bit field. There is one entry for each imported function from this import DLL. The high-order bit of each entry signals whether to import the function by name (bit = 1) or by ordinal number, that is, by position (bit = 0). The remaining 31 bits form the RVA into the *Hint/Name Table.*

Each entry in the Hint/Name Table contains the actual name of the function (not a pointer to the name) starting at offset 4. Thus, the entry lengths in the Hint/Name Table will vary. An entry is padded with another bit (if necessary) *only* to make the entry's length even, so that the next entry starts on an even boundary line.

Example: Getting PE File Information

Now that we have a basic understanding of the format of a PE file, we can create the *rpiPEInfo* utility. Figure 14-4 shows the utility, as it dissects the file *COMCTL32. DLL.*

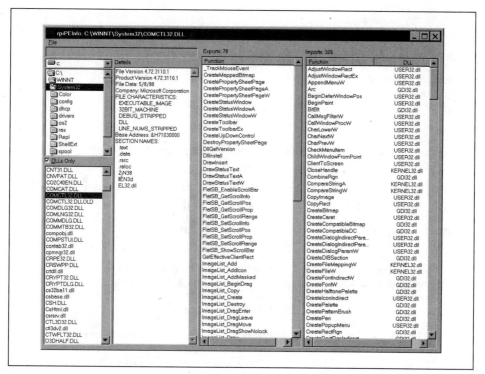

Figure 14-4. The rpiPEInfo utility

The complete source code is on the accompanying CD, so we will just cover some of the highlights. As we have seen, the PE file itself contains relative virtual addresses (RVAs) for most items. We also remarked that these addresses are relative to the file's image in memory, which is not the same as its disk image. Accordingly, the approach taken in the *rpiPEInfo* utility is first to map the executable file in question into memory and then translate relative virtual addresses (RVAs) into virtual addresses (VAs).

To map a PE file into memory, we can use the *MapAndLoad* function exported by the *IMAGEHLP.DLL* library:

```
BOOL MapAndLoad(
    IN LPSTR ImageName,
    IN LPSTR DllPath,
    OUT PLOADED_IMAGE LoadedImage,
    IN BOOL DotDll,
    IN BOOL ReadOnly);
```

or, in VB:

```
Public Declare Function MapAndLoad Lib "Imagehlp.dll" ( _
    ByVal ImageName As String, _
    ByVal DLLPath As String, _
    LoadedImage As LOADED_IMAGE, _
    DotDLL As Long, _
    ReadOnly As Long) As Long
```

There is also a corresponding *UnMapAndLoad* function:

```
BOOL UnMapAndLoad(
    IN PLOADED_IMAGE LoadedImage
);
```

or, in VB:

```
Public Declare Function UnMapAndLoad Lib "Imagehlp.dll" ( _
    LoadedImage As LOADED_IMAGE) As Long
```

The *MapAndLoad* function maps an image file into virtual memory and fills a **LOADED_IMAGE** structure with all sorts of useful stuff:

```
Public Type LOADED_IMAGE        ' 48 bytes (46 bytes packed)
    ModuleName As Long
    hFile As Long
    MappedAddress As Long       ' Base address of mapped file
    pFileHeader As Long         ' Pointer to IMAGE_PE_FILE_HEADER
    pLastRvaSection As Long     ' Pointer to first COFF section header
                                ' (section table)??

    NumberOfSections As Long
    pSections As Long           ' Pointer to first COFF section header
                                ' (section table)??

    Characteristics As Long     ' Image characteristics value
    fSystemImage As Byte
    fDOSImage As Byte
    Links As LIST_ENTRY         ' 2 longs
    SizeOfImage As Long
End Type
```

For us, the important information is the base address of the loaded image (*MappedAddress*) and the pointer to the PE file header (*pFileheader*), which, incidentally, the documentation also refers to as the *NT headers*.

To get a VA from an RVA, we use the function:

```
LPVOID ImageRvaToVa(
    IN PIMAGE_PE_FILE_HEADER NtHeaders,
    IN LPVOID Base,
    IN DWORD Rva,
    IN OUT PIMAGE_SECTION_HEADER *LastRvaSection
);
```

or, in VB:

```
Public Declare Function ImageRvaToVa Lib "Imagehlp.dll" ( _
    ByVal NTHeaders As Long, _
    ByVal Base As Long, _
    ByVal rva As Long, _
    ByVal LastRvaSection As Long) As Long
```

Note that this function requires not only the RVA, but also a pointer to the PE file header (NT headers) as well as the base address of the loaded image. This is further evidence that more is going on in translating an RVA to a VA than just adding the base address. (The last parameter to *ImageRvaToVa* is not important.) This function returns the VA.

The Structures

There are several structures (user-defined types) that we require. These structures can be found in the *Winnt.h* include file and reflect various tables in the PE file. (We changed a few names to bring them into conformance with the documentation on PE files.)

In the *rpiPEFile* program, we must declare the structures from the bottom up, in order to avoid forward reference error messages from VB. It will help to refer to Figure 14-1.

We begin with a Data Directory entry, which is used to get the RVA for the export and import tables:

```
' Data Directory entry
Public Type IMAGE_DATA_DIRECTORY  ' 8 bytes
    RVA  As Long
    size  As Long
End Type
```

Next comes the optional header—all three parts. The constant **IMAGE_NUMBEROF_ DIRECTORY_ENTRIES** (see the last member below) is defined, in one of the include files, to be equal to 16, even though the documentation says that the number of Data Directory entries is not fixed.

```
' Optional header (all three parts)
Public Type IMAGE_OPTIONAL_HEADER      ' 232 bytes
```

```
'Standard fields.
Magic  As Integer
MajorLinkerVersion  As Byte
MinorLinkerVersion  As Byte
SizeOfCode  As Long
SizeOfInitializedData  As Long
SizeOfUninitializedData  As Long
AddressOfEntryPoint  As Long
BaseOfCode  As Long
BaseOfData  As Long

'NT additional fields.
ImageBase  As Long
SectionAlignment  As Long
FileAlignment  As Long
MajorOperatingSystemVersion  As Integer
MinorOperatingSystemVersion  As Integer
MajorImageVersion  As Integer
MinorImageVersion  As Integer
MajorSubsystemVersion  As Integer
MinorSubsystemVersion  As Integer
Win32VersionValue  As Long
SizeOfImage  As Long
SizeOfHeaders  As Long
CheckSum  As Long
Subsystem  As Integer
DllCharacteristics  As Integer
SizeOfStackReserve  As Long
SizeOfStackCommit  As Long
SizeOfHeapReserve  As Long
SizeOfHeapCommit  As Long
LoaderFlags  As Long
NumberOfRvaAndSizes  As Long        '96

' Data directories
DataDirectory(0 To IMAGE_NUMBEROF_DIRECTORY_ENTRIES) _
    As IMAGE_DATA_DIRECTORY   ' 17*8 + 96 = 232
End Type
```

Next comes the PE file header without the MS-DOS stub:

```
' PE File header without MS-DOS stub
Public Type IMAGE_PE_FILE_HEADER   ' 256 bytes
    Signature  As Long                          ' 4 bytes -- PE signature
    FileHeader As IMAGE_COFF_HEADER             ' 20 bytes -- COFF header
    OptionalHeader As IMAGE_OPTIONAL_HEADER     ' 232 bytes
End Type
```

We also declared the COFF header itself, but didn't use it:

```
' COFF File header
Public Type IMAGE_COFF_HEADER       ' 20 bytes
    Machine As Integer
    NumberOfSections As Integer
    TimeDateStamp  As Long
    PointerToSymbolTable  As Long
    NumberOfSymbols  As Long
```

```
        SizeOfOptionalHeader  As Integer
        Characteristics  As Integer
    End Type
```

Finally, we have the Export Directory Table:

```
' Export Directory table
Public Type IMAGE_EXPORT_DIRECTORY_TABLE    ' 40 bytes
    Characteristics  As Long
    TimeDateStamp  As Long
    MajorVersion  As Integer
    MinorVersion  As Integer
    Name As Long
    Base As Long
    NumberOfFunctions  As Long
    NumberOfNames As Long                    ' We need this one
    pAddressOfFunctions  As Long
    ExportNamePointerTableRVA  As Long       ' We need this one
    pAddressOfNameOrdinals  As Long
End Type
```

We declared a few other structures, as you can see by looking at the source code.

Getting Version Information

The first function we call when the user clicks on a file name is *GetVersionInfo*. This function uses several functions from the *VERSION.DLL* library: *GetFileVersion-InfoSize*, *GetFileVersionInfo*, *VerLanguageName*, and *VerQueryValue*. These functions are used primarily by setup programs.

The *GetFileVersionInfo* function fills a buffer with version information about the file. To get at this information, we use *VerQueryValue*:

```
Public Declare Function VerQueryValue Lib "version.dll" Alias "VerQueryValueA" ( _
    pBlock As Byte, _
    ByVal lpSubBlock As String, _
    lplpBuffer As Long, _
    puLen As Long _
) As Long
```

passing various descriptive strings in the `lpSubBlock` parameter. For instance, passing the string "\" returns the *root block*, which is a pointer to the following structure (MS stands for most significant and LS for least significant):

```
Public Type VS_FIXEDFILEINFO
    dwSignature As Long
    dwStrucVersion As Long
    dwFileVersionMS As Long
    dwFileVersionLS As Long
    dwProductVersionMS As Long
    dwProductVersionLS As Long
    dwFileFlagsMask As Long
    dwFileFlags As Long
```

```
      dwFileOS As Long
      dwFileType As Long
      dwFileSubtype As Long
      dwFileDateMS As Long
      dwFileDateLS As Long
   End Type
```

There is a tricky part to getting the company name—we first need to search the translation array that specifies the languages that are supported by the file. Finding the correct language and code page codes for English, we can then pass *VerQueryValue* the *subblock*:

```
   "\StringFileInfo\" & sLangID & sCodePageID & "\CompanyName"
```

Getting File Characteristics

The next step is to open the file and look for the PE signature. According to the PE documentation, the offset of the PE signature is found at offset &H3C of the file. The following code in the function *GetPEFileChars* gets the 4 bytes at this offset and checks it for the correct signature:

```
   'Check for PE file signature
   Get #fr, &H3C + 1, bSigOffset
   Get #fr, bSigOffset + 1, lSignature
   If Not lSignature = &H4550 Then          ' PE\0\0 backwards in memory
       Close fr
       txtDetails = txtDetails & vbCrLf & "  No PE signature"
       Exit Function
   End If
```

It is then a straightforward matter to get the characteristics flag from the COFF header as well as some other data, such as the section names. There does seem to be a little problem here, however. You may notice that some section names are a bit strange, as in Figure 14-4. The number of sections is retrieved from the optional header and must be correct, since it is used to calculate the offset of the Section Table. Whatever.

Getting Export Names

The function used to get the exports is where the fun really starts. This function is called only for PE files. Here is an overview.

First, we map the file (*sFile*) into memory and load a **LOADED_IMAGE** structure:

```
   Dim loadimage As LOADED_IMAGE
   lret = MapAndLoad(sFile, "", loadimage, True, True)
```

From this, we can get the base address of the loaded image:

```
   baseaddr = loadimage.MappedAddress
```

Next, we copy the PE file header to our own variable, so that we can access its members:

```
Dim peheader As IMAGE_PE_FILE_HEADER
CopyMemory ByVal VarPtr(peheader), ByVal loadimage.pFileHeader, 256
```

Next, we retrieve the VA from the RVA of the first Data Directory, which is the Data Directory for the Export Directory Table. The constant `IMAGE_DIRECTORY_ENTRY_EXPORT` is defined to be 0—the index of the first Data Directory:

```
rvaExportDirTable = peheader.OptionalHeader. _
   DataDirectory(IMAGE_DIRECTORY_ENTRY_EXPORT).RVA

vaExportDirTable = ImageRvaToVa(loadimage.pFileHeader, _
   loadimage.MappedAddress, rvaExportDirTable, 0&)
```

Again we make a copy into our own structure:

```
' Export directory
Dim exportdir As IMAGE_EXPORT_DIRECTORY_TABLE
CopyMemory ByVal VarPtr(exportdir), ByVal vaExportDirTable, LenB(exportdir)
```

From this copy (see Figure 14-2), we can get the number of exported names:

```
cNames = exportdir.NumberOfNames
```

Now, *exportdir.ExportNamePointerTableRVA* is the RVA for the Export Name Pointer Table (see Figure 14-2), so we get the VA for this table as follows:

```
ExportNamePointerTableVA = ImageRvaToVa(loadimage.pFileHeader, _
   loadimage.MappedAddress, exportdir.ExportNamePointerTableRVA, 0&)
```

Now we can simply march through the Export Name Pointer Table, collecting the target strings:

```
' Start at the beginning of names
pNextAddress = ExportNamePointerTableVA

' Get the next address (to export name)
VBGetTarget lNextAddress, pNextAddress, 4

lvExports.ListItems.Clear

For i = 0 To cNames - 1

   ' Convert address of this name from RVA to VA
   lNextAddress = ImageRvaToVa(loadimage.pFileHeader, _
      loadimage.MappedAddress, lNextAddress, 0&)

   ' Convert ANSI string to BSTR
   sName = LPSTRtoBSTR(lNextAddress)
   lvExports.ListItems.Add , , sName

   ' Point to next address in table
   pNextAddress = pNextAddress + 4
```

```
' Get the address
VBGetTarget lNextAddress, pNextAddress, 4

Next
```

Finally, we call *UnMapAndLoad.*

Getting Import Names

Getting imports requires a different approach, since the table structure is different. Here is an overview. Once again we map and load the file. This could have been done once for both imports and exports, but it seemed easier to follow the code by separating the two tasks. In a similar manner as for exports, we get the VA of the Import Directory Table (see Figure 14-3):

```
rvaImportDirTable = peheader.OptionalHeader. _
    DataDirectory(IMAGE_DIRECTORY_ENTRY_IMPORT).RVA

' Call RvaToVa to get VA from RVA
vaImportDirTable = ImageRvaToVa(loadimage.pFileHeader, _
    loadimage.MappedAddress, rvaImportDirTable, 0&)
```

Then we need to cycle through the entries of this table, getting the Import Lookup Table and DLL name for each entry, until we encounter a null entry. For each **non-NULL** entry, the following **Do** loop gathers the import names:

```
Do
    VBGetTarget LookupTableEntry, pLookupTableEntry, 4
    If LookupTableEntry = 0 Then Exit Do

    ' Check most significant bit
    ' If 0 then skip since it is by ordinal not by name
    If LookupTableEntry >= 0 Then

        cNames = cNames + 1
        ' Mask MSB
        LookupTableEntry = LookupTableEntry And &H7FFFFFFF

        ' Convert RVA to VA to get address of function name
        pImportFunctionName = ImageRvaToVa(loadimage.pFileHeader, _
        loadimage.MappedAddress, LookupTableEntry, 0&)

        ' Name is at offset 2 in entry
        sFunctionName = LPSTRtoBSTR(pImportFunctionName + 2)

        Set li = lvImports.ListItems.Add()
        li.Text = sFunctionName
        li.ListSubItems.Add , , sDLLName

    End If

    ' Next entry
    pLookupTableEntry = pLookupTableEntry + 4
Loop
```

III

Windows (USER32.DLL Programming)

15

Windows: The Basics

We begin our study of Microsoft Windows with the basics, including much of the terminology associated with windows.

Terminology

Let us begin with the basic terminology of windows. Note that many of these terms are not used in a precise way and so their meanings may differ depending on the context. However, our definitions will serve as general guidelines.

*   When Windows is started, it automatically creates the *desktop window*, which is a system-defined window that paints the background of the screen and serves as the "base" for all windows displayed by all applications.

*   Every *graphical-based* Windows application (as opposed to *console-based* application) creates at least one window, called its *main window*. This window is the main interface between the application and the user.

Here are the general categories of windows:

Application window

   A window that typically has one or more of the following: a titlebar with an icon and Maximize, Minimize, and Close buttons; a menu bar; and scroll bars. One concept that many users are not familiar with, but which is important for programmers, is that of the *client area*. This is the area of a window that can receive output, such as text or graphics. Thus, for instance, the client area of a window does not include rulers, menu bars, window borders, or scroll bars. The remainder of a window is referred to as the *nonclient area*.

Control

A special-purpose window that is used for single-function (usually) communication with the user. Every control is a child of some other window, called the control's *container*.

Dialog box

A window whose main function is to contain controls, and thus provide multi-function communication with the user.

Message box

A window that is used to display a message.

Some windows are considered *top-level windows*. Unfortunately, this term is defined differently in different parts of the MSDN documentation. In one location, it is defined as a window with no parent. (We will discuss parent windows later.) In another location, it is defined as a window either having no parent or whose parent is the desktop window. Also according to the documentation, the *Enum-ChildWindows* API function will enumerate all top-level windows (if a certain parameter is set to 0). However, as we will see, the function enumerates some windows that *do* have parents other than the desktop window. The only reasonable conclusion is that the term top-level window is not used consistently. However, it seems generally to refer to a window that is not a child window.

As we will see in some detail in Chapter 16, *Windows Messages*, every window has associated with it:

A window handle

A 32-bit number that uniquely identifies the window throughout the system.

A window class

A distinction used to create the window and gives the window its initial characteristics. We will discuss window classes in Chapter 17, *Window Classes and the Window Creation Process*.

Window styles

We discuss these next.

Window Styles

In addition to a handle and a class, every window has one or more *window styles* that define the characteristics of the window, such as the presence or absence of borders, titlebars, Maximize buttons, and so on. Window styles are defined by symbolic constants, of which there are roughly 200 in number. Window styles are generally combined (by ORing the constants) to produce the desired effect. For instance, setting the style of a window to:

```
WS_MAXIMIZEBOX Or WS_MINIMIZEBOX Or WS_SYSMENU
```

gives the window Maximize and Minimize buttons as well as a *window menu* (which used to be called a *system menu*).

Note that some styles are defined as combinations of other styles. For instance, the WS_POPUPWINDOW style is defined as:

```
WS_POPUPWINDOW = WS_POPUP Or WS_BORDER Or WS_SYSMENU
```

This is very helpful, in view of the large number of styles.

Many window styles fit neatly into categories, which we discuss next.

Styles That Define General Window Characteristics

Some styles help define the *general* characteristics (as opposed to specific characteristics, such as having a Maximize button) of a window.

Overlapped windows

An *overlapped window* is a top-level window with style WS_OVERLAPPED or WS_OVERLAPPEDWINDOW. Those windows with style WS_OVERLAPPED have a titlebar and border and those with style WS_OVERLAPPEDWINDOW have a titlebar, sizing border, window menu, and Minimize and Maximize buttons.

An application's main window is generally an overlapped window.

Pop-up windows

A *pop-up window* is a window with style WS_POPUP. These are special types of overlapped windows that are used for dialog boxes, message boxes, and other temporary windows that can appear outside of an application's main window. A pop-up window may or may not have a titlebar. Otherwise, pop-up windows are the same as overlapped windows with the WS_OVERLAPPED style.

Child windows

A *child window* is a window that is defined with the WS_CHILD style. This style must be specified when the window is created. As we will see, the *CreateWindow* and *CreateWindowEx* functions have a parameter that is used to specify the handle of the parent window of the child.

A child window is confined to the client area of its parent window. Child windows are typically used to divide the client area of its parent into functional areas. A child window may have a titlebar, a window menu, Minimize and Maximize buttons, a border, and scroll bars, but it cannot have a menu.

Note that the *GetParent* function can be used to retrieve a handle to a window's parent. We will use this function in an upcoming example.

Window Border Styles

Several styles define the border characteristics of a window, as follows:

WS_BORDER

> A window with a thin-line border.

WS_DLGFRAME

> A window with a double border, typically used with dialog boxes. Such a window cannot have a titlebar.

WS_EX_DLGMODALFRAME

> A window with a double border, but possibly with a titlebar as well (if the window also has the WS_CAPTION style).

WS_EX_STATICEDGE

> A window with a three-dimensional border style. This is intended to be used for windows that do not accept user input.

WS_THICKFRAME

> A window with a sizing border.

Styles That Affect the Nonclient Area of a Window

The nonclient area of a window can include a titlebar, window menu, Minimize and Maximize buttons, sizing border, and horizontal and vertical scrollbars. Here are the relevant styles:

WS_CAPTION

> A window with a titlebar (includes the WS_BORDER style)

WS_HSCROLL

> A window with a horizontal scrollbar

WS_MAXIMIZEBOX

> A window with a Maximize button

WS_MINIMIZEBOX

> A window with a Minimize button

WS_SYSMENU

> A window with a window menu in the titlebar

WS_VSCROLL

> A window with a vertical scrollbar

Styles that Affect the Initial State of a Window

The following styles determine the initial state of a window:

`WS_DISABLED`

A window that is initially disabled

`WS_MAXIMIZE`

A window that is initially maximized

`WS_MINIMIZE`

A window that is initially minimized

`WS_VISIBLE`

A window that is initially visible

Parent and Child Styles

It is possible for one window to be a child of another window. The *clipping region* of a window is that portion of the window's client area where Windows currently permits drawing. There are two styles that affect clipping regions:

`WS_CLIPCHILDREN`

This style clips all child windows from the drawing area of the parent.

`WS_CLIPSIBLINGS`

This style clips a child window relative to its sibling windows. Thus, when one child window needs repainting, only its exposed area will be repainted, which prevents repainting on top of an overlapped sibling window.

We will discuss clipping in detail in Chapter 22, *Device Contexts I: Overview.*

Extended Styles

There are a great many *extended styles*. We mention only two:

`WS_EX_TOPMOST`

This style specifies that a window should be placed above all nontopmost windows, even when another application is in the foreground. Of course, one topmost window may cover another topmost window. For instance, some help systems let you specify that a window be topmost.

`WS_EX_TOOLWINDOW`

This style defines a *tool window*; that is, a window that is intended to be used as a floating toolbar.

We will continue our discussion of styles, and how to change them, in Chapter 17.

Owned Windows

It is possible for an overlapped or pop-up window to be *owned* by another overlapped or pop-up window. This is quite different from the parent-child relationship, since in the case of owned windows both windows must be overlapped or pop-up windows. In particular, a child window can be neither an owner nor an owned window. Dialog boxes and message boxes are owned windows by default, for instance.

The basic characteristics of an owned window are:

- An owned window always lies on top of its owner in the Z order (described shortly).

- Windows automatically destroys an owned window when its owner is destroyed.

- An owned window is hidden when its owner is minimized.

The *GetWindow* function can be used to retrieve a handle to a window's owner.

Z Order

The *Z order* refers to the order of visibility of windows on the screen. More specifically, the Z order indicates the window's relative position with respect to an imaginary z-axis that comes directly out of the monitor at right angles, toward the user, as pictured in Figure 15-1.

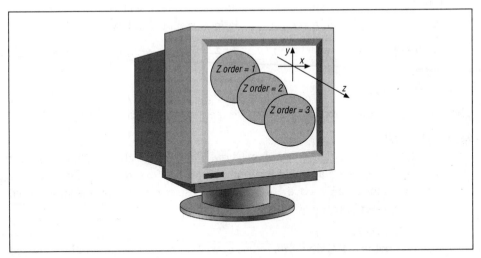

Figure 15-1. Illustrating Z order

Windows keeps the Z orders of all windows in a single list, but it does so in a structured way. In particular, the child windows of a parent window are always grouped with the parent, so when the Z order of the parent window changes, the Z orders of its children follow along. Figure 15-2 illustrates what happens when a top-level window (Window2) moves to the top of the Z order. Quite simply, it brings its children along for the ride.

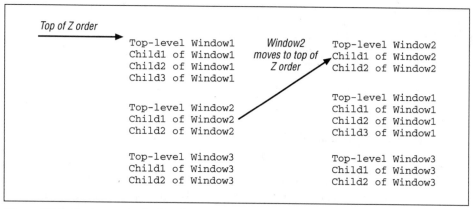

Figure 15-2. Moving up in the Z order

The topmost windows (style `WS_EX_TOPMOST`), if any, always appear at the top of the Z order and are thus always visible, unless obscured by another topmost window. There follow the parent-child groupings. When a window is created, it is placed at the top of the Z order *for its type.* Thus, a new parent window is placed just below the topmost windows, and a new child window is placed just below its parent window and therefore above any other child windows *for that parent.*

Note that this scheme gives the child windows of a single parent a relative Z ordering as well.

There are several API functions that relate to Z order. Here are a few.

BringWindowToTop

The *BringWindowToTop* function:

```
BOOL BringWindowToTop(
   HWND hWnd    // handle to window
);
```

brings a window to the top of the Z order *for its type.* If the window is a top-level window, then it is activated. If the window is a child window, its *top-level* parent window is activated and thus brought to the top of the Z order for windows of *its* type.

Note that this function does not change the type of window; that is, it will not promote a nontopmost window to a topmost window and so it will not place a top-level window over a topmost window (only over other top-level windows).

SetWindowPos

The *SetWindowPos* function can be used to change the size, position, and Z order of a window, as in the following code.

```
BOOL SetWindowPos(
    HWND hWnd,              // handle to window
    HWND hWndInsertAfter,   // placement-order handle
    int X,                  // horizontal position
    int Y,                  // vertical position
    int cx,                 // width
    int cy,                 // height
    UINT uFlags             // window-positioning flags
);
```

The *hWndInsertAfter* parameter can assume one of the following values:

HWND_BOTTOM

> Places the window at the bottom of the Z order. If the window was topmost, it loses its topmost status and is placed at the bottom of all other windows.

HWND_NOTOPMOST

> For a topmost window, places the window above all nontopmost windows and thus directly beneath all topmost windows. This flag has no effect on a nontopmost window.

HWND_TOP

> Places the window at the top of the Z order for its type. When applied to a child window, moves its top-level parent to the top of the Z order for its type. (Same as *BringWindowToTop*.)

HWND_TOPMOST

> Gives a top-level window the topmost attribute and places it at the top of the Z order. We will use this feature in several of our utilities.

GetTopWindow

The *GetTopWindow* function has syntax:

```
HWND GetTopWindow(
    HWND hWnd    // handle to parent window
);
```

This function looks at just the child windows of the specified parent and retrieves a handle to the child window at the top of the Z order among all children of that parent. If *hWnd* is NULL (0), then the function retrieves a handle to the window at the top of the Z order among *all* windows.

In a similar vein, the *GetNextWindow* function:

```
HWND GetNextWindow(
    HWND hWnd, // handle to current window
    UINT wCmd  // direction flag
);
```

retrieves a handle to the window that is next (lower down) or previous (higher up) in the Z order *of the same type* as the window in question. Thus, if *hWnd* refers to a top-level (nontopmost) window, the function retrieves a handle to the appropriate top-level window, and if *hWnd* refers to a child window, the function returns a child window (for the same parent). If no such window exists, the function returns NULL (0).

Enumerating Windows

The Win32 API provides a collection of *enumeration functions* that can be used to enumerate various objects, including windows. Let us take a look at the notion of an enumeration function, since it will come up several times in the book (and has already come up in the *rpiEnumProcs* applications).

Enumeration Functions

Here are a few examples of enumeration functions:

EnumProcesses
> Enumerates the process identifiers for each process object in the system

EnumProcessModules
> Enumerates the handles of each module in the specified process

EnumWindows
> Enumerates top-level windows

EnumChildWindows
> Enumerates child windows of a window

EnumThreadWindows
> Enumerates all nonchild windows associated with a thread

EnumFonts
> Enumerates the fonts available on a specified device

EnumFontFamilies
> Enumerates the available fonts in a given font family

EnumObjects
> Enumerates the pens or brushes available for a specified device context

EnumDateFormats
> Enumerates the long or short date formats that are available for a specified locale

EnumDeviceDrivers
> Enumerates the load address for each device driver in the system

EnumPrinterDrivers
> Enumerates all of the printer drivers currently installed

EnumPorts
> Enumerates the ports that are available for printing

Generally speaking, the main issue related to enumeration functions is how to return the enumerated data. The problem is that there is no way of knowing ahead of time how much data needs enumerating, so passing a data structure (such as an array) to an enumeration function is not very practical.

Nevertheless, some enumeration functions make us do just that. As we will see, they make us guess at the size of a buffer for the returned value and then return not only the data but also the number of bytes required to hold the data. If the buffer that we have allocated is not sufficiently large, we must increase the size of that buffer and try again. This is crude but it does work.

On the other hand, several enumeration functions take a "cop out" approach by saying, in effect, "I will tell you *separately* about each item to be enumerated, and you figure out what to do with this information."

The way that an enumeration function tells the calling program separately about each item to be enumerated is by calling a function that the calling program must supply. This function is descriptively referred to as a *callback function.*

The idea is simply that the enumeration function will call a callback function once for each item that it enumerates, passing information (such as the item's handle) in the parameters of the callback function. (In many ways, this is reminiscent of VB events—Windows fires an "event" for each object being enumerated.)

Thus, the signature (parameter types, etc.) of the callback function must be supplied to us in the documentation for the enumeration function, but it is up to us to create this function, pass its address to the enumeration function, and write code for the function to process the information returned in the parameters. Typically, an enumeration function inspects the *return value* of the callback function to see whether it should continue enumerating or just quit.

Fortunately, VB can supply the address of a callback function using the `AddressOf` operator. In fact, this is probably why the `AddressOf` operator was introduced into Visual Basic!

To illustrate, the *EnumWindows* function is declared as:

```
BOOL EnumWindows(
    WNDENUMPROC lpEnumFunc,    // pointer to callback function
    LPARAM lParam              // application-defined value
);
```

The *lpEnumFunc* parameter should be set to the address of the callback function. The *lParam* parameter can be defined by the caller and is passed to the callback function each time it is called by *EnumWindows*. One use for this value is as a counter.

The *EnumWindows* function can be translated into VB as:

```
Declare Function EnumWindows Lib "USER32" ( _
    ByVal lpFunct As Long, _
    lParam As Long _
) As Long
```

where *lParam* is passed by reference. Now, we declare a counter variable:

```
Dim c As Long
```

outside the callback function (this is key) and pass it *by reference* to *EnumWindows*.

```
EnumWindows(AddreesOf OurCallBack, c)
```

In turn, *EnumWindows* passes the variable c to our callback function, which will just increment it by 1. Since each time the callback function is called, it increments the *external* (to the callback function) variable c by 1, the variable c will contain a count of all enumerated windows when the *EnumWindows* function is done.

Example: The EnumWins Utility

The CD that accompanies this book contains the source code for a utility called *rpiEnumWins*, which enumerates all windows and places information about each in a TreeView control. Figure 15-3 shows the main window.

It is interesting to see the kinds of windows that Windows creates. One of the most amusing features of this utility is that it will draw a red rectangle on the screen at the current location of a window, whether it is visible or not.

This utility uses the API *EnumChildWindows*, which is similar to *EnumWindows*, but which will enumerate child windows as well as top-level windows. The declaration is:

```
BOOL EnumChildWindows(
    HWND hWndParent,           // handle to parent window
    WNDENUMPROC lpEnumFunc,    // pointer to callback function
    LPARAM lParam              // application-defined value
);
```

Here is what the documentation says about the *hWndParent* parameter:

> If this parameter is NULL, the parent window is the desktop window, and the function enumerates all top-level windows.

This is a bit contradictory, since it implies that all top-level windows have the desktop window as parent, which is not the case. In any case, this function seems to enumerate all top-level windows (whatever that *really* means).

The main action in the *rpiEnumWins* utility is in the callback function *EnumChildProc*. Here we gather the data about each window, such as its handle, caption,

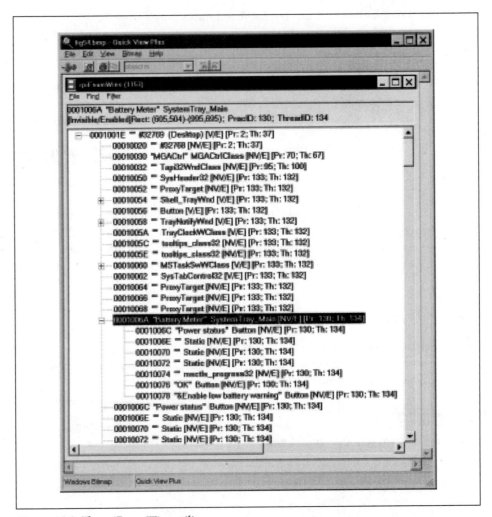

Figure 15-3. The rpiEnumWins utility

class name, window rectangle (coordinates of the window on the screen), and
process and thread IDs. A new TreeView node is created for each window. Fortunately, the Tag property of a node can be a variant, and so it can hold an entire
array of values. This is where we store all of the window's data.

```
Function EnumChildProc(ByVal hwnd As Long, lParam As Long) As Long

  ' This is called by Windows for each child window
  ' ByVal is needed in order to use hwnd
  ' lParam can be called ByVal or ByRef but make sure it matches in Declare _
    statement!

Dim lret As Long
Dim lTitleLen As Long
```

```
Dim sWinTitle As String
Dim sWinClass As String
Dim hOwner As Long
Dim s As String
Dim uNode As Node
Dim r As RECT
Dim lThreadID As Long
Dim lProcID As Long

' Gather window data
lTitleLen = GetWindowTextLength(hwnd) + 1
sWinTitle = String$(lTitleLen, 0)
lret = GetWindowText(hwnd, sWinTitle, lTitleLen)
sWinTitle = Left$(sWinTitle, lret)
sWinClass = GetClass(hwnd)
hOwner = GetWindow(hwnd, GW_OWNER)
GetWindowRect hwnd, r
lThreadID = GetWindowThreadProcessId(hwnd, lProcID)

' Increment window count
lParam = lParam + 1

s = HexFormat(hwnd) & "  """ & sWinTitle & """  " & sWinClass

' Append owner if nonzero
If hOwner <> 0 Then
    s = s & " [Owner: " & HexFormat(hOwner) & "]"
End If

Set uNode = frmEnumWins.trvWins.Nodes.Add( _
    frmEnumWins.trvWins.Nodes(idxCurrentParent).Key, _
    tvwChild, "Key" & Format$(lParam), s)

' Tag is an array
uNode.Tag = Array(hwnd, sWinTitle, sWinClass, _
    hOwner, r.Bottom, r.Left, r.Right, r.Top, lProcID, lThreadID)

' To continue
EnumChildProc = True

End Function
```

Size and Position Functions

The Win32 API has a great many functions that relate to the positioning and sizing of windows on the screen. Frankly, these functions are a bit boring, but we should at least introduce some of them here, so that you can investigate them further when needed.

SetWindowPlacement

The *SetWindowPlacement* function sets the show state and the restored, mini-mized, and maximized positions of the specified window:

```
BOOL SetWindowPlacement(
    HWND hWnd,                          // handle to window
    CONST WINDOWPLACEMENT *lpwndpl  // address of structure with position data
);
```

Here *lpwndpl* is the address of a **WINDOWPLACEMENT** structure:

```
typedef struct _WINDOWPLACEMENT {
    UINT length;              // length of this structure
    UINT flags;
    UINT showCmd;
    POINT ptMinPosition;      // upper-left corner when the window is Minimized
    POINT ptMaxPosition;      // upper-left corner when the window is Maximized
    RECT rcNormalPosition;
} WINDOWPLACEMENT;
```

Note that the *length* field of this structure *must* be filled in *before* calling *SetWin-dowPlacement*. We won't discuss all of the possible values for the members of this structure, but just note that among the possible values for *showCmd* are SW_HIDE, SW_RESTORE, SW_SHOW, SW_SHOWMAXIMIZED, SW_SHOWMINIMIZED, and SW_SHOWNORMAL. These are pretty self-explanatory.

The Windows API uses **POINT** and **RECT** structures quite often. A **POINT** structure is defined as:

```
typedef struct tagPOINT {
    LONG x;
    LONG y;
} POINT;
```

and a **RECT** structure as:

```
typedef struct _RECT {
    LONG left;
    LONG top;
    LONG right;
    LONG bottom;
} RECT;
```

The VB translations are very straightforward, since VC++ **UINT**s and **LONG**s become VB longs. The only wrinkle is that the word POINT is a VB keyword, so we should choose another word:

```
Type POINTAPI
    x As Long
    yAs Long
End Type

Type RECT
```

```
      Left As Long
      Top As Long
      Right As Long
      Bottom As Long
   End Type

   Type WINDOWPLACEMENT
      Length As Long
      flags As Long
      showCmd As Long
      ptMinPosition As POINTAPI
      ptMaxPosition As POINTAPI
      rcNormalPosition As RECT
   End Type
```

We can now declare *SetWindowPlacement* as:

```
   Declare Function SetWindowPlacement Lib "user32" Alias "SetWindowPlacement" ( _
      ByVal hwnd As Long, _
      lpwndpl As WINDOWPLACEMENT _
   ) As Long
```

As you may have guessed, there is also a *GetWindowPlacement* function that retrieves the current window settings in a WINDOWPLACEMENT structure.

MoveWindow

The *MoveWindow* function changes the position and size of a window. It is important to note that, for a top-level window, the position is relative to the upper-left corner of the screen, whereas for a child window, it is relative to the upper-left corner of the parent window's *client area.*

The declaration is:

```
   BOOL MoveWindow(
      HWND hWnd,       // handle to window
      int X,           // position of left side of window (in pixels)
      int Y,           // position of top of window (in pixels)
      int nWidth,      // width (in pixels)
      int nHeight,     // height (in pixels)
      BOOL bRepaint    // repaint flag
   );
```

or, in VB:

```
   Declare Function MoveWindow Lib "user32" Alias "MoveWindow" ( _
      ByVal hwnd As Long, _
      ByVal x As Long, _
      ByVal y As Long, _
      ByVal nWidth As Long, _
      ByVal nHeight As Long, _
      ByVal bRepaint As Long _
   ) As Long
```

The **bRepaint** flag should be set to **True** to have Windows repaint the window after it is moved or resized.

Unfortunately, all of the parameters to this function must be filled in, so even if we want to change only the window's size, we must compute the window's current position to use in the position parameters. This can be done using the *GetWindowRect* function discussed below.

SetWindowPos

We discussed the *SetWindowPos* function earlier in the chapter. This function can be used to change the size, position, and Z order of a window:

```
BOOL SetWindowPos(
    HWND hWnd,               // handle to window
    HWND hWndInsertAfter,    // placement-order handle
    int X,                   // horizontal position
    int Y,                   // vertical position
    int cx,                  // width
    int cy,                  // height
    UINT uFlags              // window-positioning flags
);
```

Note that there is no corresponding *GetWindowPos*.

GetWindowRect and GetClientRect

The *GetWindowRect* function retrieves the *window's rectangle* (or *bounding rectangle*), which is a rectangle that would precisely circumscribe the *entire* window (client and nonclient areas). The dimensions of this rectangle are *screen coordinates*, that is, coordinates (in pixels) relative to the upper-left corner of the screen. Here is the declaration:

```
BOOL GetWindowRect(
    HWND hWnd,      // handle to window
    LPRECT lpRect   // address of RECT structure that will be filled by function
);
```

The *GetClientRect* function does the same thing for the client area of the window:

```
BOOL GetClientRect(
    HWND hWnd,       // handle to window
    LPRECT lpRect    // address of structure for client coordinates
);
```

You might expect that the coordinates returned in the **RECT** structure would be *window coordinates*, that is, coordinates relative to the upper-left corner of the window, but this is not the case. Indeed, the main purpose of this function is to retrieve the size of the client area, so it simplifies matters for the function to return *client coordinates*, that is, coordinates that are relative to the client area itself. Hence, the upper-left corner will always be (0,0).

Ignorance reigns supreme

Consider for a moment the following code:

```
SetWindowPos Text1.hwnd, HWND_TOP, 0, 0, 2, 2, SWP_SHOWWINDOW Or SWP_NOMOVE
GetWindowRect Text1.hwnd, r
Debug.Print r.Top, r.Bottom, r.Left, r.Right
```

This simply sets the height and width of a text box to 2 pixels. A sample output is:

| 46 | 48 | 17 | 19 |

We might have expected the `Top` and `Bottom` values to differ by only 1 (see Figure 15-4), since the text box has height 2 pixels. However, the *GetWindowRect* function returns the coordinates (`r.Right, r.Bottom`) of the pixel just *below and to the right* of the window, as shown in Figure 15-4. Hence, this pixel is not actually part of the window!

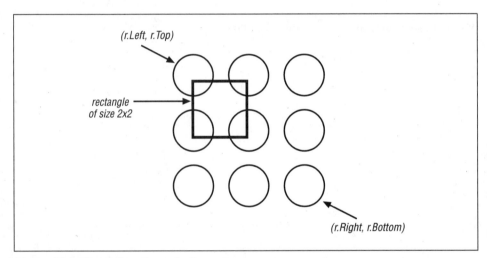

Figure 15-4. Illustrating rectangle dimensions

This was done deliberately, so that the following equations would hold:

```
r.Height = r.Bottom - r.Top
r.Width = r.Right - r.Left
```

In my opinion, this is a clear example of ignorance reigning supreme—to deliberately return misleading values for the `Bottom` and `Right` properties just so that programmers would not have to learn the correct formulas:

```
r.Height = r.Bottom - r.Top + 1
r.Width = r.Right - r.Left + 1
```

Oh well.

ClientToScreen and ScreenToClient

The functions *ClientToScreen* and *ScreenToClient* can be used to translate between client coordinates and screen coordinates. The functions have the same form. They both take a POINT structure as input and replace the values in this structure with the translated values. Thus, the POINT structure is an IN/OUT parameter. Here are the declarations:

```
BOOL ClientToScreen(
    HWND hWnd,        // window handle for source coordinates
    LPPOINT lpPoint // pointer to structure containing screen coordinates
);

BOOL ScreenToClient(
    HWND hWnd,        // window handle for source coordinates
    LPPOINT lpPoint // address of structure containing coordinates
);
```

We will use these functions in several utilities.

16

Windows Messages

The Windows operating system uses *messages* to communicate to and from the windows in the system. In general, messages can be classified as:

- Messages generated by Windows in response to user input from the keyboard or mouse

- Messages generated by an application, such as those produced by the *SendMessage* function

A message is composed of four parts:

- A window handle that identifies the *target window* of the message

- A *message identifier*, which is a 32-bit long

- Two 32-bit values called *message parameters*

These four message parts are clearly seen in the declaration of the *SendMessage* function:

```
LRESULT SendMessage(
    HWND hWnd,          // handle of destination window
    UINT Msg,           // message to send
    WPARAM wParam,      // first message parameter
    LPARAM lParam       // second message parameter
);
```

I have counted almost 1,000 different messages, and I am sure that I have missed some. These messages can be broadly categorized into a few main categories:

- Messages related to a type of control: Static, Listbox, Combo box, Button, Edit, Scrollbar, TreeView, ListView, Toolbar, Trackbar, Statusbar, Progressbar, Tool-Tip, UpDown, Tab Control

- Mouse messages

- Keyboard messages

- Clipboard messages

- Dialog messages

- MDI messages

- Others

Microsoft was kind enough to supply symbolic constants for the message identifiers. For instance, Table 16-1 shows the 45 Listbox-related message identifiers. We can tell what many of these messages do from their names:

Table 16-1. The Listbox Messages

LB_ADDFILE	LB_GETITEMHEIGHT	LB_SELECTSTRING
LB_ADDSTRING	LB_GETITEMRECT	LB_SELITEMRANGE
LB_CTLCODE	LB_GETLOCALE	LB_SELITEMRANGEEX
LB_DELETESTRING	LB_GETSEL	LB_SETANCHORINDEX
LB_DIR	LB_GETSELCOUNT	LB_SETCARETINDEX
LB_ERR	LB_GETSELITEMS	LB_SETCOLUMNWIDTH
LB_ERRSPACE	LB_GETTEXT	LB_SETCOUNT
LB_FINDSTRING	LB_GETTEXTLEN	LB_SETCURSEL
LB_FINDSTRINGEXACT	LB_GETTOPINDEX	LB_SETHORIZONTALEXTENT
LB_GETANCHORINDEX	LB_INITSTORAGE	LB_SETITEMDATA
LB_GETCARETINDEX	LB_INSERTSTRING	LB_SETITEMHEIGHT
LB_GETCOUNT	LB_ITEMFROMPOINT	LB_SETLOCALE
LB_GETCURSEL	LB_MSGMAX	LB_SETSEL
LB_GETHORIZONTALEXTENT	LB_OKAY	LB_SETTABSTOPS
LB_GETITEMDATA	LB_RESETCONTENT	LB_SETTOPINDEX

As we will see in some detail later in this chapter, every window is based on a *window class*. Each window class has an associated *window procedure* (also called a *window function*). This procedure must be supplied by the programmer; that is, by the VC++ programmer—VB takes care of this for the VB programmer.

The window procedure is called by the system in order to notify a window that it has a message. Thus, a window procedure is a *callback* procedure. The procedure has the general form shown here. The parameters are filled in by the system with the four parts of a message described earlier.

```
// Window procedure for window class
LRESULT CALLBACK WndProc(HWND hwnd, UINT iMsg, WPARAM wParam, LPARAM lParam)
{
    switch(iMsg)    // act based on window identifier
    {
```

```
            // process any resize messages
            case WM_SIZE:
               // code here to process message
               return 0;

            // process the destroy message
            case WM_DESTROY:
               // code here to process message
               return 0;
         }
         // Call Windows default window procedure
         return DefWindowProc(hwnd, iMsg, wParam, lParam);
      }
```

Messages are handled on a per thread basis. That is, the system determines which thread owns the target window of the message and passes the message to that thread. The thread determines which window procedure should be called and, in effect, asks the system to call that window procedure by calling the *Dispatch-Message* function. This will become clearer as we look at the process in more detail.

The Message Queues of a Thread

Each thread has a collection of *message queues* that are used to queue incoming messages, that is, messages sent by the system (perhaps in response to user action or another thread calling *SendMessage*). As Figure 16-1 illustrates, there are four queues:

The posted-message queue

Queues *posted messages*, that is, messages that are received via the *Post-Message* API function.

The sent-message queue

Queues *sent messages*, that is, messages that are received via the *SendMessage* API function (and its relatives).

The reply-message queue

Queues messages that are received as a reply to a sent message (posted messages do not reply).

The virtualized input queue

Queues messages that result from hardware input, such as from the keyboard or mouse.

A special structure called THREADINFO holds pointers to these queues along with some additional information that we will discuss later in this chapter. Note, however, that this structure is undocumented. The only source of information that I could obtain for it is Jeffrey Richter's book *Advanced Windows, Third Edition* from Microsoft Press. Thus, I suppose I should say that my information is only as current as his. Normally, I would not discuss undocumented features of the operating system, but this one does help tie the discussion together very nicely, so I will make an exception.

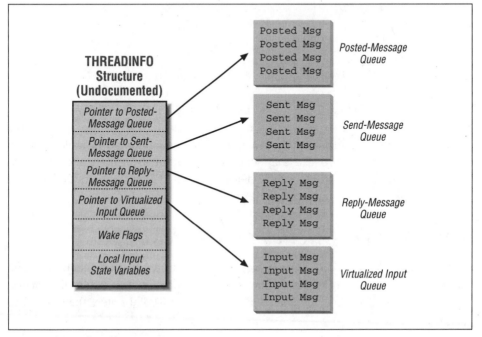

Figure 16-1. A thread's input queues

The Windows Messaging System

Figure 16-2 shows the overall layout of the Windows messaging system. Let us look at the components of this system.

We should note that the documentation simply refers to *the* message queue for a thread. I presume that it does so because it does not acknowledge the existence of separate posted, sent, reply, and virtual input queues.

The documentation also suggests that sent messages are not queued at all, but that the system just calls the window procedure for the target window immediately. This is true when the *SendMessage* function is being called from the thread that owns the target window. In this case, the thread simply calls the window procedure for the target window just like any other procedure. On the other hand, if the target window belongs to a foreign thread (in the same process or in another process), the message must be placed in the target thread's sent-message queue. (In 16-bit Windows, sent messages were never queued.)

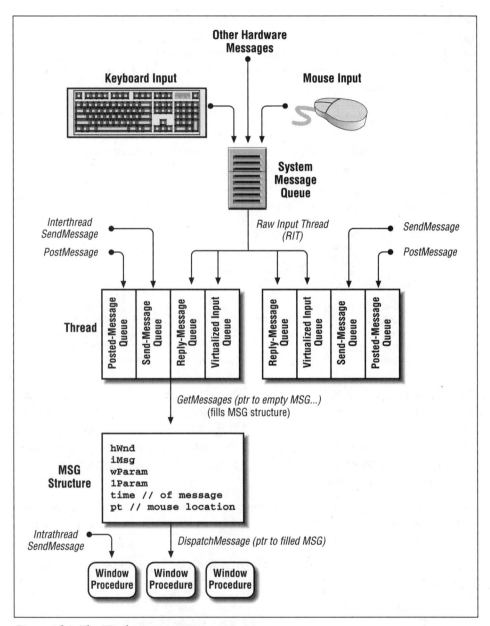

Figure 16-2. The Windows messaging system

Getting to a Thread's Message Queues

As we have said, messages are generated in response to user action (keyboard and mouse) and also by application code. Hardware input messages, such as those generated by the keyboard or mouse, are placed in the system message queue by the hardware device driver. From there, a special system thread called the *Raw Input Thread*, or RIT, removes the messages, determines the thread that owns the target window, and places the message in the appropriate message queue for the thread. Note that posted and sent messages are placed in the appropriate thread message queue directly.

Message Loops

When a VC++ programmer creates a program, he or she must create a *message loop*, which has the following appearance:

```
// Message loop for window
while( GetMessage(&msg, hwnd, 0 , 0) )
{
   TranslateMessage(&msg);
   DispatchMessage(&msg);
}
```

The *GetMessage* function is:

```
BOOL GetMessage(
   LPMSG lpMsg,            // address of MSG structure to receive message
   HWND hWnd,              // handle of window to check for messages for
   UINT wMsgFilterMin,     // first message in acceptable message range
   UINT wMsgFilterMax      // last message in acceptable message range
);
```

This function retrieves a message from the thread's message queues, provided that it is intended for the window with handle *hwnd* and provided that the message number lies in the acceptable range between *wMsgFilterMin* and *wMsgFilterMax*. These parameters provide a way to filter messages. For instance, if *wMsgFilterMin* is set to WM_KEYFIRST, and *wMsgFilterMax* is set to WM_KEYLAST, then only keyboard messages are retrieved.

Setting both filtering parameters to 0 removes all filtering and allows all messages to be retrieved. Also, setting the *hwnd* parameter to NULL specifies that all messages for this thread should be retrieved.

The *GetMessage* function then fills the lpMsg structure with information about the message. This structure is defined by:

```
typedef struct tagMSG {
   HWND hwnd;             // handle to the target window of message
   UINT message;          // message number
   WPARAM wParam;         // message-specific parameter
   LPARAM lParam;         // message-specific parameter
   DWORD time;            // time the message was posted
   POINT pt;              // cursor position when message was posted
} MSG;
```

When *GetMessage* returns, it returns a nonzero value unless the message is WM_QUIT, in which case the return value is 0. Hence, the **while** loop will continue until a quit message is received.

If *GetMessage* returns a nonzero value, the *TranslateMessage* function will do some translation related to keyboard input if necessary (we won't discuss this further), and the *DispatchMessage* function:

```
LONG DispatchMessage(
    CONST MSG *lpmsg // pointer to MSG structure with message
);
```

asks Windows to call the window procedure for the class, feeding it the parameters from the filled-in MSG structure for the message. Note that *DispatchMessage* does not return until the message has been processed and the window procedure returns.

Note, however, that it is possible for a function *within* a window procedure to send a message that results in the window procedure being called again. For instance, if a window procedure calls *UpdateWindow*, this function sends a WM_PAINT message to the window, thus invoking the window procedure while it is still processing the message that caused the call to *UpdateWindow*. In this case, processing of the first message is halted until the second message (WM_PAINT) is processed.

This requires that a window procedure be *reentrant* (capable of being called while its code is being executed). Among other things, this may require that the procedure save its current state so that it can restore that state to continue where it left off.

A Closer Look at GetMessage

When a message is placed in one of a thread's message queues, the system also sets one or more *wake flags* in the thread's THREADINFO structure. This will cause the thread to wake so that it can process the message. A thread can also call the API function *GetQueueStatus*:

```
DWORD GetQueueStatus(
    UINT flags // queue-status flags
);
```

or, in VB:

```
Declare Function GetQueueStatus Lib "user32" ( _
    ByVal fuFlags As Long _
) As Long
```

to check on the types of messages that are pending. Table 16-2 shows the various wake flags and their meanings.

Table 16-2. Wake Flags

Value	Meaning
QS_ALLEVENTS	An input, **WM_TIMER**, **WM_PAINT**, **WM_HOTKEY**, or posted message is in a queue.
QS_ALLINPUT	Any message is in a queue.
QS_ALLPOSTMESSAGE	A posted message (other than those listed here) is in the posted-message queue.
QS_HOTKEY	A **WM_HOTKEY** message is in a queue.
QS_INPUT	An input message is in the input queue.
QS_KEY	A **WM_KEYUP**, **WM_KEYDOWN**, **WM_SYSKEYUP**, or **WM_SYSKEYDOWN** message is in the input queue.
QS_MOUSE	A **WM_MOUSEMOVE** message or mouse-button message is in the input queue.
QS_MOUSEBUTTON	A mouse-button message is in the input queue.
QS_MOUSEMOVE	A **WM_MOUSEMOVE** message is in the input queue.
QS_PAINT	A **WM_PAINT** message is in a queue.
QS_QUIT	A Quit message is pending.
QS_POSTMESSAGE	A posted message (other than those listed here) is in the posted-message queue.
QS_SENDMESSAGE	A message sent by another thread or application is in the sent-message or reply-message queue.
QS_TIMER	A **WM_TIMER** message is in a queue.

You are probably wondering by now how the *GetMessage* function determines from which of possibly several nonempty queues to retrieve a message. The answer, according to Richter's book (with a few embellishments), is that *GetMessage* follows the steps outlined below, *in this order*. These steps also show the priority given to the various types of messages and explain why sent messages are taken before posted messages, for instance.

1. If the QS_SENDMESSAGE flag is on, the next sent message is retrieved from the sent-message queue, and the appropriate window procedure is called. This is repeated until no more sent messages remain. The QS_SENDMESSAGE flag is then turned off. *GetMessage* does not return during this process, and so no further code following the call to *GetMessage* is executed.

2. If the QS_POSTMESSAGE flag is on, the next posted message is retrieved from the post-message queue, and the MSG structure (the parameter to *GetMessage*) is filled. If this was the only posted message, the QS_POSTMESSAGE flag is cleared. In any case, the *GetMessage* function returns a nonzero value other than –1 (which is reserved to indicate an error).

3. If the QS_QUIT flag is set, the MSG structure is filled and the flag is cleared. *GetMessage* returns FALSE (0).

4. If the QS_INPUT flag is set, the MSG structure is filled. The status of each of the input-related flags (QS_KEY, QS_MOUSEMOVE, etc.) is cleared if there are no more messages of the corresponding type in the input queue. *GetMessage* returns a nonzero value other than –1 (which is reserved to indicate an error).

5. If the QS_PAINT flag is set, the MSG structure is filled. *GetMessage* returns a nonzero value other than –1 (which is reserved to indicate an error).

6. If the QS_TIMER flag is set, the MSG structure is filled. The timer is reset. *GetMessage* returns a nonzero value other than –1 (which is reserved to indicate an error).

Note, in particular, that a WM_PAINT message is not processed until all sent, posted, and input messages are processed. Also, if several WM_PAINT messages pile up for the same window, they are consolidated by the system into a single message .

Posting and Sending Messages

The above description shows that all sent messages are processed before *any* posted messages (or other type of message) are processed. There is also an important distinction between the *SendMessage* and *PostMessage* functions.

The *PostMessage* function returns immediately with a Boolean value indicating success or failure of the *posting*, but the calling thread gets no information about the outcome of the message, or even whether or not the thread actually processed the message. (It could terminate before processing the message.)

Unlike the *PostMessage* function, *SendMessage* does not return (and so the calling thread waits) until the message has been processed. In this way, *SendMessage* can return information to the calling thread about the outcome of the message processing. For instance, the LB_GETTEXT message retrieves the text of an item in the listbox to which the message is sent. Obviously, *posting* an LB_GETTEXT message to a listbox is pointless.

Actually, the calling thread must do one thing while waiting for a return value from *SendMessage*—it must (and does) process messages *sent* to it. After all, if it did not do this, then the target thread could send a message to the calling thread, in which case both threads would be sitting idle, waiting for the other thread to respond. Result: deadlock.

Setting a Timeout

If the calling thread does not want to wait indefinitely for the target thread to process its message, it can use the *SendMessageTimeout* function instead of *SendMessage*. This function has declaration as follows.

```
BOOL SendMessageTimeout(
    HWND hWnd,              // handle of destination window
    UINT Msg,               // message to send
    WPARAM wParam,          // first message parameter
    LPARAM lParam,          // second message parameter
    UINT fuFlags,           // how to send the message
    UINT uTimeout,          // timeout duration
    LPDWORD lpdwResult      // return value for synchronous call
);
```

The first four parameters are the same as for *SendMessage*. The *fuFlags* parameter can be a combination of the following values:

SMTO_ABORTIFHUNG

Returns immediately if the receiving process appears to be hung.

SMTO_BLOCK

Prevents the calling thread from processing any other messages until the function returns.

SMTO_NORMAL

Does not prevent the calling thread from processing other messages while waiting for the function to return. This is the usual setting.

The *uTimeout* parameter is the time to wait, in milliseconds. The final parameter contains return information and is message-specific.

Notification Messages

The *SendNotifyMessage* function:

```
BOOL SendNotifyMessage(
    HWND hWnd,          // handle of destination window
    UINT Msg,           // message to send
    WPARAM wParam,      // first message parameter
    LPARAM lParam       // second message parameter
);
```

has the same signature as *SendMessage*, but has different behavior depending upon whether the target window is in a different thread or not. If the target window is in the calling thread, the function behaves just like *SendMessage*. However, if the target window is in a foreign thread, the function returns immediately, thus gathering no information about the results of the message. However, it differs from *PostMessage* in that the message sent has higher priority than posted messages.

The main role of *SendNotifyMessage* is to send *notification messages*. These are messages that notify the recipient of some action, but that do not require the sender to wait for a reply. These messages are very common, and Windows uses them often. For instance, WM_ACTIVATE, WM_DESTROY, WM_SIZE, and WM_MOVE messages are all notification messages. Also, as we mentioned earlier, a child control will often send a notification message to its parent, informing the parent of some action related to the child.

Example: Sending Messages to a Listbox

As you begin to write programs that manipulate the operating system more closely than VB generally permits, you will find various reasons to send messages. One of the main reasons is to have more control over controls. For instance, Visual Basic itself does not permit us to set tab stops in a listbox control, nor to add a horizontal scrollbar to a listbox. However, we can accomplish both of these tasks easily using *SendMessage.*

Setting Tab Stops

To set the tab stops in a listbox, we just send the listbox a `LB_SETTABSTOPS` message. According to the documentation, the message parameters are as follows:

wParam
> The number of tab stops to set.

lParam
> A pointer to the first member of an array of integers (i.e., VB longs) containing the tab stops, in dialog template units. The tab stops must be sorted in ascending order.

For this messages, the *SendMessage* function returns `True` if the tabs are set correctly.

The documentation also mentions that in order to respond to the `LB_SETTABSTOPS` message, the listbox must have been created with the `LBS_USETABSTOPS` style. Fortunately, VB's *ThunderListbox* listboxes seem to have this style.

The documentation goes on to say that if *cTabs* is set to 0 and *lpnTabs* is `NULL` (also 0), the listbox will have a default tab stop set at intervals of two dialog box template units. Moreover, if *cTabs* is set to 1, the listbox will have default tab stops separated by the distance specified by *lpnTabs*. On the other hand, if the array pointed to by *lpnTabs* has more than a single value, a tab stop will be set for each value in the array.

The dialog box template units that this message uses are the device-independent units used in dialog box templates. To convert measurements from dialog box template units to pixels, we can use the *MapDialogRect* function. However, these units tend to be about one-fourth the average character width, and it generally suffices to just guess and adjust.

To illustrate, Figure 16-3 shows the results of an **LB_SETTABSTOPS** message. For this, we need the declarations for *SendMessage* and **LB_SETTABSTOPS**:

```
Declare Function SendMessage Lib "user32" Alias "SendMessageA" ( _
    ByVal hWnd As Long, _
    ByVal wMsg As Long, _
    ByVal wParam As Long, _
    ByRef lParam As Long _
) As Long
Public Const LB_SETTABSTOPS = &H192
```

Example 16-1 shows the code to send the message.

Example 16-1. Using SendMessage to Set Tab Stops

```
Public Function SetTabstopsExample()

Dim i As Integer

' Set tab stops in List2 only
Dim Tabstops(1 To 4) As Long

Tabstops(1) = 4 * 10              ' approx 10 characters wide
Tabstops(2) = Tabstops(1) + 4 * 8
Tabstops(3) = Tabstops(2) + 4 * 6
Tabstops(4) = Tabstops(3) + 4 * 4
SendMessage List2.hWnd, LB_SETTABSTOPS, 4, Tabstops(1)

' Fill listboxes
For i = 1 To 4
   List1.AddItem "Item1" & vbTab & "Item2" & _
      vbTab & "Item3" & vbTab & "Item4" & vbTab & "Item5"
   List2.AddItem "Item1" & vbTab & "Item2" & _
      vbTab & "Item3" & vbTab & "Item4" & vbTab & "Item5"
Next

End Sub
```

Setting the Horizontal Extent

To quote the documentation:

> An application sends an **LB_SETHORIZONTALEXTENT** message to set the width, in pixels, by which a listbox can be scrolled horizontally (the scrollable width). If the width of the listbox is smaller than this value, the horizontal scroll bar horizontally scrolls items in the listbox. If the width of the listbox is equal to or greater than this value, the horizontal scroll bar is hidden.

For this message, the *wParam* parameter is set to the scrollable width, in pixels. For Windows 9x, this is limited to a 16-bit value (are they kidding?) and *lParam* is 0. There is no return value.

The declaration for **LB_SETHORIZONTALEXTENT** is:

```
Public Const LB_SETHORIZONTALEXTENT = &H194
```

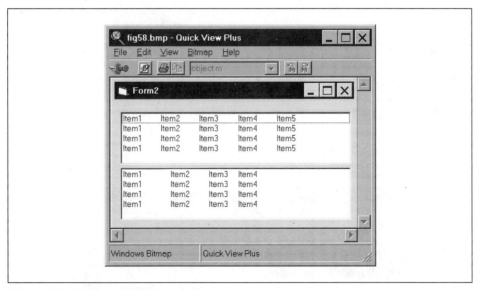

Figure 16-3. Setting tab stops in a listbox

The following code results in the listbox shown in Figure 16-4:

```
List1.AddItem "I would I could quit all offenses with as clear " & _
              "excuse as well as I am doubtless I can purge " & _
              "myself of many I am charg'd withal."

SendMessage List1.hWnd, LB_SETHORIZONTALEXTENT, 500&, 0&
```

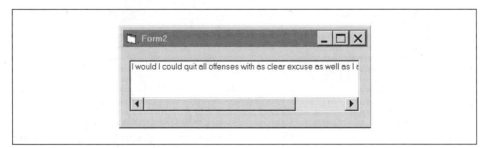

Figure 16-4. Setting the horizontal extent of a listbox

Extracting Listbox Data

From time to time, I have found the need to extract the entries from a listbox or combo box of another application. This has been very useful to me in writing books. For instance, in my books on programming Microsoft Access, Word, and Excel, and on creating Visual Basic Add-ins, I have wanted to grab a list of the properties or methods of various objects in the corresponding object models.

Figure 16-5 shows the Microsoft Word Visual Basic help system, with an open Topics Found dialog box for the properties of the **Range** object. Since this object has 65 properties, I find it helpful to extract the list of these properties so that I can peruse it more easily than scrolling through the ridiculously small Topics Found listbox. Figure 16-5 also shows the *rpiControlExtractor* application, which has extracted the list of properties. Of course, once this list is in my own listbox, I can do what I want with it. (This application should probably be called the *Control Data Extractor*, since it doesn't extract controls, it extracts a control's data, but I opted for the shorter term.)

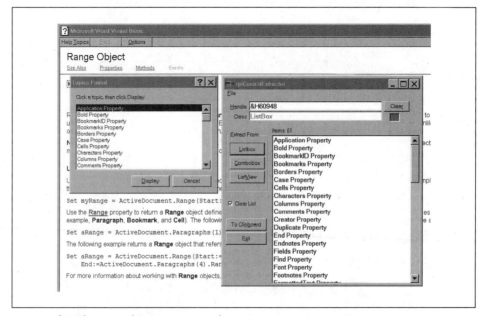

Figure 16-5. The Control Extractor at work

The Control Extractor application can extract data from a listbox, a combo box, or a ListView control. The former controls (the listbox and combo box) are old-style controls that existed in 16-bit Windows, whereas the ListView control is a newer 32-bit control. As we will see, this has a profound effect on the problem of getting the data from a foreign control (control in another process).

In fact, we will need to postpone a discussion of the code required to extract data from a foreign ListView control until Chapter 20, *DLL Injection and Foreign Process Access*. Also, the process of extracting from combo boxes is very similar to that of listboxes, so we will consider only the latter. (Of course, the source code for *rpiControlExtractor* contains code for all three types of controls.)

For a listbox, control data extraction is done by sending a **LB_GETTEXT** message to the control. To send this message, we set the *wParam* message parameter to the zero-based index of the item to retrieve and *lParam* to the address of a memory buffer in which to place the item. This memory buffer is the cause of some problems.

In particular, Example 16-2 contains the code that executes when the user presses the (Extract From) Listbox command button. It assumes that the handle of the listbox is in the global variable *hControl*.

Example 16-2. Extracting the Contents of a Listbox

```
Sub ExtractFromListBox()

Dim cItems As Integer
Dim i As Integer
Dim sBuf As String
Dim cBuf As Long
Dim lResp As Long

' Get item count from control
cItems = SendMessageByNum(hControl, LB_GETCOUNT, 0&, 0&)

' Display count in label
lblItems = "Items: " & cItems

If cItems <= 0 Then Exit Sub

' Clear listbox first?
If chkClearList.Value = 1 Then lstMain.Clear

' Put items into listbox
For i = 0 To cItems - 1

    ' Get length of item
    cBuf = SendMessageByString(hControl, LB_GETTEXTLEN, CLng(i), 0)

    ' Allocate buffer to hold item
    sBuf = String$(cBuf + 1, " ")

    ' Send message to get item
    lResp = SendMessageByString(hControl, LB_GETTEXT, CLng(i), sBuf)

    ' Add item to local listbox
    If lResp > 0 Then
        lstMain.AddItem Left$(sBuf, lResp)
    End If

Next i

lstMain.Refresh

End Sub
```

Interprocess Marshalling

The issue of interprocess communication is a very important one to those of us who like to hack. After all, much of what we want to do involves invading a foreign process—sending commands and sending or receiving data.

Referring to the *ExtractFromListbox* procedure, the `LB_GETTEXTLEN` message works across process boundaries because the only data returned is the return value of the function. This value is returned on the calling process's stack. In particular, it does not require allocating a memory buffer.

On the other hand, the `LB_GETTEXT` message requires the address of a memory buffer. Now, the calling process can allocate a memory buffer only in its own memory space, not in the address space of the process that contains the listbox. But the window procedure of the foreign process *thinks* that the address in the `lParam` parameter is in its own address space (that is, the only address space it knows about), so it will try to place the item at that location in its address space. It would certainly seem that this will cause an access violation. In any case, it certainly won't return the item text to the calling process. However, the code works, and the listbox item is in fact placed in the buffer of the calling process!

The reason is that Windows actually watches out for certain messages, such as `LB_GETTEXT`, and is kind enough to marshall the data (in this case the listbox item) from the target address space to the calling address space. (*Marshalling* means packaging data and sending it across process boundaries. This happens a lot in OLE Automation.)

It is not clear exactly which messages are automatically marshalled by Windows and which are not, so you need to experiment. For instance, buffers for messages sent to older-style 16-bit controls, such as listboxes and combo boxes, appear to be marshalled in order to preserve compatibility with 16-bit Windows, where marshalling was not even an issue (it was not required).

However, Windows does not marshall data extracted from a new 32-bit ListView control, since in this case there is no compatibility issue. The Control Extractor application will need to find another approach. Indeed, we will need to find some way to allocate memory in the foreign process and then copy data to and from this foreign memory, in particular, when we come to write the *rpiControlExtractor* code for extracting from a foreign ListView control.

Actually, the hard part can be the allocation of foreign memory. Note that under Windows NT, this is not difficult, because Windows NT implements the function *VirtualAllocEx*:

```
LPVOID VirtualAllocEx(
    HANDLE hProcess,        // process within which to allocate memory
    LPVOID lpAddress,       // desired starting address of allocation
```

```
    DWORD dwSize,            // size, in bytes, of region to allocate
    DWORD flAllocationType, // type of allocation
    DWORD flProtect         // type of access protection
);
```

which is designed specifically for this purpose! Unfortunately, this function is *not* implemented in Windows 9x. We will need to go to considerably more trouble to allocate foreign memory in a way that will work in all versions of Windows. As mentioned, this will be done in Chapter 20.

Copying Data Between Processes

Once foreign memory has been allocated, there are a variety of ways to copy data between the processes. In fact, I find it a bit curious that Microsoft has made it easy to copy data between processes, but not to set up a foreign memory buffer to hold that data. Let us discuss some of these methods now. We will have occasion to use them later in the book.

One possibility for interprocess data transfer is to use *WriteProcessMemory* and *ReadProcessMemory*. The *WriteProcessMemory* function is:

```
BOOL WriteProcessMemory(
    HANDLE hProcess,        // handle to process whose memory is written to
    LPVOID lpBaseAddress,   // address to start writing to
    LPVOID lpBuffer,        // pointer to buffer to write data to
    DWORD nSize,            // number of bytes to write
    LPDWORD lpNumberOfBytesWritten   // actual number of bytes written
);
```

Note that the foreign process handle must have **PROCESS_VM_WRITE** and **PROCESS_VM_OPERATION** access to the foreign process. Such a handle can be obtained by using the *OpenProcess* function, discussed in Chapter 11, *Processes*. The *ReadProcessMemory* function is:

```
BOOL ReadProcessMemory(
    HANDLE hProcess,        // handle to the process whose memory is read
    LPCVOID lpBaseAddress,  // address to start reading
    LPVOID lpBuffer,        // address of buffer to place read data
    DWORD nSize,            // number of bytes to read
    LPDWORD lpNumberOfBytesRead   // address of number of bytes read
);
```

In the case of *ReadProcessMemory*, the handle must have **PROCESS_VM_READ** access to the foreign process.

Another way to send data to a foreign process is to use the *SendMessage* function to send a **WM_COPYDATA** message. In this case, the *wParam* parameter is a handle to a foreign window (that is, a window in the foreign process), and the *lParam* parameter is a pointer to a **COPYDATASTRUCT** structure:

```
typedef struct tagCOPYDATASTRUCT {
    DWORD dwData;
```

```
        DWORD cbData;
        PVOID lpData;
    } COPYDATASTRUCT;
```

The *dwData* parameter can be any 32-bit data value; *cbData* is the number of bytes to send; and *lpData* is a pointer to a buffer, in the calling process that contains the *cbData* bytes to send.

The correct form of *SendMessage* is:

```
SendMessage(hTargetWindow, WM_COPYDATA, hSendingWindow, _
            Address of COPYDATASTRUCT)
```

Sending this message causes Windows to create a buffer in the foreign process, place the data into that buffer, and adjust the value of *lpData* to point to that foreign buffer. (Of course, that buffer is not foreign to the target window's window procedure.)

We will see an example of using this message when we discuss hooks in Chapter 19, *Windows Hooks*. Here are some points to keep in mind:

- We must use *SendMessage* to send this message and not *PostMessage*. The reason is that Windows will deallocate the foreign buffer as soon as the message is processed, and the procedure is not designed to wait around for a posted message to be processed.

- The data in the buffer (as well as *dwData*) should not contain pointers, for the simple reason that the target of any such pointers is *not* marshalled and is thus not accessible to the foreign process.

- The target process should consider the data as being read-only. The final parameter to *SendMessage*, that is, the pointer to the foreign copy of COPYDATASTRUCT, is valid only during the processing of the message. The target process should not free this memory. Also, if the target process wants to save the data, it should copy that data to another location.

The Local Input State

Under Win32, each thread in the system is a kind of virtual computer in itself. Accordingly, each thread needs to at least *think* it has sole possession of the keyboard, mouse, monitor, and other hardware.

To put this into effect, each thread is given its own *local input state* as part of its THREADINFO structure, as shown in Figure 16-1. This consists of the following information related to the focus, the keyboard, and the mouse:

- The currently active window for the thread.

- The window that has the *keyboard input focus* (or just *input focus*).

- The current state of the keyboard (for example, is the Alt key pressed or is CAPLOCKS on?).

- The current state of the *caret* (the bitmap that marks the location of the insertion point).

- The window that currently has the *mouse capture*, that is, the window that currently receives mouse messages. (It need not be the window underneath the mouse pointer.)

- The current *cursor* (the bitmap that marks the location of the mouse pointer) and its visibility.

It is important to understand that the notions of active window and input focus exist for each thread separately. In other words, each thread owns a window that it considers the active window and a window that it considers as having the input focus. On the other hand, the user sees the computer as a whole, not as a collection of separate virtual computers. To the user, only one window is "active" at a time and only one window has the "input focus." Here are the facts.

The Foreground Thread

At any given time, the Raw Input Thread (RIT) directs keyboard input and mouse input to the virtual input queue of one thread. The thread that is currently receiving this attention is called the *foreground thread*. When the user switches applications, the RIT will redirect output to a different thread, thus causing a change in which thread is the foreground thread. The API function *SetForegroundWindow* can be used to change which thread is the foreground thread.

Recall, however, our discussion in Chapter 11, concerning the change in behavior of *SetForegroundWindow* under Windows 98 and Windows 2000. To reiterate, under Windows 95 and Windows NT 4, the *SetForegroundWindow* function does bring an application to the foreground. However, under Windows 98 and Windows 2000, all that happens is that the target application's main window will become the active window *for that thread* and the titlebar will flash! Recall also that we discussed the *rpiSetForegroundWindow* function that is designed to duplicate the original functionality of *SetForegroundWindow*.

Keyboard Input

For each thread, at any given time, there is at most one window that would be processing keyboard messages if the thread happened to be the foreground thread. The window that processes keyboard messages (if any) is said to have the *input focus* for the thread. The input focus for a given thread can be changed by calling *SetFocus*. Also, the handle of the window that currently has the input focus can be retrieved by calling *GetFocus*. Again, we emphasize that this is on a per-thread basis. (We will consider an example of keyboard input in the "Experiments" section later in the chapter.)

Mouse Capture

Mouse input is a bit more involved than keyboard input. The reason is that a mouse-drag operation starts at one location and ends at another location, and these two locations need not be over windows in the same thread!

For each thread, there are essentially three possible states with regard to mouse focus:

- No mouse capture
- Thread-wide mouse capture
- System-wide mouse capture

Under normal conditions (no button pressed and no strange code executing), no window has the mouse capture. In this case, any mouse messages are placed in the input queue of the thread that owns the window under the mouse cursor at the time the message was generated, and the message is then processed by that window.

Whether or not the window does anything with this message is another story. In VB, we must place code in the MouseDown, MouseUp, or MouseMove events if we wish to process the mouse messages. In VC++, the programmer must place code in the appropriate window procedure.

On the other hand, mouse capture can take place on two levels: system-wide and thread-wide.

When we click on a control in a VB project, that control is given a *system-wide* mouse capture until we release the button. The reason is that clicking on a control may be preparatory to dragging the mouse pointer (as in drawing), in which case the initial window should receive all mouse messages until and including the release of the mouse button that signals the end of the drawing procedure. (Visual C++ programmers must arrange for mouse capture by calling *SetCapture* when a mouse button is depressed—VB does that for us.)

The *SetCapture* function can also be used to give a window the mouse capture, but this is only a thread-wide capture. If the mouse ventures over a window in a foreign thread, that window will begin receiving mouse messages. However, as soon as the mouse returns to *any* window owned by the thread that called *SetCapture*, the window with the mouse capture will receive all mouse messages. To turn off mouse capture for that thread, we must call *ReleaseCapture*. (We will consider an example of mouse capture in the "Experiments" section later in the chapter.)

Active Windows and the Foreground Window

As we have seen, Windows uses a parent-child relationship for its windows. Thus, one window can be the child of another window. Windows that do not have parents are called *top-level* windows. In each thread, the top-level window that is the parent of the window with the keyboard input focus is said to be the *active window* for the thread.

The *foreground window* is the active window for the foreground thread. It is the window that typically has the blue titlebar, to distinguish it from other windows. Unfortunately, much of the documentation uses the term active window for the foreground window. (This is true, for instance, in the Appearance tab of the Display applet on the Control Panel.) However, it is vital to maintain a distinction between *an active window* and *the foreground window*.

It should be clear from this discussion that using *SetFocus* works only within a given thread. Thus, it cannot be used to switch applications, that is, to set the foreground application. Under Windows 95 and Windows NT 4, *SetForeground-Window* can be used in this way, since it changes the foreground window and therefore redirects hardware input to the thread that owns the target window. However, see the discussion about the change in behavior of *SetForeground-Window* for Windows 98 and Windows 2000 in the section "The Foreground Thread" earlier in the chapter.

Experiments

The best way of examining the Windows messaging system and learning how it handles user input is to experiment. Accordingly, this section contains three experiments that allow you to see that different windows can have the input focus and the mouse capture at the same time; to determine that each thread has its own input focus; and to examine the difference between system-wide and thread-wide mouse capture.

Experiment one

To see that the window with the input focus and the window with the mouse capture can be different, you can create a simple VB project as follows. Create a form with one Command button and two text boxes. Add the code shown in Example 16-3.

Example 16-3. The Window with the Input Focus and the Mouse Capture

```
Option Explicit
Private Declare Function SetCapture Lib "user32" (ByVal hwnd As Long) _
                    As Long
Private Declare Function SetFocusAPI Lib "user32" Alias "SetFocus" _
                    (ByVal hwnd As Long) As Long
```

Example 16-3. The Window with the Input Focus and the Mouse Capture (continued)

```
Private Declare Function GetActiveWindow Lib "user32" () As Long

Private Sub Command1_Click()
' Set input focus to Text1
SetFocusAPI Text1.hwnd
' Set mouse capture to Text2
SetCapture Text2.hwnd
Debug.Print GetActiveWindow = Me.hwnd
End Sub

Private Sub Text2_MouseMove(Button As Integer, Shift As Integer, _
                            X As Single, Y As Single)
Text2 = X
End Sub
```

Now start the project and click the command button. Then move the mouse and type at the keyboard at the same time. You should see numbers changing in Text2 and keystrokes being added to Text1. This shows that Text1 has the input focus, but Text2 has the mouse capture (both relative to this thread).

Experiment two

You can also perform an interesting experiment that demonstrates the fact that each thread has its own input focus as follows. Create a VB project with a form that contains a single text box and a single timer control (see Figure 16-6).

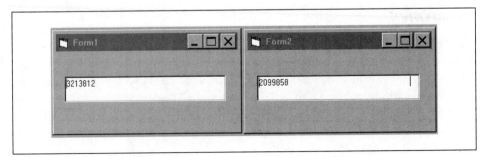

Figure 16-6. Demonstrating input focus

Set the timer's Interval property to 1000. Add the code from Example 16-4 to the form.

Example 16-4. Establishing that Each Thread Has Its Own Input Focus

```
Option Explicit
Private Declare Function SetFocusAPI Lib "user32" Alias "SetFocus" _
                    (ByVal hwnd As Long) As Long
Private Declare Function GetActiveWindow Lib "user32" () As Long

Private Sub Timer1_Timer()
' Set input focus to Text1
```

Example 16-4. Establishing that Each Thread Has Its Own Input Focus (continued)

```
SetFocusAPI Text1.hwnd
' Display active window handle
Text1 = GetActiveWindow
End Sub
```

Now repeat this with a second VB project, renaming the form's caption to Form2 to distinguish it from the form in the first project. Run both projects. After 1 second, both text boxes should have a blinking cursor, indicating that they both have the input focus, but for different threads. (Figure 16-6 does not do this justice.) Moreover, each thread has its own active window, as indicated by the different handles in each text box. Only one of the two forms can be the foreground window, however, as indicated by the blue titlebar.

Experiment three

To demonstrate mouse capture, create a project with a single form, as in Figure 16-7. Place a timer on the form as well, and set the interval property to 250. The complete code for the project appears in Example 16-5.

Example 16-5. System-wide and Thread-wide Mouse Capture

```
Option Explicit
Private Declare Function SetCapture Lib "user32" (ByVal hwnd As Long) _
                                                As Long
Private Declare Function GetCapture Lib "user32" () As Long
Private Declare Function ReleaseCapture Lib "user32" () As Long

Private Sub Command1_Click()

' Set mouse capture to Text1
SetCapture Text1.hwnd

End Sub

Private Sub Command2_Click()
ReleaseCapture
End Sub

Private Sub Form_MouseMove(Button As Integer, Shift As Integer, _
                        X As Single, Y As Single)
Text1 = X + Y
End Sub

Private Sub Text1_MouseMove(Button As Integer, Shift As Integer, _
                        X As Single, Y As Single)
Text1 = X + Y
End Sub

Private Sub Timer1_Timer()
txtCapture = GetCapture
End Sub
```

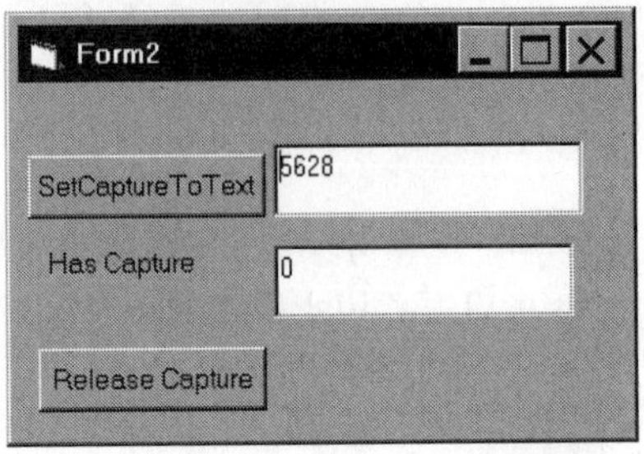

Figure 16-7. Demonstrating mouse capture

Now, as you move the mouse over the form, the value in Text1 (the upper text box) will change, indicating that the form is processing WM_MOUSEMOVE messages. However, the *GetCapture* function is reporting 0, meaning that no window has the mouse capture. This is why the value in Text1 does not change when the mouse pointer goes over the Command button or one of the text boxes, or goes outside of the form. This is normal (noncapture) mouse operation.

Next, hold down the left mouse button while the mouse pointer is over the form and drag the pointer around the screen, especially to a window belonging to another application. Notice that the handle of the form is placed in Text2, and Text1 gets the value of X+Y no matter where the pointer goes. Thus, VB has given the form system-wide mouse capture.

Finally, click the Command button. This gives a thread-wide mouse capture to Text1 as a result of the call to *GetCapture*. Move the mouse around the screen again, including over foreign windows. As long as the mouse is over *any* window in the current VB project (thread), the values in Text1 change, but as soon as the mouse ventures over a foreign window, the changes stop since the mouse is no longer captured by the Command button.

17

Window Classes and the Window Creation Process

We have seen how the operating system communicates with a window using messages. In this chapter, we take a closer look at the nature of a window itself. We will discuss window classes and how a window is actually created. This is the process that every VC++ programmer must understand. Visual Basic takes care of all of this for the VB programmer. Nevertheless, advanced VB programmers should have some understanding of these issues in order to program the Windows API.

To get a deeper understanding of what a window is and how it works, it is instructive to follow a brief (that is, as brief as possible) Visual C++ program that creates a window class and a window based on this class. Don't worry about understanding every line of code—we are after a general understanding here.

The basic steps in window creation under VC++ are as follows (although we will change the order a bit):

- Define a window class.
- Register the class.
- Set up the window procedure for the class.
- Create a window based on this class.
- Set up the message loop for the window.

Window Classes

Every window is an instance of a *window class*. In this sense, windows are object-oriented. Creating a window class is not hard. We begin by declaring a variable of type WNDCLASS. This is a structure with the following definition.

```
typedef struct WNDCLASS {
    UINT style;                 // window style
    WNDPROC lpfnWndProc;        // window procedure
    int cbClsExtra;
    int cbWndExtra;
    HANDLE hInstance;           // instance handle of process
    HICON hIcon;                // icon for window
    HCURSOR hCursor;            // mouse cursor for window
    HBRUSH hbrBackground;       // background color of window
    LPCTSTR lpszMenuName;       // menu for window class
    LPCTSTR lpszClassName;      // class name
};
```

This structure defines the properties of the window class, and thus of each window that is based on this class. In particular, the structure has members to set the icon, mouse cursor, background color, and menu for the class. The last member is used to give the class a name. In fact, the most important members of this structure are the class name and the window procedure.

Note that we can change or augment the properties of any given window once it is created. The window class properties act only as a starting point.

Here is some actual VC++ code:

```
WNDCLASS wndclass;

// Define window class
wndclass.style          = CS_HREDRAW | CS_VREDRAW;
wndclass.lpfnWndProc    = WndProc;
wndclass.cbClsExtra     = NULL;
wndclass.cbWndExtra     = NULL;
wndclass.hInstance      = hInstance;
wndclass.hIcon          = NULL;
wndclass.hCursor        = NULL;
wndclass.hbrBackground  = (HBRUSH)GetStockObject(LTGRAY_BRUSH);
wndclass.lpszMenuName   = NULL;
wndclass.lpszClassName  = TEXT("rpiClass1");
```

The *style* member is defined as the conjunction (ORing) of two values. (A horizontal bar is the OR operator in VC++.) The CS_HREDRAW style causes Windows to redraw the window if its width is changed, and similarly for the CS_VREDRAW style. Thus, all windows based on this class will have these redrawing properties.

The next step is to register the class with Windows. This is done using the *RegisterClass* function, which takes a pointer to the WNDCLASS structure for the class (the & means "address of"):

```
// Register class
RegisterClass(&wndclass)
```

Predefined Window Classes

Fortunately, Windows defines several window classes that we can use for creating windows. These are:

- Button
- Combo box
- Edit (Text box)
- Listbox
- MDIclient (an MDI client window)
- RichEdit (Version 1.0)
- RichEdit_Class (Version 2.0)
- Scrollbar
- Static (A label, rectangle, or line used to label, box, or separate other controls. Static controls receive no input and produce no output, which is why they are called *static*.)

The Window Procedure of a Window Class

We have already discussed the fact that messages are processed in the window procedure of a window class. It is worth emphasizing that it is the window *class* that has a window procedure and not individual windows. Thus, all windows based on a certain class use the same window procedure.

Here is an example of a window procedure. This example watches for only two types of messages: a WM_DESTROY message is sent to a window when it is being destroyed, and a WM_SIZE message is sent to a window after it has been resized by Windows (probably in response to user action with the mouse).

```
// Window procedure for this class
LRESULT CALLBACK WndProc(HWND hwnd, UINT iMsg, WPARAM wParam, LPARAM lParam)
{
    // a temporary string
    char temp[50];

    switch(iMsg)     // like the VB Select Case structure
    {
        // process any resize messages
        case WM_SIZE:
            _itoa( (lParam & 0x0000FFFF) , temp, 10 );
            SetWindowText(hwnd, temp);
            return 0;
```

```
        // process the destroy message
        case WM_DESTROY:
            // Generate a quit message
            PostQuitMessage(0);
            return 0;
    }
    // Call Windows default window procedure
    return DefWindowProc(hwnd, iMsg, wParam, lParam);
}
```

If a WM_DESTROY message arrives, our window procedure sends a WM_QUIT message to terminate the thread that created the window (and thus the application if it is single-threaded). If a WM_SIZE message arrives, our window procedure grabs the width of the client area of the window (this is the portion of the window that does not include the caption or borders), which is returned in the lower 16 bits of the *lParam* parameter, and places it in the window's caption—just for something to do.

We should emphasize that programmers seldom call a window procedure directly. The window procedure is a *callback function*, that is, it is called by Windows in order to pass the message information (window handle, message ID, *wParam*, and *lParam*) to the application for processing.

Finally, note that the final act of our window procedure is to call the *default window procedure*, which will supply default processing of all messages that are not processed by our window procedure (in this case, all messages except WM_SIZE and WM_DESTROY—the VC++ return statement exits the window procedure). Of course, window procedures in most applications will be far more complicated than this one, possibly having code that depends upon the window that is the target of the message (as given by the *hwnd* parameter). In fact, for many Windows applications, the main action takes place in the window procedure!

Creating a Window

Once a window class is defined and registered, we can create a window based on this class. This is done using the *CreateWindow* function:

```
HWND CreateWindow(
    LPCTSTR lpClassName,      // pointer to registered class name
    LPCTSTR lpWindowName,     // pointer to window name
    DWORD dwStyle,            // window style
    int x,                    // horizontal position of window
    int y,                    // vertical position of window
    int nWidth,               // window width
    int nHeight,              // window height
    HWND hWndParent,          // handle to parent or owner window
    HMENU hMenu,              // handle to menu or child-window identifier
    HANDLE hInstance,         // handle to application instance
    LPVOID lpParam            // pointer to window-creation data
);
```

Notice that the parameters to this function are quite similar to the parameters of the WNDCLASS structure.

The *CreateWindow* function requires the class name for the window and sets various properties of the window, such as its initial placement. The window name is used as a caption for those windows that have captions (application windows and command buttons, for instance).

The *CreateWindow* function returns a handle to the newly created window. Here is an example:

```
// Create window
hwnd = CreateWindow(
    wndclass.lpszClassName,              // window class name
    TEXT("rpi Window"),                  // window name
    WS_OVERLAPPEDWINDOW | WS_VSCROLL,    // window style
    CW_USEDEFAULT,                       // initial left of window
    CW_USEDEFAULT,                       // initial top of window
    CW_USEDEFAULT,                       // initial width of window
    CW_USEDEFAULT,                       // initial height of window
    NULL,                                // parent window handle
    NULL,                                // window menu handle
    hInstance,                           // process instance handle
    NULL                                 // creation parameters
);
```

Window Styles

As we have seen, every window has a *style*. This is a combination of the style defined for the window class as well as the setting of the *dwStyle* parameter in the *CreateWindow* function. The *dwStyle* parameter can be a combination of several style constants, both general constants and those that apply specifically to a particular type of window, such as a command button. Here are some examples of general style constants:

WS_BORDER
    Creates a window that has a thin-line border

WS_CAPTION
    Creates a window that has a titlebar (includes the WS_BORDER style)

WS_CHILD
    Creates a child window

WS_DLGFRAME
    Creates a window that has a border of a style typically used with dialog boxes

WS_HSCROLL
    Creates a window that has a horizontal scrollbar

WS_MAXIMIZE
    Creates a window that is initially maximized

`WS_MAXIMIZEBOX`

Creates a window that has a Maximize button

`WS_SYSMENU`

Creates a window that has a window menu on its titlebar

In addition, each type of predefined class has styles. For instance, the majority of button styles are shown here.

To create a checkbox

`BS_AUTO3STATE`

A three-state checkbox that changes its state when the user selects it

`BS_CHECKBOX`

A checkbox with text

To create a radio button (option button)

`BS_RADIOBUTTON`

A small circle with text

`BS_AUTORADIOBUTTON`

A radio button for which Windows automatically sets the button's state to checked and automatically sets the state for all other buttons in the same group to unchecked

To create a command button (push button)

`BS_DEFPUSHBUTTON`

A push button that behaves like a `BS_PUSHBUTTON`-style button, but is also the default button (can be selected by hitting the ENTER key)

`BS_PUSHBUTTON`

A push button

To place text

`BS_LEFTTEXT`

Places text on the left side of the radio button or checkbox

`BS_BOTTOM`

Places text at the bottom of the button rectangle

`BS_CENTER`

Centers text horizontally in the button rectangle

`BS_MULTILINE`

Wraps button text to multiple lines, if required

`BS_VCENTER`

Places text in the middle (vertically) of the button rectangle

Other

BS_GROUPBOX

A rectangle in which other controls can be grouped

BS_OWNERDRAW

An owner-drawn button (The programmer is responsible for the control's appearance.)

BS_BITMAP

Specifies that the button displays a bitmap

BS_ICON

Specifies that the button displays an icon

BS_TEXT

Specifies that the button displays text

The most important thing to notice about the button styles is that what VB programmers think of as different controls—command buttons, checkboxes, and option buttons—are in reality just buttons with different styles.

Changing a Window's Style

The *SetWindowLong* function can be used to set the style of a window after the window has been created. As it happens, some styles can be effectively changed after the window has been created and others cannot (the result is either nothing or disaster).

The only way to see whether changing a window's style will work is to try it. Here are a couple of examples that you might want to try. Just place a command button and two text boxes on a form:

```
Dim lStyle As Long

' Command button caption aligned at bottom
lStyle = GetWindowLong(Command1.hwnd, GWL_STYLE)
SetWindowLong Command1.hwnd, GWL_STYLE, lStyle Or BS_BOTTOM

' Textbox converts all input to lower case
lStyle = GetWindowLong(Text1.hwnd, GWL_STYLE)
SetWindowLong Text1.hwnd, GWL_STYLE, lStyle Or ES_LOWERCASE

' Textbox accepts only digits
lStyle = GetWindowLong(Text2.hwnd, GWL_STYLE)
SetWindowLong Text2.hwnd, GWL_STYLE, lStyle Or ES_NUMBER
```

The main point to note about this code is that we must first get the current style so that we can make the necessary changes. It would be a mistake to simply set a window's style to, say, **BS_BOTTOM**, because this would clear all other style settings.

Windows and VB Controls

Visual Basic controls are windows. The older controls have class names that begin with the word *Thunder*, because this was Microsoft's internal code name for Visual Basic 1.0. Note that some design-time controls are different than the corresponding runtime controls and thus may have different class names. Runtime control class names are based on the design-time name, but also include reference to the version of VB. For instance, a design-time listbox has class name *ThunderListBox*, whereas a VB5 runtime listbox has class name *ThunderRT5ListBox* and a VB6 runtime listbox has class name *ThunderRT6ListBox*. Table 17-1 shows the design-time class names for some common VB controls.

Table 17-1. Controls and Their Design-time Class Names

Control	Class Name
Check	*ThunderCheckBox*
Combo	*ThunderComboBox*
Command	*ThunderCommandButton*
Dir	*ThunderDirListBox*
Drive	*ThunderDriveListBox*
File	*ThunderFileListBox*
Form	*ThunderForm*
Frame	*ThunderFrame*
Label	*ThunderLabel*
List	*ThunderListBox*
MDIForm	*ThunderMDIForm*
Option	*ThunderOptionButton*
Picture	*ThunderPictureBox*
Scroll (Horiz)	*ThunderHScrollBar*
Scroll (Vert)	*ThunderVScrollBar*
Text	*ThunderTextBox*
Timer	*ThunderTimer*
TabStrip	*TabStrip20WndClasss*
Toolbar	*msvb_lib_toolbar*
ProgressBar	*ProgressBar20WndClass*
StatusBar	*StatusBar20WndClass*
TreeView	*TreeView20WndClass*
ListView	*ListView20WndClass*
ImageList	*ImageList20WndClass*
Slider	*Slider20WndClass*

Example: Spying on Windows

The *rpiSpyWin* application, whose complete source code is on the CD, is a little utility for getting information about a specific window. Figure 17-1 shows the main (and only) window for this program. In particular, the utility retrieves the window handle, class name, caption, styles, location, window ID, and process and thread IDs of any visible window. (The *window identifier*, or *window ID*, is a number that is passed to the *CreateWindow* function and identifies a child window from among its siblings. This value is occasionally useful in calling API functions, so I have included it here in case you run across it.)

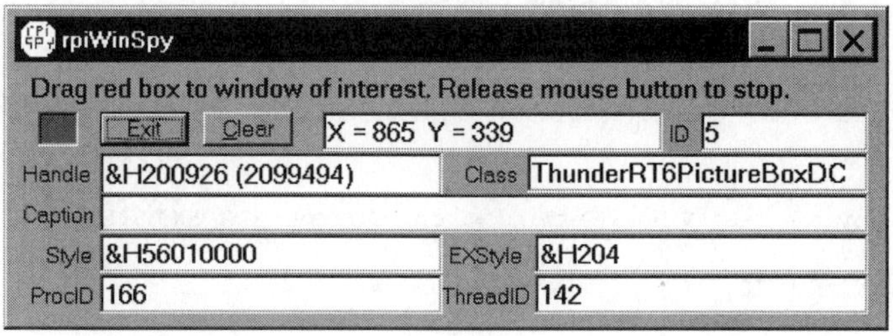

Figure 17-1. The Windows spying utility

The utility takes advantage of the system-wide mouse capture that Windows creates when we drag a window with the mouse. So to use *rpiSpyWin*, just hold down the left mouse button over the red box and move the mouse. When you have found the window of interest, just release the mouse button. Incidentally, if *rpiWinSpy* leaves some residual lines on the screen, just move the mouse pointer over the red box again.

Almost all of the program's action takes place in the MouseMove event for the red picture box:

```
Private Sub picSpy_MouseMove(Button As Integer, Shift As Integer, _
x As Single, y As Single)

Dim xValue As Long, yValue As Long
Dim pt As POINTAPI

' Convert X and Y to screen coordinates (pixels)
' X and Y are twips with respect to the upper left corner of drag window
' Top and Left are in twips with respect to client area of form
xValue = (x + picSpy.Left) \ Screen.TwipsPerPixelX
yValue = (y + picSpy.Top) \ Screen.TwipsPerPixelY

pt.x = xValue
pt.y = yValue
ClientToScreen Me.hwnd, pt
```

```
txtX = "X = " & pt.x & "   Y = " & pt.y
'txtY = pt.y

' Get window handle from mouse location
hCurrent = WindowFromPoint(pt.x, pt.y)

If hCurrent <> hPrevious Then
    ' Change of window

    txthWnd = "&H" & Hex$(hCurrent) & " (" & hCurrent & ")"

    ' Get class name
    txtClass = GetClass(hCurrent)

    ' Get caption
    txtCaption = GetCaption(hCurrent)

    ' Get style
    txtStyle = "&H" & Hex$(GetWindowLong(hCurrent, GWL_STYLE))

    ' Get extended style
    txtEXStyle = "&H" & Hex$(GetWindowLong(hCurrent, GWL_EXSTYLE))

    ' Get window ID
    txtID = GetWindowLong(hCurrent, GWL_ID)

    ' Get rectangle
    lretSpy = GetWindowRect(hCurrent, rectCurrent)

    ' Invert the borders of previous rectangle
    ' Top line
    rectTemp = rectPrev
    rectTemp.Bottom = rectPrev.Top + PEN_WIDTH
    InvertRect hDCScreen, rectTemp
    ' Bottom line
    rectTemp = rectPrev
    rectTemp.Top = rectPrev.Bottom - PEN_WIDTH
    InvertRect hDCScreen, rectTemp
    ' Left side
    rectTemp = rectPrev
    rectTemp.Right = rectPrev.Left + PEN_WIDTH
    InvertRect hDCScreen, rectTemp
    ' Right side
    rectTemp = rectPrev
    rectTemp.Left = rectPrev.Right - PEN_WIDTH
    InvertRect hDCScreen, rectTemp

    ' Invert the borders of new rectangle
    ' Top line
    rectTemp = rectCurrent
    rectTemp.Bottom = rectCurrent.Top + PEN_WIDTH
    InvertRect hDCScreen, rectTemp
    ' Bottom line
    rectTemp = rectCurrent
    rectTemp.Top = rectCurrent.Bottom - PEN_WIDTH
    InvertRect hDCScreen, rectTemp
```

```
        ' Left side
        rectTemp = rectCurrent
        rectTemp.Right = rectCurrent.Left + PEN_WIDTH
        InvertRect hDCScreen, rectTemp
        ' Right side
        rectTemp = rectCurrent
        rectTemp.Left = rectCurrent.Right - PEN_WIDTH
        InvertRect hDCScreen, rectTemp

        ' Update previous
        hPrevious = hCurrent
        rectPrev = rectCurrent
    End If

End Sub
```

The first thing that we must do is translate the incoming mouse coordinates, which are relative to the upper-left corner of the picture box, to values that are relative to the upper-left corner of the main form's client area. Note that twips must also be translated to pixels. (Most API functions use pixels.) Then we must translate from client coordinates to screen coordinates.

The screen coordinates in pixels can be used to get the handle of the window that is under the mouse pointer, using the *WindowFromPoint* function. If this handle has changed since the last mouse move, the window's class name, caption, and other data are obtained and placed in the text boxes. The *GetClass* function is basically just a wrapper for the API function *GetClassName*:

```
Function GetClass(lhwnd As Long) As String

' Return class name of lhwnd window

Dim lret As Long
Dim sClassName As String

GetClass = "Cannot get class name."

sClassName = String$(256, 0)

lret = GetClassName(lhwnd, sClassName, 257)
If lret = 0 Then
    Exit Function
Else
    GetClass = Left$(sClassName, lret)
End If

End Function
```

The *GetCaption* function uses the API functions *GetWindowTextLength* and *GetWindowText*:

```
Function GetCaption(lhwnd As Long) As String

Dim sText As String
```

```
Dim lCaption As Long
Dim hnd As Long

lCaption = GetWindowTextLength(lhwnd)

' Allocate string buffer
sText = String$(lCaption + 2, 0)
lCaption = GetWindowText(lhwnd, sText, lCaption + 1)   ' include NULL
GetCaption = Left$(sText, lCaption)

End Function
```

To get the styles, we just use the *GetWindowLong* function.

The *GetWindowRect* function retrieves the dimensions of a window. In particular, it fills a **rect** structure:

```
Type rect
    Left As Long
    Top As Long
    Right As Long
    Bottom As Long
End Type
```

The most interesting part of the application is the use of the API function *InvertRect*, which inverts the pixels in a given rectangle by performing a logical negation on each pixel. Thus, a second inversion returns the pixels to their original value. When the window handle changes, the procedure returns the previous rectangle to normal and inverts a new rectangle that surrounds the new window. Note that *InvertRect* inverts all of the pixels in the *interior* of the rectangle, so we had to make up four small rectangles to represent the sides of the window under the mouse.

Incidentally, I got the idea for using *InvertRect* by using the *rpiPEInfo* utility to spy on the imported functions for a commercial screen-capturing utility that does essentially the same thing. This is a good way to get ideas.

One more item is worth mentioning. The *rpiWinSpy* window is given the topmost property using the *SetWindowPos* API function. This means that the window will remain above all other windows (except other topmost windows), even when the window loses its focus.

18

Windows Subclassing

In the next few chapters, we want to discuss some more advanced topics, including subclassing windows, installing Windows hooks, and accessing memory in foreign processing through DLL injection. We begin in this chapter with subclassing.

Subclassing a Window or Window Class

We have already seen that the API function *SetWindowLong* can be used to change a window's style. It can also be used to change the window procedure for any window. The declaration is:

```
LONG SetWindowLong(
    HWND hWnd,         // handle of any window
    int nIndex,        // index of value to set
    LONG dwNewLong     // new value
);
```

In VB, this is:

```
Declare Function SetWindowLong Lib "user32" Alias "SetWindowLongA" ( _
    ByVal hWnd As Long, _
    ByVal nIndex As Long, _
    ByVal dwNewLong As Long _
) As Long
```

We can change the window procedure for a window by setting the *nIndex* parameter to one of the following values:

GWL_WNDPROC

>   Sets a new address for the window procedure

DWL_DLGPROC (for dialog boxes)

>   Sets a new address for the dialog box procedure (Every dialog box has a *dialog procedure*, rather than a window procedure. However, the two are similar.)

Note that the return value of *SetWindowLong* is the address of (i.e., handle to) the previous window or dialog procedure. This is important.

Using this function, we can replace the window procedure for a particular window by a procedure of our own making. However, we have no way of knowing which messages were processed by the original window procedure. This makes it vital to be able to call the original procedure after our procedure is done doing its mischief.

Fortunately, the *CallWindowProc* function is made to order for this purpose:

```
LRESULT CallWindowProc(
    WNDPROC lpPrevWndFunc,      // pointer to previous procedure
    HWND hWnd,                  // handle to window of this class
    UINT Msg,                   // message
    WPARAM wParam,              // first message parameter
    LPARAM lParam               // second message parameter
);
```

This function passes a message to the window procedure indicated by the *lpPrevWindowProc* argument. This parameter should be set to the return value of *SetWindowLong*, thereby passing the message to the original window procedure for the class associated with the window.

The process of replacing a window procedure by another procedure and passing unprocessed messages on to the original procedure is called *subclassing* the window. It is important to emphasize that the new window procedure must call the original procedure to process all messages that are not processed by the new procedure.

Let us emphasize that *SetWindowLong* affects only the window whose handle is placed in the *hWnd* parameter. To subclass an entire class, we can use *SetClassLong*:

```
DWORD SetClassLong(
    HWND hWnd,          // handle of window of the class
    int nIndex,         // index of value to change
    LONG dwNewLong      // new value
);
```

and set *nIndex* to GCL_WNDPROC. In this case, all windows *in the calling process only* that are created *after* the call to *SetClassLong* are subclassed.

Superclassing

Incidentally, there is a related concept called *superclassing*. This refers to the process of creating a *new class* that processes some messages and then calls the window procedure of another class. The new call is called a *superclass* of the original class. This may sound the same as subclassing, but the difference is that in subclassing, we do not create a new class, but just modify an existing class.

Example: Subclassing the VB Checkbox Class

Subclassing under Visual Basic is not difficult, but it must be done carefully since any misstep will almost surely lead to the well-known General Protection Fault.

To illustrate the subclassing process, the following example subclasses a VB checkbox control. As you know, clicking with the mouse on a VB checkbox normally cycles the value of the checkbox between the checked (value 1) and unchecked (value 0) states only—it does not put the checkbox in the grayed state (value 2). However, we can easily subclass the VB checkbox control so that clicking on the mouse will cycle the value from checked to grayed to unchecked.

Figure 18-1 shows the main window of the *rpiSubClass* example (whose source code is on the CD).

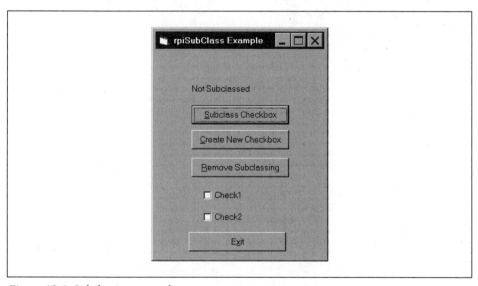

Figure 18-1. Subclassing example

Clicking the Subclass Checkbox button runs the following procedure:

```
Sub SubClass()

' Subclass check box
hPrevWndProc = SetWindowLong(Check1.hwnd, GWL_WNDPROC, AddressOf WindowProc)

' For subclassing the entire class
''hPrevWndProc = SetClassLong(Check1.hwnd, GCL_WNDPROC, AddressOf WindowProc)

If hPrevWndProc <> 0 Then
    bIsSubclassed = True
```

```
        lblStatus = "Subclassed"
    End If

    End Sub
```

Clicking the Remove Subclassing button executes the *Remove* procedure:

```
Sub Remove()

Dim lret As Long

' Remove Subclass if appropriate
If bIsSubclassed Then

    lret = SetWindowLong(Check1.hwnd, GWL_WNDPROC, hPrevWndProc)

    ' For Unsubclassing the entire class
    ''lret = SetClassLong(Check1.hwnd, GCL_WNDPROC, hPrevWndProc)

    bIsSubclassed = False
    lblStatus = "Not Subclassed"
End If

End Sub
```

The window procedure is:

```
Public Function WindowProc(ByVal hwnd As Long, ByVal iMsg As Long, _
    ByVal wParam As Long, ByVal lParam As Long) As Long

Select Case iMsg
    ' Process left mouse button and exit
    Case WM_LBUTTONDOWN

        ' Search through controls collection
        ' to see if this handle belongs to a checkbox
        For Each ctl In frmSubClass.Controls
            If TypeName(ctl) = "CheckBox" Then
                If ctl.hwnd = hwnd Then
                    ' Change the value
                    If ctl.Value <= 1 Then
                        ctl.Value = ctl.Value + 1
                    Else
                        ctl.Value = 0
                    End If
                    ' No default processing
                    Exit Function
                End If
            End If
        Next
End Select

    ' Call original window procedure
    WindowProc = CallWindowProc(hPrevWndProc, hwnd, iMsg, wParam, lParam)

End Function
```

This window procedure processes the **WM_LBUTTONDOWN** message by checking to see if the control whose handle is *hwnd* is actually a checkbox. We must be very careful here, because some controls (such as the label control) do not have handles and will cause an exception when we try to reference the hWnd property.

Try running the program and clicking on Check1 a few times. Then click on the Subclass Checkbox button and click Check1 a few more times. Then click on the Remove Subclassing button.

Note that since we are using *SetWindowLong*, the subclassing applies only to the checkbox Check1, because this is the control whose handle is placed in the *hWnd* parameter. There is no effect on Check2.

Now comment out the two references to *SetWindowLong* and uncomment the references to *SetClassLong*. If you run the program and try clicking on the two checkboxes, you will notice that there is no effect on either one. This is because these controls existed *prior to* the call to *SetClassLong*. However, the subclassing will work on the checkbox created by hitting the Create New Checkbox button!

In closing, allow me to suggest that both caution *and* restraint should be exercised when subclassing entire classes.

19

Windows Hooks

A *hook* is a technique for observing various portions of the Windows message stream. Windows defines more than a dozen different types of hooks, the locations of several of which are shown in Figure 19-1 (along with subclassing).

The principle behind hooks is quite similar to that of subclassing. If a message passes through a portion of the Windows messaging system in which a hook is installed, the system will call a *hook procedure* which we must implement.

Global and Thread-Specific Hooks

A hook may be *thread-specific*, in which case it hooks messages (of the specified hook type) sent only to a particular thread, or it may be *global* (or *system-wide*), in which case it hooks all messages (of the specified hook type) throughout the system. Hooks of some types can be set for either individual threads or globally, whereas other hook types (such as journal hooks) must be global.

The difference between thread-specific hooks and global hooks is quite significant. In the first place, global hooks reduce performance on a system-wide basis and are usually used for debugging purposes.

More seriously, a global hook procedure will need to be called from any thread throughout the system that receives an appropriate message type. Hence, the hook procedure must be placed in a module that is accessible to all threads in the system—that is, a DLL.

Indeed, whenever a thread in one process sets a hook on a thread in another process, the issue of cross-process communication must be addressed. To illustrate, imagine that Thread A in Process A wants to set a mouse hook on Thread B in Process B. Thread A must call the *SetWindowsHookEx* function (discussed soon) to

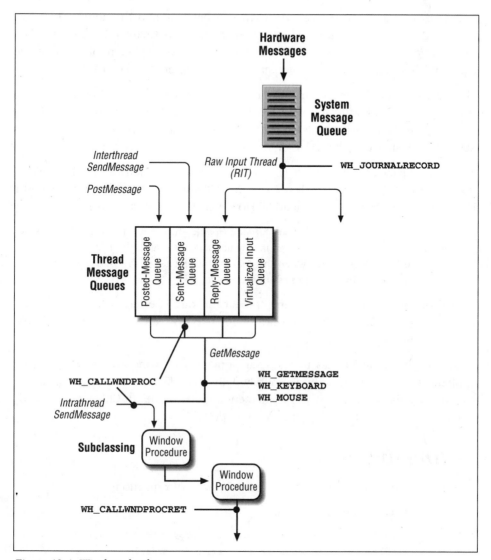

Figure 19-1. Windows hooks

set the hook, passing this function the thread ID of Thread B. However, it is the hook procedure in Thread B that is called when a mouse message is sent to Thread B.

This raises two issues: how does Thread A get the hook procedure into the address space of Process B, and, once this is done, how does Thread A get the results of any processing done by the hook procedure in Process B?

The answer to the first question is that Windows takes care of this when Thread A calls *SetWindowsHookEx*. But for the system to do so, the hook procedure must be in a DLL, so that Windows can *inject* (map) that DLL into the address space of Process B. (We will discuss DLL injection in detail in Chapter 20, *DLL Injection and Foreign Process Access.*) Unfortunately, this takes global hooks out of the realm of Visual Basic, because we cannot write a traditional DLL in VB.

Thus, a global hook can potentially cause the injection of a DLL into every existing process space. Fortunately, if the DLL can be loaded at its default base address in each case, then it is not necessary to commit additional physical memory to a new virtual instance of the DLL.

Also, the official documentation is a little vague as to when these DLLs will be released. Clearly, a process will not call the API function *FreeLibrary* to unload a DLL that it is not aware is even loaded! However, Richter says in his book:

> When a thread calls the *UnhookWindowsHookEx* function, the system cycles through its internal list of processes into which it had to inject the DLL and decrements the DLL's lock count. When this lock count reaches 0, the DLL is automatically unmapped from the process's address space.

Indeed, some experimentation seems to bear this out. Injected DLLs appear to disappear in a ghostly fashion when no longer needed. Nevertheless, global hooks should be used with circumspection.

Our plan now is to discuss the general principles of Windows hooks and then implement a thread-specific hook entirely within VB. Then, with the help of a simple DLL written in VC++, we will implement a global hook. In Chapter 20, we will discuss the process of DLL injection in more detail.

Setting the Hook

To set a Windows hook, we use the *SetWindowHookEx* function:

```
HHOOK SetWindowsHookEx(
    int idHook,            // type of hook to install
    HOOKPROC lpfn,         // address of hook procedure
    HINSTANCE hMod,        // handle to application instance
    DWORD dwThreadId       // identity of thread to install hook for
);
```

or, in VB:

```
Declare Function SetWindowsHookEx Lib "user32" Alias "SetWindowsHookExA" ( _
    ByVal idHook As Long, _
    ByVal lpfn As Long, _
    ByVal hmod As Long, _
    ByVal dwThreadId As Long _
) As Long
```

If successful, the *SetWindowsHookEx* function returns a handle to the newly created hook. The *idHook* parameter specifies the type of hook to install. We will discuss some hook types soon. If the hook is intended to be thread-specific, then the *dwThreadId* parameter is the thread ID of the target thread. If the hook is intended to be global, then *dwThreadID* should be set to NULL (0). The values of the other two parameters depend upon the scope of the hook. There are two possibilities.

If the hook is a *local hook*, that is, if it is a thread-specific hook for a thread in the process that is calling *SetWindowsHookEx*, then the hook procedure will also be in the calling process. Hence, it can be referred to by its address. In this case, *lpfn* is the address of the hook procedure and *hMod* is NULL (0).

On the other hand, if the thread is thread-specific for a foreign thread, or if the hook is global, then *lpfn* is the address of the hook procedure within the DLL that contains that procedure, and *hMod* is the instance handle of this DLL, that is, the base address of this DLL. To be absolutely clear, these values (*lpfn* and *hMod*) will, of course, be for the copy of the DLL that is loaded in the *calling process*. However, Windows will translate these values to the correct values for each process that is forced (by the hook) to load the DLL. Put another way, the base address of the DLL and the address of the hook procedure in the calling process will together determine the offset of the hook procedure within the DLL:

```
offset of hook proc = address of hook proc - base address of DLL
```

This offset can be used to find the hook procedure regardless of where the DLL is loaded into a given process space.

When an application no longer requires a hook, it should call *UnhookWindowsHookEx*:

```
BOOL UnhookWindowsHookEx(
    HHOOK hhk // handle to hook procedure to remove
);
```

Hook Procedures

Hook procedures have the form:

```
LRESULT CALLBACK HookProc(
    int nCode,
    WPARAM wParam,
    LPARAM lParam
);
```

where *nCode* is a *hook code* that depends upon the hook type. The other parameters also depend on the hook type, but generally contain information about the message. For instance, *wParam* may be the message number and *lParam* may be a pointer to further message information.

Hook Types

Windows implements more than a dozen type of hooks (as shown in Figure 19-1). Note that some hooks are allowed to modify a message, whereas others can only examine the message. Here is a sampling:

WH_CALLWNDPROC

>   Windows calls a WH_CALLWNDPROC hook procedure before passing a message generated by a call to *SendMessage* to the receiving window procedure. Note that this hook is allowed to examine a hooked message, but not modify it.

WH_CALLWNDPROCRET

>   Windows calls the WH_CALLWNDPROCRET hook procedure after the window procedure has processed a message generated by *SendMessage*. This hook works only within the process that generated the message. This type of hook also gives information about the results of the message-processing by the window procedure.

WH_GETMESSAGE

>   Windows calls the WH_GETMESSAGE hook procedure when the *GetMessage* function has retrieved a message from a thread's message queue, but before passing the message to the destination window procedure. This type of hook is allowed to modify hooked messages.

WH_JOURNALRECORD *and* WH_JOURNALPLAYBACK

>   Windows calls the WH_JOURNALRECORD hook procedure when a message is removed from the system message queue. Thus, it monitors hardware (mouse and keyboard) messages only. This hook is generally used, in conjunction with the WH_JOURNALPLAYBACK hook, to record and later play back user input. The WH_JOURNALRECORD hook is a *global hook*—it cannot be used to hook an individual thread. A WH_JOURNALRECORD hook procedure must not modify hooked messages.

WH_KEYBOARD

>   Windows calls the WH_KEYBOARD hook procedure when an application calls *GetMessage* (or *PeekMessage*) and the retrieved message is a keyboard message (WM_KEYUP or WM_KEYDOWN).

WH_MOUSE

>   Windows calls the WH_MOUSE hook procedure when an application calls *GetMessage* (or *PeekMessage*) and the retrieved message is a mouse message.

WH_SHELL

>   Windows calls the WH_SHELL hook procedure when the Windows shell application is about to be activated and when a top-level window is created or destroyed.

Hook Chains

It is important to understand that more than one hook of a particular type may exist in the system at any given time. Indeed, several applications may have installed, say, WH_MOUSE hooks. For this reason, Windows maintains a separate *hook chain* for each type of hook. A hook chain is just a list of pointers to the hook procedures for that hook type.

When a message occurs that is associated with a particular type of hook, Windows passes that message to the first (most recently created) hook procedure in the hook chain for that hook type. It is up to the hook procedure to determine what to do with the message. However, as noted earlier, some hooks are allowed to alter or delete messages, whereas others are not.

If a hook procedure wants to (or must) pass the message along the hook chain, it calls the function *CallNextHookEx*:

```
LRESULT CallNextHookEx(
    HHOOK hhk,         // handle to current hook (returned by SetWindowsHookEx)
    int nCode,         // hook code passed to hook procedure
    WPARAM wParam,     // value passed to hook procedure
    LPARAM lParam      // value passed to hook procedure
);
```

As you can see, this basically just passes on the message information to the next hook procedure in the hook chain.

Example: A Local Hook

Implementing a local hook is not hard. Figure 19-2 shows the main window of our example utility *rpiLocalHook*.

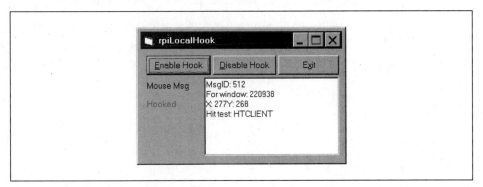

Figure 19-2. A local mouse hook example

The entire code behind the form is:

```
Option Explicit

Sub EnableHook()
    ghHook = SetWindowsHookEx(WH_MOUSE, AddressOf MouseProc, 0&, App.ThreadID)
End Sub

Sub DisableHook()
    UnhookWindowsHookEx ghHook
End Sub

Private Sub cmdDisable_Click()
    DisableHook
    ghHook = 0
    lblIsHooked = "Not Hooked"
    lblIsHooked.ForeColor = &H0
End Sub

Private Sub cmdEnable_Click()
    EnableHook
    lblIsHooked = "Hooked"
    lblIsHooked.ForeColor = &HFF
End Sub

Private Sub cmdExit_Click()
    Unload Me
End Sub

Private Sub Form_Unload(Cancel As Integer)
    If ghHook <> 0 Then DisableHook
End Sub
```

The action here is in the *EnableHook* procedure, wherein lies the call to *SetWindowsHookEx*:

```
ghHook = SetWindowsHookEx(WH_MOUSE, AddressOf MouseProc, 0&, App.ThreadID)
```

The supporting standard module contains the mouse hook procedure. Example 19-1 is the entire code for this module.

Example 19-1. SetWindowsHookEx

```
Option Explicit

Public ghHook As Long
Dim mhs As MOUSEHOOKSTRUCT
Dim sText As String

Public Const WH_MOUSE = 7

Type POINTAPI
    x As Long
    y As Long
End Type
```

Example 19-1. SetWindowsHookEx (continued)

```
Type MOUSEHOOKSTRUCT
    pt As POINTAPI
    hwnd As Long
    wHitTestCode As Long
    dwExtraInfo As Long
End Type

Declare Function SetWindowsHookEx Lib "user32" Alias "SetWindowsHookExA" ( _
    ByVal idHook As Long, _
    ByVal lpfn As Long, _
    ByVal hmod As Long, _
    ByVal dwThreadId As Long _
) As Long

Declare Function CallNextHookEx Lib "user32" ( _
    ByVal ghHook As Long, _
    ByVal ncode As Long, _
    ByVal wParam As Integer, _
    ByVal lParam As Long _
) As Long

Declare Function UnhookWindowsHookEx Lib "user32" ( _
    ByVal ghHook As Long _
) As Long

Declare Sub CopyMemory Lib "kernel32" Alias "RtlMoveMemory" ( _
    Destination As Any, _
    Source As Any, _
    ByVal Length As Long)

'-----
Public Function MouseProc(ByVal ncode As Long, ByVal wParam As Long, _
    ByVal lParam As Long) As Long

' Documentation says to do this
If ncode < 0 Then
    ' Forward message and get out
    MouseProc = CallNextHookEx(ghHook, ncode, wParam, lParam)
    Exit Function
End If

' Get MOUSEHOOKSTRUCT pointed to by lParam
CopyMemory mhs.pt.x, ByVal lParam, LenB(mhs)

' Fill text box with message data
sText = "MsgID: " & wParam
sText = sText & vbCrLf & "For window: " & Hex$(mhs.hwnd)
sText = sText & vbCrLf & "X: " & mhs.pt.x & "Y: " & mhs.pt.y
sText = sText & vbCrLf & "Hit test: " & GetConstant(mhs.wHitTestCode)
frmMain.txtMsg.Text = sText

' Forward to next hook
```

Example 19-1. SetWindowsHookEx (continued)

```
MouseProc = CallNextHookEx(ghHook, ncode, wParam, lParam)

End Function

'-----
Function GetConstant(vValue As Variant) As String

' Function returns name of constant for given value.

Dim sName As String

Select Case vValue

    Case 18
        sName = "HTBORDER"
    Case 15
        sName = "HTBOTTOM"
    Case 16
        sName = "HTBOTTOMLEFT"
    Case 17
        sName = "HTBOTTOMRIGHT"
    Case 2
        sName = "HTCAPTION"
    Case 1
        sName = "HTCLIENT"
    Case -2
        sName = "HTERROR"
    Case 4
        sName = "HTGROWBOX"
    Case 6
        sName = "HTHSCROLL"
    Case 10
        sName = "HTLEFT"
    Case 9
        sName = "HTMAXBUTTON"
    Case 5
        sName = "HTMENU"
    Case 8
        sName = "HTMINBUTTON"
    Case 0
        sName = "HTNOWHERE"
    Case 11
        sName = "HTRIGHT"
    Case 3
        sName = "HTSYSMENU"
    Case 12
        sName = "HTTOP"
    Case 13
        sName = "HTTOPLEFT"
    Case 14
        sName = "HTTOPRIGHT"
    Case -1
```

Example 19-1. SetWindowsHookEx (continued)

```
    sName = "HTTRANSPARENT"
Case 7
    sName = "HTVSCROLL"

End Select

GetConstant = sName
End Function
```

Note that *lParam* points to a MOUSEHOOKSTRUCT structure variable that contains message data. The *dwHitTestCode* data is interesting, since it describes where the mouse pointer is when the message is generated: on a window border, on a scrollbar, on a menu, and so on. For more on these values, see the MSDN documentation for the message WM_NCHITTEST.

Example: A Global Hook

As discussed earlier, to set a global hook, we need to make the hook procedure accessible to all threads, which means placing the hook procedure in a DLL. Since VB cannot produce traditional DLLs, we need to use another programming environment, such as VC++.

The *rpiGlobalHook* application consists of two parts. The global hook is actually implemented in a pair of modules—a form module called *frmRpiHook* and a standard module called *basRpiHook*. The form *frmRpiHook* is shown in Figure 19-3. This form is intended to be loaded but remain hidden. Thus, it functions somewhat like a class module, but also provides a window (the form itself) that can be subclassed.

Figure 19-3. The global hook form

These two modules can be added to any VB project in order to implement a global mouse hook. The *rpiGlobalHook* application also contains this *installing project*, in the form of the *frmMain* form shown in Figure 19-4 and the *basMain* standard module.

Remember that our goal here is to demonstrate the technique of creating a global hook, not to produce a commercial-quality product. Such a product could be created as an ActiveX control. Also, we have not included any error checking in this simple example.

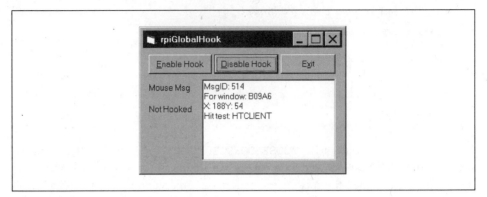

Figure 19-4. A global mouse hook example

Figure 19-5 shows the entire project.

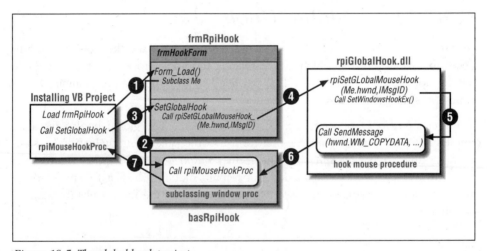

Figure 19-5. The global hook project

Here are the steps shown in Figure 19-5:

1. When the user clicks the Enable Hook button, the installing project loads the form *frmRpiHook* shown in Figure 19-3.

2. The Load event of *frmRpiHook* subclasses itself by calling *SetWindowLong* and passing it the address of the window procedure in *basRpiHook*.

3. The installing program then calls the *SetGlobalHook* procedure, which is implemented in the *frmRpiHook* form.

4. This function calls the DLL function *rpiSetGlobalMouseHook*, passing it the handle of the form (its own handle) and the message IDs of the messages to process. Note that you must put this DLL in your Windows System directory or change the `Lib` clause in the appropriate declarations in the source code before this program will work.

5. The DLL function *rpiSetGloablMouseHook* sets up the global mouse hook by calling *SetWindowsHookEx*, thus setting up the hook's mouse procedure in the DLL.

6. When a mouse message is generated, the system injects the DLL into the target process space, and the message is passed to the mouse procedure in the target process. If the message ID matches the `lMsgID` argument, the mouse procedure sends a `WM_COPYDATA` message to the window procedure of the subclassed form *frmRpiHook*.

7. The window procedure calls the function *rpiMouseHookProc*, which is defined by the user in the installing project.

Note that steps 1–5 (and step 7) take place in the installing application's process, and Step 6 takes place in the process that is the target of the mouse message, but the `WM_COPYDATA` message is marshalled from the target process to the installing process.

Now let us look at some of the actual code. .

frmRpiHook

The code behind the form *frmRpiHook* is:

```
Option Explicit

Private mhHook As Long
Private mhPrevWndProc As Long


' -----
Public Property Get hHook() As Long
    hHook = mhHook
End Property


' -----
Public Property Get hPrevWndProc() As Long
    hPrevWndProc = mhPrevWndProc
End Property


' -----
Public Function SetGlobalHook(ByVal lMsgID As Long) As Long
' Call DLL to set hHook property
' Returns handle to hook (0 indicates error)
mhHook = rpiSetGlobalMouseHook(Me.hwnd, lMsgID)
SetGlobalHook = mhHook
End Function


' -----
Public Function FreeGlobalHook() As Boolean
    FreeGlobalHook = (rpiFreeGlobalMouseHook <> 0)
End Function
```

```
' -----
Private Sub Form_Load()
' Subclass the form
mhPrevWndProc = SetWindowLong(Me.hwnd, GWL_WNDPROC, AddressOf WindowProc)
End Sub


' -----
Private Sub Form_Unload(Cancel As Integer)

' Remove subclassing
SetWindowLong Me.hwnd, GWL_WNDPROC, mhPrevWndProc

' When unloading form, check for a valid hook and free it
If hHook <> 0 Then FreeGlobalHook
Set frmRpiHook = Nothing

End Sub
```

The form has two properties:

hHook

> The handle of the hook (if set). Read-only.

hPrevWndProc

> Handle to form's original window procedure. Read-only.

And two methods:

SetGlobalHook

> Calls DLL to set hook for messages.

FreeGlobalHook

> Calls DLL to free hook.

The **SetGlobalHook** method is:

```
Public Function SetGlobalHook(ByVal lMsgID As Long) As Long
' Call DLL to set hHook property
' Returns handle to hook (0 indicates error)
mhHook = rpiSetGlobalMouseHook(Me.hwnd, lMsgID)
SetGlobalHook = mhHook
End Function
```

This method calls the *rpiSetGlobalMouseHook* function in our DLL, passing it the handle of the subclassed form (this form) and the message IDs of the messages that we want to process. Similarly, the *FreeGlobalHook* method calls the *rpiFree-GlobalMouseHook* DLL function. We will take a look at these DLL functions soon.

basmRpiHook

The accompanying standard module *basRpiHook* contains the required declarations, along with the window procedure for the subclassed form. It is necessary to put the window procedure in a standard module because the VB **AddressOf** operator requires its argument to be in a standard module. If it weren't for this, we could place the entire project in the form module. What a shame.

Here is the code for the window procedure:

```
Public Function WindowProc(ByVal hwnd As Long, ByVal iMsg As Long, _
    ByVal wParam As Long, ByVal lParam As Long) As Long

' Window procedure for subclassed form.

If iMsg = WM_COPYDATA Then
    ' lParam has pointer to COPYDATASTRUCT structure.
    ' Get it out immediately

    ' First copy COPYDATASTRUCT
    CopyMemory cds.dwData, ByVal lParam, LenB(cds)

    ' Then copy MOUSEHOOKSTRUCT
    CopyMemory mhs.pt.x, ByVal cds.lpData, LenB(mhs)

    ' Call user-implemented mouse hook procedure
    rpiMouseHookProc mhs.hwnd, cds.dwData, mhs.pt.x, _
        mhs.pt.y, mhs.wHitTestCode, mhs.dwExtraInfo

    ' Do not pass message this on to form
    Exit Function

End If

' Call original window procedure
WindowProc = CallWindowProc(frmRpiHook.hPrevWndProc, _
    hwnd, iMsg, wParam, lParam)

End Function
```

When the global mouse hook is set, all mouse messages are observed by our DLL. For each message, the DLL sends a WM_COPYDATA message to the window procedure *WindowProc*, which processes the incoming message, calls the user-implemented *rpiMouseHookProc* (in the installing project), and kills this message. All other messages are passed on to the default window procedure for the form.

The data in the parameters of *WindowProc* is as follows:

hwnd

The handle of the subclassed form. This is not of much use to us.

iMsg

The message number, which is always WM_COPYDATA.

wParam

The handle of the sending window, which is always 0 because there is no sending window (the DLL does the sending).

lParam

> A pointer to a variable of type COPYDATASTRUCT, marshalled from the target process by the call to *SendMessage* using WM_COPYDATA.

The COPYDATASTRUCT is:

```
Type COPYDATASTRUCT
    dwData As Long    ' message ID of the hooked mouse message
    cbData As Long    ' count of bytes pointed to by lpData--equal to 20
    lpData As Long    ' pointer to variable of type MOUSEHOOKSTRUCT
End Type
```

The MOUSEHOOKSTRUCT structure is:

```
Type MOUSEHOOKSTRUCT
    pt As POINTAPI              ' POINT structure with mouse coordinates
    hwnd As Long                ' handle of the window receiving the mouse message
    wHitTestCode As Long        ' describes location of mouse
    dwExtraInfo As Long         ' extra info with message, normally 0
End Type
```

Finally, the DLL expects the user-implemented mouse hook procedure to have the form:

```
Public Sub rpiMouseHookProc(ByVal hwnd As Long, _
    ByVal iMsg As Long, _
    ByVal x As Long, _
    ByVal Y As Long, _
    ByVal wHitTestCode As Long, _
    ByVal dwExtraInfo As Long)
```

rpiGlobalHook.dll

Now for the DLL, which is written in VC++. Fortunately, it is not complicated. The source code is also on the accompanying CD.

First, here is the *rpiSetGlobalHook* procedure, which essentially just calls *SetWindowHookEx*. It also saves the handle to the hook, the handle to the subclassed form, and the message IDs to process in *shared* variables; that is, variables that are shared by all processes that load the DLL.

```
int WINAPI rpiSetGlobalMouseHook(int hSubclassedForm, int iMsgID)
{
    // Sets a mouse hook and returns its handle, or 0 for failure.
    // Input is handle to subclassed form and message ID's to hook.
    // Sets the shared variable ghSubclassedForm containing handle
    // of subclassed form, the msgID and the ghHook variable.

    // If hook already set, do not set it again
    if (!ghHook == 0)
        return 0;

    ghHook = SetWindowsHookEx(
        WH_MOUSE,
```

```
                    (HOOKPROC)MouseProc,
                    hDLLInst,
                    0);

                    // Save subclassed form handle
                    ghSubclassedForm = (HANDLE)hSubclassedForm;

                    // Save the message ID(s)
                    lMsgID = iMsgID;

                    return (int)ghHook;
              }
```

The *rpiFreeGlobalMouseHook* is even simpler:

```
     int WINAPI rpiFreeGlobalMouseHook()
     {
         HRESULT hr;

         // Free hook hh. Return 0 on failure.
         hr = UnhookWindowsHookEx(ghHook);
         ghHook = 0;

         return hr;
     }
```

Finally, we come to the mouse procedure for the hook. As mentioned earlier, this procedure gathers up the mouse message data and sends it off to the subclassed form in the VB project using a **WM_COPYDATA** message, which is automatically marshalled by Windows. It then calls the next hook procedure in the hook chain.

```
     LRESULT WINAPI MouseProc(int nCode, WPARAM wParam, LPARAM lParam)
     {
         // If nCode<0 then do not process the message
         if (nCode < 0)
             return CallNextHookEx(ghHook, nCode, wParam, lParam);

         // Check for message ID filter
         if ( (lMsgID == 0) || (lMsgID & wParam) ) // || is logical OR, & is bitwise AND
         {
             // Set up data to copy in message
             copydata.dwData = wParam;        // message ID here
             copydata.lpData = (MOUSEHOOKSTRUCT*)lParam;
             copydata.cbData = sizeof(MOUSEHOOKSTRUCT);

             // Send message
             if (!ghSubclassedForm == 0) {
             SendMessage(ghSubclassedForm, WM_COPYDATA,
                 NULL, (LPARAM) &(copydata.dwData) );
             }
         }

         return CallNextHookEx(ghHook, nCode, wParam,lParam);
     }
```

The Installing Application

The code for the installing process's form, that is, the code behind the form in Figure 19-3, is:

```
Option Explicit

Dim hMouseHook As Long
Const WM_LBUTTONDOWN = &H201
Const WM_RBUTTONDOWN = &H204

' -----
Private Sub cmdEnable_Click()

' Load hook form but no need to show
Load frmRpiHook

' Set hook

''frmRpiHook.SetGlobalHook WM_LBUTTONDOWN + WM_RBUTTONDOWN
' For all mouse messages
frmRpiHook.SetGlobalHook 0

' Save handle to hook for later freeing
hMouseHook = frmRpiHook.hHook

lblIsHooked = "Hooked"
lblIsHooked.ForeColor = &HFF

End Sub

' -----
Private Sub cmdDisable_Click()
    frmRpiHook.FreeGlobalHook
    hMouseHook = 0
    lblIsHooked = "Not Hooked"
    lblIsHooked.ForeColor = &H0
End Sub

' -----
Private Sub cmdExit_Click()
    If hMouseHook <> 0 Then frmRpiHook.FreeGlobalHook
    Unload Me
End Sub

' -----
Private Sub Form_Unload(Cancel As Integer)
    ' This will remove subclassing and free hook
    Unload frmRpiHook
End Sub
```

Finally, the user code for processing the mouse messages is in a standard module for the installing application. This procedure processes the mouse information in the same manner as that of the local hook example:

```
Public Sub rpiMouseHookProc(ByVal hwnd As Long, ByVal iMsg As Long, _
    ByVal x As Long, ByVal y As Long, ByVal wHitTestCode As Long, _
    ByVal dwExtraInfo As Long)

Dim sText As String

' Fill text box with message data
sText = "MsgID: " & iMsg
sText = sText & vbCrLf & "For window: " & Hex$(hwnd)
sText = sText & vbCrLf & "X: " & x & "Y: " & y
sText = sText & vbCrLf & "Hit test: " & GetConstant(wHitTestCode)
frmMain.txtMsg.Text = sText

frmMain.txtMsg = sText

End Sub
```

Unlike the local hook example, we can now move the mouse over any window in the system and hook the generated mouse messages.

20

DLL Injection and Foreign Process Access

The global hook example in the previous chapter demonstrates the process of *DLL injection*. To recap, when a global hook is set, the system will *inject* (that is, map or load) the DLL containing the hook procedure into the address space of any process that receives a hooked message, thus enabling the hooked thread to call the hook procedure.

This has some interesting implications beyond its intended use. In particular, there is nothing that requires the injected DLL to contain only hook procedures—we can put any code that we want into the DLL. Thus, we can force any process in the system to run code of our own choosing!

We are going to use this idea to create a very interesting application. Its current purpose is to allocate memory in a foreign process, that is, to allocate *foreign memory*. However, its design is more general than this, for it allows us to force a foreign process to run any code we choose to include in the injected DLL, which is why I named the DLL *rpiAccessProcess.dll*.

After discussing the application, we will consider examples of the use of foreign memory allocation.

Accessing a Foreign Process: The Hooked Thread Graph

The *rpiAccessProcess.dll* library that accompanies this book currently exports the following functions:

rpiVirtualAlloc
  Allocates the specified amount of memory in the foreign process.

rpiVirtualFree

Frees memory allocated by a call to *rpiVirtualAlloc*.

rpiVirtualWrite

Writes a specified number of bytes to foreign memory.

rpiVirtualRead

Reads a specified number of bytes from foreign memory.

rpiSetForegroundWindow

Moves an application to the foreground. Designed to work just like Win32's *SetForegroundWindow* even under Windows 98 and Windows 2000. This function was discussed first in Chapter 11, *Processes*.

To understand how these functions work and how the application is designed, it is helpful to think of each thread that is either making or receiving a memory allocation request as a *node* in a graph, which, for lack of a better name, I call the *hooked-thread graph*. As we will see, a thread is part of the hooked-thread graph; that is, a thread is represented by a node in the graph, if it has been hooked and the DLL is loaded in the address space of its owner process.

Figure 20-1 illustrates this idea. It shows three hooked threads (which may or may not be in different processes).

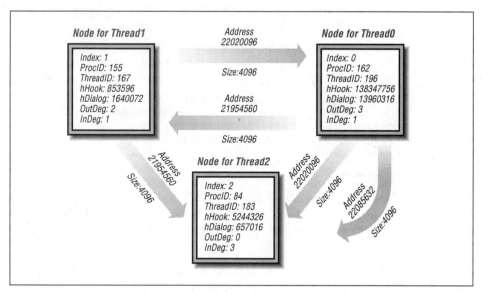

Figure 20-1. The thread graph

Each node is just a structure defined in the DLL as:

```
struct rpiNODE {
    DWORD dwThreadID;
```

```
HHOOK hHook;
HWND hDialog;
int iOutDeg;
int iInDeg;
}
```

Of course, the value of *dwThreadID*—the thread ID of the thread represented by the node—uniquely identifies the node. The member *hHook* is the handle of the hook. As we will see, each node has an associated hidden dialog box, whose handle is *hDialog*. The *iOutDeg* member is the number of arcs (explained later) leaving the node and *iInDeg* is the number of arcs entering the node. (Don't worry, this is not going to be a lesson in data structures.)

Note that the nodes in the hooked-thread graph are kept in an array, called the *nodes table*, in a shared section of the DLL. This means that all threads using the DLL have access to this common table. (As we have discussed before, a variable in a DLL can have one of three types of scope: *local* means accessible to a single procedure, *global* means accessible to a single instance of the DLL, and *shared* means accessible to all instances of the DLL. For a local or global variable, each instance of the DLL gets a separate copy of the variable, so that if one instance changes the variable, other instances are not affected.)

As we can see from Figure 20-1, the hooked-thread graph may also have directed *edges* (arrows) between nodes. An edge from Node1 to Node2 represents a *successful* request for a memory allocation made by Node1 (Thread1) on Node2 (Thread2). The edge is labeled with the size of the memory allocation and the base address of that allocation. In the DLL, an edge is just a structure:

```
struct rpiEDGE {
    DWORD dwOutThreadID;     // ThreadID of node from which edge leaves
    DWORD dwInThreadID;      // ThreadID of node into which edge enters
    DWORD dwSize;            // Size of allocation
    LPVOID lpAddress;        // Base address of allocation
}
```

The number of edges leaving a node is thus the number of times the thread has *successfully* requested memory from *any* other threads in the system. This number is called the *out degree* of the node. The number of edges coming into a node is the number of *successful* requests honored by that thread. This is called the *in degree* of the node.

As with the nodes, the edges in the hooked-thread graph are kept in an array, called the *edges table*, which is also in a shared section of the DLL.

The hooked-thread graph model of (successful) memory allocation requests makes the job of designing the application much easier. With this model in mind, we can describe how the application works.

The rpiVirtualAlloc Function

The *rpiVirtualAlloc* function is defined as:

```
LPVOID WINAPI rpiVirtualAlloc(
    DWORD dwThreadID,
    DWORD dwSize,
    int *piResultCode
);
```

or, in VB,

```
Public Declare Function rpiVirtualAlloc Lib "rpiAccessProcess.DLL" ( _
    ByVal dwThreadID As Long, _
    ByVal dwSize As Long, _
    Optional ByRef lResultCode As Long = 0 _
) As Long
```

The final parameter is optional. If we do not want to examine the result code (which indicates the type of error, if any), then we can just omit this argument.

Now suppose that a VB application calls *rpiVirtualAlloc*. The thread ID would probably have been obtained from a window handle using *FindWindow* and *GetWindowThreadProcessID*:

```
Dim lResultCode As Long
Dim hWindow As Long
Dim ThreadID As Long
Dim lAddress As Long

hWindow = FindWindow(vbNullString, WindowTitle)
ThreadID = GetWindowThreadProcessId(hWindow, 0&)
lAddress = rpiVirtualAlloc(ThreadID, 4096&, lResultCode)
```

Here is what happens:

1. If a node for the target thread does not exist, it is created. This is done by calling an internal DLL procedure named *CreateNode*, which works as follows:

    a. An empty location in the nodes table is found. (The nodes table is not packed, and so may have unused entries in various locations. Also, the table's size is hardcoded into the DLL at 100 nodes. This should be plenty.)

    b. A `WH_CALLWNDPROC` hook is installed on the target thread.

    c. All of the members of the `rpiNODE` structure except the *hDialog* member can now be filled in.

    d. The *CreateNode* function sends a harmless `WM_NULL` message to the target thread. This forces Windows to inject the DLL into the target process. The *CallWndProc* hook procedure is then called to process the `WM_NULL` message. This hook procedure checks to make sure that the *hDialog* value is 0, indicating that the dialog has not yet been created. It then calls the API function *CreateDialog* to create a dialog box. Because this is done in the hook procedure, the dialog box is created *in the target process*. The bottom portion of Figure 20-2 shows three such dialog boxes. These dialogs are intended to be hidden and so do not need to contain a text box, but for the sake of illustration, the application shows the dialogs and fills a text box with node data.

e. When the WM_NULL message returns, the *CreateNode* function checks the shared node table to make sure that the node has a nonzero *hDialog* value. This signals that the dialog has been created successfully. Then *CreateNode* returns to *rpiVirtualAlloc*.

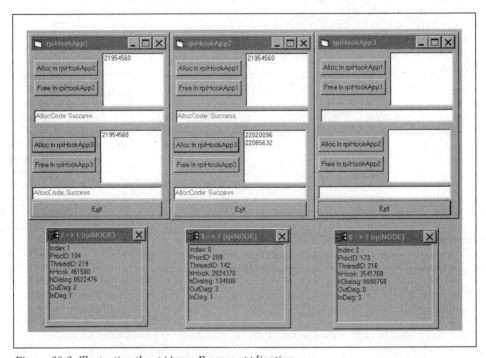

Figure 20-2. Illustrating the rpiAccessProcess application

2. This procedure is repeated for the *calling* thread. That is, if a node for the calling thread does not exist, it is created, also by calling *CreateNode*.

3. At this point, there is a node for the calling thread and a node for the target thread. The next step is to create the edge, which is done as follows:

   a. The *dwInThreadID* and *dwOutThreadID* values and the allocation size *dwSize* are set.

   b. A memory allocation request is made by sending a MSG_VIRTUAL_ALLOC (defined to be WM_APP + 1) message to the target dialog box, whose handle is the *hDialog* value of the target node. Note that Windows reserves the values WM_APP through &HBFFF for use by applications, so this value will not interfere with built-in Windows messages sent to the dialog.

c. The dialog box's dialog procedure (a *dialog procedure* is a special form of window procedure for processing dialog box messages) processes this message by calling the API function *VirtualAlloc* and then filling in the shared *lpAddress* member of the edge with the return value of this API function. The important point is that the dialog procedure is running in the *target* space, so its call to *VirtualAlloc* actually allocates memory in the target process.

4. Once the edge is created, the appropriate *iInDeg* and *iOutDeg* values are incremented, completing the edge.

Figure 20-1 shows the picture for three nodes and five edges.

The rpiVirtualFree Function

The *rpiVirtualFree* function is simpler than *rpiVirtualAlloc*. It is declared as follows:

```
int WINAPI rpiVirtualFree(
    DWORD dwThreadID,
    LPVOID lpAddress
);
```

or, in VB:

```
Public Declare Function rpiVirtualFree Lib "rpiAccessProcess.DLL" ( _
    ByVal dwThreadID As Long, _
    ByVal lpAddress As Long) As Long
```

The thread ID and address are sufficient (and necessary) to uniquely identify an edge of the hooked-thread graph, that is, a successful memory allocation request, because no two such allocations can use the same address in the same process. (The application cannot create two edges with the same *lpAddress* but different threads in the same process, because the second call to *VirtualAlloc* will fail.)

The *rpiVirtualFree* function works as follows:

1. It gets the index of the in node and out node for the edge.

2. It sends a MSG_VIRTUAL_FREE message to the target dialog box. The dialog's window procedure processes the message by calling the API function *Virtual-Free* (from the target process space) and then clearing the shared *lpAddress* member of the edge.

3. The *rpiVirtualFree* function can then delete the edge (that is, clear the rpi-EDGE structure).

4. It then decrements the appropriate in degree and out degree.

5. If either of the nodes has in degree 0 *and* out degree 0, the node is destroyed. This is done by first closing the dialog box and then unhooking the thread by calling *UnhookWindowsHookEx*.

This describes the main functionality of the hooked graph model. Once the graph is created, the edges act as a kind of *conduit* between processes. To force a target thread to run some code at the request of a calling thread, all we need to do is create a new message and add the desired code as the message-processing code in the dialog procedure. Sending the message will trigger the processing code. *Voilà*.

Testing the Allocation Functions

Figure 20-2 shows the results of a VB application that can be used to test the *rpiVirtualAlloc* and *rpiVirtualFree* functions. The source code for this application is on the CD. Basically, this application provides a way to call the DLL functions *rpiVirtualAlloc* and *rpiVirtualFree* on two other instances of itself, modified slightly to change the window title.

To try this out, just run the three variations *rpiHookApp1.exe*, *rpiHookApp2.exe*, and *rpiHookApp3.exe* located on the CD. Figure 20-2 shows these executables and the corresponding node dialog boxes created by the DLL in response to several calls to *rpiVirtualAlloc*. This reflects the layout in Figure 20-1.

Keep in mind that you need to free all allocations before closing any of these applications, unless you like General Protection Faults.

Let me know if you find some interesting extensions for this model, beyond allocating foreign memory (and fixing *SetForegroundWindow*), which we consider next.

Allocating Foreign Memory

As mentioned, the *rpiAccessProcess* DLL is currently set up to allocate foreign memory. This is done through the *rpiVirtualRead* and *rpiVirtualWrite* functions. These functions are pretty straightforward, especially compared to the allocation functions.

The rpiVirtualWrite Function

The *rpiVirtualWrite* function is:

```
int WINAPI rpiVirtualWrite(
    DWORD dwThreadID,
    LPVOID lpSourceAddress
    LPVOID lpTargetAddress,
    DWORD nSize
);
```

or, in VB:

```
Public Declare Function rpiVirtualWrite Lib "rpiAccessProcess.DLL" ( _
    ByVal dwThreadID As Long, _
    ByVal lpSourceAddress As Long, _
    ByVal lpTargetAddress As Long, _
    ByVal dwSize As Long) As Long
```

This function first checks to make sure that the edge identified by *dwThreadID* and *lpAddress* actually emanates from the calling thread's node, since we cannot allow a strange thread to write to memory allocated by another thread! (In a sense, writing memory is like *pushing* data along the edge, and it better be the correct edge.)

The *rpiVirtualWrite* function then calls the API function *WriteProcessMemory*, discussed in Chapter 16, *Windows Messages*. To do so, it calls *GetWindowThread-ProcessId*, to get the process ID from the target dialog handle, and then it calls *OpenHandle* to get a process handle, which is required by *WriteProcessMemory*.

The rpiVirtualRead Function

The *rpiVirtualRead* function is:

```
int WINAPI rpiVirtualRead(
    DWORD dwThreadID,
    LPVOID lpSourceAddress
    LPVOID lpTargetAddress,
    DWORD nSize
);
```

or, in VB:

```
Public Declare Function rpiVirtualRead Lib "rpiAccessProcess.DLL" ( _
    ByVal dwThreadID As Long, _
    ByVal lpSourceAddress As Long, _
    ByVal lpTargetAddress As Long, _
    ByVal dwSize As Long) As Long
```

As with the *rpiVirtualWrite* function, this function first checks that the edge emanates from the calling thread's node. (In a sense, reading is like *pulling* data along the edge backwards.) It then calls the API function *ReadProcessMemory*.

Example: Foreign Control Extraction

We have seen that it is not difficult to extract data from a foreign listbox or combo box, because Windows automatically marshalls the necessary data across process boundaries. However, the same does not apply to the 32-bit controls such as the ListView control. In this case, we must do the marshalling ourselves.

To get the *rpiControlExtractor* application, first discussed in Chapter 16, to work on a ListView control, we can use the *rpiAccessProcess* allocation function to allocate a buffer in the foreign process. But first we need to discuss the ListView control itself.

Each item in a ListView control is represented by an LVITEM structure:

```
typedef struct LVITEM {
    UINT mask;
    int iItem;
    int iSubItem;
    UINT state;
    UINT stateMask;
    LPTSTR pszText;
    int cchTextMax;
    int iImage;
    LPARAM lParam;
    #if (_WIN32_IE >= 0x0300)
        int iIndent;
    #endif
};
```

Here are the members we need to consider:

- The *mask* member is a set of flags that indicate which members of the structure either contain valid data or need to be set (depending upon the function being invoked). For instance, the value LVIF_TEXT specifies that the *pszText* member is either valid or needs to be filled in.

- The *item* member is the 0-based index of the ListView item of interest.

- The *subitem* member is the 1-based index of the subitem of interest. To refer to an item (rather than a subitem), set this to 0. (We will explain subitems in a moment.)

- The *pszText* member is the address of a buffer containing the item or subitem text (a null-terminated string).

- The *cchTextMax* member is the size of the buffer pointed to by the *pszText* member.

As is typical, the documentation on ListView controls, especially with respect to items and subitems, is confusing. However, the following appears to be the case.

When a ListView control is in *report mode*, it can display one or more columns. Each column after the first column corresponds to a ListView *subitem*. The first column corresponds to the ListView *item*.

Thus, the first column contains the text (also called the *label*) or icon for the item itself, and subsequent columns contain the text for the subitems. It follows that the number of subitems is one less than the number of columns. Subitems are not added or deleted by name. Instead, columns are added or deleted.

To retrieve the text of an item or subitem, we need to fill in the appropriate members of an LVITEM structure and send the control an LVM_GETITEMA message.

Here is the code:

```
uLVItem.mask = LVIF_TEXT      ' Specifies that text is requested
uLVItem.iItem = lItem         ' Index of item
uLVItem.iSubItem = lsubitem   ' Index of subitem or 0
uLVItem.cchTextMax = 255      ' size of buffer
uLVItem.pszText = lpAddress   ' Address of text buffer

' Send the message
lResp = SendMessage(hListView, LVM_GETITEMA, lItem, lpAddress)
```

The problem, of course, is that this structure must be placed in the foreign address space. Note that this includes the text buffer as well as the structure itself.

We can accomplish this as follows:

1. First, we set up two buffers in the foreign process space—a 40-byte buffer for the **LVITEM** variable:

   ```
   ' Allocate foreign buffer for 40-byte LVItem
   lForeignLVItemAddr = rpiVirtualAlloc(lThreadID, 40&)
   ```

   and a 256-byte buffer for the item (or subitem) text:

   ```
   ' Allocate foreign buffer for text of item
   lForeignTextBufferAddr = rpiVirtualAlloc(lThreadID, 256&)
   ```

2. Next, we fill a local **LVITEM** variable with the required members, using the address of the *foreign* text buffer:

   ```
   uLocalLVItem.mask = LVIF_TEXT
   uLocalLVItem.iItem = lItem
   uLocalLVItem.iSubItem = lSubItem
   uLocalLVItem.cchTextMax = 255
   uLocalLVItem.pszText = lForeignTextBufferAddr
   ```

3. The local **LVITEM** variable is copied to the foreign space:

   ```
   ' Copy local uLocalLVItem to foreign space
   lResp = rpiVirtualWrite(lThreadID, VarPtr(uLocalLVItem.mask), _
       lForeignLVItemAddr, 40&)
   ```

4. Now we can send the **LVM_GETITEMA** message to the foreign control:

   ```
   ' Send the message
   lResp = SendMessageByNum(lhwnd, LVM_GETITEMA, lItem, lForeignLVItemAddr)
   ```

5. This fills the foreign **LVITEM** structure *and* the foreign text buffer. The text buffer can be copied back to the local process:

   ```
   ' Copy the data back from foreign space
   lResp = rpiVirtualRead(lThreadID, lForeignTextBufferAddr, _
       VarPtr(bLocalTextBuffer(0)), 256)
   ```

6. Finally, we must not forget to free the foreign buffers:

   ```
   ' Free foreign memory
   lret = rpiVirtualFree(lThreadID, lForeignTextBufferAddr)
   lret = rpiVirtualFree(lThreadID, lForeignLVItemAddr)
   ```

That's basically all there is to it. The complete code is on the CD.

Example: Fixing the VB6 Help System

Frankly, I think that, *at the moment*, Microsoft's new HTML help system, introduced in Visual Studio 6, leaves much to be desired. It is definitely a step backwards in functionality. Fortunately, these shortcomings can be addressed if Microsoft has the will to do so.

I will hasten to add that there is one very important advantage to the new system for serious VB programmers—we now have access to the documentation for all of Visual Studio. Frankly, I use the VC++ and SDK documentation far more often than the VB6 documentation, even when programming in VB. Nevertheless, Microsoft should have done a better job of implementing this help system before releasing it. It has even prevented me from installing the latest versions of MSDN Library!

Let me share with you two of the help system's most inexcusable problems—one of which is so amazing that I could not believe my eyes when I first encountered it. It also involves one of the strangest mysteries I have encountered in using PCs.

Figure 20-3 shows the problems. First, as you can see, the Topics Found dialog occupies only a small portion of the screen. Why on earth doesn't Microsoft implement dialog boxes that adjust their size based on screen resolution? I can't think of any excuse for not displaying a *full screen height* list here.

The second problem is that the list of topics is not alphabetized! At least, it wasn't alphabetized when I decided to write about the problem. Let me suggest that you start your VB6 help system and select the listbox control item in the index tab. Then click on the Properties link and check the Topics Found list to see whether it is alphabetized on your system.

From the time that I installed VB6 until I began writing the words you are now reading, my topic lists were not alphabetized. So I wrote an application to deal with this. Figure 20-4 shows the result.

Here is how the *rpiFixVB6Help* application works. Suppose that a Topics Found dialog is showing. I use the key combination Ctrl-Alt-Shift-X (an easy keystroke combination on my keyboard) to start the *rpiFixVB6Help* application. The application immediately searches the current windows in the system to find a top-level window named *Topics Found*, using the *FindWindow* function:

```
hTopics = FindWindow(vbNullString, "Topics Found")
```

The application then gets the handle of the child ListView control, which is named List1:

```
' Search child windows for "List1"
hListView = FindWindowEx(hTopics, 0, vbNullString, "List1")
```

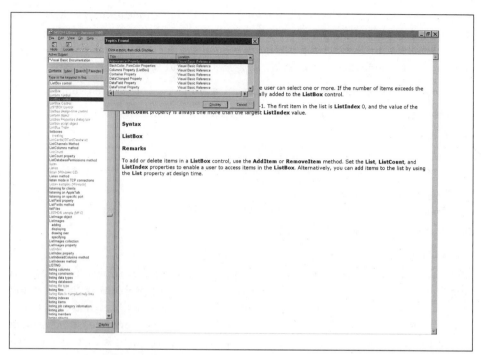

Figure 20-3. *The VB6 help system*

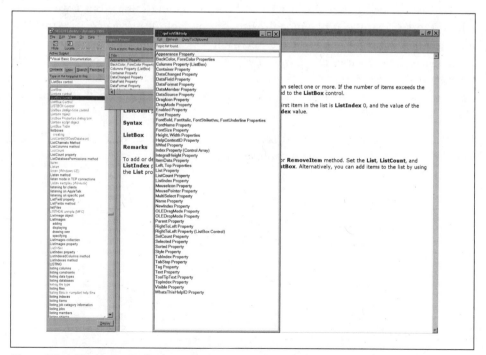

Figure 20-4. *The rpiFixVB6Help application*

Now, just as in the *rpiControlExtractor* program, the application fills its listbox (whose Sorted property is set to **True**) with the topics. Now, when I double-click on an item in this listbox, the application searches the ListView control for that item, using the same cross-process tricks as before, and sending the message:

```
lResp = SendMessageByNum(hListView, LVM_FINDITEMA, -1&, lForeignLVFindInfoAddr)
```

Then the item in the ListView control is selected and made visible by sending the appropriate messages:

```
' Send the message to select the item by setting its state
lResp = SendMessageByNum(hListView, LVM_SETITEMSTATE, lItem, lForeignLVItem)

' Ensure item is visible
lResp = SendMessageByNum(hListView, LVM_ENSUREVISIBLE, lItem, 0&)
```

Finally, the application closes down.

There is one more tale to tell with respect to this situation. Just as I cranked up the VB6 help system to get the screen shot in Figure 20-4, the Topics list appeared alphabetized! I don't know how this happened, but the problem is fixed on the computer I am using to write this book. The only guess I can make is that I recently installed a non-Microsoft application. Perhaps it overwrote some system files with either newer files that fixed the problem or older files that didn't have the problem? Who knows.

In any case, at first I thought that I had been imagining things, but I was much relieved to see that the problem still exists on my laptop! Just to be sure the laptop wasn't the anomaly, and to see if Microsoft was aware of this problem, I called Microsoft technical support. After walking the technical support person through the steps to get the Topics Found list in Figure 20-4, she said that her list was also *not* alphabetized, but didn't seem too concerned and suggested that I call the Microsoft wish list line!

In any case, if your Topics Found lists are not alphabetized, or if you would like to have full screen lists, then you can use the *rpiFixVBHelp* application.

IV

The Windows GDI (GDI32.DLL Programming)

21

Bitmaps

So far, we have discussed in some detail the rather low-level concepts of processes and threads, memory, PE files, and windows messages. In this chapter, we begin our look at graphics and text, which is much closer to the user level than the material that we have been discussing.

Windows exposes its graphics-related functions in the Windows *Graphical Device Interface*, or GDI library. The GDI functions are implemented primarily in the *GDI32.DLL* library.

Rectangles

We have had some occasion to use the **RECT** structure previously in the book. Let us repeat the declaration:

```
typedef struct _RECT {
    LONG left;
    LONG top;
    LONG right;
    LONG bottom;
} RECT;
```

The GDI makes extensive use of rectangles and the **RECT** structure, and implements a variety of functions for manipulating rectangles:

CopyRect
: Makes a copy of a rectangle.

EqualRect
: Returns **True** if two rectangles are equal.

InflateRect
: Enlarges a rectangle by increasing the value of one or more members.

IntersectRect

Gets the intersection of two rectangles.

IsRectEmpty

Returns **True** if the rectangle has no area.

OffsetRect

Moves a rectangle.

PtInRect

Returns **True** if a specified point lies within a specified rectangle.

SetRect

Sets the members of a **RECT** structure.

SetRectEmpty

Sets the members of a **RECT** structure to 0.

SubtractRect

Subtracts one rectangle from another, provided that the difference is another rectangle.

UnionRect

Returns the smallest rectangle that contains the two specified rectangles. (In case you are interested, this is *not* the union, but rather the *convex hull*, of the two rectangles.)

We will get a chance to use some of these functions in an upcoming example.

Bitmaps

The term *bitmap* (or *bitmap image*) refers to a graphical image that consists of a rectangular array of *picture elements*, or *pixels* (although transparent pixels may make the bitmap appear to be nonrectangular). Each bitmap pixel corresponds to a pixel on the display device, which we will assume to be a display monitor. (Unfortunately, many software programs like to make unauthorized changes to a bitmap in order to print the image. Thus, it is often not the case that a bitmap pixel corresponds to a single printer "pixel" or printer dot. Life would be so much simpler if the user had easily accessible control over the mapping from bitmap pixels to printer dots...but I digress here.)

The term *Windows bitmap file* (these files have extension *.BMP*) refers to a specific set of file formats that Windows uses to render bitmaps on a display device. Each pixel in the bitmap *image* corresponds to a certain number of bits in the bitmap *file*, as shown in Figure 21-1.

The number of bits per color in the bitmap file is called the bitmap's *color depth* and depends on the number of colors supported by the bitmap. A monochrome bitmap, for instance, requires only one bit per pixel, whereas a 256-color bitmap

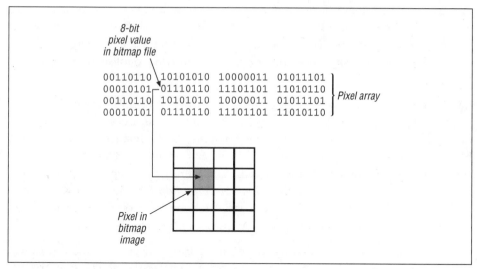

Figure 21-1. Bitmap images and bitmap files

will require 8 bits per pixel (color depth is 8). In general, a bitmap with color depth n supports 2^n colors.

As we will see, the *pixel values* in the bitmap file may or may not describe the actual colors themselves. To express a color requires 3 bytes for each primary color—one byte each for red, green, and blue. Thus, it is often the case that each pixel value specifies an *offset* into a *color table* that is also contained in the bitmap file.

Microsoft has enhanced the BMP file format several times over the years, which is why there is more than one bitmap file format extant. Files of the original BMP format are referred to as *device-dependent bitmaps*, or DDBs. This format is now generally considered obsolete, although files of this type still seem to exist in abundance. All versions of the BMP file format since the first are referred to as *device-independent bitmaps*, or DIBs. Unfortunately, the term *bitmap* is often used for these file types as well. For clarity, we will use the term *bitmap file* when we are referring to the file, and *bitmap image* when we are referring to the actual graphics image.

To confuse matters even more, when Windows loads a bitmap file into memory, it removes the file header, thus creating a *Windows bitmap memory image*. In summary, the term bitmap can refer to a bitmap graphics image, a bitmap file, or a bitmap memory image.

Scan Lines

In order to render a bitmap image on a display, the pixels (dot trios) on the inside surface of the display are scanned by electron guns, one row at a time. Hence,

each row of the bitmap file's *pixel array* (see Figure 21-1) corresponds to a portion of one of the display's *scan lines*. Sometimes a row of the bitmap file itself is
referred to as a scan line. (For more on hardware raster scanning, let me suggest
my book *Understanding Personal Computer Hardware*, published by Springer-
Verlag, New York.)

In this regard, bitmaps can be classified into two categories, distinguished by
whether the rows of pixels appearing in the bitmap file are scanned in normal
order or in reverse order. In the *top-down bitmap file*, the first row of pixels in the
bitmap file corresponds to the top row of the bitmap image. This means that the
origin of the bitmap array, that is, the pixel array entry (0,0) represents the upper-
left corner of the bitmap image. In a *bottom-up bitmap file*, the first row of pixels
in the bitmap file corresponds to the last (bottom) row of the bitmap image.
Hence, the origin represents the lower-left corner of the bitmap image.

Simply put, a top-down bitmap file builds the bitmap image from the top down,
whereas a bottom-up bitmap file builds the bitmap image from the bottom up.

Device-Independent Bitmaps

The main compatibility problem related to bitmaps is the rendering of color. The
original device-dependent bitmap (DDB) format, used in Windows 3.0 and earlier,
uses a very simple method for representing colors. Each pixel value in the bitmap's data array is an index into a *color table* that is maintained by Windows
itself. In this case, the color table is *not* part of the bitmap file. Hence, if a bitmap
is created on one system and displayed on another system with a different color
table, the original colors may be replaced. This is not good.

To mitigate this problem, the *device-independent bitmap*, or DIB, was invented. A
DIB file contains all of the color information used by the bitmap, thus making it
portable.

To understand how this is done, we must first note that colors are generally represented in a bitmap by the *RGB color model*, in which each color is described by a
3-byte (24-bit) number—8 bits to specify the intensity of red, 8 bits to specify the
intensity of green, and 8 bits to specify the intensity of blue. (The colors red,
green, and blue are the *primary* colors for the model.) Thus, for instance, the
color &HFFFFFF indicates full intensity for each color, thus producing white; &H0
produces black; and &H00FF00 produces full intensity (bright) green. You can
check this yourself by using a VB picturebox control and executing the code:

```
Picture1.BackColor = RGB(0, &HFF, 0)
```

Incidentally, there are other color models. For instance, the CYMK color model
uses the primary colors cyan, yellow, magenta, and black. The RGB color model is
used by display monitors, and the CYMK model is used by color printers. This is
one reason why it is so difficult to get screen and printer colors to match.

To understand the format of a DIB file, the place to start is with the way in which the color of each pixel is represented in the file. This depends on how many colors the bitmap supports. The common color depths for a bitmap are:

- 1 bit: 2 colors (called *monochrome*)

- 4 bits: 16 colors

- 8 bits: 256 colors

- 16 bits: 65,536 colors (called *high color*)

- 24 bits: 16,777,216 colors (called *true color*)

There is also a 32-bit color bitmap. These bitmaps actually use 24 bits for the primary RGB colors. The extra byte is devoted to the so-called *alpha channel*, which carries information about the degree of *opacity* for each pixel.

Bitmaps with color depth 1, 4, or 8 always use a *color table*, also called a *color palette*. This is a table of 3-byte RGB color values, equal in size to the number of supported colors. Each pixel value in the bitmap's data array is simply an index into this color table. Figure 21-2 illustrates the concept of a color table.

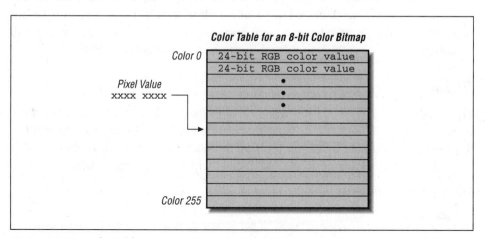

Figure 21-2. A color table

The real complexity comes with 16-bit color bitmaps, which fall into the gray area between those bitmaps that should obviously use a color table (depth 1, 4, and 8) and those that do not need a color table (depth 24 and 32). A variety of schemes are used to deal with 16-bit color bitmaps, but they basically fall into two categories. Either the pixel value is an offset into a color table or the pixel value is masked into three parts—one for each primary color. Of course, each part is less than the full 8 bits that would be used to represent all possible color intensities. For instance, the simplest color mask is to use 5 bits for each color, as in:

```
xrrrrrgggggbbbbb
```

where the most significant bit **x** is unused. Thus, the low-order 5 bits determines the intensity of blue, for instance. Note that when this 16-bit word is stored in memory, the bytes are reversed (little-endian), so it will appear as **gggbbbbb xrrrrrgg**.

It is important to note that even 24-bit and 32-bit color bitmap files may contain color tables. This is because they may need to be rendered on devices that do not support the full range of colors supported by the bitmap itself. To render a 24-bit color bitmap on a monitor that is set to display only 256 colors requires the use of a color table or some other means for replacing each of potentially over 16 million colors by one of 256 colors!

The BMP file format has evolved through at least four versions and a new version is being implemented for Windows 2000. Since it is not essential to our discussion of the Win32 GDI, we will not discuss bitmap file formats.

Bitmap Functions

The Win32 API provides a slew of functions for creating and manipulating bitmaps, and you will no doubt want to take a close look at these functions before programming your next bitmap editing application. However, our discussion will be confined to just two bitmap-related functions: *LoadImage* and *BitBlt*.

BitBlt

The *BitBlt* function is one of the workhorses of the Windows GDI. This term *BitBlt* is shorthand for *Bitmap Block Transfer*, which tells us that the purpose of *BitBlt* is to move graphical data from one location to another. However, it is also possible to specify how the source data should interact with the destination data.

The syntax for *BitBlt* is:

```
BOOL BitBlt(
  HDC hdcDest,   // handle to destination device context
  int nXDest,    // x-coordinate of destination rectangle's upper-left corner
  int nYDest,    // y-coordinate of destination rectangle's upper-left corner
  int nWidth,    // width of destination rectangle
  int nHeight,   // height of destination rectangle
  HDC hdcSrc,    // handle to source device context
  int nXSrc,     // x-coordinate of source rectangle's upper-left corner
  int nYSrc,     // y-coordinate of source rectangle's upper-left corner
  DWORD dwRop    // raster operation code
);
```

Among other things, this function requires handles to *device contexts* for both the source and the destination. We shall discuss device contexts in detail in Chapter 22, *Device Contexts I: Overview*. Suffice it to say now that a device context provides a means to use the GDI drawing functions for a particular device (which might be the display, a printer, a window, or even a chunk of memory). You may be familiar with the fact that most VB controls (including forms) have an hDC property that returns a handle to a device context. This property is all we need for this chapter.

The only other non-self-explanatory parameter is the raster operation code *dwRop*. Table 21-1 shows some of the possible values. The operators AND, OR, and NOT stand for bitwise operations. Thus, for instance,

```
1100 AND 1010 = 1000
1100 OR 1010 = 1110
1100 XOR 1010 = 0110
NOT 10 = 01
```

Table 21-1. Some Raster Operation Codes

Code	Description
BLACKNESS	Fills the destination rectangle using the color associated with index 0 in the physical palette. (This color is black for the default physical palette.)
DSTINVERT	Inverts the destination rectangle.
NOTSRCCOPY	Destination = NOT Source
NOTSRCERASE	Destination = NOT (Source OR Destination)
SRCAND	Destination = Source AND Destination
SRCCOPY	Copies the source rectangle directly to the destination rectangle. The original destination pixels are lost.
SRCERASE	Destination = Source AND (NOT Destination)
SRCINVERT	Destination = Source XOR Destination
SRCPAINT	Destination = Source OR Destination
WHITENESS	Fills the destination rectangle using the color associated with index 1 in the physical palette. (This color is white for the default physical palette.)

Example: Moving Playing Cards

Before illustrating the *BitBlt* function, let me digress briefly to explain how I first encountered this function, since it is at least partially relevant to the discussion.

Sometime in 1994 (I believe), the first continuous speech recognition software became available for the PC. At that time, I was in the process of creating a large database of several thousand high-level mathematics books for a newsletter that I publish. For this, I needed to supply each book with up to three subject classifications out of more than a hundred different subjects (I'll bet you didn't know that there were more than a hundred different subject areas of mathematics). The first few subjects are shown in Table 21-2.

Table 21-2. Subject Classification

Code	Subject
AA	Abstract Algebra
AGEO	Algebraic Geometry
ALG	Algorithms
APPL	Applied Math
APPROX	Approximation Theory
ARITH	Arithmetic
ATOP	Algebraic Topology

The idea that perhaps this could be done by voice was very exciting to me, since the alternative—typing in these subjects—was sickening. I wanted to be able to speak words such as:

> *Next Book, Algorithms, Next Subject, Applied Math, Next Subject, Approximation, Next Book . . .*

As it turned out, this worked quite well—certainly much better than I was expecting, and it got me very interested in voice recognition.

In any case, the demo program that came with the voice recognition software was a pointless little video poker game, and it occurred to me that the company might be able to better demonstrate its software by voice-enabling the traditional solitaire game that comes with Windows.

Unfortunately, there is no way to voice-enable that particular version because it does not accept keyboard input. So I set out to write a clone of Windows Solitaire using Visual Basic—one that could be completely controlled through the keyboard, with commands like JH.QS, meaning *Put the Jack of Hearts on the Queen of Spades.* This would make it a simple matter to voice-enable the program.

As it happens, this turned out to be quite a challenge.

First, I started by placing 52 picture boxes on a VB form. I didn't get very far before VB complained about being out of resources. Next, I tried using image controls instead, but there seemed to be no way to eliminate the major flicker problem when moving these controls. (There were other problems as well, but I can't remember what they were now.)

The only solution that would not require more resources than were available and would not produce noticeable flicker when the cards were moved was to use *BitBlt.*

The idea is to add a separate form with a *single* picture box called *Deck*. In that picture box, I placed the set of 52 cards, as in Figure 21-3. Whenever a card needed to be drawn somewhere on the gaming table, I just used *BitBlt* to copy it from the picture box to the main form.

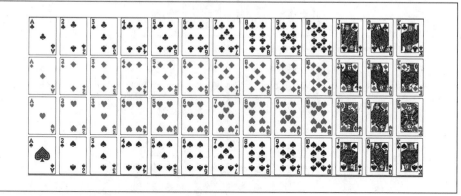

Figure 21-3. The cards for a solitaire program

To illustrate the process, the CD includes a small *BitBlt* example project called *rpiBitBlt*. The program just draws randomly chosen cards from a small deck of 20 cards onto the main form *frmTable*. You can use the mouse to drag these cards around the main window without interfering with the other cards. Figure 21-4 and Figure 21-5 show sample before and after pictures.

The bulk of the action in this program takes place in the MouseMove event.

When a card is moved, we first identify the rectangles that are uncovered by this move (*UnRect1* and *UnRect2*). Figure 21-6 shows these uncovered rectangles when the card is moved down and to the right. Of course, the location of the rectangles will depend upon the direction of movement of the card.

Here is the code that corresponds to Figure 21-6:

```
ElseIf CardLocation(iCurrentCard).Left > CardPrevRect.Left And _
    CardLocation(iCurrentCard).Top > CardPrevRect.Top Then
    ' Moved right and down
    UnRect1.Top = CardPrevRect.Top
    UnRect1.Bottom = CardLocation(iCurrentCard).Top
    UnRect1.Left = CardPrevRect.Left
    UnRect1.Right = CardPrevRect.Right

    UnRect2.Top = CardLocation(iCurrentCard).Top
    UnRect2.Bottom = CardPrevRect.Bottom
    UnRect2.Left = CardPrevRect.Left
    UnRect2.Right = CardLocation(iCurrentCard).Left
```

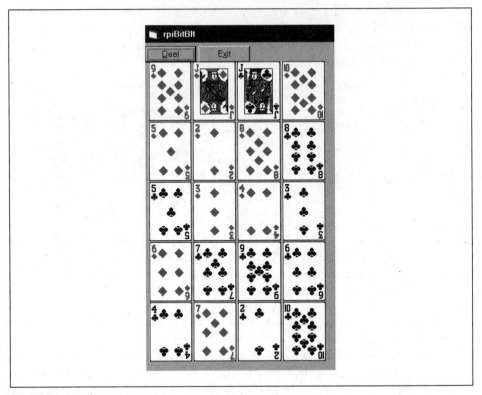

Figure 21-4. Before

Once the rectangles *UnRect1* and *UnRect2* have been identified, we next fill them
with the color of the tabletop (the form) using the *FillRect* GDI function:

```
FillRect Me.hdc, UnRect1, COLOR_BTNFACE + 1
FillRect Me.hdc, UnRect2, COLOR_BTNFACE + 1
```

(In case you are wondering about the +1, here is what the documentation says:

> If specifying a color value for the *hbr* parameter, it must be one of the standard
> system colors (the value 1 must be added to the chosen color).

Next, we copy the card being moved to its new location using a *BitBlt*:

```
' Place current card at new location
i = CardIndex(iCurrentCard)
BitBlt Me.hdc, _
   CardLocation(iCurrentCard).Left, _
   CardLocation(iCurrentCard).Top, _
   CARD_WIDTH, _
   CARD_HEIGHT, _
   frmCards.Deck.hdc, _
   DECK_X_SPACING * (i Mod DECK_COL_COUNT), _
   DECK_Y_SPACING * (i \ DECK_COL_COUNT), _
   SRCCOPY
```

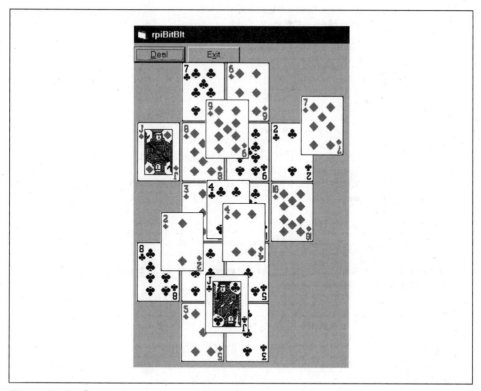

Figure 21-5. After

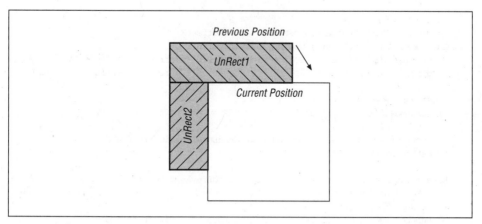

Figure 21-6. Card movement

Of course, the uncovered rectangles may intersect some of the other cards. To check that, we use the *IntersectRect* function. Here is an excerpt:

```
' Get rectangle for card
SetRect Card, CardLocation(i).Left, CardLocation(i).Top, _
    CardLocation(i).Left + CARD_WIDTH, CardLocation(i).Top + CARD_HEIGHT
```

```
         ' Get intersection of Unrect1 and card
         IntersectRect FixupRect, UnRect1, Card


         ' If not empty then redraw FixupRect
         If IsRectEmpty(FixupRect) = 0 Then
            BitBlt Me.hdc, _
               FixupRect.Left, _
               FixupRect.Top, _
               FixupRect.Right - FixupRect.Left, _
               FixupRect.Bottom - FixupRect.Top, _
               frmCards.Deck.hdc, _
               DECK_X_SPACING * (CardIndex(i) Mod DECK_COL_COUNT) _
               + (FixupRect.Left - CardLocation(i).Left), _
               DECK_Y_SPACING * Int(CardIndex(i) / DECK_COL_COUNT) _
               + (FixupRect.Top - CardLocation(i).Top), _
               SRCCOPY
         End If
```

The entire MouseMove code is shown here:

```
Private Sub Form_MouseMove(Button As Integer, Shift As Integer, _
x As Single, y As Single)

Dim i As Integer

Dim UnRect1 As RECT
Dim UnRect2 As RECT
Dim FixupRect As RECT
Dim Card As RECT

If Not bProcessMouseMove Then Exit Sub

' Adjust card location
CardLocation(iCurrentCard).Left = x - iCardOffsetX
CardLocation(iCurrentCard).Top = y - iCardOffsetY
CardLocation(iCurrentCard).Bottom = CardLocation(iCurrentCard).Top + CARD_HEIGHT
CardLocation(iCurrentCard).Right = CardLocation(iCurrentCard).Left + CARD_WIDTH


' Get uncovered rectangles
If CardLocation(iCurrentCard).Left = CardPrevRect.Left Then
    ' Vertical move
    SubtractRect UnRect1, CardPrevRect, CardLocation(iCurrentCard)
    SetRectEmpty UnRect2

ElseIf CardLocation(iCurrentCard).Top = CardPrevRect.Top Then
    ' Horizontal move
    SetRectEmpty UnRect1
    SubtractRect UnRect2, CardPrevRect, CardLocation(iCurrentCard)

ElseIf CardLocation(iCurrentCard).Left > CardPrevRect.Left And _
    CardLocation(iCurrentCard).Top > CardPrevRect.Top Then
    ' Move right and down
    UnRect1.Top = CardPrevRect.Top
    UnRect1.Bottom = CardLocation(iCurrentCard).Top
    UnRect1.Left = CardPrevRect.Left
    UnRect1.Right = CardPrevRect.Right
```

```
        UnRect2.Top = CardLocation(iCurrentCard).Top
        UnRect2.Bottom = CardPrevRect.Bottom
        UnRect2.Left = CardPrevRect.Left
        UnRect2.Right = CardLocation(iCurrentCard).Left


    ElseIf CardLocation(iCurrentCard).Left > CardPrevRect.Left And _
        CardLocation(iCurrentCard).Top < CardPrevRect.Top Then
        ' Move right and up
        UnRect1.Top = CardLocation(iCurrentCard).Bottom
        UnRect1.Bottom = CardPrevRect.Bottom
        UnRect1.Left = CardPrevRect.Left
        UnRect1.Right = CardPrevRect.Right

        UnRect2.Top = CardPrevRect.Top
        UnRect2.Bottom = CardLocation(iCurrentCard).Bottom
        UnRect2.Left = CardPrevRect.Left
        UnRect2.Right = CardLocation(iCurrentCard).Left


    ElseIf CardLocation(iCurrentCard).Left < CardPrevRect.Left And _
        CardLocation(iCurrentCard).Top > CardPrevRect.Top Then
        ' Move left and down
        UnRect1.Top = CardPrevRect.Top
        UnRect1.Bottom = CardLocation(iCurrentCard).Top
        UnRect1.Left = CardPrevRect.Left
        UnRect1.Right = CardPrevRect.Right

        UnRect2.Top = CardLocation(iCurrentCard).Top
        UnRect2.Bottom = CardPrevRect.Bottom
        UnRect2.Left = CardLocation(iCurrentCard).Right
        UnRect2.Right = CardPrevRect.Right


    ElseIf CardLocation(iCurrentCard).Left < CardPrevRect.Left And _
        CardLocation(iCurrentCard).Top < CardPrevRect.Top Then
        ' Move left and up
        UnRect1.Top = CardLocation(iCurrentCard).Bottom
        UnRect1.Bottom = CardPrevRect.Bottom
        UnRect1.Left = CardPrevRect.Left
        UnRect1.Right = CardPrevRect.Right

        UnRect2.Top = CardPrevRect.Top
        UnRect2.Bottom = CardLocation(iCurrentCard).Bottom
        UnRect2.Left = CardLocation(iCurrentCard).Right
        UnRect2.Right = CardPrevRect.Right

    End If


    ' Color the uncovered rectangles with the table color
    FillRect Me.hdc, UnRect1, COLOR_BTNFACE + 1
    FillRect Me.hdc, UnRect2, COLOR_BTNFACE + 1


    ' Place current card at new location
    i = CardIndex(iCurrentCard)
    BitBlt Me.hdc, _
        CardLocation(iCurrentCard).Left, _
        CardLocation(iCurrentCard).Top, _
```

```
            CARD_WIDTH, _
            CARD_HEIGHT, _
            frmCards.Deck.hdc, _
            DECK_X_SPACING * (i Mod DECK_COL_COUNT), _
            DECK_Y_SPACING * (i \ DECK_COL_COUNT), _
            SRCCOPY


    ' Do the uncovered rectangles intersect any cards?
    ' If so, repaint cards
    For i = 0 To DECK_CARD_COUNT - 1

        ' Skip the moving card
        If i = iCurrentCard Then GoTo NotThisCard

        ' Get rectangle for card
        SetRect Card, CardLocation(i).Left, CardLocation(i).Top, _
            CardLocation(i).Left + CARD_WIDTH, CardLocation(i).Top + CARD_HEIGHT

        ' Get intersection of Unrect1 and card
        IntersectRect FixupRect, UnRect1, Card

        ' If not empty then redraw FixupRect
        If IsRectEmpty(FixupRect) = 0 Then
            BitBlt Me.hdc, _
                FixupRect.Left, _
                FixupRect.Top, _
                FixupRect.Right - FixupRect.Left, _
                FixupRect.Bottom - FixupRect.Top, _
                frmCards.Deck.hdc, _
                DECK_X_SPACING * (CardIndex(i) Mod DECK_COL_COUNT) + _
                    (FixupRect.Left - CardLocation(i).Left), _
                DECK_Y_SPACING * Int(CardIndex(i) / DECK_COL_COUNT) + _
                    (FixupRect.Top - CardLocation(i).Top), _
                SRCCOPY
        End If

        ' Get intersection of Unrect2 and card
        IntersectRect FixupRect, UnRect2, Card

        ' If not empty then redraw FixupRect
        If IsRectEmpty(FixupRect) = 0 Then
            BitBlt Me.hdc, _
                FixupRect.Left, _
                FixupRect.Top, _
                FixupRect.Right - FixupRect.Left, _
                FixupRect.Bottom - FixupRect.Top, _
                frmCards.Deck.hdc, _
                DECK_X_SPACING * (CardIndex(i) Mod DECK_COL_COUNT) + _
                    (FixupRect.Left - CardLocation(i).Left), _
                DECK_Y_SPACING * Int(CardIndex(i) / DECK_COL_COUNT) + _
                    (FixupRect.Top - CardLocation(i).Top), _
                SRCCOPY
        End If


NotThisCard:
Next
```

```
' Save for next time
CardPrevRect = CardLocation(iCurrentCard)

End Sub
```

Using Bitmaps in Menus

If anyone asks you why he or she would want to program the Win32 API under Visual Basic, you can always cite the following example as a good reason. In this example, we will place a bitmap in a VB menu, as shown in Figure 21-7.

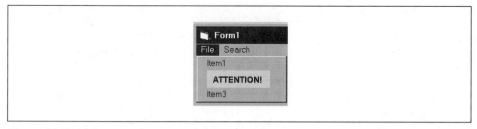

Figure 21-7. A bitmap in a menu

The key to doing this is the *ModifyMenu* function:

```
BOOL ModifyMenu(
   HMENU hMnu,          // handle to menu
   UINT uPosition,      // menu item to modify
   UINT uFlags,         // menu item flags
   UINT uIDNewItem,     // menu item identifier or handle to drop-down menu/submenu
   LPCTSTR lpNewItem    // menu item content
);
```

When the *uFlags* parameter is set to **MF_BITMAP**, the *lpNewItem* parameter is expected to contain the handle to a bitmap. Accordingly, we declare the *Modify-Menu* function in VB as follows (note that the last parameter is declared as a long):

```
Declare Function ModifyMenu Lib "user32" Alias "ModifyMenuA" ( _
    ByVal hMenu As Long, _
    ByVal nPosition As Long, _
    ByVal wFlags As Long, _
    ByVal wIDNewItem As Long, _
    ByVal lpNewItem As Long _
) As Long
```

To get a handle to a bitmap, we use the *LoadImage* function:

```
HANDLE LoadImage(
   HINSTANCE hinst,     // handle of the instance containing the image
   LPCTSTR lpszName,    // name or identifier of image
   UINT uType,          // type of image
   int cxDesired,       // desired width
```

```
    int cyDesired,      // desired height
    UINT fuLoad         // load flags
);
```

By setting *hInst* to NULL and *uLoad* to LR_LOADFROMFILE, we can put the path/ filename of a bitmap in *lpszName*.

Here is the entire code to do the job:

```
Sub MenuBitmap()

Dim hMenu As Long
Dim hSubMenu As Long
Dim lMenuID As Long
Dim hBitmap As Long
Dim hImage As Long

' Get handle of top menu
hMenu = GetMenu(Me.hwnd)

' Do we have a valid menu handle
If IsMenu(hMenu) = 0 Then
    MsgBox "Menu handle invalid", vbInformation
    Exit Sub
End If

' Get handle of submenu 0 (File menu)
hSubMenu = GetSubMenu(hMenu, 0)

' Do we have a valid submenu handle
If IsMenu(hSubMenu) = 0 Then
    MsgBox "Submenu handle invalid", vbInformation
    Exit Sub
End If

' Need menu item ID (item 1 is second item)
lMenuID = GetMenuItemID(hSubMenu, 1)

' Load bitmap
hImage = LoadImage(0, "d:\bkapi\0code\atten.bmp", IMAGE_BITMAP, 0, 0, LR_
LOADFROMFILE)

' Stick it in menu
ModifyMenu hSubMenu, 1, MF_BITMAP Or MF_BYPOSITION, lMenuID, hImage

End Sub
```

22

Device Contexts I:
Overview

The key concept in the GDI is that of a *device context*. In an effort to make drawing (by which we will mean drawing both graphics and text) as device-independent as possible, Windows uses the idea of a device context. Device contexts are used to draw not only to physical devices such as the display or a printer, but also to an individual window or even a bitmap stored in memory.

The basic procedure when using a device context is as follows:

1. Obtain a device context, either by creating a new one or using an existing one. (As we will see, Windows maintains a stock of device contexts for our use.) For a window or the screen, we can use the GDI function *GetDC* or *GetWindowDC*. For a printer, we can use *CreateDC*. This process *selects* the device context into a device, such as a window, screen, printer, or memory block. (The Visual Basic hDC property also returns a handle to a device context. We will discuss this later in the chapter. Our attention now is focused on the Windows GDI.)

2. Set the device context's attributes and graphic objects, which may include its drawing *pen*, painting *brush*, font, and so on.

3. Apply *drawing methods* to the device context. This includes outputting text.

4. Destroy (using *DeleteDC*) or free (using *ReleaseDC*) the device context if appropriate.

We will go into these steps in more detail at the appropriate time. The important point to stress now is that device contexts provide a kind of device independence. In particular, drawing code that we create for one device context, such as the screen, can also be used in other device contexts just by changing the value of the device context argument to the drawing functions. Thus, we can use essentially the same code to draw on the screen as to print to the printer, for instance.

For instance, the *Ellipse* function is used to draw an ellipse. It has five parameters, four of which specify the bounding rectangle that contains the ellipse and one of which specifies the device context into which to draw the ellipse. Thus, by changing one argument, we can draw the same ellipse in different contexts. (This will become clearer when we do some actual examples.)

How Windows Handles Window Painting

To understand the Windows GDI, we must understand how Windows decides when to paint (or repaint) a portion of a window. For this, we need to take a look at *regions*.

A Glossary of Regions

A *region* is an object that consists of a union of one or more rectangles, polygons, or ellipses. Regions have handles and can be filled, framed, moved, inverted, and so on.

To illustrate, we can create an elliptical region using the following function, which returns a handle to the region.

```
HRGN CreateEllipticRgn(
   int nLeftRect,    // x-coordinate of the upper-left corner of the
                     // bounding rectangle
   int nTopRect,     // y-coordinate of the upper-left corner of the
                     // bounding rectangle
   int nRightRect,   // x-coordinate of the lower-right corner of the
                     // bounding rectangle
   int nBottomRect   // y-coordinate of the lower-right corner of the
                     // bounding rectangle
);
```

Incidentally, this should not be confused with drawing an ellipse in a window, which can be done using the *Ellipse* drawing function. This ellipse is referred to as an ellipse *shape*.

Regions are combined using the *CombineRgn* function:

```
int CombineRgn(
   HRGN hrgnDest,     // handle to destination region
   HRGN hrgnSrc1,     // handle to source region
   HRGN hrgnSrc2,     // handle to source region
   int fnCombineMode  // region combining mode
);
```

The *fnCombineMode* parameter can assume one of the following values, which determine the precise action that takes place.

RGN_AND

Outputs the intersection of the source regions.

RGN_COPY

Copies the first region to the destination.

RGN_DIFF

Outputs the portion of *hrgnSrc1* that is not part of *hrgnSrc2*. (This is *region1 – region2*.)

RGN_OR

Outputs the union of the source regions.

RGN_XOR

Outputs all portions of the union that are *not* in *both* regions. In set-theoretic language, this is the *symmetric difference* of the two regions.

In addition to combining regions, a region can be filled, using the *FillRgn* or *PaintRgn* functions, inverted using *InvertRgn*, framed using *FrameRgn*, and moved using *OffsetRgn*.

The update region

The *update region* of a window is that region in a window that is currently out-of-date or *invalid* and therefore requires repainting.

The visible region

The *visible region* is generally the region that is visible to the user. However, the WS_CLIPCHILDREN and WS_CLIPSIBLINGS styles have an effect on what is con-sidered the visible region. If a window has the WS_CLIPCHILDREN style, then the visible region does not include any child windows. If the window has the WS_CLIPSIBLINGS style, then the visible portion of the window does not include any portion that is obscured by sibling windows.

The clipping region

The *clipping region* is the subregion of the client area of a window in which draw-ing is currently permitted. Put another way, if we attempt to draw to a window, Windows will *clip* the drawing so that it does not extend beyond the clipping region.

As we will see, when an application receives a display device context through a call to one of the GDI functions *BeginPaint*, *GetDC*, or *GetDCEx*, the system sets the clipping region for the device context to the *intersection* of the visible region and the update region. In this way, the only portion of the window that is drawn is the portion that has *visible changes*.

The window region

The term *window region* also appears in Microsoft's documentation as follows:

> The window region determines the area within the window where the operating system permits drawing. The operating system does not display any portion of a window that lies outside of the window region.

This is not quite the same as the clipping region, because the window region is apparently not restricted to the client area of the window. In any case, it would not surprise me very much if the two terms were often mixed up in the documentation, so I would advise some caution here.

Functions That Affect Window Regions

The GDI API has a variety of functions that affect the various window regions (besides the functions for combining, filling, inverting, and moving regions discussed earlier).

GetUpdateRect and GetUpdateRgn

The *GetUpdateRect* function returns the coordinates of the smallest rectangle that completely encloses the update region of the specified window. The *GetUpdateRgn* function returns the actual update region of a window by copying it into a specified region object.

GetWindowRgn and SetWindowRgn

The *GetWindowRgn* function retrieves (makes a copy of) the window region of a window. The *SetWindowRgn* function sets the window region of a window.

The *SetWindowRgn* function can be used to create nonrectangular windows. More particularly, the function can be used to set the visible portion of a window to a nonrectangular shape. You can try this out very simply by creating a VB project with two forms: Form1 and Form2. Then place the following code behind a button on Form1 (you will need to add the necessary declarations, of course):

```
' Load form2 and change window region
Dim hrgn As Long

hrgn = CreateEllipticRgn(0, 0, 100, 200)
Form2.Show

SetWindowRgn Form2.hWnd, hrgn, -1
```

InvalidateRect and ValidateRect

The *InvalidateRect* function *invalidates* a rectangle by adding it to a window's update region. The *ValidateRect* function *validates* a rectangle by removing it from the update region.

InvalidateRgn and ValidateRgn

The *InvalidateRgn* function invalidates a region by adding it to the window's update region. The *ValidateRgn* function *validates* a region by removing it from the update region.

RedrawWindow

The *RedrawWindow* function can be used to do a variety of things, including validating or invalidating a given region.

UpdateWindow

The *UpdateWindow* function updates the client area of a window by sending a WM_PAINT message to the window.

The Update Region and WM_PAINT Messages

As we have seen, the *update region* of a window is the region that is currently invalid and therefore requires repainting. Of course, this is constantly changing. For instance, if the user moves another window partially over the window in question, then Windows will add the covered portion to the update region. If a window is minimized, the entire window becomes invalid and is "added to" the update region.

Indeed, when any action takes place that affects the contents of a window, such as when the window is first created, minimized, resized, or covered by another window, the window's contents are not saved. (It would take too many resources to save the contents of all such windows.) Instead, Windows *invalidates* the affected portion of the window and adds it to the update region. Then the system sends a WM_PAINT message to the window procedure of the window. Recall our discussion of how *GetMessage* handles WM_PAINT messages. In particular, WM_PAINT messages have very low priority and are bumped by both sent and posted messages.

Note that it is up to the programmer to include code in the window procedure to perform any necessary repainting of the update region of the window. The invalid region can be obtained through a call to *GetUpdateRgn*.

Even though Visual Basic takes care of this for us, it is worth looking a bit more closely at this issue.

Typically, a programmer will begin the WM_PAINT processing code with a call to *BeginPaint*. This function retrieves a device context, which is required by various painting API functions. We will discuss device contexts in detail very soon. However, the point here is that Windows sets the clipping region to the intersection of the update and visible regions. It then fills a PAINTSTRUCT structure with (among other things) the location of the update region. Then *BeginPaint* sets the update region to NULL, that is, it validates the update region, so that further WM_PAINT messages are not generated.

The nonclient area

As expected, Windows does nothing to help repaint the client area of a window, for it does not know the contents of that area. However, the story is different with respect to the nonclient area. The default window function *DefWindowProc* that is called at the end of the window procedure will redraw the nonclient area of the window. If, however, the application wants to assume this chore, it can process the WM_NCPAINT or WM_ERASEBKGND messages.

Device Contexts

A *device context* (or DC) is an object that is used to perform drawing (of both graphics and text) on a *target device*. Target devices may be *virtual devices*, such as a memory block or a window, or *physical devices* such as the screen or a printer.

Device contexts have *attributes*, such as the background color. Some attributes are graphic objects. The GDI graphic objects are listed below:

*   Bitmap object
*   Brush object
*   Palette object
*   Font object
*   Path object
*   Pen object
*   Region object

The process for associating a graphic object with a device context is simple:

1. Create a graphic object using an API function such as *CreatePen, CreateBrush-Indirect,* or *CreateBitmap*, or use a *stock* object. (Windows maintains a collection of stock pens and stock brushes.) The properties of a graphic object are set when the object is created. For instance, the *CreatePen* function has parameters that determine the pen's width and color.

2. *Select* the object into the device context using *SelectObject*. (The analogy here is with *selecting* a pen with which to draw.)

We can use the *GetCurrentObject* and *GetObject* functions, in combination, to retrieve information about the currently selected object of a specified type in a device context. The *GetCurrentObject* function retrieves a handle to the currently selected object, and the *GetObject* function fills a structure with information about the object whose handle was retrieved by the *GetCurrentObject* function.

Note that to change certain attributes currently used by a device context, such as the pen color, we need to create and select a *new* pen into the device context or use a *different* stock pen, destroying the previous pen. (Windows 2000 implements functions such as *SetDCPenColor* that can directly change the pen color of the currently selected pen, thus saving some hassle on the programmer's part.)

Using a Device Context

As we have mentioned, the basic procedure when using a device context is as follows:

1. Obtain a device context, either by creating a new one or using an existing one. For the client area of a window or the entire screen, we use *GetDC*. For an entire window (both client and nonclient areas) or the entire screen, we can use *GetWindowDC*. For a printer, we use *CreateDC*. When using device contexts obtained from Visual Basic's hDC property, save the current state of the DC. This process *selects* the device context into a device (window, screen, printer).

2. Set the device context's attributes and graphic objects (pens, brushes, or whatever).

3. Apply drawing methods to the device context.

4. Destroy (using *DeleteDC*) or free (using *ReleaseDC*) the device context if appropriate. When using device contexts obtained from Visual Basic's hDC property, restore the original state of the DC.

Figure 22-1 illustrates a device context.

To illustrate, the following procedure will draw a red ellipse with a black interior around a command button. Since drawing output is placed on a layer beneath standard controls, the command button appears on top of the ellipse.

```
Sub EllipseIt()

Dim hPen As Long
Dim hBrush As Long
Dim hDCForm As Long
Dim r As RECT
Dim iDC As Long

' Get device context for form
hDCForm = Form1.hdc

' Save it for later restoration
iDC = SaveDC(hDCForm)
```

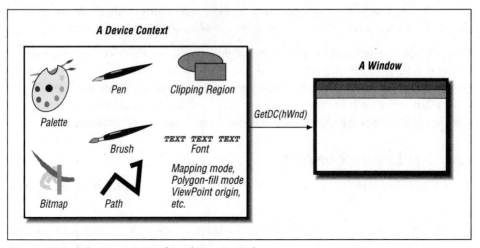

Figure 22-1. A device context selected into a window

```
' Set brush (fill) to black
hBrush = GetStockObject(BLACK_BRUSH)
SelectObject hDCForm, hBrush

' And pen to red
hPen = CreatePen(PS_SOLID, 3, &HFF)
SelectObject hDCForm, hPen

' Get coordinates of rectangle surrounding button
r.Left = Command1.Left \ Screen.TwipsPerPixelX
r.Top = Command1.Top \ Screen.TwipsPerPixelY
r.Right = (Command1.Left + Command1.Width) \ Screen.TwipsPerPixelX
r.Bottom = (Command1.Top + Command1.Height) \ Screen.TwipsPerPixelY

' Draw rectangle
Ellipse hDCForm, r.Left - 50, r.Top - 50, r.Right + 50, r.Bottom + 50

' Refresh
Me.Refresh

' Delete pen
DeleteObject hPen

' Restore DC
RestoreDC hDCForm, iDC

End Sub
```

Default Properties

To get some idea of the types of attributes possessed by a device context, Table 22-1 shows the default values that are given to a DC when it is first created. We will discuss some of these attributes later.

Table 22-1. Default Device Context Attribute Values

Attribute	Default Value
Background color	Background color setting from the Control Panel
Background mode	OPAQUE
Bitmap	None
Brush	WHITE_BRUSH (stock brush)
Brush origin	(0,0)
Clipping region	Entire window
Palette	DEFAULT_PALETTE
Current pen position	(0,0)
Device origin	Upper-left corner of the window or the client area
Drawing mode	R2_COPYPEN
Font	SYSTEM_FONT
Intercharacter spacing	0
Mapping mode	MM_TEXT
Pen	BLACK_PEN (stock pen)
Polygon-fill mode	ALTERNATE
Stretch mode	BLACKONWHITE
Text color	Text color setting from Control Panel
Viewport extent	(1,1)
Viewport origin	(0,0)
Window extent	(1,1)
Window origin	(0,0)

Device Context Modes

Device contexts have *modes* that affect how certain operations are performed. These are shown in Table 22-2.

Table 22-2. Device Context Modes

Mode	Description	Set/Get
Background mode	Specifies how background colors are mixed with existing window or screen colors when performing bitmap or text operations.	*SetBkMode, GetBkMode*
Drawing mode	Specifies how foreground colors are mixed with existing window or screen colors for pen, brush, bitmap, and text operations.	*SetROP2, GetROP2Mode*
Mapping mode	Specifies how graphics output is mapped from logical coordinates to device coordinates.	*SetMapMode, GetMapMode*

Table 22-2. Device Context Modes (continued)

Mode	Description	Set/Get
Polygon-fill mode	Specifies how the brush pattern is used to fill the interior of complex regions.	*SetPolyFillMode, GetPolyFillMode*
Stretching mode	Specifies how bitmap colors are mixed with existing window or screen colors when the bitmap is scaled down.	*SetStretchBltMode, GetStretchBltMode*

Device Contexts and Visual Basic

Visual Basic forms and picture boxes have an hDC property that returns a *private* device context for the object (we will explain the term *private* later in Chapter 23, *Device Contexts II: Types of Device Contexts*). It is also possible to get a handle to a device context for these objects using the *GetDC* function. As we will see, the handles returned by hDC and *GetDC* may or may not be handles to the same DC. This depends on the setting of the AutoRedraw property.

Note that it is important to save the state of a VB device context obtained from hDC using the *SaveDC* function and then restore that state using *RestoreDC* when finished, as we did in the previous example.

The AutoRedraw property

As you probably know, the setting of the AutoRedraw property determines whether *drawing output* is automatically redrawn by Windows when necessary, for example, when the target window is resized or is covered and then uncovered by another window. (Unlike drawing output, child windows, such as controls, are always automatically redrawn.) When graphics are automatically redrawn, they are said to be *persistent*.

In order for Windows to have the capability of supporting persistent graphics, drawing output must be stored somewhere during the life of the application. This storage area is called a *persistent bitmap* and is kept in memory.

It is important to note that forms and picture boxes can have two memory bitmaps associated with them. One is a *background bitmap* that is used to "clear" the window. This will exist once the Picture property has been set for the form or control. When AutoRedraw is **True**, there is also a persistent bitmap that receives graphics output. Thus, the setting of this property has a profound effect on drawing. Let us look at this more closely.

The hDC property, GetDC, and drawing output

When AutoRedraw is **True**, a persistent bitmap exits. In this case, the hDC property refers to the device context for this persistent bitmap. When AutoRedraw is **False**, there is no persistent bitmap and the hDC property refers to the device context for the target window. In either case, the return value of *GetDC* is a handle to the device context for the target window (the API knows nothing about VB's persistent bitmaps).

It follows that the API drawing functions will always send their output to the target window, whereas the VB drawing functions send their output to the object referred to by the hDC property, which might be either the target window (when AutoRedraw is `False`) or the persistent bitmap (when AutoRedraw is `True`).

The *HDCExample* subroutine shown below demonstrates this. First, we turn on AutoRedraw and then use the hDC property of the *pic* picture box to select a white brush. Then we draw a rectangle (see Figure 22-2), which is filled with the white brush, as expected. Note that we must invoke the **Refresh** method for the picture box in order to get VB to move the output from the persistent bitmap to the picture box itself.

Next, we turn off AutoRedraw and draw two more rectangles—one with the hDC property and one using the device context handle obtained from the *GetDC* function. In both cases, the rectangles do not use the white brush (see Figure 22-2), because we are using the device context of the picture box, not the persistent bitmap.

```
Private Sub HDCExample()

Dim hDCPic As Long

' Turn on AutoRedraw
pic.AutoRedraw = True

Debug.Print "hDC:" & pic.hdc

' Set brush to white
SelectObject pic.hdc, GetStockObject(WHITE_BRUSH)

' Draw rectangle to persistent bitmap
Rectangle pic.hdc, 0, 0, 100, 100

' Need this
pic.Refresh

' Turn off AutoRedraw
pic.AutoRedraw = False

' Get device context for window
hDCPic = GetDC(pic.hwnd)
Debug.Print "GetDC:" & hDCPic

' Draw rectangles
Rectangle pic.hdc, 100, 100, 200, 200
Rectangle hDCPic, 200, 200, 300, 300

End Sub
```

The output from the Debug.Print statement is:

```
hDC:-469695987
GetDC:1946224922
```

which shows that *GetDC* at least returns a different handle than hDC.

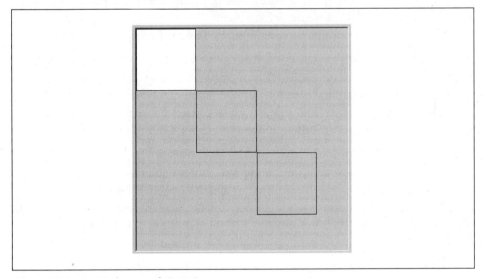

Figure 22-2. AutoRedraw and GetDC

It follows from this discussion that, when AutoRedraw is **True**, a problem arises if we try to draw with both the API drawing functions, through the device context handle obtained from *GetDC* and the VB drawing functions through the hDC property. Namely, Visual Basic will redraw the window from the persistent bitmap when it thinks necessary, thus erasing any graphics output that has gone directly to the window via the *GetDC* device context.

AutoRedraw and the Paint event

When a VB window, such as a picture box, needs redrawing for some reason (such as a change in size or being covered and uncovered, or as a result of a call to the **Refresh** method), VB will do one of two things. If AutoRedraw is **True**, then, as expected, VB will automatically redraw the window using the persistent bitmap. That is the whole point of the AutoRedraw property. Moreover, in this case, VB will *not* fire the Paint event for that window. On the other hand, if AutoRedraw is **False**, then VB instead simply fires the Paint event, leaving the programmer to deal with redrawing issues.

If we want to create persistent graphics when AutoRedraw is **False**, we must place the drawing code in the Paint event of the target window.

Note, however, that in the examples in the following discussion of GDI drawing, we will use a picture box whose AutoRedraw property is set to `False`, but we will not bother to place the drawing code in the Paint event for these examples.

The Picture and Image properties and the CLS method

By definition, the Picture property of a VB control always returns a handle to the background bitmap for the window. On the other hand, the Image property is intended to return a handle to the persistent bitmap. If this bitmap does not exist, then VB *creates* a persistent bitmap containing the same image as the background bitmap (but this is a different bitmap). The Image property then returns a handle to the newly created persistent bitmap.

Finally, we mention that the Visual Basic *Cls* method is based on the hDC property. Thus, when AutoRedraw is `True`, the persistent bitmap is cleared to the background color, and this change is also reflected in the window. When AutoRedraw is `False`, the window is cleared directly, and the persistent bitmap is drawn in that window.

Pens

Pens are graphic objects used to draw lines and curves. Many drawing functions require pens. For instance, the *LineTo* function is:

```
BOOL LineTo(
    HDC hdc,       // device context handle
    int nXEnd,     // x-coordinate of line's ending point
    int nYEnd      // y-coordinate of line's ending point
);
```

This function draws a line using the pen that is currently selected into the device context.

The Windows GDI supports two types of pens: *cosmetic* and *geometric.*

Cosmetic pens

A *cosmetic pen* is used for quick drawing operations. Cosmetic pens use fewer resources than geometric pens, but have only three attributes: width, style, and color.

The functions *CreatePen*, *CreatePenIndirect*, or *ExtCreatePen* can be used to create a cosmetic pen. Windows also maintains three *stock* cosmetic pens, denoted by `BLACK_PEN`, `WHITE_PEN`, and `DC_PEN` (Windows 98/2000 only), which are accessible using the *GetStockObject* function.

The *CreatePen* function is:

```
HPEN CreatePen(
    int fnPenStyle,    // pen style
```

```
    int nWidth,      // pen width
    COLORREF crColor   // pen color
);
```

where COLORREF is a 32-bit value of the form **&Hbbggrr** where the 16-bit value **bb** specifies the blue component of the color (from 0 to &HFF) and similarly for green and red. Thus, for example, &H0000FF is pure red.

In VB, we can use the declaration:

```
Declare Function CreatePen Lib "gdi32" ( _
    ByVal fnPenStyle As Long, _
    ByVal nWidth As Long, _
    ByVal crColor As Long _
) As Long
```

The *fnPenStyle* parameter is one of the following values:

PS_SOLID

Pen is solid.

PS_DASH

Pen is dashed. (Valid only when the pen width is a single pixel.)

PS_DOT

Pen is dotted. (Valid only when the pen width is a single pixel.)

PS_DASHDOT

Pen has alternating dashes and dots. (Valid only when the pen width is a single pixel.)

PS_DASHDOTDOT

Pen has alternating dashes and double dots. (Valid only when the pen width is a single pixel.)

PS_NULL

Pen is invisible.

PS_INSIDEFRAME

Pen is solid. When used with a drawing function that takes a bounding rectangle, such as the *Ellipse* function, the dimensions of the figure (ellipse) are shrunk so that it fits entirely within the bounding rectangle, taking into account the width of the pen. Applies only to geometric pens.

The *nWidth* parameter specifies the width of the pen, in *logical units* (explained later). We can set this to 0 to create a line whose width is a single pixel.

Geometric pens

While cosmetic pens draw very quickly (about 3 to 10 times faster than geometric pens), *geometric pens* are more flexible, having the following properties: width, style, color, pattern, optional hatch, end style, and join style.

A geometric pen is created using *ExtCreatePen*:

```
HPEN ExtCreatePen(
    DWORD dwPenStyle,        // pen style
    DWORD dwWidth,           // pen width
    CONST LOGBRUSH *lplb,    // pointer to structure for brush attributes
    DWORD dwStyleCount,      // length of array containing custom style bits
    CONST DWORD *lpStyle     // optional array of custom style bits
);
```

This function permits the creation of cosmetic or geometric pens, determined by including the `PS_COSMETIC` or `PS_GEOMETRIC` bit style in the *dwPenStyle* argument.

Brushes

A *brush* is a graphic object that is used to paint the interior of polygons, ellipses, and paths.

Windows makes a distinction between a *logical brush* and a *physical brush*. The GDI functions that create a brush return a handle to a logical brush. However, when we select that brush into a device context using *SelectObject*, the device driver for the device creates a physical brush with which to do the actual painting. (After all, a black-and-white printer cannot use a red logical brush, for instance.)

The brush origin

It is important to understand the concept of the *brush origin*. Figure 22-3 illustrates the need for this concept.

The *brush origin* is that pixel in the brush that is placed at the starting pixel in the object to be painted when the painting begins. Figure 22-3 illustrates what happens when we want to paint a window and a control on the window, using the same brush. This involves two separate painting operations.

In Window1 of Figure 22-3, the brush origin is set at the upper-left-hand pixel in the brush for both painting operations. However, when the brush origin is aligned with the pixel at the upper-left corner of the *control*, to begin painting the control, the bit pattern on the control does not align properly with the pattern on the window.

As shown in Window2 of Figure 22-3, to get the patterns to align, all we need to do is change the brush origin when painting the control to the pixel in the second row and first column of the brush.

The brush origin can be set using the *SetBrushOrgEx* function:

```
BOOL SetBrushOrgEx(
    HDC hdc,          // handle of device context
```

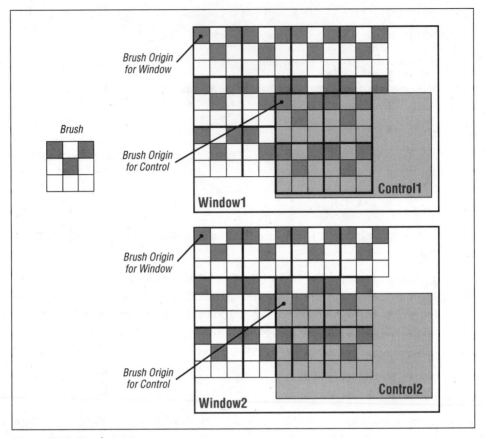

Figure 22-3. Brush origin

```
    int nXOrg,      // x-coordinate of new origin
    int nYOrg,      // y-coordinate of new origin
    LPPOINT lppt    // points to previous brush origin
);
```

Brush types

The Windows GDI implements four types of brushes: *solid*, *stock*, *pattern*, and *hatch*.

Solid brush. A *solid brush* is a logical brush that contains 64 pixels of a single color. Solid brushes are created using the *CreateSolidBrush* function.

Stock brush. The Windows GDI maintains seven predefined stock brushes. A GDI stock brush can be retrieved using the *GetStockObject* function:

```
HGDIOBJ GetStockObject(
    int fnObject    // type of stock object
);
```

The function returns a handle to a GDI object (HGDIOBJ). The *fnObject* parameter can assume one of the values in Table 22-3 (which includes the seven stock GDI brushes).

Table 22-3. Stock Object Types

Value of *fnObject*	Meaning
BLACK_BRUSH	Black brush
DKGRAY_BRUSH	Dark gray brush
DC_BRUSH	Solid color brush (Windows 98/2000)
GRAY_BRUSH	Gray brush
HOLLOW_BRUSH	Same as NULL_BRUSH
LTGRAY_BRUSH	Light gray brush
NULL_BRUSH	Null brush
WHITE_BRUSH	White brush
BLACK_PEN	Black pen
DC_PEN	Solid color pen (Windows 98/2000)
WHITE_PEN	White pen
ANSI_FIXED_FONT	Windows fixed-pitch system font
ANSI_VAR_FONT	Windows variable-pitch (proportional) system font
DEVICE_DEFAULT_FONT	Device-dependent font (Windows NT)
DEFAULT_GUI_FONT	Default font for user interface objects, such as menus and dialog boxes
OEM_FIXED_FONT	Original equipment manufacturer (OEM) dependent fixed-pitch font
SYSTEM_FONT	System font (used to draw menus, dialog box controls, and text)
SYSTEM_FIXED_FONT	Fixed-pitch system font used in Windows 3.0 and earlier
DEFAULT_PALETTE	Default palette

The Windows USER library also maintains a collection of 21 stock brushes. These brushes correspond to the colors of window elements, such as menus, scrollbars, and buttons. The *GetSysColorBrush* function is used to obtain a handle to one of these stock brushes.

Note that stock brushes do not need to be deleted when no longer needed, although it does not do any harm to do so.

Hatch brush. A hatch brush paints a pattern of vertical, horizontal, and/or diagonal lines. The Windows GDI maintains six predefined hash brushes.

Pattern brush. A pattern brush is created using a bitmap. To create a logical pattern brush, we must first create a bitmap and then call *CreatePatternBrush* or *CreateDIBPatternBrushPt* to create the pattern brush.

Paths

A *path* is a sequence of one or more figures (or shapes) that are filled, outlined, or both. Note that, unlike a pen or brush, paths do not have handles and are not created and destroyed in the sense that the other graphic objects are created or destroyed.

One and only one path can be selected into a device context at a given time. When a new path is selected into a DC, the previous path is discarded.

To create a path and select it into a DC, we must first define the points that describe the path. This is a three-step process:

1. Call the *BeginPath* function.

2. Call the appropriate drawing functions.

3. Call the *EndPath* function.

This sequence of function calls is referred to as a *path bracket*.

The *BeginPath* function is:

```
BOOL BeginPath(
    HDC hdc        // handle to device context
);
```

and the *EndPath* function is similar:

```
BOOL EndPath(
    HDC hdc        // handle to device context
);
```

The drawing functions that can be used in a path bracket are shown in Table 22-4.

Table 22-4. Drawing Functions Allowed in a Path Bracket

AngleArc	LineTo	Polyline
Arc	MoveToEx	PolylineTo
ArcTo	Pie	PolyPolygon
Chord	PolyBezier	Polyline
CloseFigure	PolyBezierTo	Rectangle
Ellipse	PolyDraw	RoundRect
ExtTextOut	Polygon	TextOut

Once a path has been selected into a DC, we can perform various operations on that path, such as:

- Drawing an outline of the path using the current pen

- Filling the interior of the path using the current brush

- Converting the curves in the path to line segments
- Converting the path to a clip path
- Converting the path into a region

23

Device Contexts II: Types of Device Contexts

There are actually four different types of device contexts:

Display
> These DCs are used to draw on windows or on the screen.

Printer
> These DCs are used to draw to a printer or plotter.

Memory
> These DCs support drawing operations on a bitmap.

Information
> These DCs support the *retrieval* of device data, such as printer data, and thus use fewer resources than DCs that draw.

We will discuss each of these types of DCs.

Information Device Contexts

The Win32 GDI supports a special type of device context called an *information device context*. These DCs are used to retrieve default device data. Information DCs are "lightweight" DCs that do not require much in the way of resources. Neither can they be used for drawing operations—as the name implies, they are strictly informational. An information DC is created using the *CreateIC* function:

```
HDC CreateIC(
  LPCTSTR lpszDriver,        // pointer to string specifying driver name
  LPCTSTR lpszDevice,        // pointer to string specifying device name
  LPCTSTR lpszOutput,        // pointer to string specifying port or file name
  CONST DEVMODE *lpdvmInit   // pointer to optional initialization data
);
```

The **DEVMODE** structure holds all sorts of information about a device:

```
Type DEVMODE
    dmDeviceName As String * CCHDEVICENAME      ' CCHDEVICENAME = 32
    dmSpecVersion As Integer
    dmDriverVersion As Integer
    dmSize As Integer
    dmDriverExtra As Integer
    dmFields As Long
    dmOrientation As Integer
    dmPaperSize As Integer
    dmPaperLength As Integer
    dmPaperWidth As Integer
    dmScale As Integer
    dmCopies As Integer
    dmDefaultSource As Integer
    dmPrintQuality As Integer
    dmColor As Integer
    dmDuplex As Integer
    dmYResolution As Integer
    dmTTOption As Integer
    dmCollate As Integer
    dmFormName As String *                      ' CCHFORMNAME = 32
    dmUnusedPadding As Integer
    dmBitsPerPel As Long
    dmPelsWidth As Long
    dmPelsHeight As Long
    dmDisplayFlags As Long
    dmDisplayFrequency As Long
    dmICMMethod As Long
    dmICMIntent As Long
    dmMediaType As Long
    dmDitherType As Long
    dmReserved1 As Long
    dmReserved2 As Long
End Type
```

To illustrate, the following code creates an information DC for a printer and then uses *GetCurrentObject* and *GetObject* to get the face name of the printer's default font:

```
Sub GetPrinterInfo()

Dim dc As Long
Dim hObj As Long
Dim f As LOGFONT

dc = CreateIC(vbNullString, "HP LaserJet 4000 Series PS", vbNullString, 0)

hObj = GetCurrentObject(dc, OBJ_FONT)

GetObjectAPI hObj, LenB(f), f
```

```
Debug.Print "Face:" & StrConv(f.lfFaceName, vbUnicode)

DeleteDC dc

End Sub
```

Memory Device Contexts

The Win32 GDI supports a special type of device context called a *memory device context*. This type of DC is used to draw to a bitmap in memory. This bitmap must be compatible with another device context; that is, the bitmap must have the same dimensions and color format as the bitmap associated with a device. For this reason, a memory DC is sometimes called a *compatible* DC. We can create a memory device context by calling the *CreateCompatibleDC* function:

```
HDC CreateCompatibleDC(
    HDC hdc     // handle to a device context
);
```

This function creates a memory device context that is compatible with the device context given by the *hdc* parameter. The return value is a handle to the memory DC.

It is important to note that when a memory DC is first created, its bitmap is just a one-pixel-by-one-pixel placeholder. Before we can begin drawing, we must select a bitmap with the appropriate width and height into the device context, by calling the *SelectObject* function.

One of the main uses of memory device contexts is to preserve a bitmap during other operations. For instance, as we have seen, Visual Basic creates and maintains a persistent bitmap in a memory device context for any form or picture box for which the AutoRedraw property is set to **True**. In this way, when the form or picture box needs repainting (if it is resized, for instance), VB can just map the persistent bitmap to the control.

Another important use of memory device contexts is to perform complex drawing operations in memory, which is faster than drawing directly to an output device. When drawing is completed, the entire bitmap image can be quickly transferred to the device using the *BitBlt* function. Let us illustrate.

The following code creates a memory DC that is compatible with a picture box (*pic*). It then colors each pixel in the memory bitmap with a random color. Finally, the bitmap is transferred to the picture box in one *BitBlt* operation. If you run this code with the line dcComp = pic.hdc commented and uncommented, you can see the difference in behavior between drawing directly to the picture box and using a memory device context. (The difference in performance is not that great in this simple example.)

```
Public Sub MemoryDCExample()

' Requires a picture box named pic

' Save DC for later restoration
hDCPic = SaveDC(pic.hdc)

' Create compatible memory DC
dcComp = CreateCompatibleDC(pic.hdc)

''dcComp = pic.hdc

WidthInPixels = pic.Width / Screen.TwipsPerPixelX
HeightInPixels = pic.Height / Screen.TwipsPerPixelY

' Create bitmap
hBitmap = CreateCompatibleBitmap(pic.hdc, WidthInPixels, HeightInPixels)
lDummy = SelectObject(dcComp, hBitmap)

' Random pixel colors between 0 and 2^24 - 1
Randomize Timer
For r = 0 To WidthInPixels - 1
   For c = 0 To HeightInPixels - 1
      l = Rnd * (2 ^ 24 - 1)
      SetPixel dcComp, r, c, l
   Next
Next

BitBlt pic.hdc, 0, 0, WidthInPixels, HeightInPixels, dcComp, 0, 0, SRCCOPY

RestoreDC pic.hdc, hDCPic
DeleteDC dcComp
DeleteObject hBitmap

End Sub
```

Printer Device Contexts

The Win32 GDI provides a special type of device context called a *printer device context* that can be used when printing with a printer or drawing with a plotter.

We can get access to a printer device context by calling *CreateDC*. When finished printing, the printer DC should be destroyed, using *DeleteDC* (not *ReleaseDC*).

The *CreateDC* function is:

```
HDC CreateDC(
    LPCTSTR lpszDriver,        // pointer to string specifying driver name
    LPCTSTR lpszDevice,        // pointer to string specifying device name
    LPCTSTR lpszOutput,        // must set this to NULL
    CONST DEVMODE *lpInitData  // pointer to optional printer data
);
```

In VB, we can write:

```
Declare Function CreateDC Lib "gdi32" Alias "CreateDCA" ( _
    ByVal lpDriverName As String, _
    ByVal lpDeviceName As String, _
    ByVal lpOutput As String, _
    lpInitData As DEVMODE _        ' can be null
) As Long
```

Under Windows 9x, the *lpszDriver* parameter is generally ignored and should be set to NULL. The one exception is that *CreateDC* will return a display device context if we set this parameter to the string 'DISPLAY,' in which case all other parameters are ignored. Under Windows NT, this parameter should be a string equal to the string 'DISPLAY' (to get a display DC) or the name of the print spooler 'WINSPOOL.'

The *lpszDevice* parameter is a string that specifies the name of the output device, as shown by the Windows Print Manager.

The *lpszOutput* parameter is not used and should be set to NULL.

The *lpInitData* parameter points to a DEVMODE structure containing device-specific initialization data for the device driver. To use the default initialization values, set this parameter to 0. The *DocumentProperties* function will retrieve this structure filled in for a particular device.

The DEVMODE structure is a bit of a nightmare. In VB, it has the following declaration:

```
Type DEVMODE
    dmDeviceName As String * CCHDEVICENAME      ' CCHDEVICENAME = 32
    dmSpecVersion As Integer
    dmDriverVersion As Integer
    dmSize As Integer
    dmDriverExtra As Integer
    dmFields As Long
    dmOrientation As Integer
    dmPaperSize As Integer
    dmPaperLength As Integer
    dmPaperWidth As Integer
    dmScale As Integer
    dmCopies As Integer
    dmDefaultSource As Integer
    dmPrintQuality As Integer
    dmColor As Integer
    dmDuplex As Integer
    dmYResolution As Integer
    dmTTOption As Integer
    dmCollate As Integer
    dmFormName As String * CCHFORMNAME          ' CCHFORMNAME = 32
    dmUnusedPadding As Integer
    dmBitsPerPel As Long
    dmPelsWidth As Long
```

```
            dmPelsHeight As Long
            dmDisplayFlags As Long
            dmDisplayFrequency As Long
            dmICMMethod As Long
            dmICMIntent As Long
            dmMediaType As Long
            dmDitherType As Long
            dmReserved1 As Long
            dmReserved2 As Long
        End Type
```

We will certainly not discuss all of these members. Note, however, that the *dmDeviceName* member is the name of the device as reported by the Print Manager.

Enumerating Printers

Windows implements the *EnumPrinters* enumeration function that enumerates the available printers on a system:

```
    BOOL EnumPrinters(
        DWORD Flags,          // types of printer objects to enumerate
        LPTSTR Name,          // name of printer object
        DWORD Level,          // specifies type of printer info structure
        LPBYTE pPrinterEnum,  // pointer to buffer to receive printer info structures
        DWORD cbBuf,          // size, in bytes, of the buffer
        LPDWORD pcbNeeded,    // pointer to variable with no. of bytes
                              // copied (or required)
        LPDWORD pcReturned    // pointer to variable with no. of printer
                              // info. structures copied
    );
```

In VB, this is:

```
    Declare Function EnumPrinters Lib "winspool.drv" Alias "EnumPrintersA" ( _
        ByVal flags As Long, _
        ByVal Name As String, _
        ByVal Level As Long, _
        pPrinterEnum As Long, _
        ByVal cdBuf As Long, _
        pcbNeeded As Long, _
        pcReturned As Long _
    ) As Long
```

The parameters to this function are rather complicated, and we refer the reader to the documentation for all of the gory details. Instead, let us do an example.

Essentially, the *EnumPrinters* function returns an array of printer information structures—one for each printer, along with supporting strings. There are five different printer information structures. The one we are interested in is:

```
    Public Type PRINTER_INFO_2
        pServerName As Long
        pPrinterName As Long
```

```
            pShareName As Long
            pPortName As Long
            pDriverName As Long
            pComment As Long
            pLocation As Long
            pDevMode As Long          ' pointer to DEVMODE
            pSepFile As Long
            pPrintProcessor As Long
            pDatatype As Long
            pParameters As Long
            pSecurityDescriptor As Long
            Attributes As Long
            Priority As Long
            DefaultPriority As Long
            StartTime As Long
            UntilTime As Long
            Status As Long
            cJobs As Long
            AveragePPM As Long
        End Type
```

Note that the *EnumPrinters* function is not recursive—it behaves like *Enum-Processes* rather than *EnumWindows* (both of which we have already discussed). Thus, the only way to tell whether we have allocated a sufficiently large buffer is to try it. The return value **pcbNeeded** points to a long that tells us the number of bytes needed. If we didn't allocate a sufficient number of bytes, then we must try again!

Here is the code to list some printer values:

```
Sub ListPrinters()

Dim lNeeded As Long
Dim lReturned As Long
Dim lData() As Long
Dim pi2 As PRINTER_INFO_2
Dim dm As DEVMODE
Dim i As Integer

ReDim lData(0 To 4000)

EnumPrinters PRINTER_ENUM_LOCAL, vbNullString, 2, _
    lData(0), 4000, lNeeded, lReturned
Debug.Print "Needed: " & lNeeded
Debug.Print "Returned: " & lReturned

If lNeeded > 4000 Then MsgBox "Increase buffer size."

For i = 0 To lReturned - 1

    Debug.Print "** Printer " & i

    ' Copy i-th PRINTER_INFO_2 structure
    CopyMemory ByVal VarPtr(pi2), _
        ByVal VarPtr(lData(i * LenB(pi2) / 4)), LenB(pi2)
```

```
        Debug.Print "Name: " & LPSTRtoBSTR(pi2.pPrinterName)
        Debug.Print "Port: " & LPSTRtoBSTR(pi2.pPortName)
        Debug.Print "Driver: " & LPSTRtoBSTR(pi2.pDriverName)
        Debug.Print "Comment: " & LPSTRtoBSTR(pi2.pDriverName)

        CopyMemory ByVal VarPtr(dm), ByVal pi2.pDevMode, LenB(dm)
        Debug.Print "Driver Ver: " & dm.dmDriverVersion

    Next

    End Sub
```

The output on my system is:

```
    Needed: 2008
    Returned: 2
    ** Printer 0
    Name: HP LaserJet 4000 Series PS
    Port: LPT1:
    Driver: HP LaserJet 4000 Series PS
    Comment: HP LaserJet 4000 Series PS
    Driver Ver: 3
    ** Printer 1
    Name: EPSON Stylus COLOR 800
    Port: LPT2:
    Driver: EPSON Stylus COLOR 800
    Comment: EPSON Stylus COLOR 800
    Driver Ver: 0
```

Getting the default printer

Under Windows 95, we can set the first parameter of *EnumPrinters* to **PRINTER_ENUM_DEFAULT** to get information about the default printer. However, this does not work under Windows NT! Also, it does not appear that *EnumPrinters* lists the printers in any special order. (It would have been nice if the default printer was always the first one enumerated.) Thus, there does not seem to be a way to get the default printer under Windows NT by using *EnumPrinters*.

However, we can get information about the default printer, using the *GetProfileString* function. Here is the code:

```
    Public Function GetDefaultPrinter()

    Dim sDefPrinter As String
    sDefPrinter = String(1024, vbNullChar)
    GetProfileString "windows", "device", "xxx", sDefPrinter, 1024
    Debug.Print sDefPrinter

    End Function
```

On my system, the output is:

```
    HP LaserJet 4000 Series PS,winspool,LPT1:
```

Enumerating Printer Drivers

Windows also implements the *EnumPrinterDrivers* enumeration function that enumerates the available printer drivers on a system:

```
BOOL EnumPrinterDrivers(
  LPTSTR pName,            // pointer to server name
  LPTSTR pEnvironment,     // pointer to environment name
  DWORD Level,             // structure level
  LPBYTE pDriverInfo,      // pointer to an array of structures
  DWORD cbBuf,             // size, in bytes, of array
  LPDWORD pcbNeeded,       // pointer to number of bytes copied (or required)
  LPDWORD pcReturned       // pointer to number of DRIVER_INFO. structures
);
```

In VB, we can write this as:

```
Declare Function EnumPrinterDrivers Lib "winspool.drv" _
Alias "EnumPrinterDriversA" ( _
  ByVal pName As String, _
  ByVal pEnvironment As String, _
  ByVal Level As Long, _
  pDriverInfo As Long, _
  ByVal cdBuf As Long, _
  pcbNeeded As Long, _
  pcReturned As Long _
) As Long
```

Once again, this is a complex function, and we just consider an example. Of the three different `DRIVER_INFO` structures, we consider only:

```
Type DRIVER_INFO_2
    cVersion As Long
    pName As Long
    pEnvironment As Long
    pDriverPath As Long
    pDataFile As Long
    pConfigFile As Long
End Type
```

Here is some code to enumerate printer drivers:

```
Sub ListDrivers()

Dim lNeeded As Long
Dim lReturned As Long
Dim lData() As Long
Dim di2 As DRIVER_INFO_2
Dim i As Integer

ReDim lData(0 To 4000)

EnumPrinterDrivers vbNullString, vbNullString, 2, lData(0), _
    4000, lNeeded, lReturned
Debug.Print "Needed: " & lNeeded
Debug.Print "Returned: " & lReturned
```

```
    If lNeeded > 4000 Then MsgBox "Increase buffer size."

    For i = 0 To lReturned - 1

        Debug.Print "** Driver " & i

        CopyMemory ByVal VarPtr(di2), _
            ByVal VarPtr(lData(i * LenB(di2) / 4)), LenB(di2)

        Debug.Print "Name: " & LPSTRtoBSTR(di2.pName)
        Debug.Print "Version: " & LPSTRtoBSTR(di2.cVersion)
        Debug.Print "Path: " & LPSTRtoBSTR(di2.pDriverPath)
        Debug.Print "DataFile: " & LPSTRtoBSTR(di2.pDataFile)
        Debug.Print "ConfigFile: " & LPSTRtoBSTR(di2.pConfigFile)
    Next

    End Sub
```

The output on my system is:

```
Needed: 854
Returned: 2
** Driver 0
Name: HP LaserJet 4000 Series PS
Version:
Path: C:\WINNT\System32\spool\DRIVERS\W32X86\2\PSCRIPT.DLL
DataFile: C:\WINNT\System32\spool\DRIVERS\W32X86\2\HP4000_6.PPD
ConfigFile: C:\WINNT\System32\spool\DRIVERS\W32X86\2\PSCRPTUI.DLL
** Driver 1
Name: EPSON Stylus COLOR 800
Version:
Path: C:\WINNT\System32\spool\DRIVERS\W32X86\2\E_CPDJ33.DLL
DataFile: C:\WINNT\System32\spool\DRIVERS\W32X86\2\E_C93J33.DLL
ConfigFile: C:\WINNT\System32\spool\DRIVERS\W32X86\2\E_CUDJ33.DLL
```

Printing

The steps involved in printing using the Windows GDI are these:

1. Create a printer device context using *CreateDC.* As we have seen, this function requires the printer name.

2. Call the *StartDoc* function to start the document:

   ```
   Declare Function StartDoc Lib "gdi32" Alias "StartDocA" ( _
       ByVal hdc As Long, _
       lpdi As DOCINFO _
   ) As Long
   ```

3. Call the *StartPage* function to start a new page:

   ```
   Declare Function StartPage Lib "gdi32" ( _
       ByVal hdc As Long _
   ) As Long
   ```

4. Call the desired GDI drawing functions to print the data to a memory buffer.

5. Call the *EndPage* function, which causes Windows to send the page to the printer:

```
Declare Function EndPage Lib "gdi32" ( _
    ByVal hdc As Long _
) As Long
```

6. Repeat the previous three steps for each page.

7. Call the *EndDoc* GDI function (*not* VB's *EndDoc* function) to end the document:

```
Declare Function EndDocAPI Lib "gdi32" Alias "EndDoc" ( _
    ByVal hdc As Long _
) As Long
```

For example, the following code will print an ellipse on my LaserJet 4000 printer:

```
Sub PrintIt()

Dim printDC As Long
Dim di As DOCINFO

' Initialize DOCINFO
di.cbSize = LenB(di)
di.lpszDocName = "document"
di.lpszOutput = vbNullString   ' or name of file to print to
di.lpszDataType = vbNullString

' Create printer DC
printDC = CreateDC(vbNullString, "HP LaserJet 4000 Series PS", vbNullString, 0)

' Start document and page
StartDoc printDC, di
StartPage printDC

' Print ellipse
Ellipse printDC, 0, 0, 600, 600

' End page and document
EndPage printDC
EndDocAPI printDC

' Delete printer DC
DeleteDC printDC

End Sub
```

There is quite a bit more to printing under the Win32 GDI than we have discussed here, but this introduction should point you in the right direction. Indeed, there are about 80 different printer-related GDI functions! Have fun.

Display Device Contexts

Display device contexts are used to draw to windows or to the screen. There are several types of display device contexts, as shown in Table 23-1.

Table 23-1. Types of Display Contexts

Type	Drawing Scope	Cached?	Obtain Via	Class Style	Comments
Common	Client area	Yes	*GetDC* or *BeginPaint*	None (default)	Uses no additional memory
Class	Client area	No	*GetDC*	CS_CLASSDC	Only one DC for all windows of this class
Parent	Entire window and parent window	Yes	*GetDC* or *BeginPaint*	CS_PARENTDC	Intended for child windows only
Private	Client area	No	*GetDC*	CS_OWNDC	New 800 byte DC created for each window
Window	Entire window	Yes	*GetWindowDC* or *GetDCEx*	NA	

Note that VB supplies a private DC through its hDC property, so generally that is what the VB programmer will use. However, for completeness' sake, we will *briefly* discuss all of the different types of DCs shown in Table 23-1.

Cached and Noncached Display Contexts

As you can see from Table 23-1, some display contexts are *cached*. Windows maintains a cache of device contexts for common, parent, and window DCs. Windows will create new cached DCs when required, but cached DCs consume memory from the application's default heap, so care must be taken not to use too many cached DCs at one time. In fact, cached DCs are intended to be used quickly and released immediately after use, by calling *ReleaseDC* (or *EndPaint*). Also, cached DCs are intended to be used in cases where few changes need to be made to the default attributes. Each time a cached DC is released back into the cache, its settings are returned to the default. (Incidentally, 16-bit Windows had a limit of five cached DCs.)

On the other hand, the noncached DCs are intended to be created and held by an application indefinitely. These DCs provide better performance since they are readily available once created. Each noncached DC consumes 800 bytes of memory.

Classes and Display Contexts

As we have seen, in order to draw to a window, we must first obtain a device context, using a function such as *GetDC, GetDCEx,* or *GetWindowDC.* The type of display device context that is supplied by Windows as a result of a call to one of these functions depends upon the style of the window class from which the window was created.

Recall that, in order to register a window class, the *RegisterClass* function requires a **WNDCLASS** structure. The `style` member of that structure is used (in part) to specify the type of default DC. We describe the possibilities next (and see Table 23-1).

Common display device contexts

A *common* DC is supplied by Windows (in response to a request for a DC) as the default when no class style specifies the DC type. Common device contexts are particularly efficient because they do not require additional memory or system resources.

Common DCs draw only in the client area of the window. Thus, the coordinate system's origin is initially set to the upper-left corner of the client area. Also, the *clipping region* is set to the client area. This means that any drawing that would extend beyond the client area is *clipped* (not drawn). If an application requests a common device context using the *BeginPaint* function, the update region is also set.

Private display contexts

The **CS_OWNDC** class style specifies that each window of this class gets a *private* display context. Windows stores each private display context in the GDI's memory heap. It is not necessary to release a private display context (using *ReleaseDC*). These DCs should be used only with mapping mode **MM_TEXT** to ensure proper window erasing (we will discuss mapping modes in Chapter 24, *Device Contexts III: Coordinate Systems*).

As mentioned earlier, VB's hDC property returns the handle to a private device context.

Class display contexts

The **CS_CLASSDC** class style specifies that the windows of that class share a single display context, which is called the *class display context.* Class display contexts offer some of the benefits of private display contexts, but save resources over private DCs. These DCs should be used only with mapping mode **MM_TEXT** to ensure proper window erasing (we will discuss mapping modes in Chapter 24).

Parent display contexts

The CS_PARENTDC class style specifies that each window of that class use its parent window's display context. Thus, as with class DCs, multiple windows share one display context, thus saving resources. The main benefit of parent DCs is that they are fast.

Coordinate Systems

In general, the GDI drawing functions require that coordinates be specified for a drawing operation. (For instance, we cannot draw a line without specifying where the line starts and where it ends.) This requires a *coordinate system*. The subject of Windows coordinate systems can be quite confusing, so let us see if we can make some sense of it.

Physical Devices

We begin with the simple observation that the ultimate goal of the GDI is to draw graphical objects (including text) on a *physical device*. Physical devices include:

- The printable area of a piece of paper in a printer
- The display area of a monitor
- A complete window
- The client area of a window

Physical space and physical coordinate systems

Each physical device has a natural *physical coordinate system* determined by the way images are displayed in the *physical space* of the device. In all cases, the physical coordinate system has the following characteristics (see Figure 23-1):

Origin
> The origin is in the upper-left-hand corner of the device.

Orientation
> The horizontal axis increases, moving to the left, and the vertical axis increases, moving towards the bottom.

Units
> The units of the physical coordinate system are *pixels* (for the monitor or a window) or *printer dots* (for the printer). We may refer to both of these units simply as pixels.

Note that when the device is the client area of a window, the physical coordinate system has its origin in the upper-left corner of the *client area* of the window.

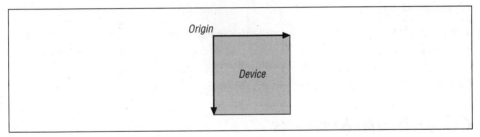

Figure 23-1. Natural physical coordinate system

Incidentally, it is tempting to refer to the physical coordinate system as the device coordinate system. However, Windows has usurped this term for a coordinate system that is identical with the physical coordinate system except that its origin need not be in the upper-left-hand corner of the device. Drat.

Monitor inches

Of course, a 600 dpi laser printer prints 600 dots per inch, so it is easy to translate printer dots to the more useful inches or millimeters. However, things are not nearly this simple for monitors.

The problem stems from the way in which resolution is described on monitors. Printer resolution is given in dots per inch, which is the most useful procedure, whereas monitor resolution is given in terms of the *total number* of pixels in the vertical and horizontal direction. The problem is that Windows has no way of knowing the actual physical dimensions of the monitor, so it cannot convert the horizontal and vertical resolutions to pixels per physical inch.

To deal with this problem, Windows defines what is sometimes referred to as a *logical inch*. As we will see, this seldom corresponds to an actual physical inch on a monitor. It is, in fact, Windows' monitor-independent version of a physical inch. (For a printer, Windows understands actual physical inches.)

Unfortunately, the term logical inch sounds like it is connected with the upcoming notion of *logical coordinate system*, so from now on we will refer to logical inches as *monitor inches* (since they apply only to monitors anyway). We emphasize that this terminology is not standard.

For a printer, a physical inch corresponds to a certain number of dots. For instance, for a 600 dpi laser printer, we have:

```
1 physical inch = 600 printer dots
```

In a sense, we could have *defined* an inch to be 600 dots on a 600 dpi laser printer. This, of course, is totally inappropriate, so we won't do it. However, monitor inches *are* defined in this way, that is, in pixels, as in:

```
1 monitor inch = 96 pixels
```

In this way, for instance, a programmer can specify a line segment of length 2 monitor inches, and Windows (or the Windows device driver) will know how many pixels (2 x 96 = 192) to use in drawing the line segment, just as it would know that in order to print the line segment on a 600 dpi laser printer, it would require 2 x 600 = 1200 dots.

How are monitor inches actually defined? The Windows Control Panel's Display applet allows the user to select from one of two display font sizes—small fonts or large fonts. Windows uses this choice to determine the size of a monitor inch. In particular, if the user chooses the small font, Windows sets the monitor inch at 96 pixels. On the other hand, if the user chooses large fonts in the Display applet, Windows sets a monitor inch at 120 pixels. Thus,

```
1 monitor inch = 96 pixels    ' small font setting in Control Panel
1 monitor inch = 120 pixels   ' large font setting in Control Panel
```

As we have said, generally speaking, monitor inches are quite different from physical inches. For instance, I am writing this book on a 21-inch monitor running at 1600 by 1200 with large fonts. Accordingly, Windows sets the monitor inch to 120 pixels, and so the display area has monitor-inch dimensions:

```
monitor width = 1600/120 = 13.3 monitor inches
monitor height = 1200/120 = 10 monitor inches
```

However, the physical dimensions of the display area are in fact 14.9 wide by 11.2 high. Thus, in this case, a monitor inch is approximately 1.12 physical inches. On the other hand, suppose that I were to raise the resolution to 1800 by 1440, which is the next setting on my display adapter. The monitor dimensions would become:

```
monitor width = 1800/120 = 15 monitor inches
monitor height = 1440/120 = 12 monitor inches
```

Now, a monitor inch in the horizontal direction measures 14.9/15 = 0.99 physical inches, but in the vertical direction, it measures 11.2/12 = 0.93 inches! This difference occurs because the resolution of 1800 by 1440 has *aspect ratio* 1800/1440 = 1.25, rather than the more usual aspect ratio of 1.33 achieved by the resolutions 640 by 480, 800 by 600, 1024 by 768, and 1600 by 1200 as well as the physical display dimensions on my monitor.

The *GetDeviceCaps* function (short for *Get Device Capacities*) can be used to get the number of pixels per monitor inch, along with other values. The declaration for this function is:

```
int GetDeviceCaps(
    HDC hdc,      // device-context handle
    int nIndex    // index of capability to query
);
```

Here are some of the most useful values of *nIndex* with respect to the monitor:

HORZSIZE
>   Width, in millimeters, of the physical screen

VERTSIZE
>   Height, in millimeters, of the physical screen

HORZRES
>   Width, in pixels, of the screen

VERTRES
>   Height, in raster lines, of the screen

LOGPIXELSX
>   Number of pixels per logical inch along the screen width

LOGPIXELSY
>   Number of pixels per logical inch along the screen height

For example, here is the output for my 21-inch monitor:

```
HORZ SIZE: 320
VERT SIZE: 240
HORZ RES: 1600
VERT RES: 1200
LOGPIXELSX: 120
LOGPIXELSY: 120
```

Actually, this is confusing. The correct formulas relating these values should be:

```
HORZ SIZE = 25.4 * HORZ RES/LOGPIXELSX
VERT SIZE = 25.4 * VERT RES/LOGPIXELSY
```

Under Windows 9x, the values would be correct, but Windows NT (which I am running) always uses the values 320 and 240, for reasons unknown to me.

24

Device Contexts III: Coordinate Systems

The Windows GDI defines three *spaces*, each with its own coordinate system, for use with drawing functions. As shown in Figure 24-1, these spaces are *world space*, *page space* (also called *logical space*), and *device space*. A drawing function draws in either world space or page space, depending upon the setting of the so-called *world transform*. Once drawing is done, Windows applies one or more *mapping functions*, or *transformations*, indicated by the symbols T_1, T_2, and T_3 in Figure 24-1, until the points reach the physical space of the device itself.

GDI Coordinate Systems

Note that the orientation of the axes in each space is the same as that of physical space. Note also that world space is supported only under Windows NT.

The mapping functions that Windows uses to map points from one space to the next can *potentially* be a composition of the following five basic transformations. However, as we will see, rotation and sheering are allowed only for the mapping T_1 from world space to page space.

- Translations

- Reflections about an axis

- Scaling (expansion or contraction along an axis)

- Rotation about the origin

- Sheering

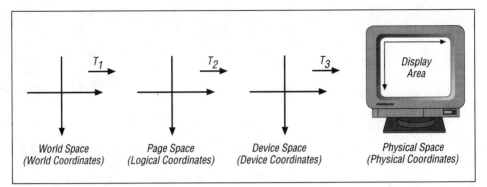

Figure 24-1. Windows coordinate systems

These transformations are pictured in Figure 24-2.

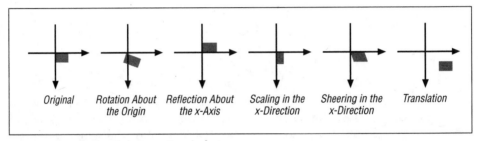

Figure 24-2. The five basic transformations

In case you are interested, in some sense, these transformations constitute *all* of the possible "nice" transformations of the plane. For those who have studied linear algebra, we can say that any *nonsingular* linear transformation of the plane can be expressed as a composition of these transformations (excluding translation) and that any nonsingular affine transformation of the plane can be expressed as a composition of these transformations (including translation). (If you are interested in why this is so, let me suggest my book *Introduction to Linear Algebra with Applications*, published by Saunders College Publishing.)

The benefit of using these mappings is that the drawing functions can be much simpler, letting the mapping function take up much of the burden of drawing. For instance, to *display* an ellipse that is not centered at the origin, we can *draw* a circle centered at the origin in page space, let the transformations flatten it in the vertical direction into an ellipse, and then translate it to the desired location. We will do some examples to illustrate this soon.

Indeed, it is important to emphasize that drawing functions use either world or page coordinates, not physical coordinates. (We also cannot draw in device space.) The point is that the drawing functions themselves know nothing about the location of the origin of the physical device, nor about its units of measurement (pixels). This is as it should be.

For instance, the code:

```
Ellipse hDC, 1, 2, 5, 10
```

draws a filled ellipse whose bounding box has upper-left corner (1,2) and lower-right corner (5,10) in *logical* (or world) coordinates. There is no reference to the location of the physical origin, or to the orientation of the axes, or to inches, millimeters, pixels, or any other dimensions. All these are taken care of by the various mappings shown in Figure 24-1.

We mentioned that Windows does not allow all five types of transformations between each pair of spaces shown in Figure 24-1. The types of transformations that Windows allows between spaces are as follows:

Device space to physical space
T_3 can only be a translation.

Page space to device space
T_2 can be a translation, followed by scaling (along one or both axes) and then a reflection (about one or both axes).

World space to page space
T_1 can be any composition of all five basic transformations: translations, rotations, scalings, sheerings, and reflections.

Virtual Space

There seems to be no compelling reason to think in terms of three separate nonphysical spaces, and it does seem to me that this viewpoint can lead to unnecessary complications. Another view we can take is that there is only one nonphysical space, which we will call *virtual space*, with its *virtual coordinate system*. As shown in Figure 24-3, all drawing is done in virtual space, using virtual coordinates. Quite simply, we draw in virtual space, using virtual coordinates, and Windows applies a *single* mapping function T, which is the composition of the three mappings in Figure 24-1, to produce the final display.

On the other hand, since Microsoft has seen fit to define the three spaces shown in Figure 24-1, we will discuss them along with our virtual space. Then you can decide how you prefer to view the process.

Device Space

Device space is special in several ways. First, we cannot draw in device space—the Windows GDI provides no such drawing functions. Second, Windows permits

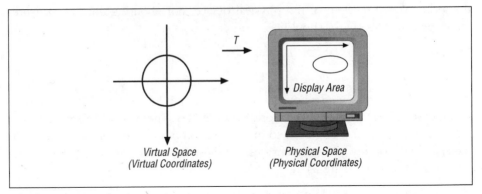

Figure 24-3. Virtual space

only a *translation* of points in device space to obtain the corresponding points in physical space—it does not permit any of the other basic transformations. To specify the translation between device space and physical space, we use the *SetViewportOrgEx* function:

```
BOOL SetViewportOrgEx(
    HDC hdc,                    // handle of device context
    int ViewportOriginX,        // x-coordinate of viewport origin in pixels
    int ViewportOriginY,        // y-coordinate of viewport origin in pixels
    LPPOINT lpPoint             // address of structure receiving original origin
);
```

(Note that *lpPoint* may be set to 0, in which case it is ignored.) The point:

```
(ViewportOriginX,ViewportOriginY)
```

defines the *viewport origin*, in device units (pixels). This is the point in physical space that the origin of device space is translated to, as shown in Figure 24-4.

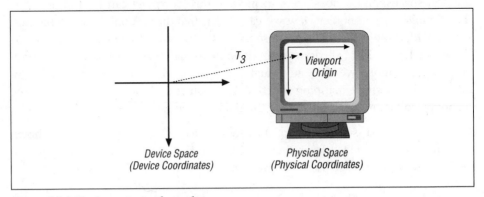

Figure 24-4. Device space to physical space

Thus, the formula for the transformation T_3 in Figure 24-1 is:

```
PhysicalX = DeviceX + ViewportOriginX
PhysicalY = DeviceY + ViewportOriginY
```

Note that Windows defines the functions *LPToDP* and *DPToLP* to see the effect of the translation between the two spaces.

It is difficult to isolate this translation in order to see it in action directly, because we cannot draw in device space. However, we will see its effect in a later example.

Page Space

As we have said, the mapping T_2 in Figure 24-1, from page space to device space, is a translation, followed by scaling (along one or both axes) and then a reflection (about one or both axes). (Any of these transformations can be the identity, of course.)

The Translation

We define the translation using the function *SetWindowOrgEx* (a rather unfortunate name):

```
BOOL SetWindowOrgEx(
   HDC hdc,                 // handle of device context
   int WindowOrginX,        // x-coordinate of window origin in logical units
   int WindowOrginY,        // y-coordinate of window origin in logical units
   LPPOINT lpPoint          // address of structure receiving original origin
);
```

This function defines the *window origin*, which is the point that is *mapped to* the origin by the translation. (Note the difference here: the window origin is mapped *to* the logical origin, whereas the viewport origin is mapped *from* the device origin.)

The formula for this translation is:

```
NewX = LogicalX - WindowOriginX
NewY = LogicalY - WindowOriginY
```

Figure 24-5 shows this initial translation.

The Scaling

The next step in the transformation from page space to device space involves a scaling in the direction of one or both of the logical axes. To scale in the x-direction, we multiply the x-coordinate of a point by a *positive* number. If the number is less than 1, the scaling is a *contraction*; if it is greater than 1, the scaling is an *expansion*.

Often, a scale factor is a noninteger. But Windows works more efficiently with integers (VB longs). Accordingly, in Windows, scale factors are set by setting *two* values, called *extents*, in each direction. These are pictured in Figure 24-5. The scale factor is taken to be the *ratio* of the extents for the given direction.

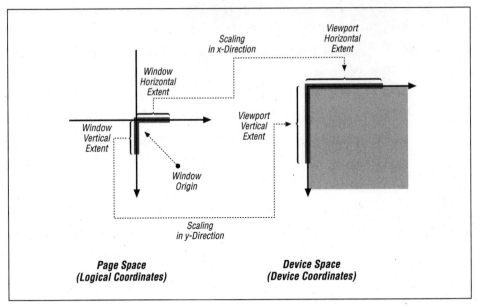

Figure 24-5. Page space to device space

Thus, in the horizontal direction, we have:

$$ScaleX = \frac{ViewportExtentX}{WindowExtentX}$$

The `ViewportExtentX` value is given in pixels, and the `WindowExtentX` value is in logical units. Hence, the scale factor `ScaleX` is in pixels per logical unit. In other words, setting the scale factor sets the number of pixels per logical drawing unit. (In a way, this is not really a scaling, because page space does not exist physically. It is simply a setting of units.) For instance, to set a scale factor of:

```
1 logical unit = 1/64 monitor inch
```

we would set (assuming a large system font and hence 120 pixels per monitor inch):

```
WindowExtentX = 64
ViewportExtentX = 120        ' 1 monitor inch
```

In this way, we can refer in the GDI drawing functions to 1 logical unit, which equals 1/64 of a monitor inch. Thus, another way to look at scaling is that it sets the *precision* or *resolution* of the drawing, that is, the *smallest physical* measurement to which we can refer.

Similarly, to perform the vertical scaling, Windows multiplies by the ratio:

$$ScaleY = \frac{ViewportExtentY}{WindowExtentY}$$

Thus, a single logical unit on the vertical axis corresponds to `ScaleY` pixels on the physical device.

We can now combine the effects of the translation and the scaling by writing:

$$\text{DeviceX} = (\text{LogicalX} - \text{WindowOriginX}) \times \frac{\text{ViewportExtentX}}{\text{WindowExtentX}}$$

$$\text{DeviceY} = (\text{LogicalY} - \text{WindowOriginY}) \times \frac{\text{ViewportExtentY}}{\text{WindowExtentY}}$$

To set the extents, we use the GDI functions:

```
BOOL SetWindowExtEx(
    HDC hdc,          // handle of device context
    int nXExtent,     // new horizontal window extent in logical units
    int nYExtent,     // new vertical window extent in logical units
    LPSIZE lpSize     // original window extent
);

BOOL SetViewportExtEx(
    HDC hdc,          // handle of device context
    int nXExtent,     // horizontal viewport extent in pixels
    int nYExtent,     // vertical viewport extent in pixels
    LPSIZE lpSize     // original viewport extent
);
```

Note that *lpSize* can be set to 0, in which case it is ignored.

The Reflection

To perform a reflection about the x-axis, for instance, we need to multiple the y-coordinate (yes, the y-coordinate) of the point by −1. Similarly, to reflect about the y-axis, we multiply the x-coordinate by −1.

Rather than specify separately in some parameter or other that reflection is requested, Windows allows us simply to change the sign of either one of the extents. It doesn't matter whether we change the window or the viewport extent—the effect on the ratio is the same. Thus, the formulas:

$$\text{DeviceX} = (\text{LogicalX} - \text{WindowOriginX}) \times \frac{\text{ViewportExtentX}}{\text{WindowExtentX}}$$

$$\text{DeviceY} = (\text{LogicalY} - \text{WindowOriginY}) \times \frac{\text{ViewportExtentY}}{\text{WindowExtentY}}$$

describe the entire transformation from page space to device space.

Virtual Space to Physical Space

The transformation from world coordinates to logical coordinates provides rotation and sheering, which are not allowed in the transformation from page space to device space. However, these transformations are used much less often than the other three basic transformations. Since world space is supported only in Windows NT, we will discuss it only briefly in the "World Space" section later in the chapter.

When world coordinates are *not* involved, and we think in terms of virtual space, the transformation from virtual to physical space is given by the formulas:

$$\text{PhysicalX} = (\text{LogicalX} - \text{WindowOriginX}) \times \frac{\text{ViewportExtentX}}{\text{WindowExtentX}} + \text{ViewportOriginX}$$

$$\text{PhysicalY} = (\text{LogicalY} - \text{WindowOriginY}) \times \frac{\text{ViewportExtentY}}{\text{WindowExtentY}} + \text{ViewportOriginY}$$

As we will discuss soon, Windows supports several *mapping modes,* of which only one—the *anisotropic mode*—allows the freedom to set all of the values in these formulas. In the other modes, Windows helps us out by setting some of these values for us, making the formulas simpler to use.

Example

Suppose we want to draw the ellipses shown on the right in Figure 24-6. The measurements on the ellipses are in monitor inches.

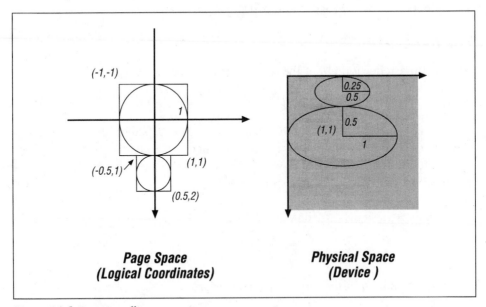

**Page Space
(Logical Coordinates)**   **Physical Space
(Device)**

Figure 24-6. Drawing ellipses

There are many ways to proceed here. One approach is to draw the circles shown on the left in Figure 24-6 and then map these circles into the desired ellipses by:

- Scaling the y-direction by a factor of 1/2

- Reflecting about the x-axis

- Translating the logical origin to the physical point (1,1)

First, we take care of some preliminaries—saving the device context of the picture box, setting the pen and brush types, getting the number of pixels per inch for the monitor, and setting the mapping mode to anisotropic (more on this later in "Mapping Modes"):

```
' Save DC for later restoration
hDCPic = SaveDC(pic.hdc)

' Set pen width
SelectObject pic.hdc, GetStockObject(BLACK_PEN)

' Set brush
SelectObject pic.hdc, GetStockObject(NULL_BRUSH)

' Get size of monitor inch
PixPerInchX = GetDeviceCaps(pic.hdc, LOGPIXELSX)
PixPerInchY = GetDeviceCaps(pic.hdc, LOGPIXELSY)

' Set mapping mode
SetMapMode pic.hdc, MM_ANISOTROPIC
```

I find it simpler to proceed as though the parameters (extents and origins) can be nonintegral values and then make the necessary adjustments afterward.

Thus, we set the scale factor to 1 logical unit per inch horizontally and 2 logical units per inch vertically. These scale factors will cause a *logical* circle to contract in the y-direction by a factor of 2, thus producing the desired elliptical shapes. At the same time, we reflect about the x-axis by setting the viewport vertical extent to a negative number:

```
SetWindowExtEx pic.hdc, 1, 2, sz
SetViewportExtEx pic.hdc, PixPerInchX, -PixPerInchY, sz
```

The translation is done by setting the viewport origin to (1,1) in monitor inches:

```
SetViewportOrgEx pic.hdc, PixPerInchX, PixPerInchY, pt
```

Now we can draw the circles, using the bounding squares shown in Figure 24-6:

```
Ellipse pic.hdc, -1, -1, 1, 1
Ellipse pic.hdc, -0.5, 1, 0.5, 2
```

Finally, we can deal with the problem that the parameters must be longs. To fix this, we need to multiply the coordinates of the bounding boxes by 2. To compensate, we need to do the same for the logical units. Here is the correct code:

```
' Set scale factors and flip
SetWindowExtEx pic.hdc, 2, 4, sz
```

```
' Set the translation
SetViewportOrgEx pic.hdc, PixPerInchX, PixPerInchY, pt

' Draw the logical ellipses (circles)
Ellipse pic.hdc, -2, -2, 2, 2
Ellipse pic.hdc, -1, 2, 1, 4
```

The output is shown in Figure 24-7.

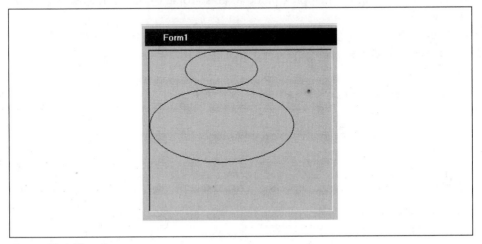

Figure 24-7. The output

Setting Up Logical Coordinates in Physical Space

Another way to look at the virtual space to physical space mapping is to look at the image of the logical coordinate axes under the mapping. The image lies in physical space, of course. To view the effect of scaling, we treat the logical axes as line *segments* of a fixed length. (Axes are actually lines, not line segments.)

Figure 24-8 shows the image of the logical coordinates under the previous transformation.

The virtue of this viewpoint is that we can think of the transformation as defining a new coordinate system in physical space. Some authors like to refer to this new coordinate system as a logical coordinate system, which is not strictly speaking correct. This coordinate system is *not* in page space—it is in physical space. Nonetheless, we will also follow this convention.

Example

To illustrate this point of view, let us consider another example. Suppose we want to create the drawing in the picture box in Figure 24-9.

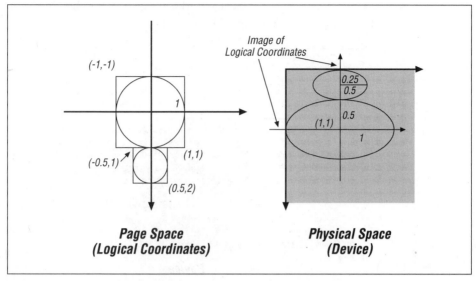

Figure 24-8. The image of the logical axes

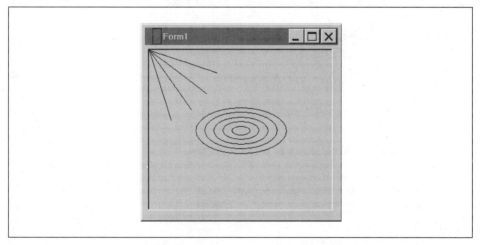

Figure 24-9. An example of GDI drawing

Here are the details of this drawing:

- There are 4 radial lines of length 1 monitor inch emanating from the physical origin of the picture box. The lines split the quadrant into equal-sized sectors.

- There are 5 ellipses centered in the picture box. The inside ellipse has a major (horizontal) axis of length 1/4 monitor inch. Each successive major axis is an additional 1/4 inch long. The minor axis of each ellipse is one-half as long as its major axis.

To make this drawing, we use one logical coordinate system for the lines and another for the ellipses, as shown in Figure 24-10.

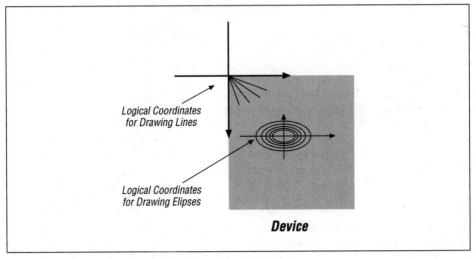

Figure 24-10. Setting up logical coordinates in physical space

As before, the code begins with some preliminaries:

```
' Save DC for later restoration
hDCPic = SaveDC(pic.hdc)

' Set pen type
SelectObject pic.hdc, GetStockObject(BLACK_PEN)

' Set brush
SelectObject pic.hdc, GetStockObject(NULL_BRUSH)

' Get size of monitor inch
PixPerInchX = GetDeviceCaps(pic.hdc, LOGPIXELSX)
PixPerInchY = GetDeviceCaps(pic.hdc, LOGPIXELSY)

' Set mapping mode
SetMapMode pic.hdc, MM_ANISOTROPIC
```

Next, we set up the mapping for drawing the rays. We set the scale factor at 100 logical units per monitor inch, which should provide sufficient resolution for the endpoints of the line segments, which are rounded to longs by Windows:

```
' ---------
' Draw Rays
' ---------

' No translations
SetWindowOrgEx pic.hdc, 0, 0, pt
SetViewportOrgEx pic.hdc, 0, 0, pt
```

```
' Scale factor: 100 logical unit per monitor inch
SetWindowExtEx pic.hdc, 100, 100, sz
SetViewportExtEx pic.hdc, PixPerInchX, PixPerInchY, sz

' Draw lines
For i = 1 To 4
   ' Move current point to logical origin
   MoveToEx pic.hdc, 0, 0, pt
   ' Draw ray of radius 100 logical units
   LineTo pic.hdc, 100 * Cos(1.57 * i / 5), 100 * Sin(1.57 * i / 5)
Next
```

To draw the ellipses, we change the logical coordinate system. Note that we flip about the x-axis, even though this is not really necessary, since the ellipses are symmetric about this axis.

```
' No initial translation
SetWindowOrgEx pic.hdc, 0, 0, pt

' Final Translation from (0,0) logical to midpoint of picture box
SetViewportOrgEx pic.hdc, (pic.Width / 2) / Screen.TwipsPerPixelX, _
   (pic.Height / 2) / Screen.TwipsPerPixelY, pt

' Scale factor set to 8 logical units per monitor inch horizontally
' Set vertical scale to flatten ellipses by 2 to 1
' Reflect about x-axis (this is not really necessary)
SetWindowExtEx pic.hdc, 8, 16, sz
SetViewportExtEx pic.hdc, PixPerInchX, -PixPerInchY, sz

' Draw ellipses
For i = 1 To 5
   Ellipse pic.hdc, -i, -i, i, i
Next i

' Restore DC
RestoreDC pic.hdc, hDCPic
```

Mapping Modes

In the previous examples, we were able to set the origins and extents to any values. This was permitted by setting the *mapping mode* to **MM_ANISOTROPIC**:

```
SetMapMode pic.hdc, MM_ANISOTROPIC
```

However, in many cases, we do not need this much freedom. For instance, we may want to scale the two axes proportionally, to preserve the aspect ratio (ratio of unit lengths on the two axes). This will guarantee that a circle or square drawn in page space will be mapped to a circle or square in physical space.

To accommodate a variety of common situations, Windows defines several *mapping modes*. These determine who gets to set the various origins and extents— Windows or the programmer.

As we have seen, the mapping mode is set using the *SetMapMode* function:

```
int SetMapMode(
    HDC hdc,            // handle of device context
    int fnMapMode       // new mapping mode
);
```

where *fnMapMode* can be set to one of the mapping mode constants: MM_
ANISOTROPIC, MM_ISOTROPIC, MM_TEXT, MM_HIENGLISH, MM_LOENGLISH, MM_
HIMETRIC, MM_LOMETRIC, or MM_TWIPS. These mapping modes are described in
the following sections.

Text Mapping Mode

In text-mapping mode, the extents are set to (1,1) by Windows and cannot be
changed. Thus, no scaling is performed and each logical unit corresponds to a single physical unit (pixel). The programmer can set the origins to permit custom
translations. The default origins are (0,0). When these defaults are used, page
space and physical space are essentially the same.

The Metric Mapping Modes

The modes MM_HIENGLISH, MM_LOENGLISH, MM_HIMETRIC, MM_LOMETRIC, and
MM_TWIPS are similar. In each case, the origins can be set by the programmer, and
have default values (0,0). The extents are set by Windows so that each logical unit
corresponds to a certain physical dimension. This saves us the trouble of figuring
out how many device units (pixels or printer dots) make up an inch, for instance.

Here are scale factors. Note that the prefix HI refers to high precision, whereas LO
refers to low precision.

MM_HIENGLISH
    Each logical unit corresponds to 0.001 of an inch

MM_HIMETRIC
    Each logical unit corresponds to 0.01 of a millimeter

MM_LOENGLISH
    Each logical unit corresponds to 0.01 of an inch

MM_LOMETRIC
    Each logical unit corresponds to 0.1 of a millimeter

MM_TWIPS
    Each logical unit corresponds to one-twentieth of a printer's point (approxi-
    mately 1/1440 inch)

Finally, each of these mapping modes also involves a reflection about the x-axis.
Hence, in order to draw in *visible* physical space, we must draw using *negative*
values of y. For instance, the results of the code:

```
' Set origins
SetWindowOrgEx pic.hdc, 0, 0, pt
SetViewportOrgEx pic.hdc, 0, 0, pt

' Set mapping mode
SetMapMode pic.hdc, MM_LOENGLISH

' Move to logical origin
MoveToEx pic.hdc, 0, 0, pt

' Draw line
LineTo pic.hdc, 100, -100

' Draw text
TextOut pic.hdc, 100, -100, "test", 4

' Draw rectangle
Rectangle pic.hdc, 50, -50, 10, -10
```

are shown in Figure 24-11.

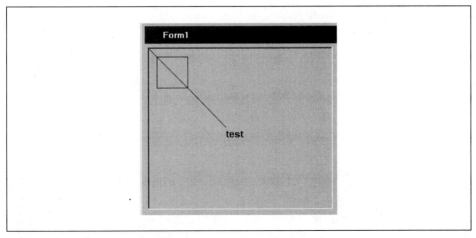

Figure 24-11. MM_LOENGLISH mode

Note finally that to achieve the scale factors described above for the English and metric mapping modes, Windows sets the window and viewport extents for us. Although we will not go into the details of how this is done, it is interesting to note that the procedure is different under Windows 9x than under Windows NT.

Anisotropic Mapping Mode

In this mode, as we have seen, the programmer is free to set the window and viewport origins and extents. Hence, this mode gives the most freedom of choice to the programmer.

Isotropic Mapping Mode

Isotropic mode is like anisotropic mode except in one respect. Windows adjusts the extents so that the logical units on each axis represent the same *distance* on the physical device. If the pixels are square (and only if the pixels are square), this can be accomplished by assuring that a logical unit is mapped to the *same number* of pixels in each direction. Windows will *shrink* the necessary viewport extent to accomplish this goal.

Of course, the purpose of isotropic mode is to ensure that aspect ratios are preserved, so that, for example, a logical square will display as a square on the physical device and a logical circle will display as a circle.

We can observe for ourselves how Windows changes the viewport extents with some simple code that uses the *GetViewportExtents* function:

```
' Set mapping mode
SetMapMode pic.hdc, MM_ISOTROPIC

SetWindowOrgEx pic.hdc, 0, 0, pt
SetViewportOrgEx pic.hdc, 0, 0, pt

' 1000 logical units for both width and height of picture box
SetWindowExtEx pic.hdc, 1000, 1000, sz
SetViewportExtEx pic.hdc, pic.Width / Screen.TwipsPerPixelX, _
    pic.Height / Screen.TwipsPerPixelY, sz

' Draw rectangle
Rectangle pic.hdc, 100, 100, 900, 900

Debug.Print "Viewport Extents Setting: " & pic.Width / Screen.TwipsPerPixelX _
    & " / " & pic.Height / Screen.TwipsPerPixelY
GetViewportExtEx pic.hdc, sz
Debug.Print "Viewport Extents: " & sz.cx & " / " & sz.cy
```

Running this code shows that Windows adjusts the vertical viewport extent, because the picture box is taller than it is wide:

```
Viewport Extents Setting: 176 / 391
Viewport Extents: 176 / 176
```

Note that when using this mode, it is important to call *SetWindowExtEx* before setting *SetViewportExtEx*.

World Space

Since world space is supported only by Windows NT, we will discuss it only briefly.

The transformation from world space to page space can be a composition of any of the five basic transformations: translation, rotation, reflection, scaling, and sheering. Thus, it is the most general transformation possible and also duplicates some of the functionality of the other transformations.

The world space to page space transformation is set using the *SetWorldTransform* function:

```
BOOL SetWorldTransform(
   HDC hdc,                    // handle of device context
   CONST XFORM *lpXform   // address of transformation data
);
```

Here **XFORM** is a structure:

```
struct _XFORM {
    FLOAT eM11;
    FLOAT eM12;
    FLOAT eM21;
    FLOAT eM22;
    FLOAT eDx;
    FLOAT eDy;
}
```

that defines the transformation. (Despite the documentation, a world transformation is *not* a linear transformation unless the translation is 0.) The point (x,y) is mapped to the point (x',y') using the following formulas:

```
x' = x * eM11 + y * eM21 + eDx
y' = x * eM12 + y * eM22 + eDy
```

In matrix language, this can be written as follows:

$$\begin{bmatrix} x' & y' \end{bmatrix} = \begin{bmatrix} x & y \end{bmatrix} \begin{bmatrix} eM11 & eM12 \\ eM21 & eM22 \end{bmatrix} + \begin{bmatrix} eDx & eDy \end{bmatrix}$$

Let us write this formula in the form:

$$P' = PM + D$$

where:

$$M = \begin{bmatrix} eM11 & eM12 \\ eM21 & eM22 \end{bmatrix}, D = \begin{bmatrix} eDx & eDy \end{bmatrix}$$

The values of *eDx* and *eDy* are just the amounts to translate in the x- and y-directions, respectively. As to the matrix *M*, it can be built using matrix multiplication. First, we need to decide the order in which we want to apply the rotation, reflection, scaling, and sheering. Then we create a matrix to do each of these jobs and multiply these matrices together to get *M*.

Here are the specifics.

Rotation

To rotate in the direction from positive x-axis towards positive y-axis through the angle *A*, use the matrix:

$$R(A) = \begin{bmatrix} \cos A & \sin A \\ -\sin A & \cos A \end{bmatrix}$$

Reflection

To reflect about the x-axis or y-axis, use the matrices *FX* and *FY*, respectively:

$$FX = \begin{bmatrix} 1 & 0 \\ 0 & -1 \end{bmatrix}, FY = \begin{bmatrix} -1 & 0 \\ 0 & 1 \end{bmatrix}$$

Scaling

To scale in the x-direction or y-direction by an amount *r*>0, use the matrices *SX(r)* and *SY(r)*, respectively:

$$SX(r) = \begin{bmatrix} r & 0 \\ 0 & 1 \end{bmatrix}, SY(r) = \begin{bmatrix} 1 & 0 \\ 0 & r \end{bmatrix}$$

Sheers

To sheer in the x-direction or y-direction by an amount *r*, use the matrices *HX(r)* and *HY(r)*, respectively:

$$HX(r) = \begin{bmatrix} 1 & 0 \\ r & 1 \end{bmatrix}, HY(r) = \begin{bmatrix} 1 & r \\ 0 & 1 \end{bmatrix}$$

To illustrate, the following code produces the output in Figure 24-12.

```
Public Sub RotatingText()

' Save DC for later restoration
hDCPic = SaveDC(pic.hdc)

' Set pen width
SelectObject pic.hdc, GetStockObject(BLACK_PEN)

' Set brush
SelectObject pic.hdc, GetStockObject(NULL_BRUSH)

' Get size of monitor inch
PixPerInchX = GetDeviceCaps(pic.hdc, LOGPIXELSX)
PixPerInchY = GetDeviceCaps(pic.hdc, LOGPIXELSY)
```

```
' Set mapping mode
SetMapMode pic.hdc, MM_ANISOTROPIC
SetGraphicsMode pic.hdc, GM_ADVANCED

' Set scale for logical to physical
SetWindowExtEx pic.hdc, 80, 80, sz
SetViewportExtEx pic.hdc, PixPerInchX, PixPerInchY, sz

' Start in middle of device
SetViewportOrgEx pic.hdc, pic.Width / 2 / Screen.TwipsPerPixelX, _
    pic.Height / 2 / Screen.TwipsPerPixelY, pt

' Draw ellipse
Ellipse pic.hdc, -18, -18, 18, 18
Const pi = 3.14159

For i = 0 To 15

    xf.eDx = 0
    xf.eDy = 0
    xf.eM11 = Cos(i * pi / 8)
    xf.eM12 = Sin(i * pi / 8)
    xf.eM21 = -xf.eM12
    xf.eM22 = xf.eM11
    SetWorldTransform pic.hdc, xf
    TextOut pic.hdc, 0, 0, "      rotating text", 18

Next

End Sub
```

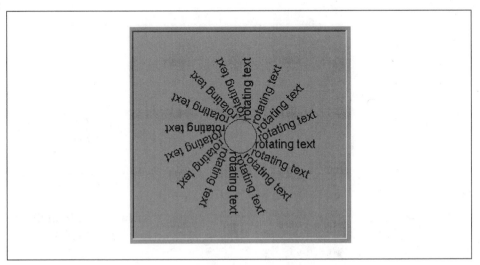

Figure 24-12. Rotating text using world space

Finally, you will be happy to hear that the Windows GDI supplies some functions to help with matrix multiplication: *CombineTransform* and *ModifyWorldTransform*.

25

Fonts

In Windows, a *font* is a collection of characters that have a common design. The terminology that Windows uses to describe fonts is not necessarily the same as that used by a typographer, but we will follow the Windows terminology.

The *typeface* of a font refers to the specific design of the characters in the font. For instance, Times New Roman and Arial are two different typefaces. One of the main design features of a typeface is the presence or absence of *serifs*, which are small lines that are designed to help the eyes make a smooth transition from one character to the next, thus making reading less stressful. Figure 25-1 shows the difference between a serif and a sans serif font.

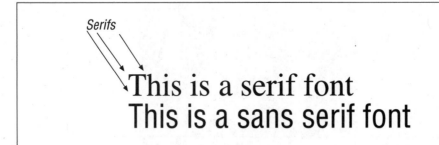

Figure 25-1. Serifs and non serifs

The term *style* refers to the weight and slant of a font. Weights range from thin to black in the following order: *thin, extralight, light, normal, medium, semibold, bold, extrabold, heavy,* and *black.*

The *slant* of a font is characterized as *roman, oblique,* or *italic.* A roman style font has no slant; an oblique style font has a slant that is created simply by sheering the characters in a roman font; an *italic* style font is one that is designed to be slanted.

To quote the documentation:

> In Windows, the *size* of a font is an imprecise value. It can generally be determined by measuring the distance from the bottom of a lowercase "g" to the top of an adjacent uppercase "M," ... A font's size is specified in units called points. A point is .013837 of an inch. Following the point system devised by Pierre Simon Fournier, it is common practice to approximate a point as 1/72 inch.

Font Families

In Windows, fonts are grouped by *family*, which is a set of fonts having a common stroke width (width of thick and thin lines making up the characters) and serif characteristics. There are five families in Windows, each identified by a symbolic constant:

Decorative (FF_DECORATIVE)
> Novelty fonts

Modern (FF_MODERN)
> Monospace fonts

Roman (FF_ROMAN)
> Proportional fonts with serifs, such as Times New Roman

Script (FF_SCRIPT)
> Fonts designed to look like handwriting

Swiss (FF_SWISS)
> Proportional fonts without serifs, such as Arial

Dontcare (FF_DONTCARE)
> A generic family name, used when information about a font does not exist or does not matter

Font Technologies

In Windows, there are four technologies for rendering fonts on the display or printer: *raster* (or *bitmap*), *vector* (or *stroke*), *TrueType*, or *OpenType*. The difference between these technologies centers on how the *glyphs* are stored in the font file. (A *glyph* is the data or commands that define a character.)

The characters of a raster font are stored as bitmaps. As a result, scaling a raster font generally gives very poor results. The characters of a vector font are stored as line segments. However, vector fonts tend to be drawn more slowly than True-Type and OpenType fonts and appear very thin, since the lines that make up the characters are one-pixel wide.

TrueType and OpenType characters are stored as line segments and curves, along with *hints* that are used to adjust the rendering of the characters based on point size. Hence, these fonts can be scaled up or down without losing their intended appearance. (OpenType fonts allow PostScript character definitions as well as True-Type character definitions.)

The glyphs for a font are stored in a *font-resource file* (or just *font file*). For raster and vector fonts, this data is divided into two parts: a header describing the font's metrics, and the glyph data. These files have extension *FON*. Each TrueType and OpenType font has two associated files—a short header file with extension *FOT* and the font data with extension *TTF*.

Character Sets

We discussed the ASCII, ANSI, and Unicode character sets earlier in the book. Most Windows fonts use character sets that belong to one of the following groups:

- Windows (ANSI)
- Unicode
- OEM (original equipment manufacturer)
- Symbol
- Vendor-specific

The OEM character set is usually used for console applications (in a text-based window). Symbol character sets contain special symbolic characters in the upper half (characters 128–255), such as those used in mathematics and the sciences.

Logical and Physical Fonts

In order for a particular font to be used in an API function, that font must exist on the user's machine. This presents a potential problem, since we have no way to predict which fonts are installed on a given computer. To deal with this issue, Windows uses the notions of *logical* and *physical fonts*.

Physical fonts can be divided into two types: *GDI fonts*, which are stored in files on the computer's hard disk, and *device fonts*, which are internal to (or resident in) a given device.

An application requests a font by creating a font object using the *CreateFont* or *CreateFontIndirect* function. The font attributes that are required by these functions define a *logical* font. When the logical font is selected into a device context using *SelectObject*, Windows replaces this logical font by a *physical* font on the user's system that forms the "closest" match to the logical font.

To do this, Windows applies a *font-mapping algorithm*. The process is call *font realization*. TrueType fonts are simply rendered on the device. Simply put, for non-TrueType fonts, Windows chooses the closest device font by assigning a relative importance to various font characteristics, the most important of which are (in decreasing order of importance): typeface name, character set, variable versus fixed pitch, family, height, width, weight, slant, underline, and strikeout.

Font Structures

There are more than two dozen structures associated with fonts, but two of them stand out. The LOGFONT structure describes a logical font:

```
Public Const LF_FACESIZE = 32

Type LOGFONT
    lfHeight As Long
    lfWidth As Long
    lfEscapement As Long
    lfOrientation As Long
    lfWeight As Long
    lfItalic As Byte
    lfUnderline As Byte
    lfStrikeOut As Byte
    lfCharSet As Byte
    lfOutPrecision As Byte
    lfClipPrecision As Byte
    lfQuality As Byte
    lfPitchAndFamily As Byte
    lfFaceName(1 To LF_FACESIZE) As Byte
End Type
```

and the TEXTMETRIC structure describes a physical font:

```
Type TEXTMETRIC
    tmHeight As Long
    tmAscent As Long
    tmDescent As Long
    tmInternalLeading As Long
    tmExternalLeading As Long
    tmAveCharWidth As Long
    tmMaxCharWidth As Long
    tmWeight As Long
    tmOverhang As Long
    tmDigitizedAspectX As Long
    tmDigitizedAspectY As Long
    tmFirstChar As Byte
    tmLastChar As Byte
    tmDefaultChar As Byte
    tmBreakChar As Byte
    tmItalic As Byte
    tmUnderlined As Byte
    tmStruckOut As Byte
    tmPitchAndFamily As Byte
    tmCharSet As Byte
End Type
```

The *CreateFont* function is used to create a logical font object. Its parameters mimic the members of a LOGFONT structure.

```
Declare Function CreateFont Lib "gdi32" Alias "CreateFontA" ( _
    ByVal nHeight As Long, _
    ByVal nWidth As Long, _
    ByVal nEscapement As Long, _
    ByVal nOrientation As Long, _
    ByVal fnWeight As Long, _
    ByVal fdwItalic As Long, _
    ByVal fdwUnderline As Long, _
    ByVal fdwStrikeOut As Long, _
    ByVal fdwCharSet As Long, _
    ByVal fdwOutputPrecision As Long, _
    ByVal fdwClipPrecision As Long, _
    ByVal fdwQuality As Long, _
    ByVal fdwPitchAndFamily As Long, _
    ByVal lpszFace As String _
) As Long
```

The *CreateFontIndirect* function does essentially the same thing:

```
Declare Function CreateFontIndirect Lib "gdi32" Alias "CreateFontIndirectA" ( _
    lpLogFont As LOGFONT _
) As Long
```

We will not go into the details of what all of these structure members mean. (Many of them are fairly evident.)

Getting the Current Logical/Physical Font

The *GetTextMetrics* API function returns a TextMetric structure for the currently realized physical font of a device context. The syntax is:

```
BOOL GetTextMetrics(
    HDC hdc,                // handle of device context
    LPTEXTMETRIC lptm       // address of text metrics structure
);
```

or, in VB:

```
Declare Function GetTextMetrics Lib "gdi32" Alias "GetTextMetricsA" ( _
    ByVal hdc As Long, _
    lpMetrics As TEXTMETRIC _
) As Long
```

To get the logical font that was selected into a device context, we need to proceed a bit more circuitously. The *SelectObject* function:

```
HGDIOBJ SelectObject(
    HDC hdc,                // handle of device context
    HGDIOBJ hgdiobj         // handle of object
);
```

returns a handle to the *previous* object of the specified type that was selected into the device context. Accordingly, we can temporarily select a new font into the device context, just to get the return value of *SelectObject*. We then immediately restore the original logical font:

```
Const SYSTEM_FONT = 13
Dim hCurrentFont As Long
Dim lf As LOGFONT

' Get handle to current font
hCurrentFont = SelectObject(Me.hdc, GetStockObject(SYSTEM_FONT))
' Get current font info
GetObjectAPI hCurrentFont, LenB(lf), lf
' Restore font
SelectObject Me.hdc, hCurrentFont

Debug.Print StrConv(lf.lfFaceName, vbUnicode)
```

Enumerating Fonts

The *EnumFontFamiliesEx* function can be used to enumerate the fonts on a system:

```
int EnumFontFamiliesEx(
    HDC hdc,                // handle to device context
    LPLOGFONT lpLogfont,    // pointer to logical font information
    FONTENUMPROC lpEnumFontFamExProc,
                            // pointer to callback function
    LPARAM lParam,          // application-supplied data
    DWORD dwFlags           // reserved; must be zero
);
```

This enumeration function uses a callback function, as does *EnumWindows*, for instance. Thus, we need a function to call *EnumFontFamiliesEx*:

```
Sub EnumFonts()

Dim cFonts As Long
Dim lgFont As LOGFONT

lgFont.lfCharSet = DEFAULT_CHARSET

EnumFontFamiliesEx Me.hdc, lgFont, AddressOf EnumFontFamExProc, cFonts, 0

End Sub
```

By setting the value

```
lgFont.lfCharSet = DEFAULT_CHARSET
```

the *EnumFontFamiliesEx* function will enumerate all fonts using all character sets.

Next, we need the *callback* function:

```
Public Function EnumFontFamExProc(ByVal lpelfe As Long, _
    ByVal lpntme As Long, ByVal FontType As Long, ByRef lParam As Long) As Long
```

```
Dim elfe As ENUMLOGFONTEX
Dim sFullName As String

' Get a copy of the structure
CopyMemory elfe, ByVal lpelfe, LenB(elfe)

sFullName = Trim0(StrConv(elfe.elfFullName, vbUnicode))
sFullName = sFullName & "-" & _
    Trim0(StrConv(elfe.elfStyle, vbUnicode)) & "-" & _
    Trim0(StrConv(elfe.elfScript, vbUnicode))

Form1.List1.AddItem sFullName

' Increment font count
lParam = lParam + 1

' Continue with enumeration
EnumFontFamExProc = 1

End Function
```

This will produce the list of fonts shown in Figure 25-2.

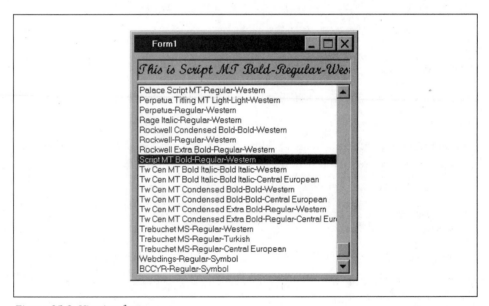

Figure 25-2. Viewing fonts

Finally, to see a sample of the selected font in a picture box (see Figure 25-2), we have the following code, which uses *CreateFont* to create the selected font object, and *SelectObject* to select that font into the picture box:

```
Private Sub List1_Click()

' Create font and select it into Text1
```

```
Dim hFont As Long
Dim v As Variant

If List1.ListIndex = -1 Then Exit Sub

pic.Refresh

' Get the face name
v = Split(List1.List(List1.ListIndex), "-", -1)

' Create the logical font
hFont = CreateFont( _
    -MulDiv(14, GetDeviceCaps(hdc, LOGPIXELSY), 72), _
    0, _
    0, _
    0, _
    FW_NORMAL, _
    0, _
    0, _
    0, _
    ANSI_CHARSET, _
    OUT_DEFAULT_PRECIS, _
    CLIP_DEFAULT_PRECIS, _
    DEFAULT_QUALITY, _
    DEFAULT_PITCH, _
    v(0))

' Select it into the picture box
SelectObject pic.hdc, hFont

' Draw text in picture box
TextOut pic.hdc, 0, 0, "This is " & List1.List(List1.ListIndex), _
    Len("This is " & List1.List(List1.ListIndex))

' Delete font when done
DeleteObject hFont

End Sub
```

V

Appendixes

The Clipboard

As you know, the clipboard is a Windows feature that enables us to pass data between applications. Visual Basic has a Clipboard object that allows VB programmers to use the clipboard in VB programs. Nevertheless, I can think of two really good reasons for using the Win32 API clipboard functions.

The Windows Clipboard

One reason is that the VB Clipboard object is part of the *Visual Basic* object model (*vb5.olb* and *vb6.olb*), not the Visual Basic for Applications object model (*vba5.dll* and *vba6.dll*). Accordingly, the Clipboard object is not available when programming in VBA, such as when programming in Microsoft Office. There have been many times when I wanted to use the Clipboard object when programming in Microsoft Word, Excel, or Access, but this does not seem possible without using the Win32 API clipboard functions. (Naturally, my first thought was to simply add a reference to the *vb6.olb* object library to the VBA project. However, when I tried this with Word 97, I was rewarded with a General Protection Fault. Moreover, the system would not let me back into my document, so I had to reboot the computer!)

The second reason for using API clipboard functions is to create a *clipboard viewer*, using Visual Basic. One of the most useful little utilities is a clipboard viewer that will collect *multiple* items for pasting into programs. (As you know, the standard clipboard viewer saves only the last item copied to the clipboard.)

We will address both of these issues in this appendix.

As you know, the clipboard can hold data of several different formats at the same time. We will restrict our attention to text, however. The various forms of text are represented by the following symbolic constants.

```
Public Const CF_TEXT = 1    ' ANSI text
Public Const CF_OEMTEXT = 7
Public Const CF_UNICODETEXT = 13
```

Note that it is only possible (and only necessary) to place one *text* format on the clipboard at a time (or one bitmap format, and so on). Windows will convert between text formats based on an application's paste request. For instance, if we place CF_TEXT (ANSI text) on the clipboard and another application asks for CF_UNICODETEXT, Windows will convert the ANSI text to Unicode for the request.

Copying Text to the Clipboard

The process for copying text to the clipboard is described as follows:

1. Allocate memory for the data (*GlobalAlloc*).

2. Lock the memory (*GlobalLock*).

3. Copy the data to the memory (*CopyMemory*).

4. Unlock the memory (*GlobalUnlock*).

5. Open the clipboard (*OpenClipboard*).

6. Clear its current contents (*EmptyClipboard*).

7. Set the clipboard data (*SetClipboardData*).

8. Close the clipboard (*CloseClipboard*).

Here are the details.

Allocate memory for the data

The first step is to allocate memory for the data using the *GlobalAlloc* function:

```
HGLOBAL GlobalAlloc(
   UINT uFlags,      // allocation attributes
   DWORD dwBytes     // number of bytes to allocate
);
```

Incidentally, while it is true that the current documentation states that *GlobalAlloc* ". . . is provided only for compatibility with 16-bit versions of Windows," we *must* use this function here, so this statement is not strictly true.

In VB, we can write:

```
Declare Function GlobalAlloc Lib "kernel32" ( _
   ByVal uFlags As Long, _
   ByVal dwBytes As Long _
) As Long
```

The *uFlags* parameter must be set to the constant:

```
GMEM_SHARE Or GMEM_MOVEABLE
```

To zero out the allocated memory, we can also include the **GMEM_ZEROINIT** constant, so we will use the following definitions:

```
Public Const GMEM_SHARE = &H2000&
Public Const GMEM_MOVEABLE = &H2
Public Const GMEM_ZEROINIT = &H40
Public Const FOR_CLIPBOARD = GMEM_MOVEABLE Or GMEM_SHARE Or GMEM_ZEROINIT
```

Note that the *GlobalAlloc* function returns a *handle* to the allocated memory. This is not the same as a *pointer* to (address of) the memory. The reason we get a handle rather than a pointer is that Windows may move the memory to another location at some point (the memory is allocated as **GMEM_MOVEABLE**, as required by the clipboard functions).

Lock, copy, and unlock

However, before we can use the memory block, we do need a pointer to that block. This requires that we ask Windows to temporarily *lock* the location of the memory. To get a pointer, we call *GlobalLock*:

```
LPVOID GlobalLock(
   HGLOBAL hMem   // handle to the global memory object
);
```

or, in VB,

```
Declare Function GlobalLock Lib "kernel32" ( _
   ByVal hMem As Long _
) As Long
```

The next step is to copy the data intended for the clipboard to the allocated memory. (If this data is text, it must be null terminated.) The *CopyMemory* function will do nicely here. (See the upcoming example.) The pointer returned by *GlobalLock* is the source address that is required by *CopyMemory*. Once the data is copied into the allocated clipboard memory, we must unlock that memory, using *Global-Unlock*:

```
BOOL GlobalUnlock(
   HGLOBAL hMem   // handle to the global memory object
);
```

or, in VB:

```
Declare Function GlobalUnlock Lib "kernel32" ( _
   ByVal hMem As Long _
) As Long
```

Note that this function requires the handle to the memory block, not the pointer. If for some reason we were careless enough to misplace the handle, we can retrieve it from the pointer, using *GlobalHandle*:

```
HGLOBAL GlobalHandle(
   LPCVOID pMem   // pointer to the global memory block
);
```

Open, empty, set, and close

Now we are ready for the clipboard API functions. The next step is to open the clipboard with *OpenClipboard*:

```
BOOL OpenClipboard(
    HWND hWndNewOwner    // handle to window opening clipboard
);
```

or, in VB:

```
Declare Function OpenClipboard Lib "user32" ( _
    ByVal hwnd As Long _
) As Long
```

This function requires the handle to a window that will *own* the clipboard data. The function returns `False` if another application has opened the clipboard. This is worth checking for.

Next, we set the clipboard data using *SetClipboardData*:

```
HANDLE SetClipboardData(
    UINT uFormat, // clipboard format
    HANDLE hMem    // data handle
);
```

or, in VB:

```
Declare Function SetClipboardData Lib "user32" ( _
    ByVal uFormat As Long, _
    ByVal hMem As Long _
) As Long
```

Note that *hMem* is the *handle* to the memory block, not the pointer. The *uFormat* parameter is a symbolic constant that describes the clipboard format.

Finally, we close the clipboard:

```
BOOL CloseClipboard(VOID)
```

or, in VB:

```
Declare Function CloseClipboard Lib "user32" () As Long
```

There are a few points about this process that we should emphasize:

- Do not forget to unlock the memory block before passing it to the clipboard.

- It is important not to leave the clipboard open any longer than is absolutely necessary.

- After calling *SetClipboardData*, the memory block no longer belongs to our application, so we should not access that memory. The handle and the pointer should be considered invalid. Windows will clean up any memory when it is no longer needed. We should *not* free this memory using *GlobalFree* (or any other method).

An Example

Let us give it a try. The following procedure places text on the clipboard:

```
Sub CopyTextToClipboard(sText As String)

Dim hMem As Long, pMem As Long

hMem = GlobalAlloc(FOR_CLIPBOARD, LenB(sText))
pMem = GlobalLock(hMem)
CopyMemory ByVal pMem, ByVal sText, LenB(sText)
GlobalUnlock hMem

If OpenClipboard(Me.hwnd) = 0 Then
    MsgBox "Clipboard opened by another application."
Else
    EmptyClipboard
    SetClipboardData CF_TEXT, hMem
    CloseClipboard
End If

End Sub
```

Pasting Text from the Clipboard

The process for retrieving text from the clipboard is described as follows:

1. Determine whether the clipboard contains data in text format (*IsClipboardFormatAvailable*).

2. Open the clipboard (*OpenClipboard*).

3. Get a handle to the global memory containing the data (*GetClipboardData*).

4. Lock the memory (*GlobalLock*).

5. Copy the text from the clipboard's memory block to memory belonging to the application (*CopyMemory*).

6. Unlock the clipboard's memory (*GlobalUnlock*).

7. Close the clipboard (*CloseClipboard*).

The following function returns any text on the clipboard. Note the use of *GlobalSize* to determine the size of the clipboard's memory block used to hold the text.

```
Function PasteTextFromClipboard() As String

Dim hMem As Long, pMem As Long
Dim lMemSize As Long
Dim sText As String

' Check for text on clipboard
If IsClipboardFormatAvailable(CF_TEXT) = 0 Then
    MsgBox "No text on clipboard", vbInformation
    PasteTextFromClipboard = ""
```

```
      Exit Function
   End If


   ' Open clipboard
   If OpenClipboard(Me.hwnd) = 0 Then
      MsgBox "Clipboard open by another application.", vbExclamation
   Else
      hMem = GetClipboardData(CF_TEXT)
      ' If no text, close clipboard and exit
      If hMem = 0 Then
         CloseClipboard
         MsgBox "No text on clipboard", vbInformation
         Exit Function
      Else
         ' Get memory pointer
         pMem = GlobalLock(hMem)
         ' Get size of memory
         lMemSize = GlobalSize(hMem)
         ' Allocate local string
         sText = String$(lMemSize, 0)
         ' Copy clipboard text
         CopyMemory ByVal sText, ByVal pMem, lMemSize
         ' Unlock clipboard memory
         GlobalUnlock hMem
         ' Close clipboard
         CloseClipboard
         ' Return text
         PasteTextFromClipboard = Trim0(sText)
      End If
   End If

End Function
```

Other Interesting Clipboard Functions

Here are a few other clipboard functions that you may want to investigate.

CountClipboardFormats
   Returns the number of clipboard formats currently on the clipboard

EnumClipboardFormats
   Enumerates the current clipboard formats

GetClipboardOwner
   Returns the handle of the current clipboard owner

GetOpenClipboardWindow
   Returns the handle of the window that has opened the clipboard

Example: Creating a Clipboard Viewer

A *clipboard viewer* is a window that receives notification of changes in the clipboard. At any given time, there may be more than one active clipboard viewer, but

Windows will send notifications only to the viewer that was last installed in the *clipboard viewer chain*, so it is the responsibility of each installed viewer to pass notification messages to the next viewer in the chain.

To install a clipboard viewer, we can just call the *SetClipboardViewer* function:

```
HWND SetClipboardViewer(
  HWND hWndNewViewer   // handle to clipboard viewer window
);
```

Here *hWndNewViewer* is the handle of the new viewer. The return value (if successful) is the handle of the current clipboard viewer (before the function call), which thus becomes the second viewer in the chain. This value must be saved, because it is the window handle to which the new viewer must pass along clipboard messages.

Once the viewer is installed, it will receive WM_DRAWCLIPBOARD messages whenever the clipboard changes. At this time, the viewer can (in its window procedure) retrieve the clipboard data.

Calling *ChangeClipboardChain* will cause Windows to remove a clipboard viewer from the viewer chain. The syntax is:

```
BOOL ChangeClipboardChain(
  HWND hWndRemove,   // handle to window to remove
  HWND hWndNewNext   // handle to next window
);
```

The *hWndRemove* parameter should be set to the handle of the viewer to be removed, and the *hWndNewNext* parameter should be set to the handle of the viewer that follows it in the chain. A call to this function prompts Windows to send a WM_CHANGECBCHAIN message to the *current* viewer. Note that this may or may not be the viewer that called *ChangeClipboardChain* or even the viewer that is to be removed. In fact, any application can remove any clipboard viewer if it knows that viewer's handle as well as the handle of the next viewer in the chain.

The parameters to this message are:

```
wParam = hWndRemove
lParam = hWndNewNext
```

That is, the parameters to *ChangeClipboardChain* are passed along to the window procedure.

This issue is a bit subtle, so we should discuss it more carefully. Figure A-1 shows a clipboard chain with four viewers.

Suppose an application calls *ChangeClipboardChain*:

```
ChangeClipboardChain hWndX, hWnd(X+1)
```

to remove ViewerX (where X = 1, 2, 3, or 4).

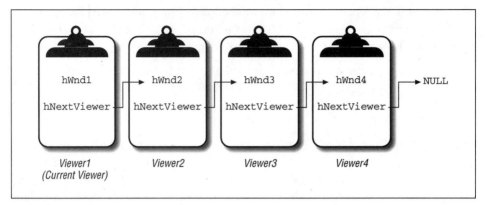

Figure A-1. A clipboard viewer chain

As a result, Windows removes ViewerX from the clipboard chain and sends a WM_CHANGECBCHAIN message to Viewer1 (the current viewer). There are three possibilities to consider.

If ViewerX is Viewer1, then it is Viewer1 that has been removed. Windows now thinks Viewer2 is the current viewer and so no further action is necessary. In particular, Viewer1 does not need to process the WM_CHANGECBCHAIN message, but note that it would do no harm for it to pass the message along the chain to Viewer2. Note also that Viewer1 can tell if it is the one being removed by checking to see if *hWndX* (= *hWndRemove* = *wParam*) is its own handle.

If ViewerX is Viewer2, then Viewer1 needs to do a bit of processing. The reason is that Viewer1 holds a handle to the next viewer in the chain (Viewer2). Since this next viewer is the one that has been removed, this handle is no longer the handle to the next viewer in the chain. So Viewer1 just needs to point its variable *hNextViewer* to Viewer3 as follows:

```
If wParam = hNextViewer Then    ' wParam = hWndRemove = hWnd2
   hNextViewer = lParam         ' lParam = hWnd3
End If
```

Finally, if ViewerX is neither the current viewer (Viewer1) nor the next one in line (Viewer2), then Viewer1 must pass the message along to Viewer2, so it can go through this little bit of terpsichorean maneuvering.

Note that we can simplify the code a bit by passing the message along without processing in all cases *except* where ViewerX is Viewer2, as in the following code:

```
If wParam = hNextViewer Then
   ' Unlink viewer
   hNextViewer = lParam
Else
   ' Just pass the message along
   SendMessage hNextViewer, WM_CHANGECBCHAIN, wParam, lParam
End If
```

In summary, all there is to creating a clipboard viewer is to:

1. Call *SetClipboardViewer*.

2. Process the WM_CHANGECBCHAIN and WM_DRAWCLIPBOARD messages.

Of course, under VB, we need to subclass a window so that we *can* process these messages!

The accompanying CD includes the *rpiClipViewer* application that hooks into the clipboard chain and places all text that is copied to the clipboard into a listbox (actually, it is currently set to keep only the last 100 items). Thus, if we need to retrieve an item placed on the clipboard a few "copies" ago, it is there for the asking. Figure A-2 shows the main window for *rpiClipViewer*.

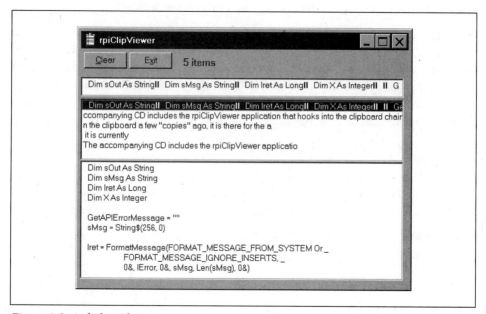

Figure A-2. A clipboard viewer

The text box at the bottom shows the item selected in the listbox, but with the carriage returns expanded for easier reading. Double-clicking on an item in the listbox (or using the ENTER key) will send that item to the clipboard for pasting.

The Load event for this form is:

```
Private Sub Form_Load()

Dim hnd As Long

' Check for running viewer and switch if it exists
hnd = FindWindow("ThunderRT6FormDC", "rpiClipViewer")
If hnd <> 0 And hnd <> Me.hwnd Then
```

```
        SetForegroundWindow hnd
      End
  End If

  BecomeClipboardViewer

  bAddToList = True

  Me.Show

  End Sub
```

This code shows one way to determine whether there is already a current instance of the clipboard viewer running. If so, the application just switches to that instance. We discussed the issue of testing for a running application in Chapter 11, *Processes.* This approach is a bit sneaky, so let us review it briefly.

One approach to testing for a running application is to use *FindWindow* to see if a window of the appropriate caption exists. However, as soon as the Load event fires, such a window will exit, so the code above just returns the handle of itself! The way to circumvent this problem is to set the main form's caption at design time to something other than its final value, say *rpiClipView* instead of *rpiClip-Viewer.* Then we can change the caption in the form's Activate event:

```
  Private Sub Form_Activate()
  Me.Caption = "rpiClipViewer"
  End Sub
```

which is not fired until after the Load event's code is executed! Note also the use of the END statement to terminate the Load event if the application is already running.

The *BecomeClipboardViewer* function just subclasses the listbox and calls *Set-ClipboardViewer:*

```
  Sub BecomeClipboardViewer()

  ' Subclass command button
  Subclass
  If Not bIsSubclassed Then
     MsgBox "Subclass failed", vbCritical
     Exit Sub
  End If

  ' Install button as clipboard viewer
  hNextViewer = SetClipboardViewer(lstItems.hwnd)

  End Sub
```

To do the subclassing, we use *SetWindowLong:*

```
  Sub Subclass()

  ' Subclass button
```

```
hPrevWndProc = SetWindowLong(lstItems.hwnd, GWL_WNDPROC, AddressOf WindowProc)
If hPrevWndProc <> 0 Then
   bIsSubclassed = True
End If

End Sub
```

The Unload event calls the following function to unhook the clipboard viewer:

```
Sub UnbecomeClipboardViewer()

ChangeClipboardChain lstItems.hwnd, hNextViewer
RemoveSubclass

End Sub
```

Here is the window procedure for the clipboard viewer (listbox):

```
Public Function WindowProc(ByVal hwnd As Long, ByVal iMsg As Long, _
    ByVal wParam As Long, ByVal lParam As Long) As Long

Dim sItem As String

Select Case iMsg

    Case WM_DRAWCLIPBOARD

        ' Get clipboard text and put it into text box
        sItem = PasteTextFromClipboard
        If sItem <> "" Then frmClipViewer.txtCurrent = sItem
        If sItem <> "" And bAddToList Then
           ' Add item to listbox
           cItems = cItems + 1
           frmClipViewer.lstItems.AddItem sItem, 0
           ' If exceeded maximum, remove last item
           If cItems > MAX_ITEMS Then
              frmClipViewer.lstItems.RemoveItem MAX_ITEMS - 1
              cItems = cItems - 1
           End If
           ' Select item
           If frmClipViewer.lstItems.ListCount >= 1 Then
              frmClipViewer.lstItems.Selected(0) = True
           End If
           ' Update label
           frmClipViewer.lblItemCount = cItems & " items"
        End If

        ' Send message to next clipboard viewer
        If hNextViewer <> 0 Then
           SendMessage hNextViewer, WM_DRAWCLIPBOARD, wParam, lParam
        End If

        Exit Function

    Case WM_CHANGECBCHAIN
```

```
' Check to see which viewer is being removed.
' Is it the next one in line?
' wParam contains handle of viewer being removed.
If wParam = hNextViewer Then
   hNextViewer = lParam
Else
   SendMessage hNextViewer, WM_CHANGECBCHAIN, wParam, lParam
End If

Exit Function

End Select
' Call original window procedure
WindowProc = CallWindowProc(hPrevWndProc, hwnd, iMsg, wParam, lParam)

End Function
```

B

The Windows Shell

In this chapter, we will give a brief overview of the Window shell. Our purpose is to acquaint you with the general features of the shell. These features are not terribly difficult to implement, and if you have made it this far through the book, you should have no real trouble extracting any further information about the shell that is not covered in this chapter directly from the documentation.

A *shell* is a Windows application that provides control over other applications. The functions of the Windows shell are primarily contained in the *shell32.dll* library. Installation of a particular version of Internet Explorer also alters (or enhances?) the current Windows shell.

The shell library *shell32.dll* supports a variety of features, such as:

- The dragging-and-dropping of files from the File Manager

- File associations

- Extraction of icons from executable files

- The System Tray

- File operations, such as sending a file to the recycle bin

- Miscellaneous shell functions (such as adding a document to the most recently used documents list)

We emphasize that the implementation of various shell features depends on the version of *shell32.dll* and *comctl32.dll* that is currently installed on the system, and this depends on the version of Windows and Internet Explorer that is installed. According to the documentation, version numbers are as follows:

- Version 4.00: Windows® 95/4.0

- Version 4.70: Internet Explorer 3.x

- Version 4.71: Internet Explorer 4.0

- Version 4.72: Internet Explorer 4.01

- Version 5.00: Windows NT 5.0 and Internet Explorer 5.0

The documentation does not make it clear as to what precisely the version number applies. It does say that the versions of *shell32.dll* and *comctl32.dll* should be the same (except for Version 5.00), but this may or may not be the case on a given system. For instance, the *rpiPEInfo* utility discussed earlier in this book reports the following for my system:

```
Shell32.dll: File Version 4.0.1381.4
Comctrl32.dll: File Version 4.72.3110.1
```

(My system has Internet Explorer 4.0—Version 4.72.3110.8—installed.) Since I did not deliberately install a new version of either of these files directly, something seems amiss. At the very least, this whole issue makes it difficult to write shell-related applications that will run on the majority of extant systems.

Now let us discuss some of the features of the Windows shell.

Drag-and-Drop

The Windows shell makes it relatively simple to enable a VB control to recognize files that are dragged from Windows Explorer and dropped on that control. The main catch is that Windows notifies the control that a file (or files) has been dragged and dropped by sending that control a message. Thus, we need to subclass the control!

The code in the *rpiShell* example demonstrates how to enable drag-and-drop features under VB. Figure B-1 shows the main window (this project also demonstrates file associations and registry manipulation, discussed in Appendix C, *The Registry and Private Profiles*).

To demonstrate drag-and-drop, just hit the enable button and drag a single file from an Explorer window to the picture box on the right of the buttons. The fully qualified name of the file will appear in the text box.

The code for this feature is quite simple. Aside from subclassing the picture box (we discussed subclassing in Chapter 18, *Windows Subclassing*), we need to call the *DragAcceptFiles* API shell function, whose VB declaration is:

```
Declare Sub DragAcceptFiles Lib "shell32.dll" _
   (ByVal hWnd As Long, ByVal fAccept As Long)
```

Here *hWnd* is the handle of the window to which messages are sent by the shell, and *fAccept* should be set to True to enable drag-and-drop and False to disable it.

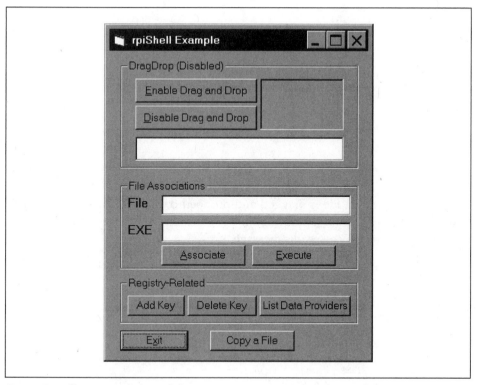

Figure B-1. Illustrating drag-and-drop

The following code takes care of subclassing and enabling drag-and-drop
(*bIsSubClassed* is a module-level variable):

```
Sub EnableDrag()

' Subclass the picture box
hPrevWndProc = SetWindowLong(Picture1.hWnd, GWL_WNDPROC, AddressOf WindowProc)

If hPrevWndProc <> 0 Then

    bIsSubclassed = True
    fraDragDrop.Caption = "DragDrop-Enabled"

    ' Set drag and drop
    DragAcceptFiles Picture1.hWnd, True

End If

End Sub
```

The following code turns off both drag-and-drop and subclassing:

```
Sub DisableDrag()

Dim lret As Long
```

```
' Remove Subclass if appropriate
If bIsSubclassed Then

    lret = SetWindowLong(Picture1.hWnd, GWL_WNDPROC, hPrevWndProc)

    bIsSubclassed = False
    fraDragDrop.Caption = "DragDrop-Disabled"

    ' Clear drag and drop
    DragAcceptFiles Picture1.hWnd, False

End If

End Sub
```

As mentioned, when a file is dragged and dropped over the picture box, the Windows shell will send a **WM_DROPFILES** message to the picture box. The following window procedure processes this message.

```
Public Function WindowProc(ByVal hWnd As Long, ByVal iMsg As Long, _
    ByVal wParam As Long, ByVal lParam As Long) As Long

Dim lpbuffer As String
lpbuffer = String$(1024, 0)

Select Case iMsg

    Case WM_DROPFILES
        ' Grab the file's name
        DragQueryFile wParam, 0, lpbuffer, 1024
        ' Print it
        frmShell.txtDragDrop.Text = lpbuffer
        ' Release resources
        DragFinish wParam

End Select

' Call original window procedure
WindowProc = CallWindowProc(hPrevWndProc, hWnd, iMsg, wParam, lParam)

End Function
```

In response to a **WM_DROPFILES** message, we need to call one or both of the shell functions *DragQueryFile* or *DragQueryPoint*. The former returns the name (and path) for the dragged file, and the latter returns the location that the file was dropped within the picture box. Also, we must release used resources by calling *DragFinish*. Here are the declarations:

```
Declare Function DragQueryFile Lib "shell32.dll" Alias "DragQueryFileA" ( _
    ByVal HDROP As Long, ByVal UINT As Long, _
    ByVal lpStr As String, ByVal ch As Long) As Long
```

```
Declare Function DragQueryPoint Lib "shell32.dll" ( _
    ByVal HDROP As Long, lpPoint As POINTAPI) As Long
```

```
Declare Sub DragFinish Lib "shell32.dll" (ByVal HDROP As Long)
```

The *hDROP* parameter that appears in each function is passed to us in the *wParam* parameter of the window procedure. It identifies the dropped file or files. (Our example deals with just a single dropped file, but you can easily enhance it to deal with multiple files dropped at one time.)

File Associations

As a Windows user, you are no doubt familiar with the fact that Windows can associate a file extension with an application (executable file). In this way, double-clicking on a file in an Explorer window, or choosing Open from the context-sensitive pop-up menu (raised by a click of the right mouse button) will cause Windows to execute the associated application and feed it the file in question.

The Windows shell permits us to take advantage of Windows file associations in VB applications. In particular, we can use the *FindExecutable* shell function to retrieve the complete path and filename of the application (executable) that is associated with a given file. Then we can use *ShellExecute* to open the file, using that application.

The VB declaration for FindExecutable is:

```
Declare Function FindExecutable Lib "shell32.dll" Alias "FindExecutableA" ( _
    ByVal lpFile As String, ByVal lpDirectory As String, _
    ByVal lpResult As String) As Long
```

Here *lpFile* is the name of the file in question, *lpDirectory* is the name of a directory that is made the default directory. This optional value (it can be **NULL**) is used to find the file specified by *lpFile* when *lpFile* does not contain a complete path. Finally, *lpResult* parameter is a string buffer that will receive the fully qualified name of the application's executable. It must have length at least **MAX_ PATH** (= 260).

The *rpiShell* application shown in Figure B-1 also illustrates the use of *FindExecutable*. The code behind the Associate button is simply:

```
Private Sub cmdAssociate_Click()

Dim sFile As String
Dim sEXE As String
sEXE = String$(MAX_PATH, 0)

sFile = txtFile
If sFile = "" Then Exit Sub
```

```
FindExecutable sFile, vbNullString, sEXE

txtEXE = sEXE
End Sub
```

The *ShellExecute* function can either open a file or print it. The VB declaration is:

```
Declare Function ShellExecute Lib "shell32.dll" Alias "ShellExecuteA" ( _
    ByVal hwnd As Long, _
    ByVal lpOperation As String, _
    ByVal lpFile As String, _
    ByVal lpParameters As String, _
    ByVal lpDirectory As String, _
    ByVal nShowCmd As Long _
) As Long
```

As an example, referring to Figure B-1, the code behind the Execute button is:

```
Private Sub cmdExecute_Click()

Dim sFile As String
Dim lResp As Long

sFile = txtFile

lResp = ShellExecute(Me.hwnd, "open", sFile, vbNullString, _
    vbNullString, SW_SHOWNORMAL)

End Sub
```

Note that the documentation indicates that the final parameter should be set to 0 for a document file, but this does not seem to work on my system!

The *ShellExecute* function can also be used to open a folder in Windows Explorer, using one of the following syntaxes, which differ only in the second parameter:

```
ShellExecute(handle, vbNullString, <PathToFolder>, _
    vbNullString, vbNullString, SW_SHOWNORMAL);

ShellExecute(handle, "open", <PathToFolder>, _
    vbNullString, vbNullString, SW_SHOWNORMAL);

ShellExecute(handle, "explore", <PathToFolder>, _
    vbNullString, vbNullString, SW_SHOWNORMAL);
```

The first two versions of *ShellExecute* will open the specified folder. For instance, the code:

```
ShellExecute Me.hWnd, "open", "d:\temp", _
    vbNullString, vbNullString, SW_SHOWNORMAL
```

displays the dialog shown in Figure B-2.

The third call to *ShellExecute* opens a *new* Windows Explorer window and displays the contents of the specified folder.

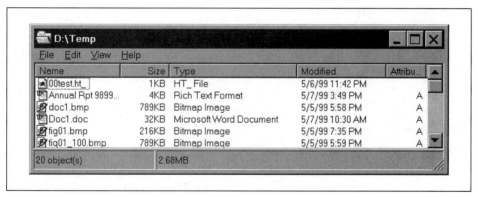

Figure B-2. Illustrating ShellExecute

The System Tray

The Windows shell also implements functions for dealing with the Windows System Tray, located on the taskbar.

It seems safe to assume that you are familiar at some level or other with the Windows System Tray. The Windows shell makes it easy to place icons in the System Tray and use them to execute code in response to mouse activity. For this, we use the *Shell_NotifyIcon* function:

```
Public Declare Function Shell_NotifyIcon Lib "shell32" _
Alias "Shell_NotifyIconA" ( _
   ByVal dwMessage As Long, _
   ByRef pnid As utNOTIFYICONDATA _
) As Boolean
```

This function can be used to add, modify, or delete an icon from the System Tray. Accordingly, the *dwMessage* parameter can be one of the following:

- NIM_ADD
- NIM_MODIFY
- NIM_DELETE

The *pnid* parameter is the address of a **NOTIFYICONDATA** structure, the content of which depends on the value of *dwMessage*:

```
Public Type NOTIFYICONDATA
   cbSize As Long
   hwnd As Long
   uID As Long
   uFlags As Long
   uCallbackMessage As Long
   hIcon As Long
   szTip(1 To 64) As Byte
End Type
```

The members of this structure are:

cbSize

> Size of this structure, in bytes, which is 88. (It is more professional to use the *LenB* function.)

hWnd

> Handle of the window that will receive notification messages associated with the System Tray icon.

uID

> An application-defined identifier of the System Tray icon. Can be 0.

uFlags

> A combination of flags indicating which of the other members of the structure contain valid data. The possibilities are:

> NIF_ICON

>> The *hIcon* member is valid.

> NIF_MESSAGE

>> The *uCallbackMessage* member is valid.

> NIF_TIP

>> The *szTip* member is valid.

uCallbackMessage

> This is a message ID. Windows will send this message to the window identified by the *hwnd* member when a mouse event occurs within the bounding rectangle of the System Tray icon.

hIcon

> Handle to the icon to add, modify, or delete.

szTip

> The tooltip text to display for the icon.

According to the documentation, we should set the callback function to an otherwise unused mouse event. The example in the documentation is the MouseMove event of the form, which seems reasonable. This is done by setting:

```
nid.hwnd = Me.hWnd
nid.uCallbackMessage = WM_MOUSEMOVE
```

In this case, when a mouse event occurs for the System Tray icon, Windows will fire the MouseMove event of the form. Moreover, it sends the mouse message ID in the X parameter of the form's MouseMove event, as follows:

```
X = MessageID*Screen.TwipsPerPixelX
```

so to recover the message ID, we must divide by **Screen.TwipsPerPixelX**. (See the upcoming example.)

An Example

To illustrate, the following code will add or delete an icon from the System Tray and respond to left-button double-clicks or right-button up events. The Load event sets up the NOTIFYICONDATA structure:

```
Private Sub Form_Load()

Dim sTip As String

' Fill in NOTIFYICONDATA structure
sTip = "Test tip"
CopyMemory nid.szTip(1), ByVal sTip, LenB(sTip)

nid.cbSize = LenB(nid)
nid.hwnd = Me.hwnd
nid.uID = 0
nid.hIcon = Me.Icon.Handle
nid.uFlags = NIF_ICON Or NIF_MESSAGE Or NIF_TIP

' Set callback message to mouse move
nid.uCallbackMessage = WM_MOUSEMOVE

End Sub
```

Just for the sake of illustration, the form's MouseMove event responds to System Tray icon mouse events by sending a line to the Immediate window.

```
Private Sub Form_MouseMove(Button As Integer, Shift As Integer, X As Single, Y As Single)

' When mouse is passed over tray icon,
' X value is MessageID * Screen.TwipsPerPixelX

Select Case X / Screen.TwipsPerPixelX

Case WM_LBUTTONDBLCLK
   Debug.Print "Double Click"
Case WM_RBUTTONUP
   Debug.Print "Right"
End Select

End Sub
```

Finally, the following code adds or removes the icon from the System Tray:

```
Private Sub cmdAdd_Click()
   Shell_NotifyIcon NIM_ADD, nid
End Sub

Private Sub cmdDelete_Click()
   Shell_NotifyIcon NIM_DELETE, nid
End Sub
```

I will leave it to you to come up with some interesting uses for the System Tray and its icons. Let me know if you find a *really* good one.

File Operations

The Windows shell implements a function called *SHFileOperation* which allows us to copy, rename, or delete a file or folder in a manner that resembles that of Windows Explorer. In particular, copying a file will display the familiar file copying progress dialog (assuming that the copying process takes long enough for Windows to display the dialog), and deleting a file will send it to the Recycle Bin. The function declaration, along with a needed user-defined type declaration, is:

```
Type SHFILEOPSTRUCT
    hwnd As Long
    wFunc As Long
    pFrom As String
    pTo As String
    fFlags As Long
    fAnyOperationsAborted As Long
    hNameMappings As Long
    lpszProgressTitle As String
End Type

Declare Function SHFileOperation Lib "Shell32.dll" Alias "SHFileOperationA" ( _
    lpFileOp As SHFILEOPSTRUCT) As Long
```

We will not go into the details of this function, except to give an example of deleting and copying.

The following code will send a file to the Recycle Bin:

```
Dim DelFileOp As SHFILEOPSTRUCT
Dim result As Long

' Initialize the structure
With DelFileOp
    .hwnd = 0
    .wFunc = FO_DELETE
    ' path and name of file to delete
    .pFrom = <filepathname>
    .fFlags = FOF_SILENT Or FOF_ALLOWUNDO Or FOF_NOCONFIRMATION
End With

' Do it
result = SHFileOperation(DelFileOp)

If result <> 0 Then      'Operation failed
    MsgBox "SHFileOperation error"
Else
    If DelFileOp.fAnyOperationsAborted <> 0 Then
        MsgBox "Operation Aborted"
    End If
End If
```

The *wFunc* parameter of the SHFILEOPSTRUCT structure can be set to any one of FO_COPY, FO_DELETE, FO_MOVE, or FO_RENAME. The *fFlags* parameter can be set to a combination of values that specify particular settings, such as whether or not to require confirmation for the operation in question. The *fAnyOperations-Aborted* flag is filled in by Windows with True if the user aborted the operation.

The following code, also in the *rpiShell* project, will copy a file, displaying the familiar progress dialog that is used by Windows Explorer (provided the copying operation takes long enough for the dialog to appear):

```
Private Sub cmdFileCopy_Click()

Dim FileOp As SHFILEOPSTRUCT
Dim result As Long

With FileOp
   .hWnd = 0
   .wFunc = FO_COPY
   .pFrom = InputBox("Enter path and name of file to copy")
   .pTo = InputBox("Enter destination")
   .fFlags = FOF_NOCONFIRMATION
End With

result = SHFileOperation(FileOp)

If result <> 0 Then
   MsgBox Err.LastDllError
Else
   If FileOp.fAnyOperationsAborted <> 0 Then
      MsgBox "Operation Aborted"
   End If
End If

End Sub
```

The Recycle Bin

The Windows 98 and Windows 2000 shell supports two functions for dealing directly with the Recycle Bin: the *SHQueryRecycleBin* function returns the number of items and the total size in bytes of a Recycle Bin, and the *SHEmptyRecycleBin* function empties a Recycle Bin. Note that these functions are not supported under Windows 95 or Windows NT 4.

The declaration of *SHQueryRecycleBin* is:

```
Declare Function SHQueryRecycleBin Lib "shell32.dll" Alias _
   "SHQueryRecycleBinA" (ByVal sRootPath As String, _
   lpRBInfo As SHQUERYRBINFO) As Long
```

where *sRootPath* is a string that begins with the drive containing the Recycle Bin (as in "c:\temp" for the C drive) and SHQUERYRBINFO is declared in C as follows.

```
struct _SHQUERYRBINFO {
    DWORD cbSize;
    __int64 i64Size;       // the total size of the items in the recycle bin
    __int64 i64NumItems;   // the number of items in the recycle bin
}
```

This is our first encounter with the 64-bit data type `__int64`. We can translate the structure into VB as:

```
Type SHQUERYRBINFO
    cbSize As Long
    lSizeLow As Long
    lSizeHigh As Long
    lCountLow As Long
    lCountHigh As Long
End Type
```

The declaration for *SHEmptyRecycleBin* is:

```
Declare Function SHEmptyRecycleBin Lib "shell32.dll" Alias _
    "SHEmptyRecycleBinA" (ByVal hWnd As Long, ByVal sRootPath As String, _
    ByVal dwFlags As Long) As Long
```

where *hWnd* is the handle of a window (use Me.hWnd) to receive any dialog messages, *sRootPath* is the same as in *SHQueryRecycleBin*, and *dwFlags* controls the display of confirmation and progress dialogs as follows:

SHERB_NOCONFIRMATION

No confirmation dialog will be displayed.

SHERB_NOPROGRESSUI

No progress dialog will be displayed.

SHERB_NOSOUND

No sound will be played when the operation is complete.

C

The Registry and
Private Profiles

The Windows API implements a few dozen functions for manipulating the Windows registry. In addition, Win32 supports *private profile files*, also called INI files. In this chapter, we will discuss both of these methods for storing persistent data. (Personally, I prefer to use private profile files, because I don't like to tamper with the Windows registry—a file that is essential to the proper operation of Windows itself.)

The Windows Registry

We should begin with a quick overview of registry terminology. Figure C-1 shows a picture of a portion of the Windows registry as shown by the Registry Editor. The items in the left pane of the Registry Editor are called *keys*. For instance, the open key in Figure C-1 is:

    HKEY_LOCAL_MACHINE\SOFTWARE\Microsoft\Browser\CurrentVersion

The registry keys are arranged in a hierarchical key-subkey relationship, with six *top-level keys*:

HKEY_CLASSES_ROOT
> This is not an actual key, but rather a *link* to the key HKEY_LOCAL_MACHINE\ SOFTWARE\Classes (and its subkeys). The link is created each time Windows is started. This portion of the registry contains definitions of document types, file associations, and class-related information.

HKEY_CURRENT_USER
> This key is a link to the portion of HKEY_USERS that refers to the current user.

HKEY_LOCAL_MACHINE
> Contains information related to the system's hardware and software configuration. The data for this key is physically stored in the file *system.dat*.

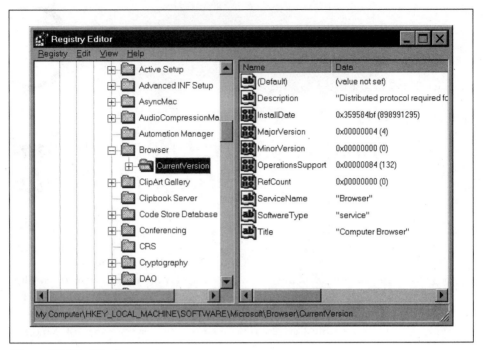

Figure C-1. The Windows registry

HKEY_USERS

Data for each user is stored in the registry file *user.dat.* When a user logs on, his or her data is moved into the registry under the **HKEY_USERS** key. In fact, at any one time, the **HKEY_USERS** key contains information for both the default user and the currently logged-on user. In this way, one user cannot view or change the user information for another user.

HKEY_CURRENT_CONFIG

This is a link to information about the current system configuration in the **HKEY_LOCAL_MACHINE** key.

HKEY_DYN_DATA

Used by plug-and-play to hold dynamic data.

Each key has one or more associated *values.* The right-hand pane in Figure C-1 shows the values for the selected key. A value has two parts: a *value name* (or just *name*) and a *value data* (or just *data*). (This is rather unpleasant terminology, but so be it.) For instance, the selected key in Figure C-1 has 10 values. The data in a key value can have one of three forms: *string, binaryz,* and *dword.*

String data is always displayed in quotes in the registry editor. Binary data is written as a series of hexadecimal bytes, as in:

```
74 e6 59 ff
```

Finally, DWORD data is also written in hexadecimal, but begins with the characters 0x. A DWORD value is interpreted as a single hex value, rather than as a binary word. The InstallDate value in Figure C-1 is an example of DWORD data.

Before discussing the registry-related API functions, I would like to express a personal opinion about the registry, even though I know that it is probably not a popular one.

I write many applications that require saving data from session to session; that is, saving *persistent* data. In the old days, many commercial applications used the *Win.ini* file to store their persistent data, even though private profile (INI) files were as easily accessible, through the use of dedicated API functions, which we will discuss later in the appendix. I found this practice very annoying, since it bloated the *Win.ini* file considerably. These days, Microsoft recommends using the registry to store persistent data for applications.

Personally, I think this is, in general, a mistake. The registry is absolutely vital to the health of Windows itself. Problems with the registry can result in disaster to the entire system. Frankly, I just don't see the sense in placing private data for an application in a device that is so critical to the operation of the entire system, especially when private INI files are still easily accessible. It just seems to me like playing with fire. Which of us can say that we never make coding mistakes and which of us is willing to say that there are no bugs in the registry-related portion of Win32? Why take the chance?

Indeed, I find private INI files very useful. Occasionally, I will open such a file with Wordpad and make wholesale changes. This is often easier than using the application's user interface. Of course, it can be a dangerous procedure, and I always *strongly* recommend against it for users of my programs.

Let me share with you one other reason for avoiding the registry. I once had an angry call from a user of one of my programs (a file manipulation program called Smart Directory). He said that after installing my program and using it for a few days, his system became unstable. He concluded that I must have altered the registry in an inappropriate way. Fortunately, I could assure him that this was not the case, since my program contains no code that accesses the registry!

This notwithstanding, there are times when I want to access the registry. Occasionally, I change an *existing* registry value. Also, there are times when it can be very useful to extract a list of key values. We will see such an example in a few moments.

The Registry-Related API Functions

Let us take a look at the registry API functions. Aside from the *RegConnectRegistry* function, which is used to establish a connection to a registry handle on another computer, the registry API functions can be divided into two groups: key-related functions and value-related functions.

Key-related functions

The key-related API function are listed below.

RegCloseKey

Closes an open registry key.

RegCreateKeyEx

Creates a new key.

RegDeleteKey

Deletes a key from the registry.

RegEnumKeyEx

Enumerates the subkeys of a key.

RegFlushKey

Writes the attributes of an open key to the registry.

RegLoadKey

Creates a subkey under **HKEY_USER** or **HKEY_LOCAL_MACHINE** and stores registration information from a specified file into that subkey. The data in the file must be in the form of a so-called *hive*, which is a collection of keys, subkeys, and values, rooted at one of the top keys of the registry.

RegNotifyChangeKeyValue

Notifies the caller about changes in a registry key (but not deletion of the key).

RegOpenKeyEx

Opens a registry key.

RegQueryInfoKey

Retrieves information about a registry key.

RegReplaceKey

Replaces the information for a given key and its subkeys with information from a file so that when the system is restarted, the key and subkeys will have the values stored in the file.

RegRestoreKey

Reads the registry information in a specified file and copies it to the registry, overwriting any existing registry information for the specified keys.

RegSaveKey

Saves registry information to a file.

RegUnloadKey

The reverse of *RegLoadKey*.

Value-related functions

The value-related API functions are as follows:

RegDeleteValue
> Removes a value (name and data) from the registry.

RegEnumValue
> Enumerates the values of an open registry key.

RegQueryValueEx
> Retrieves the value data for a specified value name for a key.

RegQueryMultipleValues
> Retrieves multiple data values for a specified key.

RegSetValueEx
> Sets a value for a specified registry key.

Examples

Let us now look at some examples of registry API functions. Before proceeding, we strongly advise backing up your registry. Note that some of the registry functions refer to the *class name* of a key. Here is what the documentation says about class keys:

> Pointer to a null-terminated string that specifies the class (object type) of this key. This parameter is ignored if the key already exists. No classes are currently defined; applications should pass a null string. Windows 95 and Windows 98 use this parameter only for remote registry keys; it is ignored for local registry keys. Windows NT supports this parameter for both local and remote registry keys

I presume that this means that we should ignore class names.

Creating and deleting a new registry key

To create a new key, we use *RegCreateKeyEx*, whose declaration is:

```
Declare Function RegCreateKeyEx Lib "advapi32.dll" Alias "RegCreateKeyExA" ( _
    ByVal hKey As Long, _
    ByVal lpSubKey As String, _
    ByVal Reserved As Long, _
    ByVal lpClass As String, _
    ByVal dwOptions As Long, _
    ByVal samDesired As Long, _
    ByVal lpSecurityAttributes As Long, _
    phkResult As Long, _
    lpdwDisposition As Long) As Long
```

The interested reader can refer to the documentation for a description of each parameter. The following *AddKey* procedure creates the key:

```
HKEY_LOCAL_MACHINE\SOFTWARE\Roman Press Inc\Test
```

and adds a value with name "Font" and string data 'Arial'. Note the use of the *FormatMessage* function to return error text. (We have used this function many times before.) The complete code is in the *rpiShell* project on the CD.

```
Sub AddKey()

Dim hKey As Long, lDisp As Long
Dim lResp As Long

' Create key
lResp = RegCreateKeyEx( _
    HKEY_LOCAL_MACHINE, _
    "SOFTWARE\Roman Press Inc\Test", _
    0, _
    vbNullString, _
    REG_OPTION_NON_VOLATILE, _
    KEY_ALL_ACCESS, _
    0, _
    hKey, _
    lDisp)

If lResp <> ERROR_SUCCESS Then MsgBox GetAPIErrorText(lResp)

' Set the value
lResp = RegSetStringValueEx(hKey, "Font", 0, REG_SZ, "Arial", 6)
If lResp <> ERROR_SUCCESS Then MsgBox GetAPIErrorText(lResp)

' Close the key
RegCloseKey hKey

End Sub
```

The *RemoveKey* procedure removes this key. Note that unlike the creation process, this is a two-step process, since we must remove two keys.

```
Sub RemoveKey()

Dim lResp As Long

lResp = RegDeleteKey(HKEY_LOCAL_MACHINE, "SOFTWARE\Roman Press Inc\Test")
If lResp <> ERROR_SUCCESS Then MsgBox GetAPIErrorText(lResp)

lResp = RegDeleteKey(HKEY_LOCAL_MACHINE, "SOFTWARE\Roman Press Inc")
If lResp <> ERROR_SUCCESS Then MsgBox GetAPIErrorText(lResp)

End Sub
```

Enumerating registry keys and values

The procedure *ListDPs*, shown below, illustrates the process of key enumeration. The purpose of this procedure is to list information about all OLE DB data providers on the system. Figure C-2 shows a typical registry entry for an OLE DB data provider. The root key for the provider is a subkey of the HKEY_CLASSES_ROOT\ CLSID key. To identify a data provider, we look for a subkey named 'OLE DB Provider'. (For more on OLE DB and ADO, let me suggest my book *Access Database Design and Programming*, Second Edition, also published by O'Reilly.)

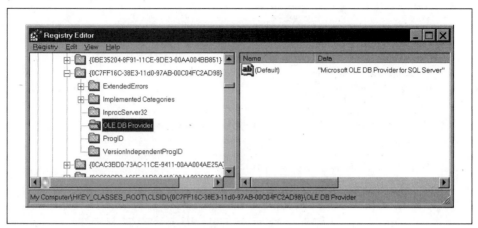

Figure C-2. A registry entry for an OLE DB provider

The source code for the *ListDPs* procedure is in the *rpiShell* project.

```
Private Sub ListDPs()

' Search the registry for Data Providers

Const BUF_LEN As Long = 2048

Dim lret As Long
Dim hCLSIDKey As Long
Dim hClassKey As Long
Dim hClassSubKey As Long

Dim bufKeyName As String * BUF_LEN
Dim bufKeyName2 As String * BUF_LEN

Dim lbufValue As Long
Dim bufValue As String * BUF_LEN
Dim lValueType As Long

Dim ft As FILETIME
Dim lxKey As Long, lxKey2 As Long

Dim bProvider As Boolean

' Open CLSID key for read-only
lret = RegOpenKeyEx(HKEY_CLASSES_ROOT, "CLSID", 0, KEY_READ, hCLSIDKey)

If lret <> ERROR_SUCCESS Then
    MsgBox "Cannot open CLSID key", vbCritical
    Exit Sub
End If
```

```
lxKey = -1        ' Key index

Do
    DoEvents

    ' Next subkey index
    lxKey = lxKey + 1

    ' Set up buffer for key name
    bufKeyName = String(BUF_LEN, 0)

    ' Get next subkey of CLSID
    lret = RegEnumKeyEx(hCLSIDKey, lxKey, bufKeyName, BUF_LEN, _
        0, vbNullString, 0, ft)

    If lret <> ERROR_SUCCESS Then Exit Do

    ' ------------------------------------------------------------
    ' Check subkeys of this subkey for the "OLE DB Provider" key
    ' If this subkey is found, we want to print all subkeys of this key
    ' ------------------------------------------------------------
    ' Open the key
    lret = RegOpenKeyEx(HKEY_CLASSES_ROOT, "CLSID\" & Trim0(bufKeyName), _
        0, KEY_READ, hClassKey)
    If lret <> ERROR_SUCCESS Then
        MsgBox "Cannot open key " & Trim0(bufKeyName)
        RegCloseKey hCLSIDKey
        Exit Sub
    End If

    ' Enumerate subkeys, looking for "OLE DB Provider"
    bProvider = False
    lxKey2 = 0

    Do
        ' Set up a buffer
        bufKeyName2 = String(BUF_LEN, 0)

        ' Enumerate the subkeys
        lret = RegEnumKeyEx(hClassKey, lxKey2, bufKeyName2, _
            BUF_LEN, 0, vbNullString, 0, ft)
        If lret = ERROR_SUCCESS Then
            ' Test for "OLE DB Provider" key
            If LCase$(Trim0(bufKeyName2)) = "ole db provider" Then
                bProvider = True
                Exit Do
            End If
        End If
        lxKey2 = lxKey2 + 1

    Loop While lret = ERROR_SUCCESS

    ' ----------------------------
    ' If a provider, print all keys
    ' ----------------------------
```

```
If bProvider Then

    Debug.Print ""
    Debug.Print "***NEW PROVIDER***"
    Debug.Print "CLSID = " & Trim0(bufKeyName)
    lxKey2 = 0

    Do
        lbufValue = 0
        bufValue = String(BUF_LEN, 0)
        bufKeyName2 = String(BUF_LEN, 0)

        lret = RegEnumKeyEx(hClassKey, lxKey2, bufKeyName2, _
            BUF_LEN, 0, vbNullString, 0, ft)
        If lret <> ERROR_SUCCESS Then Exit Do

        ' Open the key
        lret = RegOpenKeyEx(HKEY_CLASSES_ROOT, _
            "CLSID\" & Trim0(bufKeyName) & "\" & Trim0(bufKeyName2), _
            0, KEY_QUERY_VALUE, hClassSubKey)

        If lret = ERROR_SUCCESS Then

            ' Get the default value

            ' First get the size of the data and the value type
            lret = RegQueryValueEx(hClassSubKey, vbNullString, 0&, _
                lValueType, 0&, lbufValue)

            ' Is the data a string?
            If lValueType = REG_SZ Then

                ' Get the actual string data
                lret = RegQueryValueExStr(hClassSubKey, vbNullString, 0&, _
                    lValueType, bufValue, lbufValue)

                ' If it is not ExtendedErrors then print it
                If Trim0(bufKeyName2) <> "ExtendedErrors" Then
                    Debug.Print Trim0(bufKeyName2) & " = " & Trim0(bufValue)
                End If

            End If

            RegCloseKey hClassSubKey

        End If

        lxKey2 = lxKey2 + 1
    Loop

End If

Loop
```

```
RegCloseKey hCLSIDKey

End Sub
```

The output for this procedure on my system is:

```
***NEW PROVIDER***
CLSID = {0C7FF16C-38E3-11d0-97AB-00C04FC2AD98}
InprocServer32 = C:\Program Files\Common Files\system\ole db\SQLOLEDB.DLL
OLE DB Provider = Microsoft OLE DB Provider for SQL Server
ProgID = SQLOLEDB.1
VersionIndependentProgID = SQLOLEDB

***NEW PROVIDER***
CLSID = {3449A1C8-C56C-11D0-AD72-00C04FC29863}
InprocServer32 = C:\Program Files\Common Files\system\msadc\MSADDS.DLL
OLE DB Provider = MSDataShape
ProgID = MSDataShape.1
VersionIndependentProgID = MSDataShape

***NEW PROVIDER***
CLSID = {c8b522cb-5cf3-11ce-ade5-00aa0044773d}
InprocServer32 = C:\Program Files\Common Files\System\OLE DB\MSDASQL.DLL
OLE DB Provider = Microsoft OLE DB Provider for ODBC Drivers
ProgID = MSDASQL.1
VersionIndependentProgID = MSDASQL

***NEW PROVIDER***
CLSID = {dee35060-506b-11cf-b1aa-00aa00b8de95}
InprocServer32 = C:\Program Files\Common Files\system\ole db\MSJTOR35.DLL
OLE DB Provider = Microsoft Jet 3.51 OLE DB Provider
ProgID = Microsoft.Jet.OLEDB.3.51
VersionIndependentProgID = Microsoft.Jet.OLEDB

***NEW PROVIDER***
CLSID = {dfc8bdc0-e378-11d0-9b30-0080c7e9fe95}
InprocServer32 = C:\Program Files\Common Files\system\ole db\MSDAOSP.DLL
OLE DB Provider = Microsoft OLE DB Simple Provider
ProgID = MSDAOSP.1
VersionIndependentProgID = MSDAOSP

***NEW PROVIDER***
CLSID = {e8cc4cbe-fdff-11d0-b865-00a0c9081c1d}
InprocServer32 = C:\Program Files\Common Files\system\ole db\MSDAORA.DLL
OLE DB Provider = Microsoft OLE DB Provider for Oracle
ProgID = MSDAORA.1
VersionIndependentProgID = MSDAORA

***NEW PROVIDER***
CLSID = {E8CCCB79-7C36-101B-AC3A-00AA0044773D}
InprocServer32 = C:\oledbsdk\bin\SAMPPROV.DLL
OLE DB Provider = Microsoft OLE DB Sample Provider
ProgID = SampProv
VersionIndependentProgID = SampProv
```

Private Profiles

I have already mentioned that I much prefer to use private profile files (INI files) to store persistent data for my applications. Accordingly, let us briefly mention some of the API functions that are used to maintain these files.

The API Private Profile Functions

A private profile file, also called an INI file because its extension is generally *INI*, is just a text file with a specific format, as follows:

```
; comments are lines beginning with a semicolon

[section1]
key1=value1
key2=value2
  .
  .
  .
[section2]
key1=value1
key2=value2
  .
  .
  .
```

In particular, an INI file has *sections* that are labeled with the name of the section in square brackets. Under each section is a list of **key=value** pairs.

The Win32 API supports several functions for manipulating private INI files. Here is a list:

GetPrivateProfileInt

Gets an integer value from a key/value pair:

```
Declare Function GetPrivateProfileInt Lib "kernel32" _
    Alias "GetPrivateProfileIntA" ( _
    ByVal lpApplicationName As String, _
    ByVal lpKeyName As String, _
    ByVal nDefault As Long, _
    ByVal lpFileName As String _
) As Long
```

GetPrivateProfileSection

Gets the entire section in the form of an array of key/value pairs:

```
Declare Function GetPrivateProfileSection Lib "kernel32" _
    Alias "GetPrivateProfileSectionA" ( _
    ByVal lpAppName As String, _
    ByVal lpReturnedString As String, _
    ByVal nSize As Long, _
    ByVal lpFileName As String _
) As Long
```

GetPrivateProfileString

Gets a string value from a key/value pair:

```
Declare Function GetPrivateProfileString Lib "kernel32" _
    Alias "GetPrivateProfileStringA" ( _
    ByVal lpApplicationName As String, _
    ByVal lpKeyName As String, _
    ByVal lpDefault As String, _
    ByVal lpReturnedString As String, _
    ByVal nSize As Long, _
    ByVal lpFileName As String _
) As Long
```

WritePrivateProfileSection

Writes an entire section:

```
Declare Function WritePrivateProfileSection Lib "kernel32" _
    Alias "WritePrivateProfileSectionA" ( _
    ByVal lpAppName As String, _
    ByVal lpString As String, _
    ByVal lpFileName As String _
) As Long
```

WritePrivateProfileString

Writes a string value to a key/value pair:

```
Declare Function WritePrivateProfileString Lib "kernel32" _
    Alias "WritePrivateProfileStringA" ( _
    ByVal lpApplicationName As String, _
    ByVal lpKeyName As String, _
    ByVal lpString As Any, _
    ByVal lpFileName As String _
) As Long
```

Since I use these functions often, I have written some simple wrappers that I find easier to use:

```
Function INIDeleteSection(SectionName As String, IniFile As String) As Long

' Write to null section name
INIDeleteSection = _
    WritePrivateProfileString(SectionName, vbNullString, "", IniFile)

End Function


' -----
Function INIDeleteKey(SectionName As String, KeyName As String, _
    IniFile) As Boolean

' Write to null key
INIDeleteKey = _
    WritePrivateProfileString(SectionName, KeyName, vbNullString, IniFile)

End Function


' -----
```

```
Function INIEnumKeys(SectionName As String, BufferLen As Integer, _
    IniFile As String) As Variant

' Enumerate all keys for a section
' Return: null separated string or error value
' Can check error with If IsError(...
' USE A LARGE BUFFER!

Dim sBuf As String, lReturn As Long

sBuf = String$(BufferLen, 0)

lReturn = GetPrivateProfileString(SectionName, vbNullString, "", sBuf, _
    BufferLen, IniFile)

If lReturn = BufferLen - 2 Then
    INIEnumKeys = CVErr(1)
Else
    INIEnumKeys = Left$(sBuf, lReturn)
End If

End Function


' -----
Function INIEnumSections(BufferLen As Integer, IniFile As String) As Variant

' Enumerate all sections
' Return: null separated section names or error value
' Can check error with If IsError(...
' USE A LARGE BUFFER!

Dim sBuf As String, lReturn As Long

sBuf = String$(BufferLen, 0)

lReturn = GetPrivateProfileString(vbNullString, vbNullString, "", sBuf, _
    BufferLen, IniFile)

If lReturn = BufferLen - 2 Then
    INIEnumSections = CVErr(1)
Else
    INIEnumSections = Left$(sBuf, lReturn)
End If

End Function


' -----
Function INIGetSection(SectionName As String, BufferLen As Integer, _
    IniFile As String) As Variant

' Enumerate all key/values in a section
' Return: null separated key/values or error value
' Can check error with If IsError(...
' USE A LARGE BUFFER!
```

```
Dim sBuf As String, lReturn As Long

sBuf = String$(BufferLen, 0)

lReturn = GetPrivateProfileSection(SectionName, sBuf, BufferLen, IniFile)

If lReturn = BufferLen - 2 Then
    INIGetSection = CVErr(1)
Else
    INIGetSection = Left$(sBuf, lReturn)
End If

End Function


' -----
Function INIWriteSection(SectionName As String, StringToWrite As String, _
    IniFile As String) As Long

' Write a section.
' Requires null-terminated sections with final null at end of string
' Return nonzero on success

INIWriteSection = WritePrivateProfileSection(SectionName, StringToWrite, IniFile)

End Function


' -----
Function INIGetBoolean(SectionName As String, KeyName As String, _
    Default As Boolean, IniFile As String) As Boolean

' If key value is 0 or false then return False
' If key value is 1, -1 or true then return True
' Else return Default

Dim lReturn As Long, s As String, sBuf As String
sBuf = String$(50, 0)

lReturn = GetPrivateProfileString(SectionName, KeyName, CStr(Default), _
    sBuf, 24, IniFile)

s = LCase$(Left$(sBuf, lReturn))

If s = "0" Or s = "false" Then
    INIGetBoolean = False
ElseIf s = "1" Or s = "-1" Or s = "true" Then
    INIGetBoolean = True
Else
    INIGetBoolean = Default
End If

End Function


' -----
Function INIGetInt(SectionName As String, KeyName As String, _
    Default As Integer, IniFile As String) As Integer
```

```
    INIGetInt = GetPrivateProfileInt(SectionName, KeyName, Default, IniFile)

End Function

Function INIGetLong(SectionName As String, KeyName As String, _
    Default As Long, IniFile As String) As Long

INIGetLong = GetPrivateProfileInt(SectionName, KeyName, Default, IniFile)

End Function

' -----
Function INIGetString(SectionName As String, KeyName As String, _
    BufferLen As Integer, Default As String, IniFile As String) As Variant

' Return: string or error value
' Can check error with If IsError(...

Dim sBuf As String, lReturn As Long

sBuf = String$(BufferLen, 0)

lReturn = GetPrivateProfileString(SectionName, KeyName, _
    Default, sBuf, BufferLen, IniFile)

If lReturn = BufferLen - 1 Then
    INIGetString = CVErr(1)
Else
    INIGetString = Left$(sBuf, lReturn)
End If

End Function

' -----
Function INIWriteString(SectionName As String, KeyName As String, _
    StringtoWrite As String, IniFile As String) As Integer

INIWriteString = _
    WritePrivateProfileString(SectionName, KeyName, StringtoWrite, IniFile)

End Function
```

Index

Numbers

Z

About the Author

Steven Roman is a Professor Emeritus of mathematics at the California State University, Fullerton. He has taught at a number of other universities, including the Massachusetts Institute of Technology, the University of California at Santa Barbara, and the University of South Florida.

Dr. Roman received his B.A. degree from the University of California at Los Angeles and his Ph.D. from the University of Washington. Dr. Roman has authored 32 books, including a number of books on mathematics, such as *Coding and Information Theory*, *Advanced Linear Algebra*, and *Field Theory*, published by Springer-Verlag. He has also written a series of 15 small books entitled *Modules in Mathematics*, designed for the general college-level liberal arts student.

Besides his books for O'Reilly (*Access Database Design and Programming*, *Writing Word Macros*, *Writing Excel Macros*, and *Developing Visual Basic Add-Ins*), Dr. Roman has written two other computer books, entitled *Concepts of Object-Oriented Programming with Visual Basic* and *Understanding Personal Computer Hardware*, an in-depth look at how PC hardware works, both published by Springer-Verlag. Dr. Roman is interested in combinatorics, algebra, and computer science.

Colophon

Our look is the result of reader comments, our own experimentation, and feedback from distribution channels. Distinctive covers complement our distinctive approach to technical topics, breathing personality and life into potentially dry subjects.

The animal on the cover of *Win32 API Programming with Visual Basic* is an entellus langur, also known as a hanuman langur. The entellus is the largest of the langurs, members of the Old World monkey family. These monkeys are found in northwestern India, Bangladesh, Sri Lanka, and the southern Himalayas. In India the entellus langur is a revered animal. An Indian legend tells the story of Prince Rama, an incarnation of the god Vishnu, and his wife Sita. Sita was abducted and taken to an island. The king of the monkeys, Sugriva, and his minister, Hanuman, helped to free Sita and return her to her husband. As punishment, Sita's captor sentenced Hanuman to be burned at the stake. He was able to free himself, but not before his hands and face were burned. The legend says that all of Hanuman's descendants carry those burn marks on their hands and face to this day.

Entellus langurs are not as sociable as some other monkeys are. Although they live in groups of 8 to 125 individuals, they rarely band together for protection, instead seeking out solitary sanctuary. They can live in one of several social arrangements, but the single-male group is the most common. In these groups, there is one adult male living among several adult females and their offspring. Other groupings include multiple-male groups, in which several males of varying ranks live among females and young, and all-male groups, usually comprised of adult males who have been driven out of other groups. Competition for the single-male position can be fierce.

Entellus langurs eat a mostly vegetarian diet. Leaves are their principal food, but they also eat flowers, fruit, and seeds, and occasionally insects and fungi. Although quiet, the entellus langur can be an extremely active monkey. They are most active in the early morning, when they begin their first food forage of the day, and in the late afternoon, their second foraging time. During the hot afternoons they nap in a shady spot, and at night they sleep on the edges of tree limbs, returning to the same spot to sleep every night. They leap from tree to tree, letting out joyous whoops as they go, and can jump distances of up to 10 meters.

Jeffrey Liggett was the production editor for *Win32 API Programming with Visual Basic*; Beverly Goldfarb was the copyeditor; Judy Hoer and Anna Snow provided production assistance; Cindy Kogut was the proofreader; David Futato, Jeffrey Holcomb, and Claire Cloutier LeBlanc provided quality control. Robert Romano and Rhon Porter created the illustrations using Adobe Photoshop 5 and Macromedia FreeHand 8. Mike Sierra provided technical support. Ellen Troutman Zaig wrote the index.

Hanna Dyer designed the cover of this book based on a series design by Edie Freedman. The illustration was produced using a 19th-century engraving from the Dover Pictorial Archive. Kathleen Wilson produced the cover layout using Quark-XPress 3.32 and the ITC Garamond font. Whenever possible, our books use RepKover™, a durable and flexible lay-flat binding. If the page count exceeds RepKover's limit, perfect binding is used.

Alicia Cech designed the interior layout based on a series design by Nancy Priest. The inside layout was implemented in FrameMaker 5.5.6 by Mike Sierra. The text and heading fonts are ITC Garamond Light and Garamond Book. This colophon was written by Clairemarie Fisher O'Leary.

How to stay in touch with O'Reilly

1. Visit Our Award-Winning Web Site

http://www.oreilly.com/

★ "Top 100 Sites on the Web" — *PC Magazine*
★ "Top 5% Web sites" — *Point Communications*
★ "3-Star site" — *The McKinley Group*

Our web site contains a library of comprehensive product information (including book excerpts and tables of contents), downloadable software, background articles, interviews with technology leaders, links to relevant sites, book cover art, and more. File us in your Bookmarks or Hotlist!

2. Join Our Email Mailing Lists

New Product Releases

To receive automatic email with brief descriptions of all new O'Reilly products as they are released, send email to:
listproc@online.oreilly.com
Put the following information in the first line of your message (*not* in the Subject field):
subscribe oreilly-news

O'Reilly Events

If you'd also like us to send information about trade show events, special promotions, and other O'Reilly events, send email to:
listproc@online.oreilly.com
Put the following information in the first line of your message (*not* in the Subject field):
subscribe oreilly-events

3. Get Examples from Our Books via FTP

There are two ways to access an archive of example files from our books:

Regular FTP

* ftp to:
  ftp.oreilly.com
  (login: anonymous
  password: your email address)
* Point your web browser to:
  ftp://ftp.oreilly.com/

FTPMAIL

* Send an email message to:
  ftpmail@online.oreilly.com
  (Write "help" in the message body)

4. Contact Us via Email

order@oreilly.com
To place a book or software order online. Good for North American and international customers.

subscriptions@oreilly.com
To place an order for any of our newsletters or periodicals.

books@oreilly.com
General questions about any of our books.

software@oreilly.com
For general questions and product information about our software. Check out O'Reilly Software Online at **http://software.oreilly.com/** for software and technical support information. Registered O'Reilly software users send your questions to: **website-support@oreilly.com**

cs@oreilly.com
For answers to problems regarding your order or our products.

booktech@oreilly.com
For book content technical questions or corrections.

proposals@oreilly.com
To submit new book or software proposals to our editors and product managers.

international@oreilly.com
For information about our international distributors or translation queries. For a list of our distributors outside of North America check out:
http://www.oreilly.com/www/order/country.html

O'Reilly & Associates, Inc.
101 Morris Street, Sebastopol, CA 95472 USA
TEL   707-829-0515 or 800-998-9938
        (6am to 5pm PST)
FAX   707-829-0104

International Distributors

UK, EUROPE, MIDDLE EAST AND AFRICA (EXCEPT FRANCE, GERMANY, AUSTRIA, SWITZERLAND, LUXEMBOURG, LIECHTENSTEIN, AND EASTERN EUROPE)

INQUIRIES
O'Reilly UK Limited
4 Castle Street
Farnham
Surrey, GU9 7HS
United Kingdom
Telephone: 44-1252-711776
Fax: 44-1252-734211
Email: josette@oreilly.com

ORDERS
Wiley Distribution Services Ltd.
1 Oldlands Way
Bognor Regis
West Sussex PO22 9SA
United Kingdom
Telephone: 44-1243-779777
Fax: 44-1243-820250
Email: cs-books@wiley.co.uk

FRANCE

ORDERS
GEODIF
61, Bd Saint-Germain
75240 Paris Cedex 05, France
Tel: 33-1-44-41-46-16 (French books)
Tel: 33-1-44-41-11-87 (English books)
Fax: 33-1-44-41-11-44
Email: distribution@eyrolles.com

INQUIRIES
Éditions O'Reilly
18 rue Séguier
75006 Paris, France
Tel: 33-1-40-51-52-30
Fax: 33-1-40-51-52-31
Email: france@editions-oreilly.fr

GERMANY, SWITZERLAND, AUSTRIA, EASTERN EUROPE, LUXEMBOURG, AND LIECHTENSTEIN

INQUIRIES & ORDERS
O'Reilly Verlag
Balthasarstr. 81
D-50670 Köln
Germany
Telephone: 49-221-973160-91
Fax: 49-221-973160-8
Email: anfragen@oreilly.de (inquiries)
Email: order@oreilly.de (orders)

CANADA (FRENCH LANGUAGE BOOKS)
Les Éditions Flammarion ltée
375, Avenue Laurier Ouest
Montréal (Québec) H2V 2K3
Tel: 00-1-514-277-8807
Fax: 00-1-514-278-2085
Email: info@flammarion.qc.ca

HONG KONG
City Discount Subscription Service, Ltd.
Unit D, 3rd Floor, Yan's Tower
27 Wong Chuk Hang Road
Aberdeen, Hong Kong
Tel: 852-2580-3539
Fax: 852-2580-6463
Email: citydis@ppn.com.hk

KOREA
Hanbit Media, Inc.
Sonyoung Bldg. 202
Yeksam-dong 736-36
Kangnam-ku
Seoul, Korea
Tel: 822-554-9610
Fax: 822-556-0363
Email: hant93@chollian.dacom.co.kr

PHILIPPINES
Mutual Books, Inc.
429-D Shaw Boulevard
Mandaluyong City, Metro
Manila, Philippines
Tel: 632-725-7538
Fax: 632-721-3056
Email: mbikikog@mnl.sequel.net

TAIWAN
O'Reilly Taiwan
No. 3, Lane 131
Hang-Chow South Road
Section 1, Taipei, Taiwan
Tel: 886-2-23968990
Fax: 886-2-23968916
Email: taiwan@oreilly.com

CHINA
O'Reilly Beijing
Room 2410
160, FuXingMenNeiDaJie
XiCheng District
Beijing, China PR 100031
Tel: 86-10-66412305
Fax: 86-10-86631007
Email: beijing@oreilly.com

INDIA
Computer Bookshop (India) Pvt. Ltd.
190 Dr. D.N. Road, Fort
Bombay 400 001 India
Tel: 91-22-207-0989
Fax: 91-22-262-3551
Email: cbsbom@giasbm01.vsnl.net.in

JAPAN
O'Reilly Japan, Inc.
Kiyoshige Building 2F
12-Bancho, Sanei-cho
Shinjuku-ku
Tokyo 160-0008 Japan
Tel: 81-3-3356-5227
Fax: 81-3-3356-5261
Email: japan@oreilly.com

ALL OTHER ASIAN COUNTRIES
O'Reilly & Associates, Inc.
101 Morris Street
Sebastopol, CA 95472 USA
Tel: 707-829-0515
Fax: 707-829-0104
Email: order@oreilly.com

AUSTRALIA
WoodsLane Pty., Ltd.
7/5 Vuko Place
Warriewood NSW 2102
Australia
Tel: 61-2-9970-5111
Fax: 61-2-9970-5002
Email: info@woodslane.com.au

NEW ZEALAND
Woodslane New Zealand, Ltd.
21 Cooks Street (P.O. Box 575)
Waganui, New Zealand
Tel: 64-6-347-6543
Fax: 64-6-345-4840
Email: info@woodslane.com.au

LATIN AMERICA
McGraw-Hill Interamericana
Editores, S.A. de C.V.
Cedro No. 512
Col. Atlampa
06450, Mexico, D.F.
Tel: 52-5-547-6777
Fax: 52-5-547-3336
Email: mcgraw-hill@infosel.net.mx

O'REILLY®

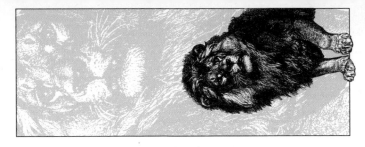

O'REILLY WOULD LIKE TO HEAR FROM YOU

Which book did this card come from?

_____

Where did you buy this book?
- ❏ Bookstore
- ❏ Direct from O'Reilly
- ❏ Bundled with hardware/software
- ❏ Computer Store
- ❏ Class/seminar
- ❏ Other _____

What operating system do you use?
- ❏ UNIX
- ❏ Windows NT
- ❏ Macintosh
- ❏ PC(Windows/DOS)
- ❏ Other _____

What is your job description?
- ❏ System Administrator
- ❏ Network Administrator
- ❏ Web Developer
- ❏ Programmer
- ❏ Educator/Teacher
- ❏ Other _____

❏ Please send me O'Reilly's catalog, containing a complete listing of O'Reilly books and software.

Name _____ Company/Organization _____

Address _____

City _____ State _____ Zip/Postal Code _____ Country _____

Telephone _____ Internet or other email address (specify network) _____

Nineteenth century wood engraving
of a bear from the O'Reilly &
Associates Nutshell Handbook®
Using & Managing UUCP.

POST CARD

BUSINESS REPLY MAIL

FIRST CLASS MAIL   PERMIT NO. 80   SEBASTOPOL, CA

Postage will be paid by addressee

O'Reilly & Associates, Inc.
101 Morris Street
Sebastopol, CA 95472-9902